A Question
of Values

Critical Perspectives
on World Politics
—————— ◇ ——————
R. B. J. Walker, *Series Editor*

A Question of Values
Johan Galtung's Peace Research

Peter Lawler

LYNNE
RIENNER
PUBLISHERS

BOULDER
LONDON

JX
1904.5
L39
1995

Published in the United States of America in 1995 by
Lynne Rienner Publishers, Inc.
1800 30th Street, Boulder, Colorado 80301

and in the United Kingdom by
Lynne Rienner Publishers, Inc.
3 Henrietta Street, Covent Garden, London WC2E 8LU

Library of Congress Cataloging-in-Publication Data
Lawler, Peter, 1952–
   A question of values : Johan Galtung's peace research / Peter
Lawler.
   (Critical perspectives on world politics)
   Includes bibliographical references and index.
   ISBN 1-55587-507-6 (alk. paper)
   1. Peace—Research. 2. Galtung, Johan. I. Title. II. Series.
JX1904.5.L39 1994
327.1'72'072—dc20   94-8624
                                                                CIP

British Cataloguing in Publication Data
A Cataloguing in Publication record for this book
is available from the British Library.

Printed and bound in the United States of America

        The paper used in this publication meets the requirements
   ∞ of the American National Standard for Permanence of
        Paper for Printed Library Materials Z39.48-1984.

Contents

Preface

It is only in the last thirty years or so that some scholars have chosen to apply the label "peace research" to their work. Since then various peace research institutions have sprung up, a range of dedicated academic journals have emerged, and some universities have chosen to adopt peace research or peace studies as part of their curricula. Few of these developments have occurred without some attendant controversy, and peace research continues to attract skepticism from various quarters even though it is not a label that could be applied to an unequivocal set of core assumptions. Although the heat has dissipated from the disputes that marked the foundational years, peace researchers continue to debate over method, concepts, and the very purpose of it all. The content of contemporary peace research is determined as much by the geographical location of specific institutes or scholars and their immediate intellectual milieu as by any understandings that they might share beyond a generalized concern with the problem of violence—war in particular—and the possibility of its reduction or elimination. To some it is a distinct discipline, to others a field of multidisciplinary or interdisciplinary inquiry, and for others still, merely indicative of an imprecise normative orientation.

A substantive history of peace research would be brief indeed—not to mention duller—if the input of Johan Galtung did not appear throughout. He was there at the beginnings of institutionalized peace research and remains a major contributor today. His writing has generated a unique lexicon utilized by many if not most peace researchers. Inscribed upon his work are all of the debates that have both impelled peace research onward and occasionally scarred it. The evolution of his work provides, then, one history, not the only one of course, of the field as a whole. In certain respects, as a peripatetic multilingual polymath, Galtung might himself be cast as the embodiment of a boundary-crossing peace researcher. Should this appear to be an overly heroic reading, it should also be noted that the status of the famous peace researcher is laced with ambiguity, as expressed in the title of one of the few monographs on his work: *Johan Galtung: Vaekkelspraedikant eller Superstar?* (Johan Galtung: Preacher or Superstar?). Yet, the same author described the publication of the first volume of Galtung's *Essays in Peace Research* as "a major event in the social sciences."

In spite of its volume and breadth, Galtung's work has attracted relatively little commentary. Given this, one of my objectives is simply that of exegesis. I present here one interpretation of the core themes in Galtung's writings and the extent to which they can be said to form a coherent model for researching peace. My reading is selective, partly for reasons of space but also in reflection of certain preoccupations. It arises out of and is guided throughout by a particular concern with what I call the question of values and their place in the analysis of world order. It is because of this focus that my assessment of Galtung's work is largely critical, although I happily concede that others coming from a different direction might arrive at very different conclusions.

Although not an intellectual biography, my survey of Galtung's work proceeds chronologically. Chapters 1 and 2 are concerned with the foundational phase of his peace research in the late 1950s and early 1960s and focus specifically on its positivist sociological leanings. Chapter 3 looks at the rupture in the peace research community in the late 1960s and the emergence of the concept of "structural violence." The next three chapters look at Galtung's work during the 1970s: Chapter 4 examines Galtung's structural theory of imperialism; Chapter 5 looks at a lesser-known aspect of his work—the reconstruction of scientific method; and Chapter 6 considers Galtung's grounding of social values in needs-talk. Chapter 7 scrutinizes Galtung's contribution to the World Order Models Project—*The True Worlds,* published in 1980—and Chapter 8 looks at more recent work on civilizations, culture, and Buddhism. In the final chapter I provide an overview of the preceding discussion, attempt some judgment on Galtung's work as a whole, and conclude with some prescriptive comments on the future of peace research.

* * *

The writing of this book in its original guise as a doctoral thesis for La Trobe University, Australia, incurred the usual range of debts. My thanks go to Roy May of the then Coventry (Lanchester) Polytechnic for encouraging me to undertake postgraduate studies. Michael Banks of the London School of Economics introduced me to normative thinking about international relations and peace research in particular. My supervisor at La Trobe, Joe Camilleri, excelled in his guidance and support and continues to do so. Herb Feith, formerly of Monash University, has been a constant source of encouragement and provided me with the first opportunity to lecture on Galtung and peace research. Impromptu conversations with Walter Isard and Håkan Wiberg on the dispute within peace research proved most illuminating. All of the thesis examiners provided very useful critical commentaries, but I especially appreciated Rob Walker's criticisms, which were followed by invaluable assistance in helping me to approach the conversion of a thesis into a book. It was courtesy of Professor Walker that I was introduced to Lynne Rienner and her staff, and I am very glad for that since I have received an unexpectedly pleasant introduction into the world of academic publishing, not to mention the wonders of e-mail. The comments provided by the reader of a revised manuscript, Larry George, were invaluable, although I have not provided the "po-mo" critique of Galtung's work that he hoped for. Many of my former colleagues in the Department of Politics at Monash have made the writing of this book less arduous, and I am especially grateful for the patience and support of Pauline Dwyer and Lesley Whitelaw as well as the sound advice of Professor Hugh Emy. Richard Devetak provided invaluable commentary on various drafts of several chapters, and Paul James provided friendship, intellectual stimulation, and lifts home beyond the call of duty. My thanks also go to Carolyn O'Brien for last-minute assistance with matters editorial.

Finally, two people are especially worthy of my appreciation. The first is my former colleague Andrew Linklater, who has never failed to offer advice, justifiable criticism, and friendship when required and across any distance to boot. The second is Thérèse O'Loughlin. She knows why I owe her so much, and it is to her that I dedicate this book.

Peter Lawler

Introduction

Some years ago Johan Galtung assessed the various types of research activity that could be undertaken by peace researchers and accorded a low priority to "commentary"—the critical examination of the work of others.[1] It is understandable that someone concerned with such large and vital issues would find the traditional academic activity of dissecting other people's work overly scholastic, trivial even. Galtung himself has rarely engaged in extended criticism. Nonetheless, I am ultimately persuaded by the counterargument: If we are in the business of taking seriously the quest for peace, we had better do it well or risk the quick dismissal of our efforts—a fate that has befallen so much normative thinking about world politics. In any case, critical examination is at the same moment an act of dissemination.

Self-evidently, exegesis and criticism do not take place in a historical or intellectual vacuum. Were I to begin by looking at Galtung's most recent work, I might well read a postmodern sensibility into it and trace that back to his earliest writings. That is not what I did, although I would be most interested to read the results of someone else taking such a route. Instead, I approached Galtung's writings (and peace research in general) with a view to discerning their contribution to normative theorizing about international relations. Upon immersing myself in his earliest work on sociology and peace research, I realized that Galtung's arguments for the possibility of peace research were wrapped around an argument about the scientific study of the social. Consequently, the bulk of my analysis is driven by the intersection of the two discourses of normative international relations thinking and social science. It was only in the latter stages of my own research, which, in turn, involved looking at Galtung's recent work, that I was struck by how much it resonated with themes emerging in postmodern writings on world politics. I came quickly to the conclusion that Galtung would refuse the label of postmodernist or some such term. Nonetheless, this third discourse unavoidably presents itself for consideration and

1

provides, at the very least, a number of themes helpful in the task of reading Galtung.

PEACE RESEARCH AND INTERNATIONAL RELATIONS

For all of its breadth and variety, peace research cannot but come up against the dominant assumptions of the discipline of international relations. Both claim a central preoccupation with large-scale violence, even if this by no means exhausts their respective contents. It would be offensive to many contemporary international relations scholars to be defined *against* peace research because many of them would, to all intents and purposes, share its method or normative and political orientation. Nonetheless, it is still commonplace to refer to a canonical "tradition" of international relations, and such references are, to paraphrase Walker, by no means innocent with regard to peace research.[2]

Within the tradition of international relations, peace research is usually relegated to the realm of so-called idealism, to be contrasted with that of realism. This dualism is textually reiterated in a variety of forms and remains highly resistant to change. Terms such as *cosmopolitanism* sometimes serve in place of *idealism; power politics* is a common synonym for *realism*. The distinction is also frequently and inaccurately characterized as a contestation between Kantian optimism and Rousseauian despair. More nuanced accounts offer a threefold categorization of the field wherein a "society of states" is postulated as a sort of halfway house between the sociableness of domestic society and an asocial international anarchy.[3] In finessing an account of the field, however, even this account is in the business of establishing firm margins: "As with all appeals to a middle road, the intended compromise reinforces the legitimacy of the two poles as the limits of permitted discourse."[4]

By and large, so the story goes, realism has been triumphant. For its advocates the realist discourse—replete with references to power, sovereignty, the perpetual threat of war, the primacy of the national interest, and the necessitous nature of human action—is seen to correspond best with the historical actuality of relations between states. The astute analyst of international relations is charged with comprehending the ways things are rather than speculating on what they should become. In contrast to idealist visions of a unified global community characterized by the harmonious interactions of peoples rather than armed sovereign states (never mind that such an unequivocal vision is actually hard to find in the classical or contemporary "idealist" literature), the realist depicts a world characterized by recurrence and repetition in which a concern for survival overrides the search for the global good life. The study of how the constraining international environment—governed by the logic of anarchy—generates suspicion, competition, and sometimes war is deemed to be the proper concern of international theory. By extension, statecraft becomes the judicious application of such insight into necessity to the practical pursuit of interests of state and the preservation of security.

As an idealist discourse, peace research commits the sin, from the realist point of view, of being normatively motivated and overly optimistic about the possibility of change. That peace researchers are by definition morally driven is hard to deny; whether they are optimists is another matter altogether. In any case, realism does not speak with a consistent voice on this matter, there being numerous permutations on its core themes that serve to undermine its tidy self-image. Some realists express a certain anguish over the immutable nature of international relations, whereas others retain a calm face in the presentation of the overwhelming structural logics that govern the external relations of the sovereign state. The popular reading of the realist canon depicts it as holding that international relations and morality are antithetical, but closer scrutiny shows that although some realists are dismissive of an international morality, many do not unequivocally deny its impact on foreign policy.[5] They depict a world of two moralities, one for domestic society and another, lesser and more narrowly conceived, for external relations. The content of the latter is determined by the obligations perceived to emerge from the former. The sovereign state looks morally inward; it is bound by an obligation to uphold the national interest, and its external actions are largely to be judged in light of this. In this sense it is consistent with realist principles to deem the selfish actions of states as somehow ethical nonetheless.

To stalk the middle ground of a society of states is to acknowledge an ethical dimension to international relations that extends beyond an inward-looking self-interest. Here statist egoism is seen to be mitigated by the presence of limited realms of institutionalized cooperation and mutual understanding represented by such phenomena as international law, the tendency of most states to uphold agreements, the practical and moral regulation of war, and the discourse of diplomacy.[6] Even so, for the more conservative proponent of this thesis, the ethical dimension of statecraft beyond an internally generated obligation to pursue the interests of state is collapsed into an external obligation to uphold international order. States are united in a *practical* rather than *purposive* association, the values of which are "those appropriate to relations among persons who are not necessarily engaged in any common pursuit but who nevertheless have to get along with each other. They are the very essence of a way of life based on restraint and toleration of diversity."[7] As with the realist, the boundaries of states and the principle of sovereignty are decisive. We are reminded that the fundamental error of those who seek to theorize the reform or transformation of world order is to suppose that the domestic "kingdom of freedom" provides a universalizable model for the realization of a world society.

In light of these sentiments, it is not surprising that the very idea of peace research has been given a mixed reception, in spite of the fact that its origins do not lie primarily in classical idealism nor has it been exclusively preoccupied with grand schemes of global reform or the nature of international morality. Indeed, it provides only one site from which challenges to the post-1945 dominance of realist moral skepticism have emerged and continue to do so. It is fashionable now to suggest (once again) that a realist-dominated "tradition" has just about had its day. The contemporary discipline of international relations, it is said with increasing frequency, offers a menu of perspectives that vary significantly in their interpretation of world politics and in the emphasis they place on its ethical dimensions or the possibility of its transformation. One example of postrealist thinking—which, I should point out, partly informs my own viewpoint—develops upon the idea of a society of states. Here the ethical dimensions of international relations are seen to extend beyond a question of coexistence to imbue the concept of international order with a richer content. International morality is depicted as a complex balancing act involving the interplay of ethical obligations arising out of national interests, the preservation of international order, and the increasingly compelling interests of humanity.[8] Indeed, it is in such a formulation that I think the image of rationalism as a via media between realism and cosmopolitanism really begins to take shape. Such a view is encouraged by a reading of contemporary global circumstances that emphasizes patterns of global change as encouraging the "seizing" of what Richard Falk has called "the Grotian moment."[9] On this basis, for example, Linklater takes seriously the idea of "good international citizenship" as a means of capturing the complex obligations confronting the sovereign state and exploring ways in which "foreign policy could be harnessed to the project of the Enlightenment." Linklater's interest in international citizenship seeks to go beyond the confines of statist rationalism and reinvigorate arguments for an ethical universalism that is cognizant of the exclusionary tendencies of classical cosmopolitanism. Drawing upon Kant and Habermas, he suggests that by focusing on the shifting outlooks of certain states, emerging out of the extension of notions of citizenship beyond the confines of the domestic community, we can detect a process of "moral learning" in world politics.[10] Contrary to the stasis of the realist account, pathways to world community might be discernible in full cognizance of the limitations of possibility emphasized by realism and rationalism, but in a manner that is corrosive of both their moral skepticism and reticence to concede that fundamental change on a global scale is possible.

Such argument provides one basis among many for critically examining the substantive contribution of peace research to the analysis of world politics. In general, the growth of overtly normative and reformist international relations scholarship underpins the view that a combination of recent empirical trends and theoretical innovations intimates the possibility of a world community emerging in which the egoistic state becomes tamed and the borderline between domestic order and international anarchy begins to dissolve. If this is the case, then it holds out the promise of the extension of a rational modernity beyond the water's edge and the dissolution of the distinctive features of international politics. On face value at least, this provides grist to the mill of something called peace research. In recent years the overlap and interchange between peace research and certain schools within the discipline of international relations has been marked—so much so, that the preservation of a distinct boundary is not only difficult to sustain but hard to justify. In certain respects contemporary peace research can be read as simply the exploration of practical applications of an amalgam of normatively driven perspectives on international relations.[11]

Unfortunately, although such a reading has had certain attractions for me, I now concede that it obscures as much as it illuminates. To overemphasize emergent commonalities between peace research and the discipline of international relations risks obliterating the quite distinctive path that many peace researchers have trodden, in particular Johan Galtung. It is both too kind and too unkind to peace research. Three reasons for resisting it suggest themselves. First, it paints an altogether too tidy image of a great journey from realism to something else, from skepticism to reformism in which the continuing power of power politics is underestimated and peace research is reduced to an appendix.

Second, for most peace researchers, interdisciplinariness is an undoubted virtue, even a normative requisite; for many international relations scholars, and not only those of more orthodox bent, part of peace research's problem is that it fails to theorize adequately its object domain.[12] In spite of normative affinities with reformist international relations scholarship, one of the paradoxical features of the emergence of contemporary peace research is the continuing (although not exclusive) influence of a scientific approach to social research and the disavowal of overtly philosophical or moral discourse, or what usually passes for political theory. The preference among peace researchers for a scientific outlook—especially in the early years—was not peculiar to them. International relations has also been marked, often to tedious extremes, by debate as to the extent to which it constitutes a science. But those debates were regulated through reference to a considerable body of existing scholarship. Coming from such disciplines as psychology, economics, and sociology, many peace researchers have eschewed reference, critical or otherwise, to either the international relations literature or debates within political theory or philosophy more generally.

A third reason for resisting too great an emphasis on the precise relationship between peace research and the international relations tradition is that both have come under the scrutiny of a body of intellectual practices now usually referred to as postmodern or poststructural. This provides another backdrop against which any analysis of Galtung's peace research is to be conducted.

MODERNITY AND ITS DISCONTENTS

Drawing from the editorial of an architectural journal, Harvey captures the tectonic cultural movement under way:

> "Generally perceived as positivistic, technocentric and rationalistic, universal modernism has been identified with the belief in linear progress, absolute truths, the rational planning of social orders, and the standardisation of knowledge and production." Post-modernism, by way of contrast, privileges "heterogeneity and difference as liberative forces in the redefinition of cultural discourse." Fragmentation, indeterminacy and intense distrust of all universalising and "totalising" discourses (to use the favoured phrase) are the hallmark of postmodernist thought.[13]

Modernity is increasingly cast as a negative category, exclusionary of anything that does not fit with a suffocating universalizing vision of a thoroughly rationalized life-world and destructive of the multiple forms of identity and existence once available to us. Furthermore, the roots of postmodern anxiety reach deep, feeding into a fundamental questioning of how we apprehend or experience the world and "our place, or placelessness, in it." Thinking about peace and world order cannot remain immune.

David Harvey's suggestion that postmodernism is startling because of "its total acceptance of ephemerality, fragmentation, discontinuity and the chaotic" might be exaggerated and insufficiently sensitive to variations within a genre, but it captures the mood nonetheless.[14] This is marked by a refusal of the reference points supplied by modernist thought and practice, seeking "not to judge modernity by its own criteria but rather to contemplate and deconstruct it."[15] The reading of "texts" (now a term of far wider purview than in traditional usage) no longer requires reference to an authoritative "determining judgment" or the use of established, sanctioned categories in confirmation of existing hierarchies of knowledge or truth claims; rather it is an interventionist act of interrogating, questioning, and playing with meaning as a means of uncovering or creating new interpretations that are themselves as open to the same forms of scrutiny. In the act of deconstruction what is not said—that which is excluded, denied, forgotten, or repressed—is exposed, not as an as yet unrevealed essence but as another possible reading out of the infinite number of readings available. The sovereign voice of the author is displaced; meaning and interpretation lose their *author*-ity and security and acquire a fluidity and contextuality that cannot be anchored to firm foundations outside of the text itself.

If one dares to attribute an essence to postmodernism at all, then it lies, paradoxically, in its antiessentialism, a refusal of the comfort of foundations and the all-encompassing, all-explaining grand narrative—the totalizing center. As a consequence, much of the authority of post-Enlightenment "modern" scholarship is dissipated. But the assault on the modern is not restricted to the intellectual plane; postmodernism offers a myriad of iconoclastic readings of the concrete practices of modernity and historical interpretations of them. In the sociological writings of Foucault, for example, we are given an interpretation that looks to the exclusionary dimension of modernity as a process of enforced universalization in which the determination of truth and right conduct arises not from the accumulation of unassailable knowledge through the application of reason, but from the pervasive exercise of power. If power and knowledge are so intertwined, then there appears no possibility of an archimedean standpoint from which the claims to rationality of universalizing discourses of emancipation, be they in the form of theories of international relations or Galtungian peace research, can be assessed. There appears to be little possibility for the grounding of universal critical principles or an ethics. Rather, we are confronted with a series of legitimating "myths," each containing an indefensible (in the strict sense) normative kernel.

Not surprisingly, there have been critical reactions to all of this. In particular, the despair, even nihilism, and antihumanism that are often read into the stronger articulations of a postmodern sensibility (frequently attributed to the legacy of Nietzsche) presage the abandonment of anything approximating an emancipatory politics. Uncertainty and profound skepticism appear to undermine any serious effort to transcend the chaotic pastiche of daily life; at best we are left with "play" and individuated amusement in the face of a world characterized by impenetrable logics of overpopulation, starvation, ecological destruction, and omnicide. Yet, it is by no means the case that all of those who work within a postmodern frame have simply embraced despair and frivolity. It can be argued that deconstruction is an ethical act, even if the move between it and a politics appears to be tenuous. Rosenau distinguishes between "skeptical" and "affirmative" postmodernists and sees the latter as remaining committed to visionary political projects premised upon the creation of "a philosophical, ontological intellectual practice that is non-dogmatic, tentative and non-ideological."[16] The loss of certitude as to the possibility of unequivocal progress and advancement does not require the complete abandonment of diverse strategies of resistance, the making of ethical choices, or the utility of issue-specific political coalitions and strategies. Postmodernity, on this view, generates the search for nonfoundational, contingent ethics and a new, perhaps more authentic, politics. Thus, White suggests that postmodernism—as illustrated by Foucault's genealogies of the intersection of power and knowledge, for example—may well "turn our humanist self-congratulations into self-doubt," but it also induces a heightened "sense of responsibility to otherness."[17] The theme of acknowledging the voice of the excluded other—of decentering various manifestations of sovereign orthodoxy, common to much postmodern writing—presents itself as a contingent but workable political and moral principle. At the very least, it places culture and identity at the heart of social and political inquiry, no longer taken as either given or merely ephemeral. If an answer to the question "how should we live" is to be found at all, then it must first be conceded that the question itself is malleable and plausible responses to it will only come from the constant interplay of voices and strategies, recourse to an unequivocal source of authoritative, transcendent knowledge being no longer available.

In reference to international relations theory, Walker argues that to celebrate identity difference "is to stress the possibility of new forms of political community and political practice that are open to the variety of people's experiences and histories, not closed off by the claims of state or the claims of hegemonic universalism."[18] Postmodernist readings of world politics disrupt the traditional demarcation of realism and idealism and other cognate dualisms. If its incursion is taken seriously, and I think that it must be, then the authority of established conceptual taxonomies as benchmarks for assessing peace research starts to weaken. The canon of international relations that confined modernity within states rather than between them is exposed as a modernist caricature. Postmodern critiques do not advocate the complete dismissal of orthodox scholarship; rather they argue that it should be mined for its insights into the global dimensions of the problematic of modernity and not as an "ahistorical apology for the violence of the present." What is resisted is the characteristic presumption of international relations orthodoxy that the fundamental division that matters is that between inside and outside the state. They seek, Ashley avers, to displace "the state-as-absolute-boundary." Such displacement is not intended to help discover where the boundary really is, or has moved to, but to ask a different question: "How by way of what practices, by appeal to what cultural resources and in the face of what resistances is this boundary imposed and ritualised?"[19] It becomes incumbent upon not only realist skeptics but also various reformists to reflect upon their constitutive assumptions.

Someone coming to Galtung's most recent work first might well conclude that it is inspired very much by the recent poststructuralist turn. It speaks of cosmologies, cultures, and civilizations and eschews state centrism—often angrily. It is highly critical of occidental intellectual practices and positivism in particular, yet it also utilizes much of the language of social science. A marked feature is a rejection of the wholesale adoption of any of the metanarratives of Western modernity, but at the same time there can be detected allusions to the reasonableness of the Nordic middle way. It embraces rather than attempts to dissolve contradictions within itself through reference to Buddhist metaphysics of all things. To read such eclecticism (or pastiche) as spiritually akin to postmodernism would not be implausible, but it would be a thin interpretation. Although the various phases of his oeuvre are very much of their time—and the most recent is no exception—there are also important linkages and commonalities that need to be kept in mind. Galtung himself operates with a historical account of the development of his model of peace research, frequently omitting, moreover, the possessive case. Even in his most recent work, decisive aspects of his earliest model of peace research—which certainly could not be described as outside of a modernist frame of reference—reappear to confound the reader. But if Galtung's peace research is not obviously postmodern, postmodernists nevertheless might do well to look at it for reasons both of critique and sympathy.

Galtung's consistent refusal of international relations orthodoxy concerning actors, processes, and outcomes in world politics frequently resonates with postmodern readings, even if he does not employ the same terms of discourse or make reference to seminal texts. Indeed, in many respects he has been well ahead of the contemporary game. Over time, his work has come to express considerable disquiet with established reformist counterpoints to realist pessimism, particularly with regard to their universalizing constitutive assumptions and their unspoken culturally specific prejudices. One of the virtues of the postmodern interregnum is that it requires those who seek to translate preferred values into practice to subject their assumptions to rigorous and continuous scrutiny. They must ask of themselves whether the preferred world order, the guiding blueprint, or the proclaimed methodological, intellectual, or practical "key" to the extension of modernity and reason beyond the water's edge does not arbitrarily supplant one set of sovereign assumptions for another—this trek to the end of history rather than that. This is a theme that suffuses Galtung's more recent work, and on occasions he employs it to criticize his own earlier efforts.

If a common praxeological theme in postmodern writings can be discerned, it is I think composed of these features: a critique of the epistemological assumptions and categorical assumptions (concerning actors, space, and time) of orthodox international relations scholarship—an affirmation, celebration even, of *difference* as a constitutive principle of international politics without falling back into state-centric reductionism; a critique of the stultifying consequences of a globalizing and homogenizing capitalism (or the universalist pretensions offered by a singular alternative); and a focus on the cultural dimensions of world politics. If a political project can be gleaned from all of this, at a minimum it consists in a multifaceted resistance to a mix of traditional intellectual moves and concrete practices that are seen to have resulted in the offering of a stark choice: incorporation within or marginalization outside of a sovereign model of global social order. In the more affirmative variants can be found an overtly constructive dimension involving the rearticulation of community in novel forms at the local and global levels that have hitherto been displaced to the margins by the sovereignty of the discourse of the sovereign state.[20]

Again, these are concerns that have animated Galtung's writings. But if connections with postmodern writings could be drawn at all, they would be with those of an affirmative leaning only. Equally, my reading of his work does not chastise him for this. For my purposes the value of contemporary critiques of modernity lies in the resources they provide to interrogate Galtung's peace research, sometimes to criticize it, but also simply to illustrate its evolution and contemporariness. (I find it rather paradoxical that postmodern lines of critique are rapidly coalescing into a "perspective" on world politics with all of the exclusionary implications its advocates so dislike). Galtung believes in foundational social values, and it is precisely the success or failure of his articulation or defense of them that provides the focus and the motivation for my particular journey through his copious writings. Indeed, it was the idea of a "science of peace" in the service of realizing universal values that energized his earlier writings. In contrast to the two broad pieces of interpretive scenery provided by the discipline of international relations and postmodernism, the idea of a science of peace provides a third, more narrowly focused backdrop.

PEACE RESEARCH AS SCIENCE

The antecedents of Galtungian peace research can be found in various appeals for the establishment of a "science" of peace, a notion premised upon a belief in the redemptive power of scientific knowledge. In the United States and United Kingdom, respectively, Quincy Wright and Lewis Richardson led the way with their application of quantitative techniques to the study of large-scale conflict.[21] Social psychologists, in particular Herbert Kelman and Theo Lentz, also began to explore the psychological, attitudinal dimensions of violent conflict. A Quaker and mathematician, Richardson argued that "science ought to be subordinate to morals." Somewhat contradictorily, he also attempted to remove any normative bias from his work on the grounds that science itself demanded moral neutrality in the name of objectivity.[22] Wright was a noted expert on international law who in his monumental work *A Study of War,* published in 1942, presented the results of a fifteen-year interdisciplinary research project, commenced at the University of Chicago in 1926. He surveyed the history and causes of wars from primitive warfare through to the atomic age, the latter being considered in a revised edition published in 1965. Anthropological data and scaling techniques were employed in the hypothesization of a definitive relationship between aggression and level of civilization.[23]

The little-known work of Lentz most clearly foreshadowed the foundational model of a self-consciously labeled peace research. In the preface to his prophetically titled *Towards a Science of Peace*, published in 1955, the eminent British scientist and first Director-General of the United Nations Educational, Scientific, and Cultural Organization (UNESCO), Julian Huxley, reflected upon the promise of science and provided one of the clearest expositions of the sentiments that were to motivate subsequent scientific peace research. He referred to a growing search for a "new ideology" that would apply scientific knowledge to the problems confronting the modern world. These problems included the prevention of war, the development of transnational organization, and the conservation of global resources. Huxley saw objective scientific knowledge as reason incarnate and the path to human progress. Science was a universal discourse with a core principle of free discussion at all social levels, whose promise had only come to be revealed in the modern period. Replacing earlier "mythological and theological inventions" and empirically unsubstantiated philosophical speculation, Huxley believed humanity now possessed a "reasonably accurate, comprehensive and scientifically-based picture of [its] destiny."[24] Science had extended its domain from the natural world into the psychological and social aspects of reality and in so doing flagged the further extension of scientific rationalization into the realm of the social. His confidence in the emancipatory potential of scientific knowledge and its ability to transcend the uncertainties of earlier speculative and philosophical forms of thought sharply recalled the historical depiction of the evolution of knowledge that was central to the arguments of the founders of positivism. Although such views might now be dismissed as both quaint and dangerous—redolent of popular images of wild-haired scientists claiming to have in sight the solutions to the ills of a grubby humanity— they were the imaginings of profoundly moral men to be judged against the backdrop of cold war, rapid escalations in the technology of war, and the evident indulgences of international political discourse at the time.

Lentz himself saw positivist scientific method as intrinsically sound but subject to abuse. Through a process of "democratization" and expansion, he depicted scientific research as capable of divorcing itself from distorting prejudices and transcending social and political barriers. What was especially needed was scientific research that would help to restore a balance between the development of physical power and the insufficient development of what he termed human "character." For Lentz, humanity had an unrealized potential to live harmoniously, and the adage that "war is made in the minds of men" was a guiding principle of the new science of peace. To this end, he argued for extensive research into human character and attitudes, to be carried out by multidisciplinary, multinational research teams, which in contrast to the earnest amateurism of the peace movements, would be thoroughly professional and conducted within an adequate institutional setting. He expressed a paradoxical *faith* in scientific procedure as the means for releasing a human potentiality to harmonize diverse purposes and achieve universal betterment.[25]

Though Lentz and Huxley offered a developed image of a possible science of peace, they were not readily emulated by their contemporaries. The enthusiasm for "social science" was already pervasive in a number of disciplines, including international relations, but a commitment to empiricism as method did not necessarily entail a commitment to positivism in the fullest sense, and it certainly did not suppose a commitment to peace. After all, science was at the same time working hard, very hard and very successfully, for the weapons industry and defense planners, and so-called social scientists were often in the business of shoring up, not challenging, conventional political practices within or outside of the state. Others shared the concerns of Lentz and others but chose to explore less grand avenues in the expression of their disquiet. What did ensue was the rapid growth of "conflict research," largely in the United States, as an intellectual orientation that lead to the establishment of the *Journal of Conflict Research* in 1957 and the Center for Research on Conflict Resolution at the University of Michigan in 1959. Both these institutional developments reflected some of the normative sentiments of Huxley and Lentz and certainly were transdisciplinary in structure. The founders of the Michigan center—Boulding, Angell, and Rapoport—came from different academic disciplines, and all shared an enthusiasm for the application of new social scientific techniques (culled from the fields of economics, social psychology, and sociology) to the study of large-scale social conflict. Their research output fell into a limited number of categories: psychological studies of the origins, management, and resolution of conflict; game-theoretic analyses of the dynamics of conflict; statistical analyses of arms races and the correlates of war.

The real innovation lay in the growing institutionalization of multidisciplinary research teams and the cautious connection of rigorous scientific research with a normative disposition to seek out ways to reduce the incidence and extent of war. A noticeable absence was reference to the word *peace* in many of these endeavors, especially in their labeling. Thus, conflict research achieved a certain respectability, and its boundaries soon blurred with similar developments in a number of other disciplines, in particular international relations. Nevertheless, even conflict research had an oppositional political flavor because its output was, from its inception, designed to counter that of the well-established institutes of strategic studies and the pessimism and perceived moral vacuity of mainstream realist international relations. There is a certain double irony to be detected in the attempts of some scientifically minded researchers to eschew the uncertainties of philosophy and political theory yet at the same time to embrace, however hesitantly, a need to provide an ethically driven counterpoint to the political and philosophical assumptions that underpinned orthodox thinking about international relations and the provision of national security in particular.

The origins of a self-consciously distinctive field of peace research that more fully reflected the positivist vision of Huxley and Lentz and was willing to declare the fact openly lay across the Atlantic in Scandinavia. It was, more accurately, a transatlantic development involving two journeys by one man: One was from Norway to the United States in order to work in the then premier sociological community; the other, a few years later, was a return to the homeland because it provided a location more conducive and sympathetic to the realization of a vision of a new, institutionalized scholarly enterprise. In 1959, a combination of events produced the founding of what was to become the International Peace Research Institute of Oslo.[26] The driving force behind its establishment and that of the first Chair in Peace and Conflict Research at the University of Oslo was a very young Johan Galtung. The setting up of the institute was not an easy task, but it was significant in that the Norwegian government had agreed to provide substantial support through the newly established Council for Research for Conflict and Peace and the Ministry for Education. In spite of this, the new institute was to achieve genuine political autonomy. Unlike their more cautious American counterparts, members of the fledgling Scandinavian peace research community had decided to adopt the title "peace research" from the outset rather than to shelter behind the politically less controversial category of conflict research. Five years later, the Stockholm International Peace Research Institute also got under way, again with considerable government support.[27] The Scandinavian peace research community finally came of age with the founding in 1964 of the *Journal of Peace Research*, which for its first ten years was edited by Galtung and in the first issue of which the birth of peace research was announced.

NOTES

1. Galtung regards "commentary" as an easy task, since "at no point does one have to touch the problems of peace." "The Next Twenty-Five Years of Peace Research," p. 252.
2. On the "tradition" in international relations, see the comments by Walker in "The Prince and 'the Pauper.'" His discussion informs much of what follows.
3. Exemplary of this is Martin Wight's distinction between realism, rationalism, and revolutionism. See Wight, *International Theory*.
4. Walker, "The Prince and 'the Pauper,'" p. 30.
5. This is forcefully illustrated in Holmes, *On War and Morality*, ch. 2.
6. See Bull, *The Anarchical Society;* and Wight, *International Theory.*
7. Nardin cited in Keal, "Can Foreign Policy Be Ethical?" p. 4.
8. See Bull, *Justice in International Relations.*
9. Falk, "On the Recent Further Decline in International Law," p. 272.

10. Linklater, "What Is a Good International Citizen?" The phrase *good international citizen* has been used by the current foreign minister of Australia, Gareth Evans. For further discussion of Evans's usage, see Lawler, "The Good Citizen Australia?"

11. See Lawler, "Peace Research and International Relations: From Divergence to Convergence."

12. For example, see the comments made by Camilleri, in spite of his evident empathy with peace research, in his "The Evolving Agenda of Peace Research." This is also a theme that runs throughout this discussion of Galtung's work.

13. Harvey is citing the editorial of *PRECIS* 6, 1987. See his The *Condition of Postmodernity*, p. 9.

14. Ibid., p. 44.

15. Rosenau, *Postmodernism and The Social Sciences*, pp. 4–5.

16. Ibid., p. 16

17. White, "Poststructuralism and Political Reflection," p. 191.

18. Roy, Walker, and Ashley, "Dialogue: Towards a Critical Social Theory of International Politics," p. 88. It is insightful to contrast Walker's and Ashley's contributions to this dialogue with Rosenau's distinction between skeptical and affirmative postmodern voices in mind. It is hard to read Walker's engagements with modernist international relations theory and not detect a significant praxeological-political intent, as expressed in the observation that challenging the discursive practices of international relations orthodoxy is at the same moment to open up possibilities for "rethinking and reconstructing contemporary political community." Ashley's position is far more ambiguous, to me at least.

19. Ashley, "Living on Borderlines," p. 311.

20. Exemplary of this is Camilleri and Falk, *The End of Sovereignty?*

21. See Wright, *A Study of War;* Richardson, *Arms and Insecurity;* and Richardson, *Statistics of Deadly Quarrels*. Richardson began his research during World War I and completed the two monographs in 1947 and 1950, respectively. They were published in 1960 after concerted efforts by the luminaries of the nascent conflict and peace research community in the United States. For reviews of Richardson's and Wright's work, see Eckhardt, "Pioneers of Peace Research—Lewis Fry Richardson," and "Pioneers of Peace Research II—Quincy Wright."

22. Eckhardt, "Pioneers of Peace Research: Lewis Fry Richardson," pp. 271–272.

23. In the preface to the 1965 edition, Karl Deutsch describes Wright's *A Study of War* as one of the foundational texts of contemporary peace research.

24. Huxley, "Foreword," in Lentz, *Towards a Science of Peace*, pp. vi–vii.

25. Lentz's five "articles of faith" were faith in progressing toward the harmonization of human purposes; in the utility of undiscovered facts; in the discoverability of facts through the use of human intelligence; in the creative evolution and redirection of scientific research; in the existence of and applicability of the motive of universal human betterment. See Lentz, *Towards a Science of Peace*, ch. 6.

26. Founded as part of the Institute of Social Research at the University of Oslo in 1959, it became a fully autonomous institute in 1966.

27. The Stockholm Institute is probably the best known of all peace research institutes. Although entirely funded from government resources, it is autonomous, and only one of the eight members of its governing board is ever a Swede. It eschews a theoretical output in favor of data collection and analysis for public use. See Blackaby, "Peace Research and the Stockholm Institute of Peace Research." For a useful survey of the Scandinavian institutes as well as most others, see Mack, *Peace Research in the 1980's.*

1

The Sociological Origins of Galtung's Peace Research

In our vital state of need this science has nothing to say to us.
—*Husserl*

The young Galtung was very much a product of the American sociological community in the 1950s within which he completed his training and began to teach. The "behavioral revolt" was cutting a swath through the social sciences, and debate as to the proper character of sociology revolved around the claim that only positivism could provide the basis for acquiring the rigor and authority attributed to the natural sciences. Although such a belief was also to permeate Galtung's foundational arguments for peace research, it was not simply a case of appealing for greater methodological rigor. A premonition of Galtung's quest was provided in Julian Huxley's commendation of Theodor Lentz's seminal exploration of a science of peace, in which he claimed that earlier mythological or theological "inventions" and philosophical speculation could now be transcended by a "scientifically-based picture of human destiny."[1]

That a young, radical political activist in Norway should embrace a positivist understanding of social science may seem strange today. Positivism has evolved into a catchall label, often used imprecisely or as a term of opprobrium applied to any approach that overly privileges empirical knowledge or sees the pursuit of moral ends as logically distinct from empirical inquiry. For its critics, positivism is irretrievably associated with a conservative political position by virtue of its preoccupation with the actual or "real" and its antispeculative, antihistoricist, and antiphilosophical core.[2] Yet, if we accept this reduction of positivism to empiricism, a paradox presents itself when we consider the early writings of Johan Galtung. They certainly show him to be of a positivist temper, his initial arguments for peace research presenting it as a putative science. But they reveal that Galtung was also committed to the search for peace and social justice on

15

a global scale. Indeed, it was this combination that gave his vision of peace research its distinctive and problematic character.

The apparent paradox that this combination of scientific and normative discourse entails dissolves, however, if we consider the origins of positivism more carefully. In its dual commitment to science and values, Galtung's peace research constituted a recovery of the Enlightenment-inspired vision of sociology's positivist founders. Given the widespread critical reaction to positivism from the late 1960s onward, such a perspective now appears rather quaint. But it must be remembered that during the 1950s the critique of positivism was only beginning to make its presence felt upon the American sociological community within which the young Galtung moved, and it appeared to have little effect upon him. Grasping the character of his early peace research requires an examination of the historical reduction of classical positivism to an argument for empiricist methodology, in which an original Enlightenment-inspired "intent" of positivism was suppressed or lost.

POSITIVISM

"Basically," says Bernstein, "the positivist temper recognises only two models for legitimate knowledge: the empirical or natural sciences and the formal disciplines such as logic and mathematics. Anything which cannot be reduced to these, or cannot satisfy the severe standards set by these disciplines, is to be viewed with suspicion."[3] Similarly, Tudor identifies the kernel of positivism as the claim that the world can only be known scientifically: "in short, that there is a single factual reality and all else fails the test of knowledge."[4] These representative descriptions establish only that positivism is a type of empiricism, by which is meant that all knowledge must ultimately be derived from the facts of experience or from purely syntactical analytic statements that accord with the canons of logic. They do not express what Habermas identifies as the ultimate purpose of positivism, a substratum that has become less visible, less significant, or "forgotten and repressed." This was the Enlightenment-inspired notion of *Bildungsprozess* (the self-formative process of a conscious subject), with which the methodology of positive science was originally intertwined.[5]

In his discussion of the intention of early positivism, Habermas detects a paradox arising out of the tension between Comte's account of the emergence of positivism within a developmental history of thought and his claim for its epistemological virtues. Simply put, positivism does not allow for the validity of the historical explanation of its claims to superiority: It cannot give an account of itself. However, for Habermas, "this paradox disappears as soon as we discern the intention of early positivism: the pseudo-scientific propagation of the cognitive monopoly of science."[6]

Comte depicted human history as the history of the realization of the positivist spirit and the supersession of previous eras of theological and metaphysical philosophy. The arrival of sociology, a term he introduced, marked "the final triumph of positivism in human thought."[7] Scientific social knowledge would end the dominance of speculative and philosophical inquiry and its preoccupation with the imaginary, undecided, inexact, and vain. Positivism was concerned with the actual, certain, exact, and useful, the factual aspects of life that constituted the true object domain of a social science. However, Comte did not provide an ontology of the factual, which led Habermas to conclude that his argument was circular: Whatever was deemed to be a legitimate object of scientific inquiry constituted a "fact," and the domain of science was therefore defined according to its own procedural rules.[8]

The crucial feature of Comtean positivism was the emphasis on the utility of knowledge, not itself a component of epistemology but a normative rule "through which science itself receives its definition."[9] Reinforcing the point that positivism cannot fully explain itself, Habermas argues that Comte was not simply supplanting seventeenth-century rationalism with empiricism but combining the two traditions. From the former was derived the requirement for the application of "rational inference" through theory, and from the latter was taken the view that science must be technically useful: "savoir pour prevoir, prevoir pour pouvoir."[10] Comtean positivism was to be a *technical discourse* that held out the promise of control over nature and society:

> All of our sound theories (are necessarily related) to the continuous improvement of our individual and collective conditions of life—in opposition to the vain gratification of a sterile curiosity. . . . The rational comprehension of the effect of man upon nature was essentially restricted to the inorganic world. . . . Once this huge gap is adequately filled—a process that is beginning today—the fundamental significance of this great practical goal (of the sciences) for the continual stimulation . . . of the highest theories will be recognised. *For technology will then no longer be exclusively geometrical, mechanical or chemical, etc., but also and primarily political and moral.*[11]

Scientific knowledge dissolved "philosophy" as metaphysics, the assertions of which Comte saw as meaningless and "undiscussable"; but the basis for such a sweeping dismissal was itself metaphysical, for it was "the background ideology that has made possible the replacement of epistemology by the philosophy of science."[12] Because the dismissal of metaphysics entailed the rejection of reflection on the meaning of knowledge, no basis was available for demonstrating the claimed superiority of positivism. Knowledge became identical with scientific knowledge.

Comte's methodological radicalism had a conservative political purpose. The subordination of social progress to the positivistically discovered natural "laws" of social development supported conservative skepticism by mediating the desire for progress through an understanding of the bases of social order.[13] In contrast, the work of Saint-Simon, arguably the true originator of positivist philosophy in all but name, secretes a different political tone. Yet, his work can be also understood as a constraining influence on the revolutionary implications of Enlightenment progressivism. In *Lettres d'un Habitant de Genève,* Saint-Simon decried the threat posed to civilization by revolutionary anarchy, arguing instead for sweeping social reforms premised upon the two principal instruments of progress: science and industry. The "sciences of man" were conceived of as a branch of physiology, and society was depicted as an organic entity governed by natural laws. A healthy (and progressive) society was characterized by good organization that produced sufficient order and stability to enable the identification of the forces of social disintegration. The ultimate purpose of positivism was "the improvement of civilization," the constraining requirement for social order notwithstanding. Thus emerged the doctrine of "industrialism" that endowed "savants" (scientists and artists) with a spiritual power that would replace that of the clergy. This technocratic "religion of Newton" envisaged the politically autonomous application of the collective intelligence of the great minds of the era toward the creation of an enlightened, industrial society guided by the science of social organization, which in itself entailed the synthesis of all existing knowledge. Coupled with the development of a scientific understanding of social life was the development of a humanist "terrestrial morality" that superseded the increasingly untenable theological morality of the past and the inadequate legal-metaphysical moralizing of the French revolutionaries.[14]

Traces of such a faith in savants armed with scientific knowledge were to emerge in Galtung's early depiction of the role of the peace researcher. He employed physiological imagery and the concept of health to describe the international body politic, to which the peace researcher was to apply curative scientific knowledge. As a positivist, then, Galtung was heir to the Saint-Simonian rather than the Comtean legacy.

In the subsequent development of positivist sociology, the utilitarian-political content of positivism became more muted as the problems raised by the synthesis of science and values came to the fore. Durkheim also tackled the problem of bridging science and social values, within a comprehensive analysis of the social, through the analysis of what he termed "social facts" or "the facts of moral life."[15] His work also reflected political circumstances, in this case the suppression of the Paris Commune and the resulting period of political instability and uncertainty. In 1870, Durkheim wrote of the shock of political events and the need to rebuild a social order "with a real basis in the nature of things." Again, beneath the investigation of sociological method lay a political project, for "the urgency of establishing a science of societies did not delay in making itself felt."[16] Like Comte, Durkheim favored incremental social change achieved through scientific understanding of society rather than through resort to revolution that was, in his view, only indicative of an incapacity to achieve progress.

Durkheim's first intellectual objective was to establish a "science of morality," a possibility that emerged out of the depiction of morality as developmentally bound up with the historical conditions of social life. Sociology's disciplinary autonomy was derived from the demarcation of a specific class of facts pertaining to social organization, including such things as the normative and symbolic aspects of collective social life.[17] Yet, there were limits to the new science. Although it endeavored to "observe, describe, and classify" social norms and values, it could not pass judgment upon them, and the authority of moral rules was grounded ultimately in the concept of "society."[18] The identification of the social foundation of morality was defended by appeal to what Benton calls "generative causality"—that is, that observable phenomena (in this case, adherence to moral rules) reflect an underlying reality. However, the precise nature of that reality remained ultimately inexplicable within the rules of scientific rationality to which Durkheim claimed to adhere.[19]

It was in the identification of perceptible and measurable phenomena that would explicate elusive features of organized social existence, such as moral authority and social solidarity, that the political content of Durkheim's sociology lay. It might reveal the bases of social order and, therefore, progress with stability. If it were possible to identify empirically a system of moral rules and norms within a specific social formation and go on to identify similar systems within societies of the same type, that system of moral rules could be deemed as normal for that particular type of society. The dichotomy between fact and value, means and ends, could be bridged, since they both were empirical outcomes of particular societies and could not be abstractly dichotomized. Drawing upon an analogy with the study of the normal and pathological within the biological sciences, Durkheim argued that the identification of normality within any society could be facilitated through the empirical identification of a prevalent "social fact." In conditions of social change, therefore, it would be possible to reject the conception of normality deemed applicable to the type of social formation being superseded on the grounds that it was no longer applicable to the nascent social order. Moral rules may appear as general, but if the conditions for their generality no longer existed, they could no longer be considered normal.

Durkheim's account appears innately conservative in depicting the existence of coercive sanctions and rules as an observational truth, but it can also be read as an attempt to escape the accusation of conservative ahistoricism through its recognition of the historical contingency of morality. He offered an evolutionary account of social morality that highlighted the immanent as well as the socially actual: "The future is already written for him who knows how to read it."[20] But even if Durkheim had undermined individualistic and psychological accounts of moral behavior by firmly placing the understanding of morality within a holistic model of society, he remained saddled with the problem of dealing with competing claims to moral superiority within any given society. Thus, Benton argues, "by taking the vocabulary (coercion, freedom, constraint, etc.) of political ideology (where these terms have a function in distinguishing, defending, or criticising different forms of political order) and giving it an epistemological task," Durkheim exposed the unscientific and conservative character of his project. As with Comte, prescientific, ideological notions were "constitutive of the political project which Durkheim's work theorizes."[21]

Only Saint-Simon could properly claim to be a political radical, but all three of positivism's founders constructed their vision of the sociological enterprise with practical, reformist intentions in mind. They commenced the process of rendering values as objects of analysis but provided no basis for critically assessing them, except in the functional sense of determining their role in the preservation of social stability and order. In recovering the classical positivist project, Galtung's foundational model of peace research was to carry over this fundamental inadequacy.

An American Science

Warts and all, Comte's and Durkheim's explorations in the scientific study of social values laid the basis for the emergence in the twentieth century of concept of "policy science." American sociology in the late nineteenth and early twentieth centuries was imbued with a spirit of moral fervor and reform verging on evangelical passion. This was not surprising given the high proportion of American sociologists who were either sons of ministers of religion or trained in the ministry. Protestant theology fostered a secular reformism guided by the mission of establishing the kingdom of God on earth. Though skeptical of Comte's agnosticism, many of the earliest American social thinkers adopted his redemptive vision of science that fitted well with the Protestant—especially Calvinist—view that all callings were obliged in some way to serve the public good.[22] Thus, the American Social Science Association, founded in 1865, proclaimed as its objective the guiding of the public mind to the most practical means for achieving social reform.[23] Under the influence of William Sumner and Lester Ward, sociology established itself as an autonomous discipline, and the earliest university courses offered in the subject reflected the dual commitment to the development of method and the social utility of sociological inquiry. By 1900, however, a rudimentary division had appeared between those who favored sociological analysis, or "pure sociology," and those who focused on social problems and practiced "applied sociology."[24]

Ward and others helped turn early American sociological discourse away from its initial Darwinian "biological fetters." Ward saw Comte's inability to divorce his "religion" from his sociology as a weakness and castigated activism and "good works" as patently unscientific and outside of the domain of sociology. Nevertheless, the spirit of Saint-Simon was invoked in Ward's vision of planned and purposeful action ("collective telesis") by an enlightened government of bureaucratized scientism—a "sociocracy." The goal was the translation of all social and political issues into technological problems, the solutions of which could be discovered by means of hypothesis, induction, experiment, and cost accounting. This foreshadowed the development of a highly professionalized American sociological community and an increasingly technocratic view of normative issues.[25] At the same time, Ross and Veblen were establishing a more radical sociological perspective. Ross, the consummate activist-scholar, combined a distinguished academic career with that of a pamphleteer and outspoken exponent of the progressive movement. He also favored a classificatory empiricism employed to expose the various means by which social control was imposed, or conformity encouraged. Democracy was the means by which repressive controls could be replaced with enlightenment and persuasion, founded upon popular awareness of social obligations.[26] Veblen remained aloof from political activism, but behind a guise of scientific impartiality he critically examined American capitalism, particularly the dominance of an unproductive "leisure class" that lived "by the industrial community rather than in it." His prescriptive response, thoroughly Saint-Simonian, synthesized a puritan work ethic with an argument for technocracy as a path beyond a competitive and socially destructive capitalism.[27]

Although a critical stream of sociological thought was thus established, to resurface periodically, early twentieth-century American sociology came to be dominated by pragmatism and atheoretical, descriptive empiricism. The Chicago school pioneered extensive empirical research based on urban fieldwork that eschewed the development of complex sociological theory in favor of empiricism and reflected the influence of the pragmatist American philosophers and their emphasis on the instrumental function of knowledge in the conduct of everyday life.[28] Between 1930 and 1950 the development of a more holistic and systematic theoretical perspective began to challenge the dominance of inductive empiricism and also to sever the close links between sociological theory and policy-oriented empirical research. The famous Middletown research project conducted by the Lynds was one of the earliest examples of a "functional" approach that focused upon the larger social system.[29] The influence of developments in the field of social anthropology was felt through the work of Radcliffe-Brown and Malinowski, who in different ways encouraged a systems-theoretic perspective and the refinement of research methods.

Thus, sociology entered what Lipset and Smelsor term the modern era, the principal features of which were characterized by the work of Paul Lazarsfeld and Talcott Parsons.

Parsons's work bridged classical European sociology and its more pragmatic American counterpart with a functionalist, systems perspective, the origins of which can be traced to Durkheim's study of "organic solidarity." In *The Structure of Social Action,* Parsons developed an analytical perspective critical of crude behaviorism and empiricism, which amplified Weber's antinaturalist method of *Verstehen,* by focusing on the subjective and interpretative aspects of social action. Parsons argued for a uniquely sociological and voluntaristic account of social action that encompassed all of the elements of social action—in particular the effect on action of subjective value orientations—perceived to be absent, suppressed, or inadequately treated in the writings of the European social theorists.[30] An immersion in European social thought was reflected in his stress on the importance of theory in the creation of scientific knowledge. In contrast to the small-scale empiricism of the Chicago school, he constructed complex, formal theoretical representations of the total social structure. For Parsons, the "facts" of social life were "statements about experience in terms of a specific conceptual scheme which provides a meaningful ordering of that experience."[31] Sociological theory was to be deductive, conceptually elaborate, precise, and capable of demonstrating the logical connections between its conceptual elements and the empirical realm that was its object domain. Such theory determined the form and content of the questions that sociology can ask. It was not a mechanical reproduction of reality but constituted a meaningful interpretation of social order. Rejecting the utility of "pure sense data" or "raw experience," Parsons privileged theory over the empirical realm, but the independence of theoretical systems from the empirical world did not obviate the need for them ultimately to "fit the facts"; theory was not fictional in content. The objective was a general theory of social action constructed around universal categories that, though not amenable to observation, were nonetheless constitutive of reality.

By Parsons's own account, Weber influenced his understanding of the sociological enterprise and his belief in the need for the professionalization of American sociology. Sociology had a limited purview: It was not a philosophy of history and therefore not a means by which the future could be discerned as the unfolding of a long-term historical pattern. In contrast to the assumptions of classical positivists, questions about the origins and future of human society were placed outside of its domain. The purpose of sociology was to explain social action, its structure and meaning, by way of theories that could give order to the apparent chaos of experience.[32] American sociology had to learn from the Europeans and develop a more "macroscopic" perspective in contrast to the traditional focus on

specific social issues. Parsons was quite clear about the normative implications of his viewpoint, rejecting the Comtean overtones of earlier American
sociology and the influence of "liberal Protestantism." In 1959 he wrote:

> Max Weber was probably the first major theorist to assert the fundamen-
> tal importance of carefully distinguishing between problems of scientific
> generalisation and those of evaluation and policy and to work out a clear
> methodological basis for the distinction. It is only within the last genera-
> tion that acceptance of this distinction has come to be generally diffused
> within the [American] social science professions and it is still quite in-
> complete. *The strong positivistic component in the philosophical matrix
> underlying the social sciences has been one of the major impediments to
> this acceptance.*[33]

Clearly, the detachment of modern sociology from its Enlightenment-
inspired normative origins was being sought. On this point Parsons and
Habermas are in agreement: Sociology qua science cannot engage in normative argument.

Parsons depicted American sociology as having reached a "first level
of maturity as a scientific discipline." The process of "disentanglement"
from "the earlier simple identification with specific practical goals in the
society" had enabled sociology to become "an independent, relatively pure
discipline with a research and theoretical tradition of its own." However,
the process was as yet incomplete; the danger of "ideological contamination" and insufficient commitment to pure research and training remained.
Parsons detected the beginnings of a "sociological era" in which "the term
sociology is coming increasingly to be a central symbol in the popular ideological preoccupations of our time." But the rising status of sociology
was not without its problems:

> An ideology is precisely a meeting ground between a society's value-
> commitments and its empirical scientific culture . . . [where] powerful
> pressures come into conflict with standards of scientific objectivity. . . .
> [Sociology] must serve as a primary guardian of the scientific tradition,
> counteracting the many tendencies to introduce biases and distortions.
> . . . The only honest professional answer to many questions is "we don't
> know," even though many would-be sociologists loudly proclaim their
> pseudo-solutions of many problems.[34]

Although accepting that "the applied function" of sociology was legitimate, Parsons thought that it should be mediated through the professional
schools, which would train practitioners and "form centers for 'action research' aimed at yielding directly practical results." Even then, the application of sociological knowledge should preferably be carried out by members of the applied professions rather than by "scientists" (i.e., sociologists)
as such.

The recovery of theory and method, seen as essential to the development of a "mature" American sociology, further encouraged the suppression of the normative motivations that threaded through earlier American
sociological discourse. But a reaction also emerged. A number of Parsons's
contemporaries accepted the tenor of his sociology but criticized the level
of abstraction and apparent disinterest in engaging in the empirical research required to substantiate conceptual and theoretical explorations.
Robert Merton called for a greater development of "theories of the middle
range" that would more effectively bridge empirical research methods (as
represented in the work of Lazarsfeld) and theoretical development (such
as advocated by Parsons). Others, such as Homans, mounted epistemological critiques arguing that Parsonian functionalism was not a bona fide theory but a conceptual scheme, devoid of explanatory power by virtue of an
insufficiency of derivative propositional statements.[35] Functionalism
tended to hypostatize social systems and subvert human relations and
needs within an overriding concern for hypothesized systemic needs and
functions. Coser and Dahrendorf took the issue further by accusing functionalism of being one-sided in its failure to consider social conflict as a
significant social phenomenon. Dahrendorf argued that Parsons erro-
neously posed the question "What holds societies together?" rather than
"What drives them on?" An emphasis on the social functions of consensual
values (whose very consensuality is assumed rather than demonstrated),
the categorization of seemingly normal behavior as deviant, and the conceptual closure of the social system—a product of an overdrawn analogy
with biomechanical systems—had produced a sociology that suffered,
paradoxically, many of the problems of the utopian social theory that it
was intended to supersede. Both utopian theory and Parsonian functionalism had removed history from the analysis of social structure and in so
doing had conceptually frozen society.

Dahrendorf went on to remark that he may have done an injustice to
the utopian theorists. Underlying most utopian constructions was a critical purpose—a strong concern with shortcomings and injustices of existing social institutions and beliefs—that made it "an intensely moral and
polemical branch of human thinking." Parsonian functionalist sociology
exhibited a complacency that could be construed as amounting to defense
of the status quo. Dahrendorf resurrected sociology's origins in noting that
contemporary sociologists had retained the technical imperfections and at
the same time abandoned "the moral impulses of their numerous forerun-
ners." Describing "modern sociological theory" as "useless and detrimental for our discipline," he castigated both practitioners of grand theory and
less theoretically distracted empiricists for having equally dispensed with
the "prime impulse of all science and scholarship . . . the desire to solve rid-
dles of experience, the concern with problems." Against this morally vacuous enterprise, Dahrendorf advocated a sociology that was not politically

radical in its contents, for this would be patently unscientific, but was nevertheless a "sociological science that is inspired by the moral fibre of its forefathers."[36]

This call for a morally informed, purposive sociology was given a more radical cast in the critiques of Alvin Gouldner and C. Wright Mills, the vanguard of an onslaught of antifunctionalist writings in the 1960s that transformed what was initially a relatively quiet dispute, ostensibly indicative of a healthy and eclectic discipline, into a debate tinged with rancor and contempt. Mills criticized Parsonian "grand theory" for betraying the Enlightenment-inspired promise of the classical tradition of sociological writing. Parsonian sociology fetishized concepts and had helped to turn American sociology into an uncritical (if involuntary) ideological prop for the status quo. This was compounded by the bureaucratization of research institutes such that, consciously or unconsciously, social scientists had become the servants of the power elite.

For Mills, "the moral and intellectual promise of social science is that freedom and reason will remain cherished values, that they will be used seriously and consistently and imaginatively in the formulation of problems." Sociology and politics were intertwined: "Within the social sciences, political crises and intellectual crises of our time coincide: serious work in either sphere is also work in the other."[37] He sought also to rehabilitate the idea of historical sociology, "the denial of which reached its peak in sociological functionalism."[38] Though Mills's particular approach remained undeveloped, it was, in its time, one of the few alternatives to functionalism—apart from marxism—acknowledged within the American sociological community.

Similarly, humanist themes threaded through Gouldner's critique of Weber, published in 1962, in which he attacked the "all-conquering myth" of value-freedom, affirmed in all of the mainstream research, textbooks, and university courses.[39] He noted that the myth was pervasive in spite of the fact that few social scientists lived up to it, agreed on its implications, or even thought about it.[40] It had arisen out of Weber's intensely personal intellectual struggle but had become transformed into a dogma that was reiterated as "the caste-mark of the decorous." In Gouldner's view, Weber had argued for the exclusion of *political* values in the context of a specific historical juncture, and his argument should be understood as an effort to construct a modus vivendi among disputatious German academics and to preserve intellectual activity from the interference of the state. Seen thus, his pursuit of value-freedom can be interpreted as the search for intellectual autonomy helping, in fact, to create the conditions for the making of better value judgments. As far as American sociology was concerned, the doctrine had encouraged the escape of American sociologists from the social world and public responsibility. It had also encouraged an escape *into* the world, whereby value-freedom affirmed the technical status of the sociologist as unbiased expert whose services could be put on the market. Against this, Gouldner identified the existence of a "critical posture" within American sociology that was fighting an uphill battle against an inexorable drive to professionalize the discipline.

Gouldner, Mills, and others foreshadowed the evolution of a radical sociological perspective, informed by classical marxism and the Frankfurt school of critical social theory, that went far beyond the evocation of classical sociology in its critique of mainstream social and political theory. The very epistemological foundations of positivism and the concept of a politically neutral social science was subjected to intense and damaging scrutiny. Nonetheless, the depiction of sociology as a form of ideology rooted in the industrial, educational, and cultural systems of advanced capitalist societies, although well established within European intellectual circles, was to remain on the American intellectual periphery for some time.[41]

GALTUNG'S SOCIOLOGY

It was not to the emerging radical stream of sociological thought that the young Galtung looked. Its influence cannot be detected in either his early depiction of the sociological enterprise or his peace research. Galtung's initial image of peace research reflected an admixture of modern scientific sociology and the Enlightenment values that motivated the classical positivists and some American sociologists. In part, it echoed Mills's recollection of the classical tradition of sociology in its utilitarian depiction of peace research as a purposeful social science dedicated to the realization of progress; Galtung was disinterested in sociological inquiry for its own sake, although he sometimes expressed hostility to the ideological contamination of social scientific inquiry and echoed Parsons's call for professionalism. The influence of Durkheim and Parsons was also evident in Galtung's grounding of social values in the empirical analysis of existing social systems and not in philosophical argument.

The character of Galtung's vision of peace research was also complicated by the fact that in spite of its distinctly sociological flavor, it addressed the theoretical and practical domain of the discipline of international relations that had been influenced by the debate within sociology to only a limited extent. The application of sociology to the international system was not unique to Galtung, but in making the case for peace research he added an overt, ostensibly apolitical reformism that owed much more to Saint-Simon than to Parsons. Galtung brought to peace research the mindset of a social scientist and endeavored to set it on a divergent path from earlier forms of normative thinking about international relations, which in his view had been mired in an overly philosophical, reflective form of discourse. The connection between Galtung's sociological writings and his arguments for peace research is not easily made, however, because the sociological underpinnings of his peace research are rarely fully explicated or acknowledged. Nonetheless, they are central to an understanding of his arguments for a scientific peace research that grounds its own normativity within empirical analysis rather than history or pure reason.

Biographical Fragments

In 1930, Johan Vincent Galtung was born into an aristocratic Norwegian family of considerable lineage. It provided a supportive environment in which a sense of noblesse oblige was encouraged. His father was a physician and a former officer in the armed forces, who exerted considerable influence upon his son. In his youth, Galtung watched his father perform medical procedures, and two features of the physician's craft created a lasting impression. First, physicians were required to draw upon a variety of the natural sciences in order to develop the requisite skills. Second, they were obliged, by virtue of the Hippocratic oath, to apply their skills to patients without regard to social circumstances, religion, or ethnic origins. The physician provided a role model for the application of scientific knowledge in a social context as guided by a universal ethic—encapsulated in the commitment to the autotelic value of "health." This notion of a practice that transcended, in principle at least, the vagaries of social and political circumstance had a formative influence upon the young Galtung's understanding of his own social obligations and, ultimately, the role of the peace researcher. Though slated by his family to be a physician, Galtung went on to study philosophy, sociology, and mathematics at the university level. The normative outlook inspired by his particular social circumstances was to be channeled into tending to the health of the social and political realm rather than the somatic health of individuals.[42]

The guiding vision of the (social) physician informed by a politically neutral scientific body of knowledge was a venerable image, recalling medieval "realistic" utopias intended to replace speculative imaginings with secular, practical designs, the plausibility of which were predicated upon and coeval with the evolution of science.[43] As we have seen, it also threaded through the classical positivist literature. All of these visions shared the belief that armed with scientific knowledge, savants could identify the good polity yet avoid the descent into politics. Even in the 1950s, many, perhaps most, sociologists had abandoned the overt utilitarianism of their forefathers, but they continued to present scientific sociology as a politically transcendent court of cognitive appeal. Some went so far as to claim that "ought" statements were not inadmissible within social science but could in fact be dealt with as "if-then" propositions, whose predictive capacity could be scientifically assessed.[44] Although the extent to which these historical antecedents impacted on Galtung's outlook remains unclear, his early writing on peace research appealed overtly to both the ideal type of the physician and to the superiority of the scientific method. The spirit of Saint-Simon was evoked in the envisioning of the professional peace researcher extending a utilitarian, scientific sociological perspective beyond the boundaries of the metropolis or the nation-state.[45]

That Galtung's normative outlook appears to have been formed at an early age is further evidenced by his petition in 1951 to the Norwegian Ministry of Justice for the cessation of the compulsory military training that he had commenced in 1949. In contrast to his family environment, the encounter with military authority and hierarchy had not been an enjoyable experience. In his petition he wrote of wanting to take positive steps toward eliminating the recourse to military means in international politics and referred to the idea of "peace research," although with little idea then of what was meant by the term. Unable to move the powers that were, and unwilling to take the more passive option of simple conscientious objection, Galtung was eventually to spend nearly six months in jail. While in prison, he completed his collaboration with the noted Norwegian philosopher Arne Naess on a book on Gandhi's political ethics. Galtung was Naess's research assistant, and Naess became both a teacher and close friend.

Gandhi's writings had an influence upon Galtung that persists throughout his work to a degree few of his critics have recognized.[46] Along with other elements of Eastern philosophy, Gandhi's life and work constitute a wild card in Galtung's philosophical makeup and thus invite caution on the part of the reader. Some of the central themes of Galtung's work stem from a Gandhian perspective and not, as might be expected, from more familiar Western sources. Nonetheless, sorting out the traces of Gandhian thought is a difficult task because although it has become more overt in Galtung's recent work, it exists only in the background in his earlier writing.

Galtung's use of the work of Gandhi suggests that it provides a practical ethics rather than a theology or metaphysic.[47] Gandhi's emphasis on ethical *conduct,* rather than the origins or nature of ethics themselves, makes his work particularly amenable to translation into the language of contemporary social science.[48] Both Galtung and Naess stressed the possibility of synthesizing Gandhian ethics and modern social science through their "systematization" and structural-functional analysis of Gandhian pacifism. The substance of Gandhian ethics was left unexamined, internally or with reference to other ethical systems.[49] This may help to account for the paucity of substantive references to Gandhi in Galtung's earlier work, since the language of positivist sociology is ill-suited to the appreciation of the complex admixture of metaphysical principles that lay behind Gandhi's "moral ideology" of nonviolence. But in spite of the obscurity of its foundational influence, the imprint of Gandhi's thought on Galtung's work would prove to be significant.

Galtung established himself as a prolific writer at an early age, contributing to newspapers and magazines on a variety of subjects, including Gandhi, conscientious objection, and his travels as a student representative to the Soviet Union. He had been an active member of the Norwegian Labor Party but left in 1952 over the decision to join the fledgling North Atlantic Treaty Organization (NATO). His book on Gandhi was published in 1955, and in that and the following year Galtung had a number of papers on statistical methods published. In 1957 Galtung wrote and had published fourteen items on such subjects as economic development in Italy, statistical research methods and design, nonviolent resistance, and Gandhian ethics. The interest in economic development stemmed from Norway's innovative decision to provide development assistance to a fisheries project in Kerala, India. Though Galtung saw the project as the product of a politically cynical decision to placate the Norwegian left wing, it established an interest in the field of development and related issues such as the transfer of technology.[50]

In 1958 Galtung was appointed visiting assistant professor in the Department of Sociology at Columbia University. He taught a number of courses on sociology, researched and wrote on the sociology of prisons and race relations in the United States, published more papers on statistical methods, and began to write on conflict theory. In 1960 Galtung returned to Oslo to participate in the setting up of the section for research on conflict and peace of the Institute for Social Research, the precursor to the International Peace Research Institute, Olso (PRIO). Although he was only thirty-two, in 1962 PRIO published a volume of more than forty-five items written or delivered by Galtung over the previous decade.[51] An astonishingly prolific writing output has remained a hallmark of Galtung ever since.

Even from such a fragmented biography, the dualism of a strong normative perspective and an enthusiasm for scientific empirical sociology is evident, but the commitment to the latter appeared to preclude adequate explication of the former. Galtung's publications also express a further duality in the mix of writings on political issues for the Norwegian popular press and of academic papers on sociological method or empirical research published in learned journals. The classical positivist vision of the scientist was supplemented with a shading of the roles of the academic and pamphleteer (as was the case with Comte, Saint-Simon, and their American successors), readily apparent in the diverse subject matter and varied discursive tone of Galtung's writings.[52]

Sociology as Science

The introduction to one of the undergraduate courses taught by Galtung at Columbia unequivocally declares: "Sociology is a science and because of this everything that applies to science in general applies to sociology."[53] It is, moreover, a "factual" science in contrast to the "formal" sciences of logic and mathematics. Having no bearing upon empirical reality, the latter are repositories of analytical techniques applicable in the factual or empirical sciences that are located along a scale of scientific rigor with sociology occupying a middle position, "softer" than physics but "harder" than the "humanistic sciences."

As Galtung then saw it, the goal of scientific activity was not that of mastering either the social or nonsocial world, that being the province of an "applied science." However, Galtung's students were advised that the tendency within "Western ideology" to compartmentalize "truth and value" was also questionable, and the social responsibility of the scientist was coming under increasing public scrutiny.[54] Galtung offered only a minimalist definition of science as involving the formulation of *invariances* (general descriptions) and *theories* (general explanations). Not merely for the benefit of undergraduate students as yet unversed in the complexities of social scientific procedure, this definition was reiterated and amplified in academic papers. Thus, in an early scholarly publication Galtung defines the scientific procedure as having as its first objective the assertion of "general implications" of the logical form (x) [P(x) – Q(x)] (being composed of a set X, a set of conditions P, and a set of results Q). Propositions of this form lay down an invariance that, in conformity with a set of established requirements, must be precisely formulated; synthetic (have empirical referents); general; testable; and, finally, tenable. The transformation of an invariance proposition into a *law* requires an intersubjectively reproducible testing procedure. Furthermore, "there must exist a certain amount of consensus within the competence group concerning the evaluation of the degree of confirmation."[55] Ideally, such a competence group should be composed of "people who are from different schools [and] hold different opinions on related subjects."[56] This need reflects the absence of any court of appeal outside of human judgment and acts as a control on the value contamination of social scientific research arising from the involvement of social scientists in the very object domain they are investigating. Any singular hypothesis is to be *verified* or *falsified*, although no position is indicated with regard to the relative merits of these different forms of proof.

The second stage of the scientific process is the formation of theories, this being not a condition sine qua non of science but a "later stage, or at least another stage."[57] However, a characteristic looseness was displayed here. If Galtung was arguing for the possibility of scientific knowledge in an inductive, descriptive, or classificatory form outside of theory, his version of science would not survive Popper's well-known critique of induction. Alternatively, by referring to the development of theory as just "another" stage, Galtung also might be allowing for a wide range of scientific procedures including induction and deduction. It transpires that the social sciences are

inherently limited, being "more concerned with elaborate and detailed statements concerning particular members of the set X than with general propositions." In other words, the unique characteristics of the object domain of
the social sciences do not make sociology inherently unscientific but "inherently difficult if one shall abide by high standards."[58] In this case, high
standards appears to include anything other than inductive empiricism.

Furthermore, when it comes to the process of theory formation, a subjective component becomes evident. The scientific process commences
when our attention is drawn to something; this interest provides the basis
for a "suspicion" and the formulation of hypotheses. Data are obtained and
classified, which leads to the formulation of invariance hypotheses and
theory hypotheses. From the former the facts that should be found are
"logically deduced" (assumably, Galtung actually meant that invariances
induced from observation statements are confirmed), whereas from the latter tenable invariances are deduced. Such exercises in (induction and) deduction can be very precise if the hypotheses are formulated in unambigu-
ous technical or mathematical terms, or they can be "very loose and
subjective as when the hypotheses are formulated partly on the basis of
aesthetic criteria."[59] The hypotheses are then confronted with data, and
predictions about specific cases are deemed to be true or false. As a consequence, invariance hypotheses are judged to be tenable or untenable, and
theory hypotheses are judged to be fruitful or unfruitful.

Absent was any discussion of the epistemological status of the initial
observations, or suspicions, and their relationship to theory. If they are
pretheoretical in origin, then a very crude form of scientific procedure is
being constructed. Given that the concern is with *social* science, some discussion of the selection and observation of the object(s) of inquiry appears
necessary. However, Galtung appeared silently to endorse the Popperian
view that the formulation of hypotheses is not the product of rational (scientific) discussion but is properly the subject of psychology.[60] As I note
later in the chapter, Galtung does provide elsewhere a conceptualization of
the subjective origins of hypotheses that does not reduce to observation, by
utilizing the notion of "empathy" between the observing scientist and the
social order he or she is observing. In other words, science commences
from a variety of sources, none of which can claim ultimate authority, and
the task of science is to detect and eliminate subjective distortion. This
view is confirmed by references to hypotheses derived partly from "aesthetic" (political, social?) criteria.[61]

What then are the consequences for social scientists of living in their
object domain? Galtung appealed to the procedure of intersubjective confirmation as the basis for eliminating subjective influences, but he also
foreshadowed Kuhn's sociology of science by acknowledging that relevant
competence groups may suffer from uniformity. Social scientists may be
less likely to suffer from homogeneity because of their different, "softer"

training and a perceived greater interaction between personality, culture, and the individual scientific ego that encourages differentiation; yet, social scientists may be especially susceptible to being influenced by dominant "truisms and cultural trends of the time and place they live" to the degree that "an intersubjective reproducibility arises which becomes the subject of ridicule of later generations."[62] This recognition of the contingency of social scientific knowledge was not resolved in Galtung's early discussion of scientific procedure, but, with hindsight, it can be seen as a first indication of discomfort with the idea of a social science that was to become more evident in his later work when science was applied to the task of peace research.

The subordinate role of theory was confirmed by Galtung's description of its purpose as the unification of several laws pertaining to the same set, within a common structure. Thus, empirical laws were obtainable prior to (and outside of) theory, but the subsequent building of a theoretical structure could provide the basis for the (hypothetico-deductive) inference of new invariances. If a theory succeeded in both respects, it was fruitful but not tenable or true. Up to this point Galtung's account corresponds with a model of science that has been variously described as "naive inductivism," "systematic empiricism," or "a common-sense epistemology."[63] In spite of the naturalism of Galtung's scientific method, he acknowledged that "the classical physical textbook experiment was of little use in the social sciences."[64] We are encouraged to accept a minimalist understanding of (social) science as being primarily concerned with the identification of invariances. Although Galtung acknowledged problems arising out of the very nature of even a minimalist model of social scientific research (such as the difficulty of translating sociological data into a variate language; the problems of closure and standardization), he appealed to future developments in statistics that may throw new light on the relationship between variables. Again, a characteristic flippancy crept in: Although the problem of measurability haunts the scientific study of the social, it may only indicate an inferiority complex toward the natural sciences. Furthermore, Galtung's subsequent writing on peace research would reveal a preoccupation with theory building, its more problematic status notwithstanding. The requirement that theory building and invariance seeking be connected within a body of empirical data was to be rarely adhered to; the grounding of theoretical explorations usually sidestepped the issue with the assertion that *if* empirical research were carried out, it would probably be supportive of theoretical postulates.[65]

Value-Freedom and Sociology

The young Galtung conceded that the value predispositions of individual social scientists and the social context within which they work were barriers to adequate social science. In the case of the survey technique, for example, the effect of the observer on the data and its evaluation is evident. Galtung's response was blunt: No intersubjectively acceptable solution to this problem exists, save that of "thinking the effect away." But, doubt is also cast on the problem itself: "Much has been said about the normative character of the social sciences and the *Wertfreiheit* of the natural or physical sciences . . . but it seems that no generally accepted conclusion has been arrived at concerning the pertinent question whether the difference is one of kind or one of degree."[66] As members of a society, scientists are likely to have value systems that more or less reflect dominant or official social values, a situation reinforced in part by the need to finance research and publish findings. Though some technical means of alleviating the problem are suggested, Galtung's unease is apparent: "What right does the social scientist have to investigate his fellow human beings" and "to what extent can he comfort himself with their willingness to cooperate, as long as the objects do not clearly see the implications of their investigations?"[67] The social context interferes with various aspects of the scientific procedure: the selection of topics for investigation; the methodological framework utilized; funding; and the exclusion of undesired results by the researcher. Such problems are particularly acute for the social sciences because they are concerned with topics of long-standing concern to humanity and about which there has been considerable dispute. Nonetheless, the problem is consistently presented as one of degree only, in spite of the further admission that, by virtue of their social qualities, the variables in sociological inquiry are stochastic rather than determinate. However, the "reliability" of the observer and observed is deemed crucial.

A further contextual influence that has particular implications for peace research, given its international object domain, arises from the developmental condition of the specific community within which social science is being conducted. In 1959, Galtung noted that the social sciences "have developed far more rapidly in the comparatively problem-free countries in Northern Europe, than for instance in Italy, where parts of the country are deemed to be underdeveloped."[68] The issue is particularly acute if knowledge moves across social boundaries. Later critical forays in the sociology of knowledge are foreshadowed in an early discussion of the social implications of Norway's path-breaking development assistance to India wherein Galtung acknowledges that the social policy developed out of Western sociology may not be suited to a different cultural context. Although the cross-cultural suitability of Western social policy is questioned, at this point the sociological approach itself is not. Nonetheless, notice is served that the putative universality of scientifically derived knowledge and policy, which underscores the claim to social neutrality of science and its agents, may falter under examination.[69] This theme was to be taken up with far greater vigor in Galtung's later work.

The limitations of Western scientific sociology were also illustrated through a brief reference to the "unbridgeable gulf" between marxist and "Western" theories. Seeing both as claiming to have realized a value-free methodology, Galtung did not then detect any basis for fruitful inter-course.[70] Though he was later to emphasize the commonalities between marxism and other forms of Western political discourse, at this stage marx-ism was placed outside of the Western pale. The failure to acknowledge humanist, antinaturalist, and distinctly Western varieties of marxism sug-gests that either Galtung did not perceive marxism to be a fruitful source of sociological insights, or he simply did not read marxist literature. Though he was to abandon such a cursory dismissal of its utility, a ten-dency to caricature marxism was retained.

A further telling observation on the question of values affirms the ten-sion within Galtung's defense of the idea of social science. Galtung admits that it would be difficult for a pacifist psychologist to arrive at research re-sults that imply violence and war are the products of, say, an ineradicable drive in human nature. The difficulty of accepting anticipated research findings that might undermine the rationality of holding to a normative po-sition may result in an inclination not to produce them. Galtung's response was to reiterate the virtues of the criterion of intersubjectivity and note the positive consequences of the intrusion of values in science arising out of the empathy (*Einfuhlung*) between the observer and observed. Empathy, introspection, and insight are, Galtung argued, important subjective (if not necessarily acknowledged) stimulants of hypotheses. Yet, he also admitted that an introspective appreciation of the complexity of social phenomena may make research appear Sisyphean, since the shortcomings of theoreti-cal representations of the real world and the inability of scientific concep-tual language to capture the nuances of everyday social life become all too apparent.[71] Intentionally or otherwise, the discussion of this issue echoed those critiques of positivism which, in emphasizing the hermeneutic qual-ities of social analysis and the social role of conceptual languages, chal-lenge the idea that scientific naturalism can adequately grasp the phenom-enon of the social.[72] The concept of empathy proves to be a two-edged sword: It may be of value in generating scientific hypotheses, but in order for science to proceed conclusively it must be eliminated at some point. As the dilemma confronting the pacifist social scientist suggests, the excision may prove difficult indeed. The inconclusiveness of Galtung's discussion of value-freedom in social science was perhaps a result of a youthful naïveté regarding the possibility of social science qua science, coupled with a lack of conviction as to the significance of the problem of values. As he was to admit later, the fact-value distinction never particularly bothered him. Galtung's early sociological writings certainly did not reveal any interest in the numerous critical interpretations of the social scientific enterprise that would have been available at the time. Yet if the value

contamination of scientific research was self-evidently an issue for a putative peace researcher, there was a further dimension of the problem that
was of equal, perhaps greater, significance: the scientific investigation of
social values themselves. As was noted earlier, this figured large in the history of modern sociology, and it was particularly acute for Galtung because his subsequent claims for peace research were predicated upon the
assumption that a scientific attitude was conducive to, indeed preferable
for, not only the investigation of specific values but also their promotion.
The key to Galtung's treatment of this issue lies in his understanding of
structural functionalism.

FUNCTIONS AND VALUES

It must be noted here that apart from his early sociological writings
and a brief reformulation of structural functionalism written some ten
years later, Galtung's peace research tends to present itself as an example
of structural analysis. To further complicate matters, his use of the term
structural is also ambiguous and changes over time, a theme to which we
will return in subsequent chapters. Generally speaking, his discussion of
structural functionalism focuses primarily on the functional contribution of
dimensions of social structure to the maintenance of the social system of
which they form a part. In contrast, the term *structural* tends to be used to
refer to enduring, constitutive social formations and accords more with
contemporary usage.[73] Certainly, Galtung's earlier sociological writings
are more systems-theoretic than structuralist, in the tradition of Durkheim
and Parsons rather than Marx and Levi-Strauss. Overall, Galtung's work reflects the wider giving way of the term *structural functionalism*, from a position of dominance in the 1940s and 1950s, to the concept of structure.[74]

These days, in spite of the imprecision of the label, structural functionalism has followed positivism in acquiring pejorative connotations.[75]
For its critics, it connotes a perspective that is innately conservative and
concerned only with the analysis of the preservation of social systems.
Usually citing Parsons as the bête noire, critics question the tendency to
abstraction and the assumption that all components of social systems can
be understood in terms of their function in the maintenance and continuing
harmonization of the wider system. It is frequently claimed that a structural-functional perspective is ahistorical, teleological, and inimical to the
consideration of social change and excludes the consideration of human
agency.[76] The purpose of social existence dissolves into an account of systemic imperatives and appears independent of human consciousness or
the exercise of reason.[77] If such criticisms hold, structural functionalism
appears to be an unusual choice for a reform-minded sociologist-cum–
peace researcher unless such a theorist seeks to deflect the philosophical

rationalization of a normative position. That proved to be Galtung's objective.

We can glean some understanding of Galtung's interpretation of structural functionalism by noting his acknowledgment of the influence of Robert Merton, who played a central role in modifying the perspective to take account of its critics. For Merton, functional analysis was a "methodological orientation" or "analytic method," but it also had to be connected to systematic empirical evidence. He was concerned with the development of a dynamic rather than static image of society, and his brand of functionalism has been described as one of its most liberal variants.[78] He argued that functionalist analysis did not exclude, by definition, an analysis of social change, since the components of social systems can be assessed in terms of their functionality in the "adaptation or adjustment" of the wider system and not just its maintenance. One need not assume the existence of universal, functional givens for social systems; this was a legacy of the analogy with organic systems underscoring classical functionalist writing.[79] Against this, Merton considered the interaction between subjective dispositions and objective functional consequences of human behavior. He also questioned (but did not decisively reject) the assumption of the functional indispensability of all of the elements that make up a society, on the grounds that this ignored the evidence of considerable diversity in social institutions, practices, customs, and social values.[80] The efforts of Parsons and others to construct sophisticated analytical frameworks simply flew in the face of human experience.

Rejecting the criticism that it was intrinsically conservative, Merton argued that a functionalist analysis could focus upon the dysfunctional consequences of aspects of a social system and lead to the adumbration of an "ultra-radical utopia." In Merton's hands, structural functionalism did not set out to construct an *explanatory* model of social systems but only an interpretive framework. In other words, the telos of social systems was not to be grounded within an analysis of their functional prerequisites. In effect, Merton was moving toward a structural analysis and a more critical emphasis on the constraints that social systems impose on social interaction.

Galtung also rejected the assumption that functionalism was irretrievably wedded to a conservative ideology, claiming instead to employ a radical version that introduces subjectively held social values, not reducible to systemic imperatives, into the functionalist equation. In a 1959 paper Galtung described structural functionalism as a metatheory that indicates one way in which sociological data can be organized and theory constructed.[81] The methodology cannot itself be empirically tested but "can be tested against methodological criteria of simplicity and fruitfulness." However, this did not "preclude the possibility that in some presentations of structural-functional theory there may be an empirically-testable nucleus."[82] The illustration offered—"affective neutrality is functional for the carrying out of a physician's obligations"—was prophetic, for it was upon a comparable functionalist premise that the role of the professional peace researcher was to be based.

Galtung followed Merton in rejecting the orthodox functionalist reliance upon the nondemonstrable, teleological notion of an overriding *systemic* imperative to explain the functionality of social norms. A consequence of this was a tendency to analyze social practices and institutions primarily in terms of their role in upholding the objectified values of social consensus, stability, and integration (all crucial to system maintenance). By implication, all consequences implying social change risk being viewed as dysfunctional, an approach Galtung also dismissed as an example of "conservative functionalism."[83] His objective was to demonstrate the utility of structural functionalism in the analysis of social change as a functionally positive consequence of changing social values rather than the mysterious logic of system maintenance. The necessity for this move was clear enough, for only then could a normatively driven peace research with claims to scientific legitimacy establish its utility.

Citing Merton again, in the 1959 discussion Galtung defined functions as "those observed consequences which make for the adaptation or adjustment of a given system." Functionality was a criterion for *evaluation* of the consequences of social interaction. Effectively, "a function is any value in a social system," the term *value* incorporating such things as "goal," "end," "need," and "aim."[84] Functionalist analysis may, therefore, be critical of certain elements of a social system. To ascertain whether or not a form of social interaction is functional or dysfunctional requires the identification of the relevant "values, goals, and aims," bearing in mind the rejection of the equation of social values with supposedly objective systemic needs. Nevertheless, the identification of relevant values still had to be achieved without the intrusion of the sociologist's own value system or of the specific values of individuals and groups within the system. Galtung acknowledged that certain values may not be held in common or may be latent; who holds certain values and the extent to which consensus exists are recognized as important empirical and theoretical questions. In sum, the idea of system maintenance becomes socially grounded.

To illustrate the point Galtung drew an analogy with the value of "health," which appears to be a consensual and "intersubjectively communicable" standard for the medical community, itself a social subsystem. What is required is a "general standard applicable to a subclass of social systems of which [the system under scrutiny] is a member . . . this must somehow give an ideal picture of what [the system] should, could or ought to be." Galtung wanted to avoid the accusation that functional analysis was a form of value judgment and rejected the assumption that the desired standard is simply either that of preserving the status quo or changing it. Rather, an ideal type—S*—can be constructed for comparison with the actual system S. Functionality is assessed in terms of the reduction in distance between S* and S. But how is S* arrived at? The following procedure is suggested:

> The safe answer seems to be that this is up to the sociologist; and a very fruitful approach seems to be to pick out the values, goals, aims and ends of S [a social system] he deems to be pertinent and embody them in S* [an ideal type]. In some cases the best thing seems to be to ask the members of S . . . [or] . . . members of some systems including S. . . . By defining S* *we define what we consider to be good for S*.[85]

The functional attributes of a social structure are determined by reference to a set of values embedded in the collective consciousness of that system or within a wider consciousness pertaining to the class of social systems, of which that system is a member. Values against which a social system can be assessed are defended only insofar as they might be shown to be held by a suitable reference group.

The proposed procedure was interventionist. Galtung went on to suggest that the values deemed pertinent by the functional analyst because of their analytical fruitfulness "should be made explicit . . . so that others can know what his standard of evaluation is." A brief allusion to opinion surveys notwithstanding, this appears to be no more than an argument for honest subjectivity rather than a decisive resolution of the question of the ultimate origins of social values. Furthermore, Galtung did not himself engage in any attempt to explore empirically what such values might consist of, or whether they were contested within the relevant social system. Indeed, at one point he opined that the empirical identification of the values in question need not concern us. The gist of his discussion is simply that values precede functions.

Elsewhere, Galtung offered a different account that provides a clearer indication of the origins of social values (or functions) and their role in social change. Also written in 1959, his "Expectations and Interaction Processes" develops the analysis of structural-functional theory by considering the Parsonian concept of *interaction*. Social interactions are conditioned by the expectations (standards of evaluation) used by individual actors to evaluate the attributes and actions of themselves and others. Actor expectations can be compared with the object of evaluation yielding three possible results: consonance, dissonance, or a rejection of the evaluative standard. Galtung is particularly interested in the problem of dissonance and the restoration of consonance. Two extreme examples of efforts to restore consonance are evident: Change or redefine the object to fit the evaluative standard; or change the standard or expectation to fit the object. Thus, dissonance contributes to the emergence of norms. If the interactions of social actors are conditioned by the evaluations of themselves and others, then efforts to equilibrate the relationship between expectation and perception will range across a spectrum of possible mechanisms of "social control." Changing the object evaluated, such as another actor, entails preserving the normative expectation and classifying the dissonant object as deviant or wrong. Prescriptive choices are frozen in favor of adaptation through social control. Changing the evaluative standard, however, is akin to the scientific process of finding a hypothesis disconfirmed or falsified by experience. Between these two poles lies a variety of intermediate outcomes, such as mild social control coupled with some modification of the evaluative standard. Thus, social change arises out of interactions that generate dissonance between expectations and actual behavior of social actors.

Galtung's exploration of social interaction contained two illuminating themes. First, the discussion is premised upon the antimetaphysical view that norms originate exclusively in human interaction and can be comprehended only within that context. Second, although social stability is seen to require an equilibrium between expectations (norms) and interactions, in the unpacking of the process of social interaction an attempt is made to free functionalist analysis from the accusation of an inadequate treatment of social change. In principle, there is no reason to suppose that social norms cannot adapt to changing social behavior (the more usual object of investigation), thereby preserving equilibrium between expectations and behavior without recourse to the social control of behavioral deviance. In other words, the holding of new values (revised expectations) can be rationalized through reference to changes in the relevant social system. This does not, of course, fully confront the difficult issue of whether the social norms are good or bad; it simply questions the fixity of assumptions about social deviance often attributed to systems-theoretic sociology.

The interpretation of functional analysis as having creative and critical potential was most evident when Galtung revisited the perspective a decade later. In "Functionalism in a New Key," Galtung correlated functions with values again, a move that was seen to distinguish radical functionalism from liberal and conservative variants. Whereas Merton located functions in the evolutionary adaptation and adjustment of a social system, Galtungian functional analysis required the empirical identification of the relevant evaluative standards prior to the examination of the functionality of a specific social system; values (or functions) could not be derived from the system itself. In focusing upon dissonance between social norms and forms of social structure, functional analysis acquired a critical role because as reflections of collective human consciousness and action, rather than the needs of an abstracted social system, functions become "changeable, rejectable and substitutable."[86]

THE IMPLICATIONS OF GALTUNG'S SOCIOLOGY FOR PEACE RESEARCH

Although peace research was to be guided by a philosophical predisposition—it would make little sense otherwise—the first implication was that as a social science it would require the exclusion of subjective, a priori values from its methodology and research program. The guiding evaluative standard—peace—would have to be on a par with the value of somatic health, with a demonstrably consensual—"intersubjectively agreeable"—content.

Second, Galtung's overt equation of functions with values invited the construction of an image of an ideal international social system (S*), the primary object domain of peace research, against which the existing international system (S) could be judged. In this respect, peace research would go beyond pure analysis and acquire an applied function. Utilizing scientific method rather than philosophy, peace research would attempt to identify those values that would enable critical assessment of the existing international system in terms of its functionality. Since the standard against which the system is judged had to be shown to be held, peace research was charged with empirically demonstrating that its normative orientation accorded with the values of a relevant reference group.

Third, the origins and rationality of such values would be derived from perceived changes already evident in the existing international system; established "expectations" had to be shown to be dissonant with the object of evaluation. If social change was explicable within an analysis of the consonance or dissonance between expectations and interactions— something Galtung also described as a theory of the emergence of norms —then the relationship between social values and actual social behavior could be used to argue for changes in normative standards. To illustrate, let us suppose actors within a social system are perceived to be changing in directions dissonant with existing expectations or normative standards embedded in established theoretical frameworks. Rather than perceive the system to be dysfunctional and the deviant actors in need of social control to fit existing normative expectations expressed as theoretical assumptions (through the denial of the significance or legitimacy of behavioral change, for example), we might better alter our expectations to fit the changing social system. Because social systems are self-evidently dynamic, socially defined systemic needs change, and assumptions about the evaluative standards for assessing the functionality (or health) of the system must adjust accordingly. If a putative peace research can convincingly identify fundamental systemic changes, the rejection of traditional theoretical accounts of that system can follow and an alternative set of systemic norms can be postulated. Indeed, Galtung did precisely this by premising his argument for peace research upon the observation of fundamental changes in the international system, to which existing social values should adapt. Specifically, he focused on the evidence of increasing interdependence and extension of community beyond the boundaries of nation-states, which legitimated the promotion of the values of further integration and cooperation across political boundaries. Actors and their behavior were changing in systemically significant ways. The function of peace research lay, then, in both the observation of significant systemic changes and the articulation of social values that better reflected them and were therefore worthy of promotion as reasonable adaptations to a changing world. The value content of the term *peace* was to be determined sociologically rather than being derived from pure reason or ethics, asserted, or simply demanded. The appeal of this procedure for the peace researcher qua social scientist lay in the claim that international relations orthodoxy could be discounted by appealing to empirical evidence alone. Valuation would proceed from cognition.[87]

Unfortunately, Galtung's account could not but be hoisted by its own petard. The act of observing specific forms of social interaction in order to demonstrate dissonance or consonance with value-laden expectations privileges certain empirical events according to unexplained criteria. As Galtung himself conceded, observations are value-driven, yet those values could not be analyzed within the model of science adopted. Values *inform* cognition, from which values are then claimed to arise. It is one thing to question conservative functionalism's reification of social values in the guise of objective systemic imperatives; it is another to claim that social values can be constructed solely upon the basis of observed systemic change, opinion surveys, and the like. The former procedure presupposes values; the latter simply confirms that values are held. In all of his sociological writings, Galtung provided no further analysis or defense of any specific social values, other than the empirical claim that they were held, or the assumption that they *should* be held in reflection of changes in the relevant social system.

The lacuna in Galtung's sociology, which was to be carried into peace research, was any sense of the political ethics of social change; it was avowedly antiphilosophical. Even if agreement could be reached as to the broad directions in which a social system was moving, it would be a different matter establishing a normative consensus as to the desirability of such changes, the extent to which they should be responded to, or whose interests they reflected. How are we to choose, for example, between competing and incommensurate visions of systemic health? The only answer implied is that empirical evidence must be produced to show which set of values accords best with the social system under scrutiny. That brings us back full circle to the problem of the value contamination of observations. As Merton correctly observed, functional analysis could be wedded to any political ideology, but because it was a descriptive rather than explanatory discourse, it could not provide that ideology. By definition, a functionalist form of peace research would be incapable of normative self-defense because, like its positivist forefathers, it could not give an account of itself.

Though aware of the problem of defending values outside of overtly normative discourse, an inescapable issue for a pacifist sociologist inspired by Gandhi, Galtung was not overly perturbed by it. In his earlier discussion of functionalism he argued that there were "fairly intersubjectively-communicable and consensual standards"—such as sane, healthy, normal—against which social systems could be judged. To describe a social system as healthy was not a value judgment, he thought, in contrast to the claim that "healthy is good." He did not seem to question whether it was possible to apply such a term to the analysis of social systems and not have it acquire an ideological slant.[88] In any case, Galtungian peace research could not but be normative in essence, for it would reproduce the deeper, more opaque imprints of the positivist sociological discourse within which it was constructed. Positivism could offer only a chimeric alternative to philosophy and morally informed reason as the cognitive bases for a rational and good social life.

Finally, two qualifications to the tidy picture I have tried to sketch must be noted. First, Galtung's adoption of a positivist model of peace research cannot be fully explained by reference to developments in analytical discourse; there was a sociology to his sociology. Given the controversy that has historically surrounded the intellectual exploration of peace, the adoption of a scientific approach—with all of the attendant connotations of rigor and absence of moralism—made pragmatic, political sense, especially during the latter part of the first Cold War. As the process of establishing the PRIO—founded by Galtung—was to reveal, the mantle of science proved useful in the quest for public legitimation, not to mention funding.[89]

Second, the appeal of science and mathematics to Galtung lay also in their inherent novelty and creativity. The quantitative sociologist Paul Lazarsfeld impressed Galtung with his ingenuity and unabated enthusiasm and taught him that mathematics and statistics were not only creative but also fun. Similarly, Galtung admired Parsons because his theoretical explorations displayed "an audacity unheard of in a jungle of small-scale empirical platitudes."[90] The intangible qualities of creativity and audacity might sit uncomfortably with the notion of a rigorous social science, but they provided more signals that Galtung's discourse on peace research could not be fully comprehended solely by reference to its self-proclaimed epistemological and methodological principles. In spite of his enthusiasm for American sociology, in 1960 Galtung declined the offer of tenure at Columbia. He vividly recalls his farewell speech in which he thanked his colleagues at Columbia for their inspiration, but frankly informed them of his felt need to engage in "higher and better things."[91] He had been told by Talcott Parsons that his interest in such things as race relations and peace was "really not very chic."[92] Galtung went home to Norway.

NOTES

1. Huxley, "Foreword," in Lentz, *Towards a Science of Peace*, pp. vi–vii.
2. Giddens, *Positivism and Sociology*, p. 2; Giddens, "Positivism and Its Critics," in Bottomore and Nisbet, *A History of Sociological Analysis*, p. 237.

3. Bernstein, *The Restructuring of Social and Political Theory*, p. 5.

4. Tudor, *Beyond Empiricism*, p. 4.

5. Habermas, *Knowledge and Human Interests*, pp. 3–5, 6–9, 71–90. *Bildungsprozess* refers to "the formation or shaping and the [humanistic] education, cultivation and acculturation of a self-conscious subject," a process that is not chosen in advance by the self but in which the self actively participates.

6. Ibid., p. 71. It is debatable whether the problem actually constitutes a paradox or simply a case of discursive incompatibility.

7. Giddens, "Positivism and Its Critics," p. 238.

8. Habermas, *Knowledge and Human Interests*, p. 74.

9. Ibid., pp. 76–77.

10. Habermas attributes this vision of the utility of science to Bacon, ibid., p. 77; whereas Giddens traces it back to Condorcet. Giddens, "Positivism and Its Critics," p. 239.

11. Comte, "Discours sur l'Esprit Positif," cited in Habermas, *Knowledge and Human Interests*, pp. 76–77, emphasis added.

12. Habermas, *Knowledge and Human Interests*, p. 80. See also Giddens, "Positivism and Its Critics," p. 242.

13. To this end, he founded the Positivist Society: "The principle, Love; The basis, Order; The end, Progress." Comte, *System of Positive Polity*, pp. xxiv–xxv.

14. I am drawing here from Taylor, *Henri Saint-Simon;* and Taylor, *The Political Ideas of the Utopian Socialists*.

15. Benton, *The Philosophical Foundations,* p. 81. See also Lukes, *Emile Durkheim,* pp. 2–4.

16. Durkheim cited in Benton, *The Philosophical Foundations*, p. 206, note 3. See also Lukes, *Emile Durkheim*, p. 396.

17. "It [sociology] must above all have an object of its own . . . a reality which is not the domain of the other sciences." Durkheim cited in Lukes, *Emile Durkheim*, p. 9. See also Giddens, *Durkheim*, p. 63; and Giddens, *Capitalism and Modern Social Theory*, p. 86.

18. Lukes, *Emile Durkheim*, pp. 9–12 and 110–119.

19. Benton, *The Philosophical Foundations*, pp. 84–89. Benton argues that the real source of Durkheim's conception of "social facts" is a "general philosophy of nature."

20. Durkheim cited in Giddens, *Capitalism and Modern Social Theory*, p. 93.

21. Benton, *The Philosophical Foundations*, pp. 89–94. See also Rex, *Key Problems of Sociological Theory*, pp. 5–7.

22. Vidich and Lyman, *American Sociology,* pp. 1–5.

23. Coser, "American Trends," in Bottomore and Nisbet, *A History of Sociological Analysis*, pp. 287–289.

24. See Coser, "American Trends," pp. 291–293 for examples.

25. Vidich and Lyman, *American Sociology*, pp. 33–35. See also Coser, "American Trends," p. 299.

26. Mills described Ross as the classic social analyst "graceful, muckraking, upright." See Mills, *The Sociological Imagination*, p. 12.

27. Veblen in Coser, "American Trends," p. 304. Veblen encouraged the temporary flourishing of the technocracy movement founded by one of his followers, Howard Scott, an engineer. See Taylor, *The Political Ideas of the Utopian Socialists*, pp. 237–239.

28. See Rock, *The Making of Symbolic Interactionism;* also Szacki, *History of Sociological Thought*, ch. 15.

29. Lipset and Smelsor, "The Setting of Sociology in the 1950's," in Lipset and Smelsor (eds.), *Sociology: The Progress of a Decade*, pp. 2–3.

30. Savage, *The Theories of Talcott Parsons*, pp. 24–27.

31. Hamilton, *Talcott Parsons*, p. 64.

32. Ibid., p. 67.

33. Parsons, "Some Problems Confronting Sociology as a Profession," p. 550 (emphasis added).

34. Ibid., p. 555.

35. Homans, *Social Behaviour: Its Elementary Forms*, pp. 10–11.

36. I have been drawing here from Dahrendorf, "Out of Utopia," pp. 115–127. For a more moderate critique along similar lines, see Coser, *The Functions of Social Conflict*.

37. Mills, *The Sociological Imagination*, p. 192.

38. Szacki, *History of Sociological Thought*, p. 523.

39. Gouldner, "Anti-Minotaur: The Myth of a Value-Free Sociology," in Stein and Vidich (eds.), *Sociology on Trial*.

40. Ibid., p. 37.

41. The impending development of a full-blown radicalism is illustrated by two collections of essays published in the early 1960s: Horowitz (ed.), *The New Sociology;* and Stein and Vidich, *Sociology on Trial*.

42. Interview with Galtung, Berlin, July 1984 (hereafter referred to as "interview").

43. Eurich, *Science in Utopia: A Mighty Design*, chs. 2 and 3.

44. Lundberg, *Can Science Save Us?* pp. 34–41.

45. For Saint-Simon the transcendence of political and social boundaries by "l'esprit industriel" promised "l'organisation definitive de l'espece humaine." Durkheim, *Le Socialisme: Sa Definition, Ses Debuts, La Doctrine Saint-Simonienne*, p. 254.

46. See Galtung, "Introduction," *Essays in Peace Research* (hereafter *EPR*), 5, p. 23. A recent exception is Korhonen, *The Geometry of Power*.

47. Thus Galtung's (and Naess's) focus is on "satyagraha," the practical application of the principle of "ahimsa" or nonviolence, rather than on the metaphysical content of the principle itself. See Korhonen, *The Geometry of Power*, ch. 2.

48. Gandhi has been described as not only a social scientist but a "social technocrat" concerned with the realization of concrete programs of social action. See Diwakar, "Gandhi: a Social Scientist and Social Technocrat"; and Malhotra, "Gandhi and the Scientific Outlook."

49. Naess, "A Systematisation of Gandhian Ethics of Conflict Resolution." Galtung presents his sociological analysis of Gandhian pacifism in deliberate contrast to an ethical point of view, yet acknowledges that Gandhi may not be representative of pacifism per se. See Galtung, "Pacifism from a Sociological Point of View."

50. Galtung, interview.

51. Galtung, *Var Nye Verden: Artikler og Foredrag Gjennom Ti Ar* (Our New World: Articles and Speeches over Ten Years).

52. Gleditsch refers to the existence of at least two audiences but not necessarily two separate literatures. He prefers to depict a continuum with "lighter" and "heavier" ends. See Gleditsch, "The Structure of Galtungism," in Gleditsch, et al., *Johan Galtung: A Bibliography*, p. 65.

53. Galtung, "Sociology 49," p. 88. Galtung's course outlines from the 1950s were made publicly available by PRIO in 1980.

54. Galtung, "Sociology 2," pp. 121–122.

55. Galtung, "Notes on the Difference Between Physical and Social Science" (hereafter "Notes"), pp. 9–10.

56. Galtung, "Sociology 49," p. 89.

57. Galtung, "Notes," p. 10.

58. Galtung, "Sociology 49," p. 92.

59. Ibid., p. 90.

60. Popper, *Conjectures and Refutations: The Growth of Scientific Knowledge*, pp. 3–28; also Salmon, *The Foundations of Scientific Inference*, pp. 21–27.

61. Galtung, "Sociology 49," p. 6.

62. Galtung, "Notes," p. 25. This observation bears comparison with Kuhn's notion of incommensurable, historically contingent scientific paradigms. See Kuhn, *The Structure of Scientific Revolutions*, chs. 2, 3, and 5. Galtung does not clearly indicate why intersubjective reproducibility comes to be ridiculed. It can only be inferred that it arises out of changing social values and norms.

63. See Chalmers, *What Is This Thing Called Science?* and Willer and Willer, *Systematic Empiricism: Critique of a Pseudo-Science*. The term "common-sense epistemology" is from Tudor who, in the spirit of Quine's description of science as "self-conscious common-sense," offers a model of science that bears comparison with Galtung. See Tudor, *Beyond Empiricism*, ch. 2.

64. Galtung, "Notes," p. 15.

65. See, for example, Galtung, "A Structural Theory of Aggression," pp. 117–121; "A Structural Theory of Integration," pp. 366–392; "A Structural Theory of Imperialism," pp. 467–470; and "A Structural Theory of Revolution." In all of these examples, empirical evidence is either minimal, nonexistent, or presumed to be supportive of the hypotheses. Yet, all contain policy-oriented conclusions.

66. Galtung, "Notes," p. 7. The Columbia course notes are unequivocal: Sociologists might research about values, but "we do not make value-judgments in sociology as in any other science; we do not evaluate the phenomena we investigate. Value statements are not scientific propositions; they are not testable." Galtung, "Sociology 49," p. 92.

67. Galtung, "Notes," p. 20.

68. Ibid., p. 26.

69. Galtung, "A Talk Held at a UNESCO Seminar at Langkollen, Norway, 1961," in *Papers*, 3, pp. 7–18.

70. Galtung, "Notes," p. 26.

71. Ibid., p. 24.

72. See the discussion in Bernstein, *The Restructuring of Social and Political Theory*, parts 2 and 3.

73. An exception is Galtung's structural analysis of imperialism that considers briefly the nature of a "structural" approach. See Chapter 5, this volume.

74. Nevertheless, the notion of social structure is itself polyphyletic and polymorphous, and its ancestral lines are difficult to unravel. See Merton, "Structural Analysis in Sociology," in Blau (ed.), *Approaches to the Study of Social Structure*, pp. 21–52.

75. On the ambiguity of "structure," see Blau, "Parameters of Social Structure," in Blau (ed.), *Approaches to the Study of Social Structure*. On the ambiguity of "function," see Abrahamson, *Functionalism*, pp. 38–40. For a survey of different forms of structural functionalism, see Nagel, *The Structure of Science*.

76. Homans, "Bringing Men Back In," pp. 809–819. See also Emmett, *Function, Purpose and Powers*.

77. Hart, *The Concept of Law*, pp. 184–186.

78. Sztompka, *Robert K. Merton: An Intellectual Profile*, p. 129; and Giddens, "Functionalism: Apres la Lutte," in Giddens, *Studies in Social and Political Theory*.

79. Lehman, "R.K. Merton's Concept of Function and Functionalism," pp. 275–277.

80. Merton, *Social Theory and Social Structure*, pp. 85, 105.

81. Galtung, "An Outline of Structural-Functional Theory." It was not until 1969 that he retrospectively described his version of structural functionalism as radical. See Galtung, "Functionalism in a New Key."

82. Galtung, "An Outline of Structural-Functional Theory," p. 150.

83. Galtung, "Functionalism in a New Key," pp. 135–137. For the argument that in the 1950s the majority of sociologists accepted that structural-functional theory was a theory of social stability, not change, see Smith, *The Concept of Social Change*, p. 2.

84. Galtung, "An Outline of Structural-Functional Theory," p. 157. See also his "A Framework for the Analysis of Social Conflict," p. 38, and "Functionalism in a New Key," p. 140. This appears to correspond with Merton's use of the term *function* to refer to both subjective motives and objective consequences. In his later reconsideration of functionalism, Galtung retains the formula "function equals value" but classes Merton as a "liberal" structural-functionalist who depicts functions as "built into society as *stable equilibria* (nature's pointer)," whereas in Galtung's account "function equals value" becomes an axiom of "radical functionalism."

85. Galtung, "An Outline of Structural-Functional Theory," p. 156 (emphasis added).

86. Galtung, "Functionalism in a New Key," p. 158.

87. In 1955, Fromm offered a comparable perspective: "A sane society is that which corresponds to the needs of man—not necessarily what he *feels* to be his needs . . . but what his needs are *objectively*, as they can be ascertained by the study of man." Cited in Friedrichs, *A Sociology of Sociology*, p. 335, note 2.

88. Galtung, "An Outline of Structural-Functional Theory," pp. 153–154.

89. Interview. See also Galtung, "Dedication," *EPR*, 1, pp. 17–18.

90. Galtung, interview. See also Galtung, "Expectations and Interaction Processes," p. 233; and Galtung, "Dedication," *Essays in Methodology* (hereafter *EM*), 2, p. 13, and "Dedication," *EM*, 3.

91. Galtung, interview. See also the introduction to Galtung, *EPR*, 3, p. 21.

92. Galtung, interview. He also noted that Paul Lazarsfeld, in spite of his socialist background and leaning, "forgot" the importance of social purpose in his enthusiasm for developing statistical methods. See also Friedrichs, *A Sociology of Sociology*, p. 78.

2

Peace Research as Science

By 1964, the year in which the *Journal of Peace Research* was established under his editorship, Galtung had begun exploring the form, content, and institutional setting of a scientific, professional peace research. It was not to be a resurrection of what he described as traditional idealist speculation as to the desirability or possibility of an ill-defined goal of global peace. In classically positivist fashion, scientific knowledge rather than metaphysical speculation or transcendental reason was seen to be not only epistemologically superior but also the key to global social progress. By implication, the new peace researchers were not to be concerned with philosophically inventing peace as a value or establishing the moral obligation to pursue it but with deriving its content empirically and exploring the means to its realization. In other words, peace research would be primarily concerned with identifying dissonance between the value of peace and social action as the basis for adumbrating alternative social orders that might achieve greater consonance between values and social action on a global scale.

Galtung's early peace research was constructed around two principal themes: the definition of the concept of peace and the application of structural-functionalist sociology to the analysis of the international system. Both will be reviewed in this chapter. However, if the latter constituted the bulk of Galtung's earlier peace research, it was the former that most clearly reflected the deficiencies of empiricism and positivism, and it is to the definitional aspect that I first turn.

AGAINST TRADITIONAL PEACE THINKING

The novelty of peace research was established via a broad, imprecise, and rather dispersed critique of "traditional peace thinking." Many of the criticisms were made a few years after the founding of peace research and were reconstructive in tone, as illustrated by the phrase "traditional peace thinking" itself. This referred not only to classical philosophical reflections on the quest for global peace—such as Kant's "Perpetual Peace" and its twentieth-century successors—but also to the modern Anglo-American discipline of international relations almost in its entirety. Not much consideration was given to how the authors of traditional peace thinking viewed their own work. Galtung took the view that by definition the discipline of international relations was primarily, if inadequately, concerned with realizing peace.

The quest for peace was the motivation expressed by the founders of the modern discipline of international relations, and virtually all mainstream writing on international relations since has claimed peace and war, in some sense or other, as its core concern. However, it is debatable whether the realization of global peace in the sense understood by its liberal-internationalist founding figures, or the young Galtung for that matter, has remained the guiding purpose of international relations scholarship, especially given the hegemonic presence of realism since the 1940s. At the heart of realism, in all of its variations, has lain the claim that as long as an anarchic system of sovereign states exists—and few realists herald its imminent disappearance—war remains an ever present possibility. Given this, a preoccupation with realizing peace as a permanent feature of international relations appears not only naive but foolhardy. For example, Hans Morgenthau, a principal architect of postwar realist ascendancy, acknowledged that in the abstract peace was an end state that international relations scholarship sought to realize, but he insisted upon the recognition of power as the prime motivation behind state behavior.[1] Others, not necessarily of a fully realist persuasion, have emphasized the problem of international order as paramount, with peace as sometimes the necessary victim. To place such thought within a historical continuum of "peace thinking," tidily connecting Kantian and neo-Kantian schemes for global peace with modern social scientific peace research, elides the crucial distinction between the transformative intent motivating so-called idealism and the profound skepticism that informs realism and its cognates. But Galtung's critique suffered from inadequate references to concrete examples of the discourses being rejected and a reliance upon impressionistic observations about various disciplines, not only international relations, within the humanities and social sciences.[2] The reader is left with the impression that he was either unaware of the nuances of debates about international relations and what some of his contemporaries were actually saying or was simply not interested. A critical point was being made in broad strokes to establish the novelty of peace research.

Lack of precision notwithstanding, the thrust of Galtung's complaint was unequivocally positivist. It also struck its target in many respects.

Traditional thinking about peace was described as usually being "vague, confused and contradictory."[3] It was deemed to be "rarely original" and often employed to glorify certain means per se rather than to identify those means that would lead to peaceful ends. The nebulousness of peace as a concept enabled its attachment to any set of social values, policies, or strategies to support claims as to their validity; few would claim to be opposed to peace. Generally speaking, historical usage of the term was as an unscientific, value-laden category, employed for "ritualistic and expressive purposes" and not with the intent of clarifying or realizing a clearly defined end state. Galtung drew a comparison that would later come to haunt him: Peace had become coterminous with nirvana—a concept that by virtue of its diffuseness, intangibility, and quasi-religious qualities could not be analyzed or researched.[4] Nevertheless, it had been put to different uses by both the political Right and Left.

The conceptual inadequacy of the term *peace* stemmed from the historical tendency for thinking about it to remain the preserve of a classical form of intellectual discourse that, Galtung asserted, was often conducted in "an easy armchair way," without the seriousness that the subject deserved. It reflected the view that the problems associated with realizing peace could be clarified by reflection rather than consideration of empirical evidence.[5] Galtung explicitly rejected "rationalism," equating it with "a priori thinking" and "dogmatism," and in so doing, he affirmed the historical confrontation of philosophy with science, of philosophical idealism with realism. Science provided a means of arbitrating between competing and ideologically biased accounts, by which was clearly meant traditional international relations scholarship in its various forms.[6] Such thinking tended to appeal to established maxims as the basis for policy, assuming the future to be largely a replication of the past. For example, the concept of the balance of power, so central to realist discourse, was an example of deficient peace thinking that relied upon an established but critically unexamined principle. Similarly, the dictum "if you wish peace, prepare for war" had acquired the status of apodictic truth within traditional literature. This excessive orientation toward the past stemmed from the unscientific nature of traditional writing. In spite of a shared empiricist outlook, Galtung held to a more formal conception of science than most realists, who understood by empiricism the idiographic (rather than nomothetic) reference to history as a repository of facts.

Traditional thinking about peace was redeemable, in part, as a source of hypotheses amenable to scientific assessment. For Galtung, the sociological enterprise was concerned not only with accounting for the empirically existing and deriving predictions from it but also with probabilistically exploring "the total range of possible variation." It not only should be concerned with predicting what will happen ceteris paribus but also should inquire as to the conditions for different states of the relevant social system to obtain. The extant system was only one of many possibilities, and prediction was seen to "[open] the range of possibilities *for those who want to form a social order*."[7] The latter task fell within the ambit of the "social engineer" who having identified the constitutive elements of social interaction would go on to manipulate them to achieve certain social goals.

Although Galtung did not address the substance of classical international relations theory or its modern representations, he sometimes suggested, somewhat contradictorily, that the field was developing in creative directions. International relations was depicted as a "pure" science, increasingly interdisciplinary and scientific in character. As a consequence of scientization, international relations was becoming more balanced in its approach and increasingly future-oriented. The fact that traditional approaches were falling out of fashion was attributed to their orientation to the past, in contrast to more scientific and therefore future-oriented developments. However, the discussion of this development was imprecise and never clearly indicated to what extent this transformation had actually occurred or was just being proposed.

Galtung's account of traditional peace thinking echoed the somewhat more considered critique of prescientific forms of knowledge by the luminaries of positivist sociology. In contrast to the quasi-theological and metaphysical content of traditional thinking, peace research entailed a different orientation for Galtung: "The whole attention is focussed on the relation between thinking and reality: is it testable? Is it tenable?" The objective was to produce scientific knowledge, which was "independent of the idiosyncracies of the peace thinker and of the characteristics of the situation stimulating his thinking."[8] Put another way, "peace research, like all other research, should be universal in its methodology—given the problem and the method, the answer shall, ideally, be independent of space and time."[9] Peace research's interest in traditional thinking was primarily concerned with discerning its syntax—the consistency and theoretical adequacy of its assumptions—rather than its relationship to historical reality or specific thinkers.

Intersecting with the promotion of a universal methodology was a more pointed criticism of the discipline of international relations, whether in its legalist, historical, or scientific guise, for its version of particularism—state centrism. This was described as nationalism verging on chauvinism: "The whole perspective is frankly and openly asymmetrical; the whole world is seen from the vantage-point of the nation-state; and whether the research takes the form of apology or criticism, the perspective is limited to the author's immediate surroundings."[10] Two implications for the content of peace research flowed from this. First, international relations as a discipline helped to perpetuate the existing international system, but peace research would seek to change it. Second, peace research was to be global in focus, again in claimed contrast to the orthodox theory and practice of international relations.

On the first point, Galtung argued that the state-centric depiction of the international system as a realm of recurrence and repetition contributed to the reproduction of that system because of the connection between traditional thinking and practice: "Politicians who define their national interests narrowly in the classical tradition, basically as a zero-sum game with other nations . . . will probably find relatively few things of interest in peace research and rather turn to classical international relations studies for research foundations of their policies."[11] The academic study of international relations was structurally connected to its practice (the "art" of diplomacy) through the influencing of practitioners. The history of foreign policy making in the United States and Britain illustrated also an unhealthy connection with the upper social echelons, or the "center" of the respective societies. To avoid similar criticism, peace research would have to eschew personal, regional, and ideological biases; the term constantly used by Galtung to capture this objective was *symmetry*. This was a form of objectivity to be realized through the scientific requirement for the intersubjective acceptance of knowledge claims, as well as good institutional structure and research team design, such that the peace researcher "in his professional activities is without a fatherland."[12] Peace researchers were to be recruited from nonpartisan milieus, so that they might "develop into more ordinary social scientists or into technicians of a relatively de-ideologised kind."[13] The difficulty of the task was not lost upon Galtung, who acknowledged that no archimedean point "outside our conflict-ridden world" existed: "For that reason one has to at least try the approach to objectivity known as multi-subjectivity: by having researchers of different colours and convictions flock together so as to neutralise each other's idiosyncratic prejudices as much as possible or at least to make each other aware of the flaws in one's reasoning that one's own particular background do not permit one to see. Later on, other bases of objectivity . . . must be found."[14]

Galtung's uncertainty on this point reflected the crudity of the proposal. There was neither discussion of the origins of specific worldviews nor questioning of the assumption that scientific, value-free knowledge could be distilled simply from the balanced interaction of different national perspectives. Furthermore, if the modern scientific study of international relations could continue still to reflect statist bias, then science, per se, was an insufficient safeguard against it. Noticeably absent was a consideration of the cogency of theoretical or ethical arguments for state centrism made by international relations scholars. The impression created was that of a group of traditionalists who had not submitted their assumptions to scientific investigation and were therefore guilty of perpetuating a normatively unacceptable status quo. In partial mitigation of this criticism, Galtung did acknowledge that the scientific analysis of the historical success of a traditional policy, such as the balance of power, would actually prove to be rather difficult.

The criticisms of national chauvinism were mirrored in the rejection of disciplinary "imperialism." Certain forms of knowledge had built-in biases and methodological preferences that could be corrected through cross-fertilization with other disciplines. Thus, international relations offered itself as one of many resource areas available to the peace researcher. Though it was obliquely acknowledged that the research output of international relations scholars was already revealing symptoms of cross-disciplinary fertilization, peace research was explicitly to adopt an interdisciplinary approach from the outset. Above all, Galtung sought to promote the universal model of scientific procedure as a path beyond the various types of prejudices identified. Peace research was not beholden to any specific discipline and was also to avoid institutional and political connection with either governments or peace movements. Science was based upon the pillars of intersubjectivity, freedom to define and redefine problems, and the resources and time to engage in the testing of hypotheses; all of these required autonomy.[15]

The second broad implication of Galtung's critique was the need for a global sociological focus. We have seen how sociology was dominated in the early 1960s by structural functionalism as a general theory of social action. By virtue of its claims to generality, premised upon an assumed isomorphism between social systems, this perspective was intrinsically supportive of the view that peace research was concerned with a problem of universal relevance: The "field of identification" of the peace researcher was "world problems in a world perspective"; its object domain was the global social system; and its research focus was to be "*human* survival." Peace research was charged with looking for "a symmetric solution that maximises long-term international health." The peace researcher was to adopt an "identification anchored at the international level," for it was in humankind's interest to view the quest for peace as global in scope and "a technical problem of organization."[16]

The (Re)definition of Peace

Peace research required, then, a substantive definition of peace that avoided the traditional appeal to reason alone and did not adopt a partisan outlook. The first attempt at this was presented in the editorial of the foundational issue of *Journal of Peace Research*, written by Galtung and published in 1964. There peace was defined as having two aspects: *negative* peace, being the absence of war and actual physical violence, and *positive* peace, initially described as the "integration of human society." The plausibility of the dual definition was predicated upon the identification of two global empirical tendencies that undermined the pervasive Hobbesian image of an anarchical world order condemned to a perpetual condition of anticipating war.

First, "man identifies," displaying a capacity for mutual empathy and solidarity: "[He] sees himself as a member of groups where a norm of reciprocity is valid and cooperation a dominant mode of interaction. . . . In the real world integration is a fact. Man surrounds himself with a sphere of amity and mutual aid. But outside of this sphere enmity and mutual destruction may rule."[17] At face value, this statement appeared only to identify a distinction between a sociable domestic realm and an asocial international order, an observation compatible with traditional realist references to an inhospitable international state of nature. This was clearly not the intention, given a preceding comment to the effect that there was little evidence of anything like the Hobbesian image ever having existed. The more plausible intention was that of highlighting a universal human capacity to identify with others, a capacity, moreover, that was amenable to extension. The term *state* with its connotations of rigidity and fixity was not used, but rather the more flexible categories of *group* or *sphere of amity* were adopted. The task confronting a putative peace researcher, therefore, was how to extend community and achieve a consonance between innate human sociability and global social structure.

The second empirical observation was that however bellicose relations between human communities are, "man rarely uses all of his means of destruction against all enemies all of the time." There were "limitations and rules . . . elements of a game in the fight."[18] By virtue of an element of common interest, humanity tended to constrain the use of force. Again, a clear implication was that the capacity to constrain the resort to violence could be expanded, a notion that provided another practical question for peace research to address. Galtung went on to propose that if we imagined the extrapolation of these two demonstrable human proclivities, then a vision of the elimination of violence and the dissolution of the distinctions between the domestic and international social realms would emerge. The extrapolation of the first would realize a condition of positive peace, whereas extrapolation of the second would lead only to that of negative peace. In combination, however, they would produce a condition of general and complete peace. The distinctiveness of peace research lay in its commitment to researching the conditions for both positive and negative peace.

In light of Galtung's claim that "global values" existed sui generis, it can now be seen how peace research was presented in the image of a functionalist sociology. The two identifiable social tendencies combine to create an image of a global system that, contra Hobbes, displayed patterned, rule-governed behavior and a dynamic potential. Violence arises from the relations between subsystemic "groups," but humanity displays a capacity to cooperate and integrate. Cast in this light, the value of peace, like that of health, was not seen to be in need of defense: "If this is a value," claimed Galtung, "it is among the most consensual ones."[19] The value of peace connoted a functioning and integrated global social system and thus took on an objective, hardly disputable quality. By extension, the role of the peace researcher was to be that of a technician-physician dedicated to the preservation and improvement of the health of the global body politic. In contrast to traditional realist skepticism as to the possibility of extending community beyond the water's edge, peace research commenced by asking under what conditions might an extension best obtain.

Having introduced the concept of positive peace into the lexicon of peace research, Galtung devoted little effort to fleshing out or substantiating its content in the early phase of his writings. This was in spite of his bemoaning of the analytical poverty of traditional conceptualizations of peace. At various points positive peace was equated with such values as cooperation, freedom from fear or want, economic development, absence of exploitation, equality, justice, freedom of action, pluralism, and dynamism. In short, it was synonymous with a specific understanding of the global good life, yet the only defense offered consisted of some brief allusions to "primary" human needs or "fundamental rights." In the end, the tenability of the various values derived solely from the a priori plausibility of the umbrella concept of positive peace; they reflected the existence of "positive relations" between groups. Although Galtung did acknowledge that his list of values may not have represented those that nations or individuals empirically pursue, a rather considerable concession, they were nevertheless exemplary of "(relatively) consensual values in the world community of nations, other than the mere absence of violence."[20] Clearly Galtung believed such values to be prima facie rational from a global systemic viewpoint, but ultimately they would have to be shown to be held. If they were simply posited as abstracted implications of the existence of a global social system, it would be difficult for peace research to make a case for anything more than system equilibrium or maintenance without being accused of imputing values to an abstract systemic entity. As his own criticisms of structural functionalism showed, this was precisely what Galtung needed to avoid.

THE "ORIENTED" SCIENCE OF PEACE RESEARCH

Galtung slid past some of the contradictions between his model of social scientific inquiry and his claims as to the merits of peace research by employing an idiosyncratic map of the social sciences. Indeed, throughout his work Galtung displays an audacious, sometimes simply cavalier approach to category problems: If in doubt, invent it.[21] Peace research was defined as "a focussed or oriented discipline with its point of gravity among the sciences of man," whereas international relations, sociology, economics, and history were "pure" disciplines to which peace research was related, as medicine is to the biological sciences.[22] In a pure science the problem to be investigated is defined by the research process itself, whereas the problem an oriented science confronts is defined according to an "autotelic" or guiding value disposition, such as health, welfare, legality, or peace. From the supreme value can be derived a number of heterotelic values, upon whose fulfillment the realization of the supreme value ultimately depends. An oriented science asks under what situations (conditions, or values of independent variables) does a specific value (of the dependent variable) obtain? This was not to be confused with the more familiar category of applied science that, argued Galtung, was "research that has found some application in furthering values, whether it was intended to or not." The uniqueness of oriented science lay in the existence of an initial motivating value disposition; but it requires that "there must be consensus in the society, or at least in major parts of it, as to the fundamental value around which the oriented discipline is organised."[23]

There were ambiguities in Galtung's model of oriented science. There was, he argued, a correlation between the status of oriented disciplines and the level of consensus over the relevant autotelic value, yet there was also a two-way relationship between the level of consensus and the allocation of funds to specific forms of oriented research: the more consensus, the more research, and the more research, the more consensus. This raises questions about the ultimate subordination of the consensual value to the interests of the funding parties, to which Galtung provided no answers, although he was clearly aware of some of the grubbier aspects of setting up research programs and the vulnerability of the autotelic value of peace to a kind of manipulation that was supposedly to be avoided.

Further ambiguity arose from the claim that peace research was not only in the business of researching the realization of goals emerging out of the guiding value of peace but was also involved in identifying the goals themselves. A note of impatience, not to mention inconsistency, was revealed in Galtung's observation that "debates on what is really meant by peace seem to postpone . . . professional research efforts." Although the identification of values was compatible with the young Galtung's positivism, at times he characterized it as an extrascientific activity reflecting differing "ideological tastes." The understanding of hypothesis formation outlined in his sociological writings is recalled here: Theoretical hypotheses (and values would have to be produced in such a form) are subjectively generated either inductively from observations or via intuition and empathy. Thus peace research could, in fact, commence without a guiding definition of peace, other than the broad distinction drawn between positive and negative peace. Nevertheless, even conjectured values would ultimately have to be presented in a form amenable to scientific investigation. Whether they were products of an empirically substantiatable social consensus or of extrascientific musings, the most that Galtung could demonstrate was that values were held. Even this he did not do; no evidence of a consensus as to the content of the autotelic value of peace was provided. The only conclusion can be that Galtung thought it to be self-evidently reasonable.[24]

The distinction drawn between pure, applied, and oriented science may have been contrived, idealized, trivial even, but it served to push peace research further away from the reflexive consideration of the value of peace toward the technical issues of implementation.[25] In this respect, Galtung's model of peace research reflected the philosophical pragmatism that so strongly influenced the evolution of American sociology in the twentieth century. Pragmatism was supportive of "the empiricist attitude." The pragmatist, argued James, "turns his back resolutely and once and for all upon a lot of inveterate habits dear to professional philosophers." Against the preoccupation of "rationalists" with ultimate origins, a priori reasons, and absolutes, the pragmatist "look[ed] towards last things, fruits, consequences, facts."[26] Such an outlook pervaded Galtung's initial argument for peace research. With the autotelic value of peace declared, subsequent discussion concerned itself largely either with developing a sociological description of the international system or with the structure and development of the *profession* of peace research. The exploration of the "conditions of peace" was given higher priority than the refinement of the idea of peace itself, the latter task being described at one point as degenerate in the mathematical sense.[27]

The Peace Researcher as Physician

The emphasis on establishing the bona fides of professional peace research was especially evident in the analogy drawn between peace research and medical science. I have already noted that in imagining peace research Galtung was influenced by his father's profession as a physician. Indeed, Galtung came to see a number of parallels between the development of peace research and medicine. First, medicine was young—a recent alliance between the old art and craft of surgery and modern "quantitative natural science." Peace research was even younger, but it was already in the process of blending the art of diplomacy with quantitative social science, "with precisely the same debate between the 'artists and intuitionists' and the theoreticians and electronic calculators." Moreover, Galtung boasted, "the former are doomed to lose, but the latter will only succeed to the extent that they are able to understand better than the intuitionists themselves what they stand for. The result, diplomats well versed in peace science, is already emerging."[28] This suggested that peace research was in competition with the discipline of international relations, at least in its legalist and historical forms, for the control of diplomatic practice.

Furthermore, there has been a historical tendency in medicine to "dephilosophize" and shift from "armchair speculation" to the discovery of "a

web of invariances that form the basis for today's control of somatic man."
So too with peace research, where "we see the same development in our
field, away from the tract, the empirically unguided sweeping speculations
and on to the piecemeal approach." These developments were not cost-free
because they involved the loss of the longer, wider viewpoint. Not that
Galtung wanted to overstate the risks: "A typical and important aspect of
this is the willingness to call something "peace research" or "research in
human survival" and just go ahead collecting research experience without
having a satisfactory definition and a conceptual framework and a deductive theory. These formal aspects of science are indispensable in the long
run, but they may be a straitjacket if developed and applied prematurely."
      It was the professionalization of medicine that was of particular inter-
est to Galtung, for it provided a developmental model for peace research.
"The structural similarity with peace science is so great that it would be
strange if this is not also to be the future status of that science," Galtung
enthused, although he conceded that his vision was utopian. In universities, medicine had the status of a faculty rather than of an institute, department, or program. It recruited from a variety of disciplines and combined insights drawn from various resources in the treatment of somatic
health. Medicine was an umbrella discipline interchanging with a number
of "participating sciences," for which it defines problems to be solved,
learns from their serendipity and to which it contributes its own original
and applied research. Perhaps in the not too distant future, fifteen to
twenty years he suggested, peace research faculties would be flourishing
"as a matter of course, as a matter of human survival."
      To be professional was "to stand in a contractual relationship to the
rest of society," for although professionalism confers a degree of autonomy and self-regulation, it carries an obligation to render to society "services that [are] deemed to be indispensable." It was to be subject to the expectation that knowledge will be brought to bear upon the realization of
some values.[29] Professionalization entailed an "esprit de corps" and high
ethical standards; it was "a moral fact with profound implications." In
medical science, universal professional ethics are encapsulated in the Hippocratic oath, obliging physicians always to live up to their professional
raison d'être of saving life, never using professional status to obtain illicit
gratifications, never betraying confidences, and seeking the advice of colleagues when in doubt. Galtung speculated as to the possible development
of professional peace research equipped with an equally secure normative
foundation and ready to place its knowledge "at the disposal of the development of international order"—he did not hesitate to describe the professional peace researcher as a technician or social engineer. Furthermore,
professionalism dovetailed with the scientific obligation to eradicate subjectivism from the research process. It was not that peace researchers were
to be the executors of political policies, developing the means to realize

already given ends. Peace research was not merely an "applied" science, for this would "exclude the important function of science as the provider of new perspectives, of new horizons and new goals." Here classical positivist sentiments came to the fore in the requirement that peace research was also to provide visions of what a peaceful world should look like. An important task was the generation of utopias, derived from well-founded empirical perspectives, in contrast to the tradition of "desperate and *ad hoc* efforts to tackle problems as they arise." Ultimately, within the field of peace research the roles of pure or oriented researcher and practitioner would become integrated, as was perceived to have already occurred within the professions of engineering, agriculture, and medicine.[30] Peace science, it seems, could save us.

Galtung showed little awareness of the ideological overtones of professionalism or its implications for the enclosure of peace as a research domain. The validity of comparing the development of medical science and peace research depended fundamentally upon sustaining the contentious analogy between the values of health and peace. While not entertaining the illusion that the concepts of "international" and "somatic" health "had anything like the same cognitive or normative standing," since consensus over the nature of the latter clearly exceeded that over the former, Galtung argued that "this kind of consensus is not created by decree, only by hard research to know the nature of the international system better." This formulation appears to attribute to scientific research an overtly political function, since the identification of peace as an autotelic value precedes the consensus-generating research. The recognition of peace as a universal social value was constrained only by insufficient research into its precise content, and the analogy with health reflected the view that peace could come to be regarded eventually as an equally reasonable value. The assumption clearly was that we could develop a knowledge of the dysfunctional international system akin to our knowledge of the unhealthy human body, a classical structural-functionalist slide. Aside from the fact that what is meant by somatic health is itself contested (by those adhering to alternative non-Western conceptions of health, for example), the idea that scientific research could replace political and moral philosophy as the source of international consensus on the precise meaning of peace relied ultimately on the presumption of an isomorphic relationship between the international social system and biomechanical entitities.

The dictates of scientific method required peace research to translate values into testable hypotheses, and the analogy with medicine was again employed to make the point. Medical research has generated a highly differentiated understanding of illness and its treatment; peace research needed to develop a comparable understanding of "nonpeace." Peace proposals (analogous to "treatments" in medicine), many of which already existed, could be judged according to their capacity to eliminate dimensions of nonpeace.[31] In utilitarian fashion, the validity of a peace proposal was to be assessed in terms of positive consequences rather than inherent worth. But this suggested procedure only defrayed the argument: Nonpeace is a category as potentially disputable as peace, especially if defined as the negation of positive peace. Following Hippocrates, the overt normative dimension of peace research lay primarily in the ethical delimitations of its practice.

In any case, Galtung's peace research decisively failed its own test. In order for the values embodied in the idea of positive peace to escape the indictment of subjectivism—the principal inadequacy of traditional peace thinking—they would have to be scientifically evaluated. They were not. In the early phase of Galtung's peace research he restricted himself largely to the generation of extensive taxonomies of the dimensions of nonpeace and types of peace thinking and the mathematical exploration of the relationships between the two sets.[32] In one of the few discussions of the autotelic value of "peace," Galtung either grounded the values it contained within a purely descriptive account of human needs and rights or simply asserted them: "Freedom from want" was premised upon a set of "primary" human needs, whereas "justice" arose out of "basic, fundamental rights"; "equality" broadly corresponded with "justice" and arose out of the equal value of either individuals or "nations"; and "pluralism" reflected the view that "nations and the world should contain a large social and cultural diversity of forms coexisting side by side." Galtung saw no logical incompatibility in his list of global social values, only a "structural incompatibility" arising out of the fact that there existed "no empirically viable world that will maximise all [the values] at the same time."[33] The potential tension between values generated from within a professional research community and authentically public values was simply not considered.

Galtung obliquely acknowledged such problems in suggesting at one point that the list of values was better understood as a catalogue of analytical problems than as a reflection of that which humanity was historically striving to obtain. This concession reinforces the judgment that Galtung's peace research was not intended to justify its normative assumptions but to focus instead on the realization of a given set of values. The problem with positive peace arose from its location within a scientific epistemology that crippled the discussion of its inescapable normativity. At the time, a typical response by Galtung to the problem was to anticipate the development of "analytical tools" so that the values that underpinned peace research could one day be expressed in mathematical terms.[34] Problems with the analogy between the autotelic values of health and peace were dismissed as a reflection of peace research's tender age. Galtung frequently pointed out that the intention was not to get the final word on basic values or to impute to the concept of peace a definitive content. Nevertheless, because peace research was cast in a largely technical role, the justification of its normative orientation was effectively presupposed and criticism cast into the dustbin of philosophy, conveniently situated outside the laboratory of peace.

PEACE RESEARCH AS GLOBAL SOCIOLOGY

Further insight into the limitations of scientized peace research can be gleaned from a brief look at Galtung's sociological writings on international relations, which constituted the bulk of his early peace research. Supposedly analogous to the study of physiology in the natural sciences, his work on the international system consisted primarily in the application of sociological concepts, such as structure, rank, and status, to the analysis of the international system. Indeed, much of Galtung's early peace research is perhaps better comprehended as a contribution to the social scientific study of international relations rather than to a distinctive new field. There was a marked absence of normative or prescriptive content, and it was not surprising that in 1965 international relations scholar John Burton cast doubt on some of the claims to originality made by peace researchers such as Galtung.[35] In Galtungian terms, early peace research appeared actually to restrict itself to contributing to the "pure" science of international relations or the exploration of barriers to negative peace.

The case for the applicability of sociology to the study of international relations rested largely upon the assumption of an isomorphic relationship between social systems. For Galtung, sociology could contribute to the analysis of international relations in two respects: First, it could contribute to the study of the "concrete" interaction of state representatives; second, in its structural-functional guise it could abstractly model the interaction of states "as such." The interest in relations between state representatives resulted in a number of useful papers on the sociology of diplomacy at the national and international levels and the connection between social position and foreign policy orientation.[36] More abstract sociological analysis could be found within a number of papers on the analysis of stratification in the international system. Here the principle of isomorphism appeared particularly useful because the numerically small international system invited comparison with the analysis of small-scale social systems. Since, strictly speaking, the concept of isomorphism refers to a 1:1 mapping relationship between different sets, Galtung acknowledged that its application was fraught with problems, and he appeared to treat it largely as a useful source of creative insights.[37]

For Galtung, international relations was properly a "structural science," yet it was characterized by a focus on individual states at the expense of an analysis of the international system sui generis. What should distinguish international relations from "political science" was an analysis of the "interaction structure," in the same way that the study of social systems distinguished sociology from individual psychology. The comparison between political science and individual psychology was rather odd because it ignored the extensive application of systems theory to the study of national political systems. But the point seems to have been that the international system should be comprehended on its own terms rather than by induction from national systems. The principle of isomorphism promotes the idea that states engage in role-playing within an international system of interaction. Thus it was argued that the behavior of states was oriented by the social structure in which they were embedded, and their interactions were to be functionally understood as rank-dependent. Like individuals, states possessed "status sets" that conditioned their behavior and outlook, and it was hypothesized that aggressive state behavior arose out of a disequilibrium within the status sets of states, which resulted in an "unstable self-image."

Galtung's sociological analysis of stratification in the international system was novel and prescient, even if it indelibly bore Parsons's hallmark. As a contribution to peace research it was less impressive. The concept of positive peace figured little in Galtung's global sociology, but its uncertain content and status left their mark nonetheless. If sociology or international relations as "pure" sciences were to provide the analysis, then the "oriented" science of peace research was supposedly charged with developing prescriptive responses to the problems highlighted by the effects of rank disequilibrium. But the more obviously analytical exercises rarely extended beyond abstract theoretical (albeit often insightful) sketches. When Galtung's explorations in international relations did broach normative themes, they blended the concerns of the pure and oriented researcher, in his terms. The relationship between theory and prescription was not established through the application of scientific method but instead was largely assumed. This was demonstrated in a discussion of the processes of integration operating at the global level. Galtung assessed various types of integrative process—territorial, organizational, and associational—in terms of their capacity to fulfill social values, expressed as systemic functions.[38] Typically, the values in question—output, variety, security, and justice—were simply asserted. The exercise was described as purely "structural" and not presupposing "anything about motivation or ideology," even though the values deployed happened to correspond with Galtung's understanding of positive peace. Though on one level his "A Structural Theory of Integration" can be understood as an attempt to apply abstract sociology to an analysis of international relations, its central purpose was to explore alternative forms of integration other than territorial. Processes of organizational and associational integration were seen to be proceeding at a greater pace than territorial integration, producing societies that were "overdeveloped" relative to existing state boundaries. This produced a condition of "structural fatigue" in the international order, and given the geopolitical problems associated with territorial integration, substitutes would have to be found in order to resolve the "total crisis" confronting humanity. However, the discussion of integration was entirely abstract, and no attempt was made to connect the discussion with the empirical world and verify the hypotheses. Nevertheless, the conclusions drawn were fully supportive of the normative foundations of peace research as a practical activity.

A similar slide from abstract theory to prescription is evident in "A Structural Theory of Aggression," published in 1964. The discussion commences with an exploration of some hypotheses about the relationship between rank disequilibrium and aggressive behavior by states; this is followed by a short consideration of testing procedures. Then the reader is asked to "imagine that there was something to this reasoning" and go on to consider the policy implications. A subsequent paper on the same theme repeats the procedure but pays greater attention to the mathematics of interaction between status sets and provides a tentative taxonomy of rank dimensions for individuals and nations.[39] Both papers conclude in overtly prescriptive terms. The first asks the reader to pretend that the hypotheses had been confirmed by "strategically placed tests" and to accept "a value premise against aggression"; the second invokes the principle of isomorphism in transposing theses about the effects of status on the interaction of individuals to the study of the interaction of states, acknowledging at the same time that this commits "the fallacy of treating the international system as if it were a system of individual actors." The latter paper concludes by defending the idea of sociology as "the science of the socially possible," committed not only to exploring the empirically existing but also to opening the range of possibilities available to "those who wish to form a social order," such as the "social engineer."

In spite of Galtung's frequent depiction of social science as a rigorous procedure entailing a move from hypothesis formation through testing to confirmation and finally prescription, none of his early research conformed to this model. The idea of science was central to the argument for peace research, but it remained an unrealized ideal providing a legitimating rhetoric but not a practice. The roles of scientist and activist became as one.

CONCLUSION

The distinctiveness of early peace research was built around the value idea of positive peace and the concept of oriented science, yet the substantiation of the normative premises of peace research was at best ambiguous—essential but also a potential distraction. In fact, the young

Galtung wrote surprisingly little about positive peace even though its realization was cast as the leitmotiv of peace research. In spite of a positivistic rejection of unscientific traditionalism, the claims for the concept of positive peace extended little beyond an appeal to its self-evident reasonableness, premised upon the assertion of certain human capacities for cooperation and constraint. The value set that was positive peace was presented either as a plausible reflection of international consensus on the fundamentals of a universalized notion of the good life (weakly connected to unexplored notions of basic human needs and rights)—to be confirmed scientifically at some later stage—or simply as an area to be explored as peace research developed.

More accurately, the values posited reflected the weltanschauung of a Scandinavian social democrat (whose personal politics were to the left of the party platform) of a rationalist temper. Paradoxically perhaps, Galtung's vision of a global normative consensus was also compatible with H.L.A. Hart's conception of "the minimum content of natural law." Beneath the functionalist gloss of the arguments for positive peace appeared to lie a suppressed teleology wherein humanity is understood as not only "tending to maintain itself in existence, but as proceeding towards a definite optimum state which is the specific good—or the *end* (*telos, finis*) appropriate for it."[40] Interestingly, Hart connected this teleological assumption with the concept of human needs and the idea of functionality as connoting a teleological purpose. The content of law and morals arose out of a set of perceived fundamental human needs and attributes that have acquired the status of truisms: human vulnerability, approximate equality, limited altruism, limited resources, limited understanding, and strength of will. These simple truisms disclosed the "core of good sense" in natural law and gave substance to the formal conception of law and morals.

I noted earlier that orthodox functionalism appeared to locate the telos of social life within a naturalistic understanding of systemic needs. The application of a modified version of this approach to the international system, under the guise of peace research, was not entirely novel, but it was unique in its explicit optimism. It restored the notion of progress to a level of human social organization traditionally deemed to be at best only partially receptive to reform. It was a form of positivist sociology (in the fullest sense) writ very large, if only at the level of aspiration. Galtung's emphasis on the scientific foundations of peace research can be read as one contemporary version of a historical tradition of positivistic impatience with nonscientific thought. As the self-proclaimed successor to earlier global reformist perspectives, Galtungian peace research held out the promise of moving beyond indeterminate philosophical discussion over first principles into the realm of empirical research into actual conditions and possibilities. But, in the manner of its positivist forefathers, it retained the indelible, yet now rendered inexplicable, stamp of its Enlightenment

64   A QUESTION OF VALUES

origins. Science may have provided peace research with a language and method, but it could only subvert rather than substantiate its normative core. This was a fatal deficiency given that the whole endeavor was premised upon a specific and contestable normative outlook. Perhaps its most remarkable feature was the absence of any argument for undertaking the enterprise in the first place. As envisioned by Galtung, scientific peace research was forced to abdicate from its own defense.

One of the young Galtung's mentors, Robert Merton, offers an interesting explanation for the appeal of science as a transformative agent. Cognition affects behavior: Social science is distinguishable from the natural sciences insofar as predictions "peculiar to human affairs" will "enter into the situation as a *new and dynamic* factor, changing the very conditions under which the prediction initially held true."[41] Friedrichs takes up Merton's point and suggests that it inheres in the very logic of social science. He cites Engels's paraphrase of Hegel to capture the dialectic between knowledge and the empirical world: "Freedom does not consist in the dream of independence from natural laws, but in the knowledge of these laws."[42] For Engels and Marx, the laws that govern social life were to be comprehended historically; for the social scientist, they are revealed through science. Galtung did not emulate Marx's historical investigation of the evolution of human society, nor did he uphold the rules of scientific procedure. But, in his frequent appeals to his readers to accept various hypotheses as probably true or specific values as inherently reasonable, and in his conception of sociology as a creative, forward-looking science of the possible, was he not operating within a form of dialectical logic that supposed that to posit a self-evidently plausible vision was at the same time to act toward its realization? Hindsight suggests that this line of explanation has some substance to it. As will be shown in Chapter 5, Galtung was later to rework extensively his understanding of science in an effort to resolve the tension between it and politics yet retain the virtues and creativity of formal analysis.

Galtung's original vision of peace research did not exhibit much interest in history, but history, we might say, was interested in it. During the late 1960s the idea of social science in general came under sustained attack from within a revived intellectual and public radicalism, and peace research could not escape critical scrutiny. Only four years after making the foundational claims for the new science of peace, Galtung critically reexamined the fundamental assumptions of peace research and set it upon a new path.

NOTES

1. Morgenthau, *Politics Among Nations.*

2. See Galtung, "Peace Research," *EPR,* 1 (hereafter "Peace Research"); pp. 151–155; and Galtung, "The Social Sciences: An Essay on Polarisation and Integration," pp. 2–32.

3. The critique of traditional peace thinking is taken from Galtung, "Theories of Peace," pp. 91–92, "Peace Research: Science, or Politics in Disguise?" and "Peace Research: Past Experiences and Future Perspectives." The only consideration of actual "traditional peace proposals" is to be found in a limited circulation paper, which briefly considers proposals by Dubois and Dante in the fourteenth century, Kant and Rousseau, and the nineteenth-century writings of Mill, Cobden, and Saint-Simon. All are seen as primarily concerned with ensuring the future of Europe alone. All of the proposals are deemed invalid because of their unscientific, political content. See Galtung, "Theories of Peace," pp. 93–97.

4. In Chapter 8, I show how Galtung was later to acquire a very different understanding of the relationship between peace and nirvana.

5. Just prior to Galtung's commentary, a comparable judgment was made by Hinsley, who complained of the continuing reliance on "simple and radical solutions" to the problem of war and peace and the absence of any development or refinement in its treatment: "Every scheme for the elimination of war that men have advocated since 1917 has been nothing but a copy or an elaboration of some seventeenth century programme—as the seventeenth century programmes were copies of still earlier schemes." Hinsley, *Power and the Pursuit of Peace,* p. 3.

6. Galtung, "Peace Research: Science, or Politics in Disguise?" p. 228; and Galtung, "Peace Research: Past Experiences and Future Perspectives," p. 250.

7. Galtung, "Rank and Social Integration," p. 171, emphasis added.

8. Galtung, "Theories of Peace," p. 25.

9. Galtung, "International Programs of Behavioural Science," p. 169.

10. Galtung, "Peace Research: Past Experiences and Future Perspectives," p. 249.

11. Galtung, "Peace Research: Science, or Politics in Disguise?" p. 229.

12. Ibid., p. 242. For examples of institutional structures designed to alleviate national bias, see also pp. 228–231; Galtung, "Teaching and Infrastructural Problems of Peace Research," pp. 280–290; and Galtung, "International Programs of Behavioural Science," pp. 180–183.

13. Galtung, "Peace Research: Future Possibilities and Necessities," pp. 192–193.

14. Galtung, "Peace Research: Science, or Politics in Disguise?" p. 229.

15. Galtung, "International Programs of Behavioural Science," pp. 176–181. The peace movement was criticized then for its lack of professionalism, impatience, and unscientific attitude but was also seen as a source of "rabid and immature but still spontaneous and imaginative inventiveness."

16. Galtung, "Theories of Peace," p. 107.

17. Galtung, "An Editorial," p. 1.

18. Ibid.

19. Galtung, "An Editorial," p. 3. One of the few references to public opinion in support of the claim cites the survey of 500 "representative Norwegians" who showed a clear preference for a "peace philosophy" that defined peace as requiring the abolition of hunger and poverty. See Galtung, "Peace Research: Science, or Politics in Disguise?" p. 225 and note 3.

20. Galtung "Theories of Peace," p. 106. Parentheses in the original.

21. For example, the "pure" disciplines of anthropology, history, and sociology were described as focused on the value of "the sane society," collectively producing the "oriented" science of "sociatry" and the profession of "sociatrists." See Galtung, "Peace Research," p. 154.

22. Ibid., pp. 150–154.

23. The discussion of "oriented science" is taken from ibid., pp. 150–164. See also Galtung, "Theories of Peace."

24. For a critique of Galtung's "horror of inequality," see Boulding, "Twelve Friendly Quarrels with Johan Galtung," pp. 79–80.

25. Holm argues that the distinction between pure and oriented science is trivial (*trivel*) and reduces to calling past research in international relations "pure" and the newer peace research "oriented." Furthermore, it can be argued that all science draws upon previous research from the same and other fields. See Holm, *Johan Galtung: "Superstar" eller "Vaekkelsespraedikant"?* pp. 66–80.

26. James, *Pragmatism*, p. 47.

27. Galtung, "Theories of Peace," p. 115.

28. The analogy is taken from Galtung, "International Programs of Behavioural Science," pp. 170–172.

29. See also Galtung, "Peace Research," p. 157.

30. Ibid., p. 157.

31. Galtung, "Theories of Peace," pp. 138–139, especially figure 2.6-1, and pp. 157–158.

32. See Galtung, "Theories of Peace," and "A Typology of Peace Thinking," pp. 13–28.

33. Galtung, "Theories of Peace," p. 104.

34. Galtung, "Peace Research: Future Possibilities and Necessities," p. 222.

35. Burton, "Peace Research and International Relations." See also Lawler, "Peace Research and International Relations: From Divergence to Convergence."

36. See, for example, Galtung, "Foreign Policy Opinion as a Function of Social Position," and "Social Position, Party Identification and Foreign Policy Orientation: A Norwegian Case Study."

37. See his suggested dictionary of correspondences between the two levels of analysis in Galtung, "Small Group Theory and the Theory of International Relations," p. 36. For a critique see Holm, "On a Major Event in the Social Sciences," pp. 67–69.

38. Galtung, "A Structural Theory of Integration."

39. Galtung, "Rank and Social Integration."

40. Hart, *The Concept of Law*, p. 184.

41. Merton, *Social Theory and Social Structure*, pp. 129.

42. Cited in Friedrichs, *A Sociology of Sociology*, p. 181.

3

Structural Violence

Exploitation is the essence of violence.
—*Gandhi*

Just four years after the publication of the first issue of the *Journal of Peace Research*, the international peace research community became embroiled in an internal conflict. At a series of conferences held in 1968 and 1969, a group of young European peace researchers questioned the general direction peace research was taking. Particularly concerned with the manner in which some American peace researchers were analyzing the role of the United States in the Vietnam conflict, they went on to criticize the conceptual foundations of peace research more generally. Galtung was rarely referred to directly, with one notable exception, but his vision of a professional, scientific activity that was to be "symmetric" in its analysis of specific conflicts was clearly a target. The upheaval engendered a division within the peace research community as the original positivist model was transformed from innovation into an orthodoxy against which a newer, more radical perspective was being constructed. Galtung was an advocate of the peace research under question, but he also became a principal architect of a revised model while at the same time distinguishing his position from that of the critics.

The two sides in the dispute were of different intellectual generations and largely reflected distinct addresses: The scientific school consisted mostly of American researchers, whereas their critics were predominantly European. As a European advocating a scientific model of peace research influenced by American sociology, Galtung straddled the divide.[1] During the period of upheaval, he was working on the revision of his own understanding of the meaning of peace and violence at the Institute of Gandhian Studies in Varanassi, India.[2] Thus, as one member of the mainstream position was later to remark, it is an open question as to whether Galtung helped pull peace research toward a more radical stance, or was pushed.[3]

KNOWLEDGE FOR WHAT?

The backdrop to the conflict within peace research was the complex amalgam of events on both sides of the Atlantic that made the 1960s a turbulent decade. In the United States, the liberal consensus that had evolved since the mid-1950s was challenged by a series of events that contributed to a rising tide of skepticism and hostility on the part of middle-class youth toward the affluent society that had nurtured them. Establishment values came under critical review as the revolt of America's black minority catalyzed growing unrest on the campuses of some of the most prestigious universities. The issues of civil rights and U.S. involvement in Vietnam combined to generate what Hodgson has called "the great schism" in American society.[4] Universities were also a focus for sometimes spectacular dissent in the United Kingdom and Europe.[5]

The ferment of the 1960s revolved around a crisis of legitimation for the Western democracies. Not only the United States but also the United Kingdom and Western Europe were confronted by "the first bourgeois revolt against the principles of a bourgeois society that is almost successfully functioning according to its own standards."[6] The legitimation crisis reflected a high level of disenchantment with both the internal condition and external relations of the Western democracies. Habermas was not alone in detecting a growing sensitivity to "the untruth of prevailing legitimations" and a fundamental loss of sympathy for "the senseless reproduction of now superfluous virtues and sacrifices." Furthermore, the upheaval within a hegemonic group of Western societies had a global dimension: "Today protest is directed against a society that has lent the emancipatory ideals of the eighteenth century the force of constitutional norms and has accumulated the potential for their realization—while it has not abolished hunger in the world of potential abundance, while it has widened the gap between industrial and developing nations, exporting misery and military violence along with mass hygiene."[7]

Developments within social theory were both reflective and coconstitutive of dissent with the prevailing consensus in the Western world. Although a stream of thought within American sociology had been critical of the assumptions of the dominant functionalist and positivist paradigm since its inception, the 1960s witnessed "a renaissance of the classical tradition in sociology" and a revitalized emphasis on the purpose of knowledge.[8] Systems-theoretic sociology in the Parsonian mold was increasingly cast as an uncritical, technological, and scientific rationalization of the status quo.[9] Unlike in the United States, positivism had not established itself to the same degree in European theoretical circles, where there remained an unbroken tradition upon which nonpositivists could draw. From Kant, Hegel, and Marx had evolved a tradition of humanist thought that continued to thematize enlightenment, critical social thought, and human emancipation in the spirit of Marx's understanding of critique. From 1961 and the beginnings of the *Positivismusstriet* in German intellectual circles, the influence of philosophical humanism and critical social theory increased on both sides of the Atlantic.[10] Such streams of thought depicted mainstream social theory as a form of technocratic discourse that had contributed to the suppression of critical inquiry and the debasement of the classical ideal of *theoria*.[11] Social theory had been reduced to a form of technical rationality that was incapable of providing a guide to enlightened action. Indeed, it was characterized by a set of categorical dichotomies—fact and value, theory and practice, normative and empirical—that combined to exclude reflection upon the connections between theoretical inquiry and social reality, the latter being deemed to be extrinsic to the scientific observer.

Against the evolution of a universal systematic science that had applied the same conceptual apparatus to the study of animate and inanimate nature, critical social theory argued for the recovery of the critical function of social theory.[12] Its essence was the reinstatement of an understanding of knowledge that emphasized public comprehension of and participation in social life. Such a reflexive participatory understanding required "that the objectifying, value-neutral standpoint of an impartial observer give way to the subjectively open, value-committed attitude of an interlocutor in a shared practice."[13] Mainstream sociology revealed the loss of critique in its overriding focus on the description and management of the social system, the denial of the analytical significance of social class, the proclamation of the end of ideology, and the enthusiastic identification of the postindustrial society characterized by abundance based upon increasing production of material wealth.

It was not only the domestic politics of the industrialized democracies that were being subjected to critical scrutiny but also their external relations. In particular, the foreign policy of the United States and the legitimating ideology of liberal internationalism (selectively leavened with realpolitik) became targets of public and scholarly criticism. The empirical reality of an expanding international community of newly independent states and the prevalence of wars of liberation, in the context of an emergent superpower détente, began to impose itself upon scholarly research. Public and scholarly focus shifted from a concern with the East-West axis of conflict to the North-South global divide. It was not just the particular question of America's role in the Vietnam War that was at issue; also challenged was the assumption that the expansion of capitalism was crucial to the modernization of the underdeveloped world.

The predominant theory of development assumed a single path to modernity for the global periphery: the reproduction of the developmental history of the developed states. Against this view, there was evolving an alternative perspective that critically drew upon Marx's and Lenin's political economy to present a radically different picture of the consequences of the expansion of capitalism into the Third World. From the mid-1960s onward, a number of sociologists and economists in Latin America (and, later, Africa) challenged orthodox theories of modernization by depicting their own states as dependent upon and underdeveloped by Western capital. Though the literature varied in approach, the collective image presented was of a relationship of dependence between the global core of developed, industrialized states and an underdeveloped periphery.[14] Rather than ensuring their development, this dependence resulted in the imposition of a particular version of modernity upon peripheral states, grounded in economic exploitation that benefited the global core. What development did occur was uneven in its effects, benefiting a small dominant class within underdeveloped states and leaving the majority in conditions of immiseration. As a consequence, the foreign policies of the United States and its allies—in all of their modalities, economic and military—came under increasingly critical scrutiny.

THE SCHISM IN PEACE RESEARCH

American peace research in the 1960s traced its origins back to the beginnings of institutionalized conflict research, a decade earlier. Its principal figures—such as Kenneth Boulding, Anatol Rapoport, Herbert Kelman, and Walter Isard—were all senior members of their various disciplines sharing a concern with examining conflict. They viewed the problem of war as a distinct phenomenon that reflected the particularities of the international system. Although they dissented from the views associated with the orthodox study of military strategy, they remained connected with the mainstream study of international relations, albeit from a peripheral position.[15] Their normative concerns were rarely overtly presented, but war was treated as an urgent problem that necessitated the application of social scientific techniques to the exploration of conflict resolution. The predominant focus, we might now say, was on negative peace.

Peace research in the Galtungian sense was more a European phenomenon, developing primarily in the Nordic states, The Netherlands, Belgium, and to a lesser extent at first, West Germany. Though sharing a scientific orientation with the American conflict researchers, its explicit interest in the exploration of positive peace was an important distinguishing factor. As Kenneth Boulding noted just after the dispute, three positions within peace research could then be identified: narrow, broad, and radical, with Galtung representing the broad group.[16] During the debate, however, the narrow and broad positions were effectively conflated as representatives of scientistic mainstream peace research. In terms of the critique of peace research as a scientific activity, the conflation was essentially valid, but with regard to the dispute that triggered the whole debate, it was the American community that was the principal target.

In 1967 the Peace Research Society (International) (PRS[I]) hosted a conference in the United States on the Vietnam conflict and in the following year published the papers, under the title *Vietnam: Some Basic Issues and Alternatives*. These generated acrimony at a subsequent conference held by the International Peace Research Association (IPRA) in the same year and also at a 1969 PRS(I) conference, where the majority of the participants signed a declaration condemning traditional peace research as represented by the papers on Vietnam.[17] The IPRA conference had also revealed deep divisions within the peace research community, particularly between the European and American groups of peace researchers, which colored subsequent conferences of both IPRA and PRS(I) during 1969 and 1970. The Vietnam papers were condemned for uncritically reflecting an American perspective. The topics covered by the papers included counterinsurgency warfare, public attitudes to U.S. participation, game-theoretic analyses of the war, and improvement of war-escalation techniques.[18] Critics argued that many of the participants did not attempt a balanced analysis and all of them unquestioningly accepted the legitimacy of the campaign against North Vietnam. The papers were seen effectively to constitute a set of policy options for the U.S. government that were "of doubtful scientific quality" and, as such, unacceptable products of peace research.[19] In contrast, critics collectively proclaimed the responsibility of peace researchers to offer "active solidarity with the peoples struggling against imperialism and super-power supremacy, particularly with the heroic people of Vietnam."[20]

The legitimacy of this viewpoint was premised upon the evident carving up of the post-1945 world into two spheres of influence, within which the superpowers constrained the autonomous efforts of smaller states to achieve national liberation and socialism. Concepts such as "détente" and "peaceful coexistence" were seen as mere slogans that disguised the common interest of the superpowers in sustaining their spheres of influence. In presenting only the American perspective, the participants in the Vietnam conference had reduced peace research to "an unwitting tool of American policy," symptomatic of a pernicious imperialism that mobilized "technicians, men of science and intellectuals" in the service of "capitalist and neocolonial interests and purposes."[21]

Such comments were ill received by the American researchers, one of whom later described the young radicals as having "elevated loutishness to a high moral virtue" and their protest as an expression of "a kind of oedipus complex against the father figures of the older generation," guided by the use of a "hopelessly inadequate . . . body of Marxist doctrine."[22] The mainstream view was that the radicals were undermining the hard-won status of peace research. A noted European supporter of the mainstream position saw the radicals as self-styled peace researchers, for whom "pacifism has been replaced by Marxism, conflict-resolution by class-struggle, peace by revolution and if necessary bloody revolution."[23] This characterization was accepted by one of the principals of the radical group, Lars Dencik, as "essentially correct."

Boulding's reference to the generation gap separating the disputees neglected the point that the radicals did not arise out of the established conflict–peace research movement but were attracted to it from without. They were not converts from a traditional viewpoint but carriers of a radical perspective from the outset. Unlike the earlier generation that had been inspired by the Cold War, they were motivated by a different social context, drew upon a different intellectual tradition, and consequently expressed a different agenda of concerns. Though they acknowledged the origins of peace research and respected the pacifist sentiments of its founders, especially Galtung, their criticisms were nevertheless aimed at the epistemological foundations and stated objectives of scientific peace research. They sought a fundamental reconstruction of peace research and not merely an adjustment in focus. As it stood, peace research could not be a force for change because under a progressivist guise it wittingly or unwittingly contributed to the preservation of a global system of domination.

In 1970 and 1971, both organizations held conferences at which the division within peace research was openly acknowledged and peace researchers on both sides began to come to terms with the new reality and even appreciate its stimulating consequences for research. The American peace research community continued an internal debate as to its proper focus and direction, with a number of younger American peace researchers demonstrating a preference for the broader research agenda being developed in Europe.[24] By 1972, it was evident that the radical critique and Galtung's subsequent contribution had permeated the American peace research community to the extent that the bastion of mainstream scientific peace and conflict research—the *Journal of Conflict Resolution*—editorially acknowledged the significance of the concept of positive peace as well as the coexistence of various schools of peace research.[25] Intellectual conflict was decisively recast as evidence of a healthy diversity.

Schmid's Critique

There were two connected thrusts to the radicals' argument: a questioning of the idea of science as an ideologically neutral activity, concerned with analyzing a social reality extrinsic to the observer; and an attack on the practical relationship between scientific knowledge qua peace research and the formulation of foreign policy, once seen to be a positive step.

The first swipe came in a 1968 paper by Herman Schmid, a Swedish sociologist and member of the Swedish Communist Party. "Peace Research and Politics" was ostensibly a response to an invitation by Galtung, in a piece published the previous year, for peace researchers to examine the adequacy of their field.[26] After acknowledging Galtung's seminal contribution, Schmid proceeded to examine his understanding of the field and its relevance to policy formulation. In Schmid's view, the political and social conditions that had spawned peace research a decade earlier had fundamentally changed. Then, concern over the Cold War and the advent of a nuclear arms race between the superpowers had encouraged the view that scientific knowledge could and must be applied to the study of war and the integration of a divided global community. The enthusiasm for science reflected a concern with attitudinal polarization in political life and a "general disgust with politics and politicians."[27] Even so, at the time of its genesis and in spite of its overt commitment to science, peace research was viewed with suspicion because of its insistence on the importance of applying scientific knowledge to normative and political ends. Because of this, the application of peace research was largely restricted to researching the conditions of war.[28]

Eschewing any discussion of the epistemological problems arising out of peace research's claims to be scientific, Schmid characterized peace research as a science aiming to achieve a type of social control, an objective he read into Galtung's founding editorial in the *Journal of Peace Research*. Although all social science aimed at social control in a manner analogous to the natural sciences' objective of controlling nature and the organism, peace research aimed for a specific type of social control that distinguished it from traditional international relations. The latter's research focus reflected an interest in "external-horizontal" control: Decisionmakers sought to control systems similar to their own in the external environment. Typical of the kind of research that this type of control generated was the analysis of the behavior of other states by national security agencies.

In contrast, peace research reflected an interest in "internal-vertical" control, in which decisionmakers sought to control elements above or below them in the social hierarchy, within their own system. In other words, peace research was distinguished by its assumption of the existence of a global *social* system, to which insights drawn from the analysis of domestic social systems could be applied isomorphically. The nuanced distinction between a "system of states" or "international system," as found in orthodox international relations theory, and an international *social* system is crucial here. The latter formulation implies more than patterned relations between elements in a system and alludes to the possibility of system management guided by systemic needs (or values) distinct from those of domestic social systems but of a similar character.

Schmid had precisely captured the intent of Galtungian peace research: It aimed at the control and integration of the international system, just as social science sought to do in national systems. Consequently, "peace researchers could do what was never possible for the nation-oriented international relationists: draw upon the wealth of social science theory developed for the control and integration of the national system." Peace research anticipated the continuing evolution of a global social system that transcended relations between states, in contrast to the orthodoxy of focusing on the orderly reproduction of the existing international system of states.

The problem with adopting this research orientation arose out of the low level of integration of the international social system and the presumption of an identity of interest among its elements in order to facilitate the application of functionalist sociology. Schmid argued that peace research had utilized two approaches to this issue. First, it interpreted the interests of the international system to mean that all individuals and groups in the world share a common interest in survival and peace. Galtung's appeal to the Hippocratic oath as a model for peace research was an example of such an approach: Both physicians and peace researchers were working for humankind. As a historical materialist, Schmid was dismissive of such "idealistic universalism," seeing it as largely vacuous and divorced from a social reality reflecting hegemonic interests.

Second, peace research appealed to a consensual value of peace, divisible into negative and positive aspects—the former referring to the control of the international system and the latter to its further integration. For Schmid, the difference between these goals and those of conservative functionalism were negligible. Although Galtung had recognized the conservative implications of restricting the focus of peace research to negative peace, Schmid doubted that any consensus existed as to what the substantive content of positive peace was, "even among people who are engaged in collective work for peace." Positive peace was no more than an umbrella concept, the meaning of which depended upon subjectively held political values. To claim that everyone is "for peace" was tautological, the equivalent of saying that everyone was for "the good life" or the best state of things.

Why the objectives of eradicating international violence and integrating the international system might be deemed too conservative became apparent when Schmid presented his understanding of global interests. Writing during the beginning of détente between the superpowers, Schmid saw a common concern with survival as reasonable in the context of the Cold War, but the growth of conflicts and contradictions between nations and groups now required a more critical perspective. Changing circumstances gave the lie to peace research's presumption of a common global interest, rendering support for the needs of the extant international system "a political and non-neutral act." Peace researchers had to identify themselves with concrete social systems rather than universalized theoretical abstractions. Although peace research was charged with looking to "the interests of the world" rather than those of the participants in specific conflicts, there were no consensual positive values to appeal to, and peace research fell back on negative peace as the only sufficiently consensual value to "serve as the basis for the system identification of the peace researcher."

The insufficiency of the category of positive peace was compounded by the prevailing self-image of the peace researcher. Galtung's notion of peace researchers as impartial "peace specialists" serving the consensual interests of the international system had fed the assumption of symmetry between parties to a conflict, of which his claim "that conflict dynamics tend to make parties relatively similar" was exemplary. The Vietnam War made the implausibility of this perspective acutely apparent. Whereas a symmetrical approach made some sense in the case of the conflict between the superpowers, the same could not be said for the conflict between the United States and North Vietnam.

Insofar as peace research had analyzed conflict at all, Schmid claimed that it employed "subjectivist models of conflict," of which Galtung's triangular model of conflict (which at the time of Schmid's paper had only been presented orally) was paradigmatic.[29] This model logically distinguished conflict itself (a reflection of goal incompatibility) from actor behavior and attitudes, yet its existence could only be discerned if certain attitudes or behavior were present. Its inadequacy could be illustrated through reference to a master-slave relationship. The slave may have internalized the social relationship to a degree that no feelings of hostility are exhibited or even felt, perhaps believing his role definition to be the only possibility and appreciating a relatively benevolent master. Yet, it seems reasonable to suppose that there is an objective, latent conflict of interest between master and slave that through the manipulation of behavior and attitudes, leading to apparent social integration, can be manifestly eradicated.

The implications of Schmid's critique were readily apparent. In the Galtungian account, the eradication of conflict requires a search for means of social integration and attitudinal change that will erode the goal differentials deemed to lie at the heart of social conflict. But dominant, subjective goals are simply subverted within the superficially innocuous equation of peace with social integration. For Schmid, the consequences of this approach were drastic: A conflict can only be solved by "destroying one or both actors, through brainwashing or ideological influence [or] through reduction of the goal aspirations of one or both of the actors." Behind "the diffuse concept of peace" lay a value orientation that depicted conflict negatively as arising out of incompatible, subjective goal definitions that are more manipulable than the social structure. The road to peace was paved with the positive values of integration, cooperation, gradualism, compromise, and mutual trust, which were weakly connected to the notion of systemwide values but effectively collapsed into the singular value of nonviolence. Refuting Galtung, Schmid concluded that "the positive values of peace are not *sui generis* but based on a negative value of peace." In essence, peace research was a scientific representation of pacifism.

Against this, Schmid's objectivist model of peace research focused on conflicts of interest "built into the social structure where the conflict is located." Conflict is logically independent of behavior and attitudes: If the latter reflect the structural conflict between parties, then the conflict is manifest; if they do not, the conflict remains latent. A radically different role for peace researchers thus emerges: They should research structural transformation, seeking to render manifest historically latent conflict through the encouragement of polarization and even the escalation of conflict. When the relations of power between the actors have changed, "a structural change can be negotiated to a point where the system breaks down and is rebuilt with a new structure." The peace researcher goes into the business of "sharpening conflicts," which are no longer seen as cataclysmic outbreaks of deviant behavior, as implied in orthodox peace research, but as "immanent characteristic[s] of human society." Thus, peace research would become a different kind of research intended to realize the revolutionary transformation of the external environment (the international system) in favor of the subordinate subsystems, thus facilitating the preferred "external-vertical" form of control, from below of course. However, were this to occur, Schmid admitted, "it would not be very meaningful to keep the label 'peace research' given the usual connotations of the term."

The assumption that Galtungian peace research equated the interests of all people with the interests of the extant international order ignored the strong emphasis in Galtung's work on the immanence of another world within the present—a future world to be brought about in part by the efforts of peace researchers. Furthermore, Schmid showed no awareness of Galtung's commitment to the formal derivation of systemic interests from subjectively held expectations. Even if this version of functionalism was also easily criticized, it suggested, nonetheless, that Galtung was one peace researcher who never intended to presume the existence of objective systemic interests. Paradoxically, Schmid's objectivist account of structural conflict endeavored to recover a genuinely scientific (albeit in the marxian sense) understanding of conflict. However, he also recognized that his interests-based approach suffered from essentially the same flaw as that of Galtung: How are interests determined outside of subjective interpretations? It might be reasonably assumed that Schmid would appeal to

Marx's critique of political economy and locate interests within a historical understanding of capitalist social relations.[30] Instead, he simply noted
that he had no answer to the problem of defining interests but, in a most
Galtungian manner, chose to see this as a challenge rather than a reason
for abandoning research. A more telling lacuna in Schmid's discussion was
the absence of any analysis of the distinction between conflict and violence and the acceptability of the latter to a *peace* researcher.

Olsen and Jarvad also utilized the theme of an abuse of science to attack the PRS(I) Vietnam conference. In their view, so-called peace researchers showed little interest in the origins of the war or the issues at
stake but were primarily concerned with the technical question of ending
violent conflict per se.[31] The preference for escaping into game-theoretic
approaches was indicative of an unwarranted imposition of the assumption
of symmetry between the parties to the conflict. The conference reflected
the positivist view that the function of science was to create technologies
that can further "commonly accepted goals," in this case "the general goal
of peace." Yet, as scientists, the conference participants excluded themselves from formulating the desired goals on the traditional grounds of
value-freedom, and in effect the conference provided American decisionmakers with a variety of strategies for resolving the conflict in line with
their interests.

Lars Dencik—an advocate of militant peace research to his critics—
did not pull any punches and depicted peace research as a technology of
control, integration, and pacification. He followed Schmid in arguing that
a shift in global politics away from Cold War presented an opportunity to
look more closely at asymmetric conflict relationships. Characterizing the
founding figures of peace research as largely "physicists suffering from a
bad conscience," and chastising them for being overly focused upon "open
palpable violence," Dencik called for "conflict resolution proper," or "realistic peace research," which would render latent conflict visible. The assumption of a harmony of interests was described as a liberal ideological
fixation, best replaced by a "structural or objectivistic starting point" that
expressed a "deepened scientific insight." Dencik used the term "structural
silent violence" to capture the nature of latent conflict, which in his view
could be far more destructive in its consequences.[32]

VIOLENCE, PEACE, AND PEACE RESEARCH

Dencik had foreshadowed the central theme of Galtung's contribution
to the debate. Unlike in the approaches of Schmid and Dencik, however,
Galtung's objective was to reconstruct the conceptual fundamentals of
peace research yet retain a pacifist taboo on violence, while rescuing the
idea of positive peace from the charge of vapidity. The first efforts at

conceptual revision were presented in a paper entitled "Violence, Peace and Peace Research." Though its origins lay outside of the rancorous debate, this landmark of peace research can be read as a reply to Schmid. Within the extensive footnotes can be found a limited polemic, in which Galtung acknowledges Schmid's efforts to address the weaknesses of peace research but remarks that he neither agrees with Schmid's critique or proposals nor accepts the representation of his own position.[33] Nonetheless, the paper suggested something of a shared outlook between the protagonists, insofar as both sought to shift peace research away from a concern with the analysis of manifest conflicts. However, two important differences between them need to be borne in mind. First, Galtung retained a commitment to pacifism and strongly rejected the implicit espousal of certain forms of violence ("sharpening of conflict") that ran through the various versions of the radical perspective, including Schmid's. Second, in spite of rhetorical commonalities with the radicals, Galtung's principal source of philosophical inspiration was not Marx but Gandhi. However, the overt acknowledgment of Gandhi's influence was some way off.

Galtung's contribution to the dispute in peace research did not immediately address the question of science and its relationship to policymaking but took up the demand that peace research focus more on the social origins of conflict, especially invisible or latent conflict, and recognize that the concept of positive peace was essentially redundant, as it stood. In an unpublished paper written just prior to "Violence, Peace and Peace Research," he foreshadowed some impending conceptual redefinitions while continuing to cast the peace researcher in the mold of social engineer. Although accepting that peace research could no longer adopt a symmetrical position toward a conflict, he continued to insist that it could not simply reflect "the vantage points of special individuals, groups or nations." Rather it was the values that peace research sought to realize that were in need of reconstruction. Peace was still to be equated with nonviolence, but the concept of violence needed to account for latent forms of social conflict. Schmid and Dencik had argued for a bias toward the oppressed, to the extent that certain forms of manifest violence may be legitimated by the need to eradicate latent violence. Galtung sought a "less biased" perspective that retained the pacifist injunction against violence but would also exclude the type of violence used by dominant social groups, "even if that violence does not show so easily because it is already built into the social structure."[34]

Galtung's response to Schmid in "Violence, Peace and Peace Research" was indecisive, reflecting an as yet unexplained normative disposition rather than systematic argument. He was not resistant to the use of the term *interests* per se but to the implicit assumption that the interests to be pursued by peace research are the expression of values held by specific groups of actors or investigators, dominant or otherwise. This was in contrast to his writing on structural functionalism in which values were located within the subjective dispositions of the members of a specific system, a view adopted to avoid the error of conservative functionalism whereby values are depicted as the objectivized needs of a system. Galtung had now accepted that the earlier formulation neglected the problem of dominance and its impact upon supposedly consensual social values. Nevertheless, ambiguity remained: On the one hand, he claimed to reject a subjectivist model of conflict that was dependent upon the attitudes and perceptions of specific groups; on the other hand, conflict was defined as "goal incompatibility." But where did these goals and the values they represented come from? Galtung admitted to sharing with Schmid uncertainty as to how the incompatible goals might be identified. The earlier view reemerged, insofar as it was suggested that asking the parties to a conflict what their goals or interests were might be one way of determining the relevant values, but it was only one possible approach. Galtung argued also for "interests" to be understood as "values, not necessarily held by the actor . . . or the investigator, just as postulated values."

The reason for resistance to Schmid's interests-based approach was clear enough. The value of peace had to retain its original transideological character, extrinsic to the specific interests of any social group. However, this would not preclude peace research from articulating the interests of a specific group, as long as its values coincided with those undergirding peace research.[35] Even as a deracinated value, peace would retain its autotelic quality. The question next to be addressed was how to provide foundations for a set of values that were sui generis yet nonetheless reflected the needs of the oppressed. "Violence, Peace and Peace Research" offered no answer, but shortly afterward Galtung was to return to this problem and attempt to ground the values impelling peace research within a theory of fundamental human needs. This move enabled him to reconcile a bias in favor of the oppressed and a rejection of any specific ideological framework.

Above all, pacifism remained the raison d'être of peace research for Galtung; without it, what was the point? But pacifism was presented anew in stronger terms: It must not become an apology for failing to tackle the question of social conflict for fear of advocating violence, nor a code word for a descent into a behavioralism that saw conflict resolution in terms of attitudinal or behavioral modification and ignored the structural determinants of social conflict. Rather, the task was now to explore the nature of violence and develop nonviolent strategies for change. With the benefit of hindsight, here can be detected the traces of a Gandhian conception of pacifism as a positive philosophy of action, not simply a moral posture of refusal.[36]

Violence Reconsidered

Galtung commenced his analysis by acknowledging that an adequate definition of violence was a necessary precursor to a superior understanding of peace. Three principles were offered as the basis for exploration:

1. The term "peace" shall be used for social goals at least verbally agreed to by many, if not necessarily by most.
2. These social goals may be difficult but not impossible to obtain.
3. The equation *peace is the absence of violence* shall be retained as valid.[37]

The first two principles simply sidestepped the problem of defending specific values. The third principle was explicitly intended to highlight the transideological qualities of the definition of peace by defining a peaceful social order as a region, within which "a tremendous amount of variation is still possible, making an orientation in favour of peace compatible with a number of ideologies outlining other aspects of social orders." It also reaffirmed the insoluble connection between pacifism and peace research.

A general definition of violence followed: "Violence is present when human beings are being influenced so that their actual somatic and mental realizations are below their potential realizations."[38] Violence is the *cause* of the difference between the actual and the potential and increases, or prevents the decrease of, the distance between them. An important qualification is that "potential" is to be understood as a contingent category connected to the "given level of insights and resources." Thus, a difference between potentiality and actuality is only indicative of violence if it is avoidable and known to be so. Clearly, the definition of *potential* is problematical, particularly with regard to mental realizations. Realized potential—human fulfillment—is inescapably a socially and culturally constructed category. Galtung's response to this problem was weak, deflective rather than exploratory: "Our guide here would probably often have to be whether the value to be realised is fairly consensual or not."[39] As to somatic realizations, the average life span within "the social order" was offered as a crude basis for estimation.

Problems of conceptual precision notwithstanding, the definition of violence attempted to address the deficiencies of early peace research by extending its research focus beyond the realm of direct or manifest violence into anything that inhibits individual human development. Galtung focused on six dimensions of violence:

1. The distinction between physical and psychological violence
2. The distinction between negative and positive influence
3. The existence or nonexistence of an object that is hurt
4. The existence or nonexistence of a subject who acts

5. The distinction between intended and unintended violence
6. The distinction between manifest and latent violence

The first dimension is self-explanatory. The second refers to the violent potential of positive influence, such as the encouragement of consumption to the exclusion of other facets of human potential. The third dimension, also described as "truncated violence," refers to the threat of violence occurring without any evident recipient, the doctrine of a balance of power being an example. Similarly, the deliberate destruction of things with the purpose of intimidating their owners is an example of a "degenerate" form of violence, powerful nonetheless because of the sense of foreboding it can induce.

The fourth dimension is the most important, for it is here that the distinction between "personal" and "structural" violence is introduced. In both cases, individuals can be killed, "hit or hurt," and subject to intimidation, but whereas personal violence can be traced back to specific individual actors, in the second case there may be no identifiable perpetrator: "The violence is built into the structure and shows as unequal power and consequently as unequal life chances."[40] The concept of structural violence ostensibly brought Galtung closer to the radicals' emphasis on latent violence, but there were some significant differences. According to Galtung, marxism's critique of the distribution of surplus value identified one form of structural violence, but the liberal critique of the distribution of power in socialist societies identified another. In what appeared to be a backhanded swipe at the radicals, Galtung argued that in both cases individuals are prevented from realizing their potential, and therefore neither of the ideologies provided a satisfactory perspective from which to comprehend violence. "Social injustice" was deemed a suitable synonym for structural violence, but "exploitation" was rejected because it belonged to a political vocabulary and was so overloaded as to inhibit communication.

A residual scientism, an implicit consequentialist ethics, and the influence of Gandhi merged into an argument for emphasizing the structure of exploitation rather than its agents. In Galtung's hands, social injustice became an abstract analytical category, but it also reflected a Gandhian distinction between the holders of oppressive roles and the role itself. Galtung took from Gandhi a distinction between "actor-oriented" and "structure-oriented" analysis: "a view of human beings both as having free will and being willed by very strong structures." In a paper on pacifism, written ten years earlier, Galtung had noted that Gandhi offered a view of violence as "evil" but to be comprehended, nonetheless, from within the universal assumption of the spiritual equality of individuals.[41] There were two means for comprehending evil (violence) from within a Gandhian perspective of universal love: No one is possessed of the whole truth and cannot be incontrovertibly wrong, and the judgment of an enemy should distinguish between the *status action* of an enemy and the enemy as a *status holder*.[42] To attack the agents of structural violence is to meet one form of violence with another, whereas true dedication to ahimsa (nonviolence) required "the return of good for evil." Gandhi employed a theologically derived ethic of nonviolence—it was the realization of atman (self, or soul) that enabled one to distinguish acts of violence from their perpetrators.[43] Galtung offered no alternative secularized philosophical defense of nonviolence, save for the implicit utilitarianism in his focus on the consequences of violence.

Detachment from the perspectives of specific social actors and the emphasis on consequences were reinforced in the discussion of the distinction between intended and unintended violence, the fifth dimension under scrutiny. Judeo-Christian ethics and Roman jurisprudence connected guilt and intent, whereas for Galtung the proper connection was between guilt and consequence. A bias toward intention may only identify individuals and elide the significance of structural violence, although it was conceded that focusing solely on structural causes would be equally fallacious; personal, direct violence still mattered. Nevertheless, the analysis of structures and their operant logic remained abstract; the role of individuals or groups in creating exploitative structures and ensuring their reproduction was left unexplored.

The final dimension of violence under consideration was the distinction between manifest and latent violence. Here, the difference between the approaches of Galtung and Schmid became fully apparent. Schmid had argued that latent conflict becomes manifest upon a transformation of consciousness (enter the peace researcher); the slave comes to perceive the difference between enslavement and freedom and struggles for the latter. For Galtung, however, latency is not connected to consciousness, it is a structural potentiality; violence is being done to the slave regardless of any subjective comprehension of the fact on the part of any actor in the equation. The existence of, say, a social consensus presuming the possibility of happy slaves would make little difference. Furthermore, both direct and structural violence can be latent or manifest. Direct violence may become manifest in conditions of social instability; structural violence might be eradicated through revolutionary action, only to reappear as a new hierarchical order evolves. As a pacifist, Galtung clearly wanted to reject one of the practical consequences of Schmid's position, namely, that a violent revolution of the oppressed may be justified in the name of true peace.

This objective was reinforced in the discussion of the interplay between personal and structural violence. The elimination of the members of an oppressive elite would not necessarily end structural violence if new forms of it were latent within the ideological perspective of the new holders of power. Galtung's observation that structural violence was evident in postrevolutionary socialist societies in which equality had been ostensibly realized is symptomatic of the "plague on both your houses" attitude toward marxism and liberalism that pervades his subsequent work. Both ideologies were viewed as potential sources of differing forms of structural violence if they become exclusively realized in practice.

The point also connected with the observation that the two categories of violence shade into each other. An individual act of violence is a product not only of personal deliberation but also of expectations arising out of norms inculcated as a consequence of the actor's status. The Gandhian distinction between status holders and the status role is again recalled: How much personal violence is not an expression of structural violence? To use violence against violence reveals a failure to examine critically the longer-term consequences of retaining a belief in the utility of violence itself. Furthermore, Galtung claimed that there were cases when structural change occurs without recourse to personal violence—although he cited none—and the presumption of the indispensability of personal violence was to turn violence into a fetish. Even if personal violence was indispensable, this was another reason to search for alternative means of realizing structural change. Not that Galtung forced the point; he concluded that the jury was still out on the sufficiency or necessity of personal violence to eliminate structural violence.[44] No defense of the value of nonviolence was actually offered, and the empirical evidence as to its utility was acknowledged to be inconclusive.

Direct violence attracted analytical attention simply because it was dynamic and highly visible. Structural violence, however, "is silent, it does not show—it is essentially static, it is the tranquil waters." Perception of its significance was contingent upon the dynamism of the relevant social order. In a *static* society, personal violence is evident, whereas structural violence "may be seen as about as natural as the air around us." The Western juridical emphasis on personal violence reflects the historical development of an understanding of violence within traditional, static social orders. In contrast, thinking about structural violence, claimed Galtung, arose out of "highly dynamic North-West European societies" where structural violence becomes apparent because "it stands out like an enormous rock in a creek, impeding the free flow, creating all kinds of eddies and turbulences."[45] This theme received no elaboration. There was no discussion of what brings about the shift between static and dynamic social formations, or why North-West European societies (assumably the Nordic states) are so "highly dynamic," even though the issue appears worthy of further analysis. It would be illuminating to explore further the noted sensitivity of Scandinavian political culture to issues of social justice, or the relatively open reception of peace research as an institutionalized activity, for that matter. However, a residual scientism reared its obstructionist head both in the level of abstraction and in the presentation of the discussion as a contribution to a universally applicable "science of social structure."

In contrast, Schmid had embedded his analysis within an implicitly historical understanding of social change; the bringing to consciousness of "latent conflict" was part of a revolutionary praxis to which peace research should contribute.[46] As an expression of exploitation, latent conflict is clearly a product of historically specific social structures. Though marxists would differ as to the precise nature and periodization of societal transformation, the exposition of historically specific, structured forms of domination is usually understood as coconstitutive of the transformative process. Marx's normative rejection of exploitation derived from a process of critique rather than from an appeal to universal principles of *recht;* exploitation impedes the realization of humanity's historical striving for emancipation.[47] In comparison, Galtung's discussion was utterly ahistorical and descriptive. Structural violence was supposedly more evident in dynamic societies, but the connections between the categories remain unexplained. Structural violence was presented as an impediment to social transformation, but, paradoxically, it is also more discernible within societies that are changing. Indeed, the shift in peace research's focus from direct to structural violence was legitimated through reference to a changing global social context in which the threat of global war was declining, economic growth continuing, yet exploitation increasing.[48] What Galtung was arguing was that structural violence does not prevent social change but constrains the direction in which it proceeds. To substantiate this, however, the normative premises that enabled a critique of specific forms of societal dynamism had to be explicitly presented and defended.

Redefining Peace

The redrawing of the concept of violence necessitated the revision of the two-sided concept of peace, something that proved to be an openended process. Thus, positive peace came to refer to the "absence of structural violence" and semantically, therefore, transformed into a negative category. Mindful of this, Galtung suggested that it could also be referred to as "social justice," thus restoring a positive content. Since structural violence is by definition a consequence of specific forms of socioeconomic development, then the critical analysis of development now entered the discourse of peace research. In subsequent writings, however, social justice was to be replaced by "human fulfillment," in reflection of a desire to avoid an overly economistic account of the human condition. In one very brief initial exploration of the concept of positive peace, Galtung offered five criteria derived from the antonyms of types of violence: social justice–equality, trust-confidence, interaction-interdependence, pluralism, and dynamism.[49] Though the taxonomy was typically underdeveloped, it is evident that the value set draws from both liberal and marxist perspectives. Although the list of values was to be further refined, most notably in

acknowledgment of nonmaterialist dimensions of human existence, adhered to was the general principle of combining the normative emphases
of different political outlooks.

The reconstruction of the concept of positive peace acknowledged
Schmid's complaint that the original integrative model of positive peace
took too symmetric a view. Galtung also shared Schmid's perception of a
tendency within peace research to focus on negative peace because consensus as to its meaning is more easily obtained. Nevertheless, in concluding "Violence, Peace and Peace Research," Galtung affirmed the pro-
scription of personal violence even in the pursuit of social justice. Also
reiterated was the warning that excessive focus on either form of violence
is undesirable, on the grounds that it would lead to the rationalization of
extremism of left- and right-wing varieties and the possible realization of
"well-known social orders where neither of the two aspects of peace is realised." The purpose of peace research was to "promote the realisation of
values . . . hence [it] could not be identified with the ideology of a group
unless that group professed the same values."[50]

CONCLUSION

"Violence, Peace and Peace Research" adumbrated an expanded research agenda that rapidly came to represent the broader position within
the peace research community, the original radicals failing to sustain their
position. It also marked a watershed in Galtung's own work, providing a
number of clues as to its future direction. The paper also revealed a declining concern with presenting arguments in a positivist form, a residual
scientism notwithstanding, and this shift foreshadowed a subsequent reworking of the concept of science itself and its connection with values.
The emphasis on peace as a transideological value amalgam against which
the extant and, more importantly, preferred global social orders could be
judged also anticipated a dominant theme in Galtung's later writings.
Peace research was cast in the role of "fighting for," "imagining," and
"promoting" a nonviolent world, in the fuller sense that the redefinition of
peace now demanded.

In spite of its historical significance, "Violence, Peace and Peace Research" suffered from some considerable deficiencies. Its normative
premises were certainly overt but barely defended, remaining largely as assertions. Judgment of the deleterious effects of social structures and, by
extension, the fleshing out of the concept of positive peace was effected
not by appeal to a historically or socially grounded concept of unrealized
interests but to a set of deracinated values collapsed into the autotelic
value of nonviolence. The brief allusion to a consequentialist ethics was
inadequate to this task, merely presupposing an understanding of the good

or of human potential. Galtung was not interested in identifying and pun-
ishing sinners but in eradicating their sins. Missing was a robust account
of sinfulness. Without a clear articulation of Galtung's moral economy and
the priorities of human development contained therein (beyond their mere
statement), structural violence remained devoid of substantive content. As
one critic was to put it, Galtung's concept of violence reduced to "simply
the cause of what the user of the term does not like."[51] In Galtung's usage,
it retained a scientific aura insofar as it was intended to represent a quantifiable difference between the actual and the potential. As such, it appeared
simply to correspond to the optimal allocation of resources, but the lack of
any definition of the optimal only underscored the deficiency of the argument.[52] Furthermore, as Galtung clearly sought to argue, human potential
(somatic and mental realizations) was not a purely economic category but
referred to the totality of human experience. It connoted a progressivist,
emancipatory vision of the materially and spiritually secure human.

I have suggested that Gandhi provided the inspiration for Galtung's
unshakable commitment to nonviolence as a supreme value. However,
there was no indication as to whether he subscribed to Gandhi's somewhat
obscure metaphysical premises or utilized a secularized version of them.
In a 1965 paper Galtung had cautioned against adopting any established
perspective on nonviolence (including Gandhi's) because it overly contex-
tualized analysis. Professing then not to have a "clear image of what nonviolence is about," he argued for nonviolence as a "style of action."[53] "Violence, Peace and Peace Research" suggested that little had changed; it
merely alluded to the a priori reasonableness of the adopted normative outlook. This was not just a consequence of Galtung neglecting to reveal his
philosophical position but a continuing overt resistance to engaging in philosophy or ethics at all, a deficiency rendered all the more stark by the
abandonment of the principle of symmetry. Yet, subsequent work was to
show that Galtung believed there were foundations to his peace research.
He went on to depict human fulfillment, or human self-realization, in
terms of the satisfaction of an expanding taxonomy of human needs, ranging from basic material needs to those of a more spiritual and psychological kind. Once postulated, they were to be followed by a straightforward
application of consequentialist reasoning. However, the resort to needs-
talk was only to deflect the problem arising from the continuing absence of
philosophy, an issue I return to in Chapter 6. Whatever the case, "structural violence" has now entered the core lexicon of peace research and has
achieved a wider currency throughout the social sciences. It is undoubtedly an evocative phrase, providing a succinct, descriptive encoding of the
general phenomenon of exploitation. Its potency in quotidian political discourse is hard to discount.

Overall, "Violence, Peace and Peace Research" suggested that Galtung's
work was shedding its orthodox sociological coating while continuing to

express a positivist hesitancy with regard to confronting the question of values. At the time he wrote it, the role of the peace thinker was still seen as that of a physician-engineer confronted with a technical problem of global social organization, guided by a set of values now expanded to include the elimination of structural violence. Nonetheless, his approach began to draw away from its sociological origins in an important respect. The technical problem of organization confronting the peace researcher was no longer that of refining the global status quo, as it evolved according to its own supposed internal logic of integration, but consisted in exploring the means by which global social relations could be *fundamentally* transformed in reflection of positive peace as a value idea. Just as positivist sociology proved inadequate to the task of realizing the Enlightenment vision of its founders, because it could not actually comprehend it, so too did peace research begin to confront the limitations of its foundational paradigm. From this point on, the peace researcher would increasingly be cast less in the role of enlightened technocrat and more in the role of political activist—Gandhi's karmayogi. In this respect, the young radicals who brought about the upheaval in peace research could find some common ground with Galtung.

NOTES

1. Bert Rolling of the Netherlands and Kjell Goldmann of Sweden were also associated with the American position.

2. First drafts of the revised concepts of peace and violence can be found in Galtung, "The Meaning of Peace," and "Peace, Peace Theory and an International Peace Academy," written during 1968 and 1969 in Varanassi. In the first published versions, Galtung traces the ideas to papers given in Oslo, Varanassi, Tokyo, Sweden, and Italy from early 1968, which was before the radical critique. However, he also acknowledges the influence of the critique on the final draft. See Galtung, "Violence, Peace and Peace Research" (hereafter referred to as VPPR), p. 384.

3. Conversation with Walter Isard, Melbourne, August 1987.

4. Hodgson, *America in Our Time,* ch. 14.

5. P. Evans, *The Protest Virus;* Habermas, *Toward a Rational Society,* chs. 1–3.

6. Habermas, *Toward a Rational Society,* p. 28.

7. Ibid., p. 25.

8. Bottomore, *Sociology: A Guide to Problems and Literature,* p. 9. See also Bernstein, *The Restructuring of Social and Political Theory,* part iv.

9. For example, Stein and Vidich, *Sociology on Trial,* published in 1963. For a British contribution see Westergaard, "Sociology: The Myth of Classlessness," originally published in 1964.

10. See Adorno (ed.), *The Positivist Dispute in German Sociology.*

11. Husserl, *The Crisis of European Sciences and Transcendental Phenomenology,* pp. 7–9.

12. See Horkheimer, "Traditional and Critical Theory."

13. Ingram, *Habermas and the Dialectic of Reason,* p. 4.

14. See Baran, *The Political Economy of Growth;* Frank, "The Development of Underdevelopment."

15. For example, see Pruitt and Snyder (eds.), *Theory and Research on the Causes of War.* The editors describe the contributors as members of the "peace research movement" and their perspective as the "rigorous empirical enquiry into the nature and origins of violence in international conflict." There is no reference to peace. See also Newcombe and Newcombe, *Peace Research Around the World*, especially p. 10; for a later example, see Russett, ed., *Peace, War and Numbers*, especially the introduction. Dedring describes "traditional" peace research as "more or less conventional international relations research." Dedring, *Recent Advances in Peace and Conflict Research,* introduction.

16. Boulding, "Limits or Boundaries of Peace Research," pp. 5–19.

17. The full text of the statement can be found as an appendix to Dencik, "Peace Research." PRS(I) was a private organization founded by Walter Isard in 1963. After the dispute it changed its name to the Peace Science Society, to distance itself from the shift away from scientific research. More recently its founder has conceded that the dispute had beneficial effects in forcing social scientists to confront the relationship between values and science (conversation, Melbourne, August 1987). IPRA was founded in 1964 out of a complex network of national and international organizations in both the East and West. Galtung was one of the members of its first executive committee, and the IPRA has evolved into the premier international peace research organization embracing all schools of thought. See Boulding, "Reflections on the founding of IPRA." For an illuminating recollection of the dispute, I am indebted to an impromptu conversation with Håkan Wiberg, Lund University, July 1984.

18. See Isard, "Introduction."

19. Olsen and Jarvad, "The Vietnam Conference Papers."

20. Dencik, "Peace Research," pp. 194–195.

21. Ibid., p. 195.

22. Boulding, "Limits or Boundaries of Peace Research," p. 84.

23. Kjell Goldmann, cited in Dencik, "Peace Research," p. 177.

24. See Rapoport, "Can Peace Research Be Applied?" and "Various Conceptions of Peace Research"; Kent, "The Application of Peace Studies"; E. Boulding, "Peace Research: Dialectics and Development"; Stohl and Chamberlain, "Alternative Futures for Peace Research."

25. See Fink, "Editorial Notes."

26. Galtung, "Peace Research: Science, or Politics in Disguise?" p. 224.

27. Schmid, "Peace Research and Politics," p. 217. All subsequent references to Schmid are drawn from this piece.

28. See also Dedring, *Recent Advances in Peace and Conflict Research*, pp. 19–21.

29. A brief written version of the triangular model of conflict can be found in Galtung, "Peace, Peace Theory and an International Peace Academy," pp. 66–67.

30. While closely following Schmid's line of argument, the German peace researchers Krippendorf and Senghaas explicitly located their critique within a marxist analysis of global political economy. See Krippendorf, "The State as a Focus of Peace Research"; and Senghaas, "Conflict Formations in Contemporary International Society."

31. Olsen and Jarvad, "The Vietnam Conference Papers."

32. Denick, "Peace Research," pp. 178–184.

33. VPPR, pp. 109–134.

34. Galtung, "The Meaning of Peace," pp. 43–49.

35. VPPR, fn. 34.

36. Galtung did not respond directly to Schmid's claim that nonviolence is a negative rather than a positive value. If the understanding of pacifism derives from Gandhian thought, then nonviolence was always a positive value, a view adopted in Galtung, "On the Meaning of Non-Violence," pp. 355–363. See also Sharma, *Ethical Philosophies of India*, pp. 327–329; and Borman, *Gandhi and Non-Violence*, ch. 1.

37. VPPR, p. 110.

38. VPPR, pp. 110–111.

39. VPPR, p. 112.

40. VPPR, pp. 113–114.

41. Galtung, "Pacifism from a Sociological Point of View," p. 313.

42. Writing in 1959, Galtung noted that Gandhi's distinction between statuses and status holders is not as rigorously presented as a sociologist might wish. See ibid., pp. 313–314.

43. Borman traces Gandhi's conception of the ideal, nonviolent man to the *Bhagavad Gita*. See *Gandhi and Non-Violence*, pp. 16–17.

44. VPPR, p. 128.

45. VPPR, p. 117.

46. This view is alluded to rather than explicitly stated. See the analysis of the master-slave relationship, in Schmid, "Peace Research and Politics," pp. 225–227.

47. "We do not anticipate the world with our dogmas, but instead attempt to discover the new world through a critique of the old." Marx, "Letter to Ruge— September 1843," in Marx, *Early Writings*, p. 207. See also Lukes, *Marxism and Morality*.

48. VPPR, p. 118, fn. 23.

49. Galtung, "The Meaning of Peace," pp. 44–47.

50. VPPR, p. 133, fn.34.

51. Eide, "Note on Galtung's Concept of "Violence," p. 71.

52. See Galtung and Hoivik, "Structural and Direct Violence: A Note on Operationalisation," in which an attempt is made to mathematize the concepts of structural and direct violence by comparing the empirical world with an abstract ideal world. In the latter case, an optimal distribution of resources is assumed and average life expectancy calculated. It is then argued that a comparison with actual life expectancies produces a quantification of structural violence. The case for eliminating structural violence assumes, of course, the egalitarian distribution of life expectancy as a normative premise.

53. Galtung, "On the Meaning of Non-Violence," pp. 341–377.

4

The Critique of Global Structure

In the first phase, Galtung defined peace research in contrast to the fields of international relations and conflict analysis. In adding structural violence to his agenda of concerns Galtung now had to distinguish peace research from an emergent critical literature on global political economy as well. As I noted in Chapter 2, Galtung had already begun to explore global stratification through a structural analysis of international aggression, but the earlier efforts were constrained by the dictates of structural functionalism and the stultifying effects of employing a normatively barren form of orthodox sociological discourse. No account of the origins of rank disequilibrium within and between actors in the global social system was attempted; the discussion remained firmly in the realm of hypothesized descriptions. The underlying prescriptive assumption was that certain forms of global social integration could alleviate the problem of rank disequilibrium within social actors, but the connection between the posited values embedded in the original definition of positive peace and the abstract sociological description of the global social system was not adequately addressed, nor could it be. Functionalist sociology writ globally identified integration and technocratic management as the universal form of the rationalization of social relations and transformed it into a normative perspective, which was then recycled as the ethical imperative to functional analysis in the first place. Thus, Galtung's original peace research promoted "associative" strategies of peace or "mutual interdependence."[1]

Galtung was not alone in now seeking to push peace research in a more critical direction, but the work of other peace researchers appears, with hindsight, to have differed little from parallel work elsewhere on the political economy of uneven or dependent development.[2] Galtung's intentions were somewhat different; he eschewed a historical approach and deliberately sought to develop a broader conception of imperialism, one encompassing noneconomic phenomena and capable of including the socialist states. More important, his goal was not to contribute simply to the further refinement of the analysis of imperialism but to stimulate the exploration of strategic responses in the form of a novel model of development in the widest sense.

FROM RANK TO STRUCTURE

The actual experience of being a peripatetic scholar, of living the life of a peace researcher, figured large in Galtung's global sociology. For example, while working in Rhodesia in 1965 he came across statistics that suggested there had been little interracial violence between 1923 and 1965 when the then prime minister, Ian Smith, unilaterally declared Rhodesia's independence from Britain. As Galtung later observed, "In a certain sense there was harmony, cooperation and integration. But was this peace?"[3] The discrepancy between the appearance of tranquillity and the reality of racial inequality in Rhodesia stimulated an interest in structural contexts. A period spent working in Latin America was also significant in this respect. In the early 1960s Galtung took up a position as a UNESCO-sponsored professor in Chile. This experience presented him with some philosophical dilemmas arising out of teaching and researching in an underdeveloped country. One particularly influential episode was his brief involvement with the ill-fated Project Camelot, funded by the Central Intelligence Agency (CIA), which alerted Galtung to the significance of the sociocultural environment for the conduct of scientific research.[4] He was also introduced to the work of Latin American contributors to the emerging *dependencia* school of political economy. However, he was convinced at the time that they were wrong in their focus on inequitable terms of trade or the historical links between the economies of Latin America and the United States. Rather, Galtung perceived exploitation in more general terms as a product of an enforced global division of labor. The time spent in South America was instructive more for the experience, he would later note, than for his discovery of Latin American social science, "however brilliant."[5]

More influential was the seemingly innocuous activity of traveling by air. Galtung was of the view that the tendency for scientists to experience confirmatory instances of their pet hypotheses was less a vice, more a blessing. The example he offered of this was that of attempting to fly between Bogotá and Caracas, capitals of neighboring countries. After he discovered that flights between the two cities were infrequent, it was suggested to him that he fly to Caracas from Bogotá via Paris and New York, thereby ensuring his arrival on the next day. Galtung recalls that nothing had made him so aware of the "feudal" system of global interaction: "It was not an armchair conception—it was there literally speaking." From that point on, Galtung detected the pattern everywhere "so that it became a form against which any social system could be seen, a structure under-lying them all as a potential even if in actuality they had departed from it."[6] The pattern of global interaction was not necessarily the product of conscious human action, of intentional exploitation, but was built into the global social structure itself.

The period in Latin America initially stimulated the kind of analysis found in the earlier papers on global structure. But he would later ac-knowledge that in his early work the verticality of all levels of social order had been taken for granted without asking what was at the root of verti-cality.[7] He had focused on the behavioral manifestation of rank-dependent interaction as a form of conflict rather than exploitation. But the different intellectual climate brought about by the upheavals within peace research and the introduction of the concept of structural violence produced a shift in focus from the former to the latter.[8] This was most dramatically evi-denced by the publication of "A Structural Theory of Imperialism" (STI) in 1971, which unequivocally identified the new problematic as that of the violence of the global structure itself and not merely its manifestation as conflict. A retrospective comment by Galtung identified the essence of the shift: Referring in 1978 to "A Structural Theory of Aggression," written in 1964, Galtung noted that had he written the paper later, he "would cer-tainly have seen aggression that can be *built into* a social structure (as structural violence) and not only as something that *comes out* of a social structure."[9]

The late 1960s and early 1970s witnessed an explosion of interest in the political economy of North-South relations, with the dependency school evolving as a challenge to orthodox modernization theory. I will not attempt here an analysis of the intricacies of debates within development theory generally, but for purposes of setting context, some aspects of the growth of a new, more radical literature on political development are worth noting.[10] Perhaps its most definitive feature was the conceptualiza-tion of capitalism and imperialism as a world system, in contrast to a focus on national modes of production and capital accumulation. The notion that underdevelopment of the global periphery was an original condition was decisively rejected. Instead, it was seen to emerge out of the expansion of the European states into the global periphery, a thrust that commenced in the sixteenth century and peaked in the nineteenth century. The term *im-perialism* has since acquired a more general meaning of exploitative rela-tions between states and classes that did not disappear as a consequence of the political retraction of European powers in the twentieth century and is now synonymous with a globalized capitalism. But however loosely the term is now used, imperialism invariably alludes to a historical connection between the development of the North and the underdevelopment of the South, historically and presently.

Another general feature of the critical literature on global political economy is its undermining of traditional perspectives on international politics. The interpretation of imperialism as an inevitable by-product of realpolitik (or mercantilism) and geopolitical imperatives was decisively rejected, as was realism's privileging of the *politics* of relations between states. Similarly, liberalism's concept of "interdependence" was implicitly depicted as intimately connected with the orthodox view of modernization. By definition, interdependence denies or disguises the asymmetry of economic relations between the global center and periphery. Consequently, a critical shadow was also cast over early peace research that in prescriptive terms relied essentially on a version of interdependency theory. In contrast, the radical wing of peace research adopted along with their cognates in political economy an emphasis on a historically evolved global structure that significantly conditioned—some would say determined—international political relations.

In reflection of the wider debate in the social sciences, radical political economy implicitly or explicitly presented theory in antipositivist terms—as a form of critique. The problem with orthodox modernization theory was not only its empirical inadequacy and ahistoricism but also its unacknowledged normative content. Against this, theory was seen as intertwined with emancipatory political action, and the orthodox view that theory should endeavor to be independent of normative assumptions and reflective of an empirical world extrinsic to the observer was usually decisively rejected. Thus, in clear homage to Marx's eleventh thesis on Feuerbach, Andre Gunder Frank concluded his seminal essay "The Development of Underdevelopment" with the hope that scientists from the underdeveloped world would further analyze the phenomenon of underdevelopment because "it is their people who in the last analysis face the task of changing this no longer acceptable process and eliminating this miserable reality."[11]

It is only against this backdrop that Galtung's analysis of imperialism can be adequately grasped. In many respects it was highly derivative. Nonetheless, it did make some specific claims to originality and cannot be simply reduced to just another contribution to the larger debate. It did not fit neatly into any specific perspective within that debate, and in certain respects it was openly promoted as a square peg in a round hole. Above all, it was presented as a contribution to a constructivist peace research seeking to go rapidly beyond the exposition and explanation of imperialism or dependent development to the exploration of alternative patterns of international interaction. This was in marked contrast to the bulk of dependency analysis that had failed to match the rapid development of theoretical understanding with prescriptions for change, save for general expressions of a need for structural change usually cast in terms of socialist revolution.[12] Galtung's theory of imperialism was intended to be a "theory of liberation from structural violence."[13]

"THE STRUCTURAL THEORY OF IMPERIALISM"

The STI was written, in typical Galtungian fashion, over a single weekend in August 1970 and published in the *Journal of Peace Research* in 1971. It was preceded, Galtung claimed, by a lot of preparatory research, by which was meant all of his writings on international interaction and global structure. It remains the most cited of all of his publications and one of the few to attract critical analysis from outside of peace research, a consequence, Galtung later accurately judged, of the paper's timeliness as much as its intellectual content.[14]

The objective of the paper was to conceive of, explain and counteract inequality "as one of the major forms of *structural violence*" and develop a "theory of liberation" from a specific dominance system, in this case "imperialism."[15] The central premise was that the world consists of "Center" and "Periphery" nations, each of these containing its own center and periphery. (Note that in this discussion I reproduce Galtung's own usage by employing capital and lowercase letters respectively to distinguish between Center and Periphery states as a whole and their internal centers and peripheries.) From this a two-by-two matrix could be generated, providing the descriptive basis for the subsequent discussion of imperialism. An imperialist relationship was defined as "a dominance relationship between collectivities, particularly between nations."[16] It was not simply a case of one state exercising power over another; the definitive feature was the establishment of a bridgehead within Periphery states by the center of Center states—a center within the Periphery—that works for the ultimate benefit of both centers. For Galtung, imperialism was not the same as military domination or the threat of conquest; nor did it embrace the reductionism of "marxist-leninist theory," which he read as offering an overly economistic model of imperialism. Attributing to marxism-leninism the assumption that imperialism would vanish along with the demise of capitalism, Galtung viewed it as "a more general structural condition between two collectivities." Economic imperialism was but a specific manifestation of a generalizable structural relationship that was not dependent upon the existence of capitalism.[17] Strictly speaking, therefore, his account was not intended to be confused with analyses of *capitalist* imperialism, although the distinction was certainly honored more in the breach than the observance.

Galtung saw imperialism as a relationship that splits up collectivities in such a manner that the relationship between their parts can be comprehended in terms of either a conflict or harmony of interests. This could be defined objectively, since it could not be assumed that parties to a conflict necessarily knew what their true interests were. That true interest was referred to as a "living condition," to be understood in relative rather than absolute terms. Thus, a conflict of interest exists if the relationship between two parties is such that the gap in living condition is increasing, and a harmony of interest exists if it is decreasing. He provided few clues as to the contents of living condition, which appeared to be simultaneously an objective and subjective category, definable according to a set of quantifiable criteria, such as income or standard of living, as well as the less tangible criteria of quality of life and autonomy. Galtung's fundamental concern was not the precise content of living condition but the definition of a conflict of interest. At some point, he averred, "parties" to a conflict may crystallize into "actors" whereupon a latent conflict of interests is transformed into the pursuit of incompatible goals. At this point, Galtung appeared to be alluding to a notion of class consciousness but with some discomfort. Thus, if a government endeavors to increase its living condition at a greater rate than that of the wider community, then a conflict of interest can be said to exist and the government regarded as "illegitimate." Defining illegitimacy in this manner was preferred to the more usual process of deriving it from the expression of opinion in the population or legislature. The latter presupposed a capacity to reason and express oneself or to possess a political consciousness and capacity to act politically. For Galtung, such capacities could "only be presupposed at the centre of the more or less vertical societies in which people live. It is a model highly protective of the centre as a whole."[18]

Although this formulation suggested a decisive break with Galtung's earlier functionalism that had emphasized public opinion as a source of societal norms, it rested on a crude sociology of knowledge and had awkward, one could say imperial, political implications. It implied that the periphery of a state was by definition incapable of determining a government to be illegitimate, and thus it beholds the analyst to speak on behalf of the oppressed by defining their situation in objective terms in lieu of their apparent incapacity. At what point, then, would the periphery be deemed capable of comprehending its own interests? At face value, the argument exuded an elitism that ran counter to the very thrust of the critique of imperialism. With hindsight, a partial defense of Galtung can be mounted, insofar as his discussion was elitist in implication rather than intention. Underpinning it was an assumption that a theory of human needs would ultimately give content to the idea of an adequate living condition and, by extension, a definition of true or objective interests.[19]

Galtung conceded that the concept of "interest" employed was ideologically grounded in the value of equality, but this could be read through either liberal or marxist lenses. Equality could be formulated either as the "distribution or redistribution of values generated by the society," a view attributed to liberal theory, or it may be understood in marxist terms as the "absence of exploitation."[20] According to Galtung, the liberal perspective supported the retention of the essential social structure coupled with redistribution, whereas marxism demanded structural transformation. Typically refusing to endorse a specific perspective, Galtung claimed that his structural account of imperialism cut across the liberal-marxist divide and was based upon "a more general concept of harmony and disharmony of interests." It was evident, nonetheless, that his broad sympathies lay with the larger project of structural transformation.

The core of Galtung's model assumes a two-nation world and presents imperialism as a relationship between a Center state and Periphery state that has the following features:

1. A harmony of interest between the center in the Center state and the center in the Periphery state
2. Greater disharmony of interest within the Periphery state than within the Center state
3. A disharmony of interest between the periphery in the Center state and the periphery in the Periphery state[21]

Galtung did not locate his definition of imperialism within the wider literature, claiming only that it arose out of "a certain research tradition," apparently his own earlier structural explorations because the origins of the definition were traced to "a long set of findings about international interaction structures" as well as deductions arising out of "speculations relating to structural violence in general and the theory of inequality in particular."[22]

Confusingly, Galtung also claimed to have borrowed from Lenin, with whom he saw himself sharing an interest in the relationship between center and periphery. Yet, it is not at all clear that this was, in fact, Lenin's main concern; he was more interested in the conflict between European states that arose out of the expansion of capitalism into colonized territories on the global periphery and that set the stage for World War I.[23] The most evident commonality was with Lenin's notion of a labor aristocracy. However, the extent to which Lenin's analysis of the use of "superprofits" to buy the compliance of "the labour leaders and the *upper-stratum* of the labour aristocracy" (emphasis added)—letting the majority of the proletariat in Center states off the hook—is commensurate with Galtung's somewhat broader claim that there was a disharmony of interest between the two internal peripheries is a moot point. Lenin and Galtung employed very different discursive tones; one was historically specific, the other decisively not.[24] Even so, there were commonalities. Galtung suggested that there remained a partial disharmony of interest between the two sectors of Center states, in spite of a shared disharmony of interest with the periphery in the Periphery state (point 2 of the definition of imperialism appears to capture this). Indeed, Galtung emphasized that in his model the uneven levels of disharmony, or inequality, were crucial, because only then could it be seen that "the total arrangement is largely in the interest of the periphery in the Centre." In the overall scheme of things, the periphery areas in developed states see themselves "more as the partners of the centre in the Centre than as the partners of the periphery in the Periphery." Thus, "alliance formation between the two peripheries is avoided and the Centre nation becomes more and the Periphery nation less cohesive . . . and hence less able to develop long-term strategies."[25]

Absent from Galtung's discussion was the historical analysis of the internationalization of capital during the colonial era, "the economic basis of a world-historic phenomenon," that provided the core of Lenin's argument. The language of social class was also avoided. The STI was primarily formal and descriptive in style, containing only brief sweeping references to historical processes and clearly intended not to be compared closely to other accounts of imperialism but to provide a provocative model of the prevailing global social structure. Nevertheless, the spirit of Lenin's (and, more recently, Emmanuel's) argument was retained, and it was potent. Thus, the global social structure was seen to act as a disincentive to the development of empathy between the peripheries within Center and Periphery states, the periphery in the Center being effectively bought off through a mutually beneficial alliance with those who dominated it. A markedly lower gradient of inequality within Center states, compared to Periphery states, was obtained through welfare policies leading to improvements on most dimensions of living condition, with the exception of power. Galtung offered no evidence for this much debated hypothesis, the intended conclusion being that it was in the overall interest of imperialism that the interests of the periphery and the center in the Center state are at least partly commensurate.

There is an important qualification to the model outlined so far. Given the overriding shared interest of the two parts of a Center nation in the exploitation of a Periphery nation, and the fact that the center in the Periphery state is likely to be a proportionately smaller segment of the whole, do not the interests of the Center state *as a whole* conflict with the interests of the Periphery nation *as a whole*? This conclusion was rejected because it blurred the central feature of his model—the harmony of interests between the two centers—and reduced imperialism to a problem of international relations. Galtung saw imperialism as a global structure of domination, which required for its continued existence "a bridgehead for the Centre nation in the centre of the Periphery nation." If two states with horizontal internal social relations were externally connected by a relation of dominance, then this would not constitute an imperialist relationship but one better described by a term such as *looting* or *stealing*. But if a secular increase in the living condition between two such states became apparent, then the researcher should be prompted to investigate the existence of imperialism. Obviously, Galtung did not consider a nonimperialist relationship between a developed state and an underdeveloped state to be a likely occurrence.

THE MECHANISMS OF IMPERIALISM

The Vertical Interaction Relation

According to Galtung, there were two basic mechanisms (or principles) of imperialism: One reflected the interaction relationship between specific parties, and the other referred to the larger interaction structure. The first was that of the *vertical interaction relation* between centers and peripheries, assessed according to two factors: the value exchange between actors and the effects of this exchange *within* actors. Whereas liberal and marxist economists alike emphasized the exchange relationship between actors, Galtung included the effects of unequal exchange within actors, a process he later was to term "in-change."[26] Thus, an adequate "interaction budget" needs to take account of the benefits accruing to the importer of raw materials (usually a developed or industrialized state), not only from the initial terms of trade but also from the manufacturing spin-offs as raw materials are processed prior to being resold with value added. Equally, the underdeveloped state is doubly exploited by the exchange relationship and the lack of positive spin-offs, due to the tendency to import finished goods. An interaction budget needs to note also that *both* parties to an equal exchange experience costs, something that at the time Galtung rightly saw as absent from most analyses of exchange relations. The identification of negative spin-off effects within developed states, such as pollution and exploitation, foreshadowed a significant theme in subsequent writing: overdevelopment. The models of preferred developmental strategies that were to flow from the STI invariably rejected the reproduction of developed societies within the periphery, because of their deficiencies as paradigms of the good life.

Galtung went on to account for the emergence of exploitation on a global scale by way of a schematic and very brief account of three stages of exploitation, or "unequal exchange." This was claimed to be in part representative of the actual history of exploitation as well as "types of thinking about exploitation." The first stage is the looting of an undeveloped state by a developed state, usually by means of a slave-labor force. This is followed by a derisory offer of exchange by the developed state, such as beads for land, although the offer at least has some acknowledgment of indigenous ownership of the exploited territory. In the third stage a more equitable exchange relationship emerges, in which the developed state has to pay more for whatever is extracted. Galtung admitted that the shift from the second to the third stage was difficult to pinpoint precisely. It occurs as a consequence of shifts in international relations of power arising, assumably, from granting of independence to former colonies. Identification of a more equal exchange might be based upon an analysis of shifting attitudes in the weaker party, objective market values, or changes in the labor value of the products on either side of the exchange relationship. In his view, none of these explanations considered the *intra*-actor effects of exchange, yet it was the disparity between the appearance of an equal exchange relationship and the reality of inequality, detected through the employment of a comprehensive interaction budget, that is distinctive to the third and contemporary phase of imperialism. In the case of exchanging oil for tractors, for example, oil is pure nature, whereas the tractor is moving in the direction of pure culture or form. The two products are distinguished by the vastly different levels of processing of raw materials required for their manufacture and by the differing impact on the state of origin.[27] Processing acts as a multiplier that transforms the host society by stimulating the development of sophisticated production, communication, research, education, defense, and transport systems. Thus, a Center state can reinforce its dominance in the global social structure by developing a psychology of self-reliance and autonomy.[28] The deficiency of most economists was that of failing to consider the level of processing in their analyses of North-South exchange relations. Academic research traditions had evolved into a division of labor that not only mitigated against an adequate grasp of the totality of the exchange relationship between the global center and periphery but, more importantly, prevented the formulation of "a new program of trade on equal terms." For Galtung, genuinely equal trade could occur only if all of the internal and external effects of unequal exchange were equalized. A disinterest in assessing intra-actor effects of exchange relations worked to the ultimate benefit of the developed states.

More provocative was the claim that it had become "natural" for even the center in the Periphery state to see things solely in terms of *inter*action, although the explanation of this was somewhat sketchy. If elites in the underdeveloped states have primarily thought in terms of "being" rather than "becoming," if they have preferred ownership to processing, then their interaction with the developed world would appear advantageous to them. What was formerly nature was converted into money, which was further converted into a variety of things. In sum, "very little effort was needed: and that this was precisely what made the exchange so disadvantageous only became clear after some time."[29] The elites of peripheral states viewed the world through a specific and limited developmental prism. Rationality itself was grounded in an inequitable exchange relationship and masked it and rendered it seductive; the true nature of the relationship would be revealed only when it ultimately impinged upon the living conditions of the center in the Periphery state, in other words, the weaker of its principal agents. Imperialism conditioned the mind-sets of its agents and created a form of false consciousness, as part of the process of its reproduction. What Galtung did not consider was the possibility that elites in peripheral states were motivated by the shrewd, self-serving, yet possibly very accurate calculation that the benefits accruing to them under the prevailing relationship of exploitation would likely always be better than those arising out of another exchange relationship that would be more equitable from the point of view of the exploited majority. Galtung appeared loathe to point an accusatory finger, preferring to stay inside the confines of abstract structural argument.

Nonetheless, Galtung's overall point was one with which many other critics of orthodox development theory could and still would concur: Uneven exchange relations could not be rectified by fiscal adjustment of the terms of trade alone. Increased revenue might help to fund internal development strategies in partial compensation for the lack of spin-off benefits within Periphery states, but such a policy would force dependent states into a pattern of development still determined by the location of the Periphery state in the global structure. "It is hard to see," Galtung argued, "how the psychology of self-reliance can be bought for money."[30] A more just rectification would occur if dependent states were free to decide for themselves their pattern of development "without being forced by the entire social machinery." An important prescriptive theme, to be developed further in his later work, was being flagged here: Self-reliant development is the preferred strategy for states on the global periphery. Again, this signaled a decisive break with a previous emphasis on *associative* strategies of development, constructed around the themes of interdependence, integration, and cooperation. Now recognized as being blind to the structural determinants of underdevelopment, associative strategies had at the very least to be supplemented with strategies of disassociation and delinking from the global economy.

The Feudal Interaction Structure

The second mechanism of imperialism—the feudal interaction structure—has two principle features: First, multilateral interaction is monopolized by the Center state; second, interaction between Periphery states is virtually nonexistent, and their interaction with Center states is limited to bilateral relations.[31] These features may have accorded with Galtung's personal experiences, but as the data on economic relations within and between nations provided in an appendix to the STI showed, actual trade relations across the developmental divide are considerably more varied than suggested by the model.[32] Nevertheless, he went on to discuss the implications of the feudal interaction structure, in particular the concentration of trade between Periphery states and their respective centers and the concentration in commodities exported by the periphery. The latter is a fact to be explained, Galtung argued, not by the vagaries of nature but by the historical evolution of the structure of imperialism in reflection of the Center states' import needs that led to the creation of a local economy around the particular primary product.

Although Galtung evidently sympathized with the depiction of imperialism as a product of capitalism, it is important to reiterate the point that the depiction of a feudal structure was intended to capture a generalized pattern of interaction. This becomes more apparent in the discussion of noneconomic forms of imperialism, but it is also evident in the assertion that the most significant consequence of dependence is political: "The feudal interaction structure is in social science language nothing but an expression of the old political maxim 'divide et impera,' divide and rule, as a strategy used systematically by the Centre relative to the Periphery nations." Thus, Galtung went on to ask, "How could a small foggy island in the North Sea rule over one quarter of the world?"[33] Awesome though the nineteenth-century Pax Britannica was, Galtung neglected to ask the obvious next question: Why, given the self-reinforcing feudal structure of interaction, did that small foggy island lose its position of dominance?[34]

Clearly, the cognitive intent behind Galtung's analysis of imperialism was not that of refining or supplementing the kind of historical and empirical analysis undertaken by the dependency theorists to make their case. Instead, he endeavored to go a step further and construct an image of a generalized logic of domination in which the opportunities open to and the constraints upon global actors were determined by the structural characteristics of their external environment. On face value this invites comparison with the international relations literature, in particular the work of Kenneth Waltz. From a different structural starting point—the necessary existence of international anarchy in a system of functionally similar but unequal sovereign states—Waltz also seeks to theorize the reproduction of the international system.[35] But Galtung's approach differed in two important respects: First, he insisted upon the inseparability of domestic and international social relations, thereby challenging the orthodox assumption that international relations constitutes a distinctive realm. Second, the modeling of the feudal interaction system was only the first step in a larger project—the realization of positive peace, a normative impulse markedly absent from Waltz. The STI was intended to show how the mechanisms of imperialism have become so refined that overt oppression is needed less and less: "Only imperfect, amateurish imperialism needs weapons; professional imperialism is based on structural rather than direct violence."[36] The absence of overt violence and the refinement of imperialism may encourage the erroneous conclusion that a decline in the use of direct violence is indicative of more peace. Against such an assumption, Galtung presented an image of a pervasive structure of domination, the eradication of which should take first place on the agenda of peace research.

The difference between Galtung's account and the supposedly more limited purview of the dependency theorists was also illustrated by a discussion of five types of imperialism: economic, political, military, communications, and cultural, spatially connected like the points on a "Pentagon or Soviet star." In contrast to the tendency to use imperialism as a term of abuse to describe "the other camp," Galtung's preference was "to see it as a technical term, which does not mean that he who struggles for peace will not have to struggle against imperialism regardless of what shape it takes."[37] The existence of imperialism was not determined by the modality of the exchange relationship but by whether the mechanisms of imperialism were present and the relationship fulfilled the three criteria contained in the original definition. However, in a later version of the STI—published as part of *The True Worlds* in 1980—Galtung conceded that "it may well be . . . that at the present juncture in world history, in looking at international relations at large, an economic point of view would be most fruitful in explaining what is going on." But even this concession is itself conditioned by the reiteration of agnosticism on the question of the primacy of the economic aspect.

The True Worlds also introduced "social imperialism" as a sixth type, a concept taken from Chinese criticisms of the Soviet Union's attempts to impose upon China a particular societal configuration, something the Chinese viewed as "sufficiently wrong and evil in its own right."[38] Similarly, relations between Eastern and Western Europe appeared to resist explanation in purely economic terms, since in spite of remaining formally outside of the Western economic system, the political culture of Eastern Europe increasingly revealed the imprint of the West. In fact, Galtung's interpretations of East-West relations in Europe in early (1971) and later (1980) versions of the STI revealed a shifting normative position. Initially, the theme was the devious success of the West in penetrating East European political culture, whereas later the impact of Soviet imperialism in encouraging the East Europeans to look westward came to the fore. Although they were hardly rigorous, such observations reinforced the argument against the adoption of a model of imperialism that is too tied either to concrete history or to the specific case of capitalist imperialism.[39] The types of imperialism were seen as being convertible from one type to another. Just as vertical interaction produces reinforcing spin-offs (intra-actor effects), so too can it produce *spill-over* effects from one type of imperial relationship to another—the capacity to produce tractors can easily be converted into a capacity to produce tanks, which might then provide the basis for military as well as economic imperialism.[40] Imperialism had evolved into a complex whole in which no hierarchy of types should be assumed.

Galtung's intended iconoclasm was bold but weakly formulated. The primacy of the economic factor was rejected, but he focused nonetheless almost exclusively on economic domination and exploitation. He borrowed heavily from the dependency literature and marxist historiography yet at the same time sought to be distinguished from these sources. What was described as a general *theory* of imperialism was in effect an impressionistic taxonomy of the key features of global political economy, suggestive nonetheless and certainly not entirely implausible, within which was embedded a number of normative themes. For Galtung, to read the future from the past, to bow before history, is to restrict the creative potentiality of theory. In sum, the STI was the starting point of a research program rather than its conclusion.

THE STRATEGIC IMPLICATIONS OF
"THE STRUCTURAL THEORY OF IMPERIALISM"

For Galtung, imperialism was characterized by an unequal distribution not only of economic wealth and productive capacity but also of access to political power, the use of violence, communications, and cultural production. The gradient of inequality varied, however, according to the location of the state within the global structure. Within Center states, the periphery had some access to political power, to positions within the military, and to the production of culture, as a consequence of (relatively) high levels of access to education. This lower gradient of inequality was presented as the hallmark of liberal democracy, and it contributed to the preservation of the global structure of imperialism. Democracy in the Center states actually enabled the exercising of control over peripheral states because the periphery in the Center benefited from a lower gradient of inequality, which made it less likely that they would find common cause with the oppressed in the peripheral states. Implicit within this imagery was more than a doubting of proletarian internationalism as an agency of global transformation; liberal democracy was intertwined with a global structure of domination and was, therefore, an integral part of the wider problematic. Thus, yet another theme, also considerably expanded in subsequent work, was introduced: The eradication of global exploitation requires also the transformation of social relations within Center states.

A perfect example of imperialism would arise if all the definitional criteria were fulfilled, both mechanisms of imperialism were operating, and all five (later six) types of imperialism existed. Then there would be a "perfectly feudal interaction network." But, Galtung asked, has there ever been such a thing? This question revealed, in his view, the continuing applicability of positivist methodology to problems of structuralist or even marxist analyses. What he was offering was an "ideal type" to which few empirical cases appeared to correspond.[41] Although all of the criteria of imperialism could be operationalized and in principle, therefore, the theory could be tested, Galtung conceded that as a whole it was too complex except for the specific case of economic imperialism.[42] Nonetheless, he also remarked that so rich a theory should provide ample basis for empirical research, within liberal and marxist schools of thought, employing either synchronic statistical methods or diachronic case studies. Furthermore, he opined that "it would be sad if ideological and other types of conflicts between adherents of different schools should lead to any systematic neglect of the mobilising of general social science for a deeper understanding of how this system works."[43]

The uncertain status of the STI—as a description of an ideal type untied to concrete history—also did not inhibit Galtung from concluding with a programmatic survey of strategic guidelines for action. Given that resistance to imperialism, in all of its modalities, was constrained by the lack of communication and cooperation between the peripheries of the peripheral states, an alternative structure must be constructed. First, there would need to be greater "horizontalization"—exchange would need to be on more equal terms in order to eradicate vertical interaction and decrease the dependency of peripheral states. Second, strategies of defeudalization would be required. This would mean establishing exchange relations across the existing patterns, notably between peripheral states. Galtung suggested that this may necessitate the creation of some form of "viable organisation of peripheral countries for international class conflict," functionally analagous to a trade union demanding more equitable exchange relations. Such an organization would depend upon a multilateral commitment to an ideology characterized by a "rejection of past and present" and containing "visions for the future." Center-Periphery relations would need to become more symmetrical, with the "destruction" of those international organizations that did not move in this direction to be facilitated through the withdrawal of Periphery nations coupled with the establishment of alternatives consisting exclusively of Periphery nations. Further horizontalization of Center-Periphery relations could be realized by the globalization of the means of production and communication to equalize access in order to ensure that the needs of the periphery in the Periphery states were being met. In general, defeudalization would require the establishment of greater contact between the most distant of parties and outside of established blocs.[44]

Obviously, such strategies would not be viewed favorably by the beneficiaries of the existing global structure. In Galtung's eyes, the centers in the Periphery states appeared to be the most exposed groups as the pawns of the dominant centers and also coexploiters. In short, they would have to choose sides. To facilitate the process of realigning the centers of the Periphery toward their own peripheries, he suggested some strategies aimed at reducing harmony between the centers. The first suggestion—somewhat extraordinary coming from a pacifist—was not so much a strategy as a favorable circumstance. If war occurred within or between Centers, this might provide opportunities for Periphery states, as a consequence of a reduced capacity for Center states to exercise global dominance. In addition, a breakdown in the bridgehead between centers across the development divide—as a consequence of the rise of, say, a populist nationalism in the

Periphery state—may camouflage the disharmony within the Periphery state, thereby providing new strategic opportunities. Still another set of strategies focused on the reduction of disharmony within the Periphery state. Again, the pacifist voice was surprisingly muted because either violent or nonviolent revolution was cited as means for eliminating (quite literally, in the case of the former) disharmony. Alternatively, there was the more populist strategy of developing greater cooperation between peripheries in Periphery states—patterns of nongovernmental foreign policy. In general, Periphery-generated strategies were to be preferred, since they reduced the likelihood of new forms of dependence being created.

Finally, some strategies for transforming the Center states were very briefly explored. Thus, an increase of internal disharmony, possibly as a consequence of a decline in nationalist solidarity, might facilitate a shifting of the allegiance of the periphery in the Center state toward other peripheries, although Galtung had his doubts. On a more hopeful note, he suggested that the center in the Center state may actually change its fundamental goals without coercion as a consequence of increasing awareness of the costs (i.e., negative spin-offs such as a threat to world peace, pollution, and exploitation) of the imperialist structure: "There are many possibilities [that] may combine into quite likely contributions towards a disruption of the system." Ostensibly, then, a peace praxis within developed states emerges here, with clear implications for the Galtungian peace researcher. But rather than develop the point, Galtung simply reiterated his preference for Periphery-generated solutions.

CRITICISMS OF "THE STRUCTURAL THEORY OF IMPERIALISM"

That the STI was one of the few of Galtung's offerings to attract published critical response was a consequence, no doubt, of the fact that it trod on more than a few disciplinary toes. To be frank, it also provided an easy target, as some examples of critical commentary will illustrate. For Waltz, the concluding prescriptions reduced to moral imperatives that did not consider the structural constraints upon effective action faced by a coalition of underdeveloped and resource-deficient states. Indeed, Waltz employed the STI as a case study of poor international relations theory, since, among other deficiencies, it provided little in the way of an explanation of imperialism or its historical origins, the occasional brief excursion into the past notwithstanding. As Waltz correctly observed, the claim that "vertical interaction is the major source of inequality in the world" was simply asserted and reasserted. More pointedly, Waltz claimed that because the concluding assumptions were built in from the outset, the STI was not a theory at all.[45]

The lack of explanatory content has also been noted by more sympathetic critics. Palonen argued, for example, that Galtung's major indicator of exploitation—the shifting gap in living condition—only identifies the intensity of an interaction, not its direction or cause.[46] Although professing to share Galtung's normative outlook, Van den Bergh found his approach to be static and ahistorical, even though the subject matter was "structured processes of social development." Galtung offered no more than a taxonomy of types of imperialism that could not account for change, either in support of the prescriptive remedies or against them. He depicted a global order that was stable in spite of its inequity, and questions of why and how remained unanswered. Echoing Waltz, Van den Berg also criticized the lack of propositional statements, despite Galtung's frequent allusion to the need to test the hypotheses arising out of the theory.[47]

Chris Brown has examined the uncertain relationship between Galtung's perspective and varieties of the marxist tradition. In a complex critique, Brown argues that Galtung's rejection of marxism, on the grounds that it was reductionist in its economic determinism, revealed a particularly vulgar reading that few marxists would recognize. Nonetheless, Galtung was not averse to selectively drawing upon classical and neomarxist sources and appeared to accept "more or less completely" Emmanuel's theory of unequal exchange and, in later versions of the structural theory, Wallerstein's world systems approach as well.[48] The thrust of Brown's argument is that both the classical marxist tradition and the more recent dependency literature utilize developmental historical accounts of capitalist development that at the very least offer a basis for a theory of structural change. It is against this capacity that Galtung's approach invites judgment.

According to Brown, the fundamental problem is the problematic character of Galtungian structuralism. Purporting to be an abstract, generalizable concept, Galtung's "structure" was in fact primarily illustrated by reference to consequences of the European form of imperialism developed in the nineteenth century. By generalizing from the specific case, Galtung committed the very error that he attributed to marxists. To be of value in its own terms, Galtung's model had to be shown to be applicable under a variety of conditions in the empirical world, and this was not attempted. The inference that the external behavior of specific actors is governed by an encompassing structure is itself plausible, but in Galtung's case there was no consideration of the constant interplay of structure and action. The structure is created and from then on influences without being influenced. Galtung's purportedly abstract structure mysteriously acquired ontological substance, yet where it came from remained unclear. In grounding the specificity of contemporary imperialism in the political economy of European capitalism, marxian varieties of structuralism at least provided a basis for a theory of structural change. Galtung wanted to avoid the depiction of a concrete structure that was in some sense historically unique from previous forms of domination; but in so doing, his notion of structure was stripped of explanatory substance.[49] Regardless of its "dismal political record," the virtue of marxian analysis, Brown argues, lies in the combination of a sense of structure and a sense of history. Galtung's fundamental error, then, was to confuse "an argument about the nature of structural explanation in general with an argument that concerns the nature of a particular structure."

CONCLUSION

To its critics, Galtung's analysis of imperialism was ahistorical, static, imprecise, and lacking in explanatory content, deficiencies arising, arguably, from the limitations of the adopted methodology. Its sole claims to originality lay first in the identification of intra-actor effects of exchange relations—an interesting but hardly decisive addition to dependency theory—and, second, in the depiction of imperialism as a general structural phenomenon, most visible perhaps in economic relations but applicable to any mode of social interaction. What is debatable, however, is whether other theorists of imperialism or Galtung's critics would dispute this. It is hardly overextending marxist and neomarxist analyses to suggest that they clearly imply that the political economy of imperialism is reinforced or reproduced in other realms of social life, such as the political, military, and cultural. Galtung took issue with the economism of other radical critiques of imperialism but failed to provide a knock-down argument against the supposition that economic relations between the center and periphery were indeed primary. The construction of a general model of imperialism that could incorporate noncapitalist forms of domination was undertaken at the cost of supplanting explanation with description. To claim that to all intents and purposes socialist variants of imperialism have the same *effects* as capitalist imperialism is plausible enough, but this is not to say that they are the same thing. Galtung abdicated from providing a more complex account in which the differences as well as similarities between forms of domination were more fully exposed. Instead, we are given a suggestive description of various modalities of domination adding up to an image of a world in which oppression and exploitation are rife and multifaceted.

It must be conceded that the image of nonspecific imperialist domination was, descriptively at least, compelling and suited to the intellectual times. Galtung's STI can still be usefully mined for diagrammatic representations of certain arguments about the patterns of exchange between the global North and South, even if its claims to go beyond those same arguments are judged to be doubtful.[50] It can be argued, moreover, that to construct a debate between him and other writers on imperialism is not only unlikely to be very fruitful but also to miss the point. The significance of the STI can only be comprehended within the context of a revivified peace research. It purported to identify, by way of a sketched ideal type, a general condition from which to be liberated, rather than to resolve questions about when or how that condition came about. Within the discussion of imperialism lay a sketch of the future agenda of peace research, clues as to the normative framework that would henceforth guide it.

The portrayal of global imperialism fleshed out the concept of structural violence and made a case for placing it at the top of the agenda of peace research. The antithesis of the world described by the STI would provide an alternative model of world order that peace research would be charged with helping to both adumbrate and realize. The STI concluded with a plea that good social theory should identify alternative practices and agents of transformation. A theory should be evaluated not only in terms of the production of hypotheses to be tested against empirical reality (data) but "as much—or perhaps more—as a reservoir of policy implications to be tested against potential reality (goals, values)."[51] The existing global order could not realize the core values—in particular equality and autonomy—of positive peace.

That Galtung was critical of liberalism is evident throughout the STI, but in spite of some normative commonalities between Galtung, the dependency theorists, and marxism more generally, it also further illustrated Galtung's perception of marxism as a constricting perspective. Two explanations for his antipathy suggest themselves. The first, increasingly apparent in subsequent writings, is a negative judgment of the historical record of marxism as practice (or more accurately, Soviet marxism); socialist states had not and could not realize all of the values embedded in the concept of positive peace. Connected with this is a normative distaste for the privileging of specific agents of social change, which was already evident in Galtung's response to Schmid's criticisms of the early model of peace research.

A second reason for the lack of enthusiasm for marxism (and liberalism as well) stems from the view that good theory should be judged in comparison with potential reality constructed upon a set of preferred values. The STI was an early example of what was to be subsequently described as "constructivism." For Galtung, both marxist epistemology and liberal social science shared an excessive preoccupation with the past and present. As I will show in the next chapter, he increasingly would see virtue in detaching science from its obligations to observable, empirical reality. However, this conception of science was not to provide an escape route beyond two problems—one practical, the other normative—exposed by the STI.

First, by divorcing the exploration of alternative world orders from a historical analysis of alleged reality (as opposed to a descriptive sketch), strategies for moving from the present world to a preferred world would remain hollow, an issue I take up in Chapter 7. Second, the rejection of the two dominant schools of political thought as sufficient to the task of underpinning the normative dimensions of peace research meant that the values that were to be realized would be detached from notions of either *critique* or *recht*, central to marxism and liberalism, respectively, but presumed nonetheless to have universal validity. What *should be* is implicitly the antithesis of what *is*, but the assessment of what is wrong with the extant world order presupposed an unsubstantiated normative outlook. To be blunt, the STI did not provide much assistance in answering the question of why the world should be equitable; no path was provided beyond Eide's indictment of structural violence as a category devoid of meaning outside of "the chosen goal structure," or Brown's equally curt observation that "in the last resort, Galtung's position reduces to the proposition that exploitation exists whenever and wherever he determines it exists."[52]

Brown made his comment in 1981, ten years after Eide. By then Galtung had begun to address the question of values through reference to the concept of human needs. Before looking at his efforts in this respect, I shall consider the reformulation of science as an emancipatory practice.

NOTES

1. Galtung, "On the Future of the International System," pp. 616–618.
2. See, for example, Krippendorf, "Peace Research and the Industrial Revolution"; Gantzel, "Dependency Structures as the Dominant Pattern in World Society"; Senghaas, "Conflict Formations in Contemporary International Society." A more recent anthology of contemporary peace research includes two papers by dependency theorists Samir Amin and Andre Gunder Frank, even though they were not written for a peace research audience and do not refer to peace research at any point. See Pardesi, *Contemporary Peace Research*.
3. Galtung, "Twenty-Five Years of Peace Research," p. 12.
4. Project Camelot was a CIA–Department of Defense project that ostensibly sought to promote research into the relationship between processes of development in Latin American states and the potential for civil conflict and insurgency. Galtung was invited to participate but rejected the offer and was instrumental in ensuring the eventual cancellation of the project as a consequence of adverse publicity. Although he initially simply defended social science against its abuse by government agencies, the project seems to have constituted a starting point for a long-term reappraisal of social science itself. See Galtung, "After Camelot"; and Kelman, *A Time to Speak*, ch. 6.
5. Galtung, "Introduction," *EPR*, 5, p. 23.
6. Galtung, "On the Structure of Creativity," p. 213. See also Galtung and Gleditsch, "International Air Communication."
7. Galtung, "Introduction," *EPR*, 3, pp. 21–22.
8. In describing his own shift from the perspective of a "liberal . . . work[ing] within the behaviourist approach to international politics" to a critic of it, Jenkins cites Galtung's early structuralist papers as exemplars of "psychologically reductionist" behaviorism. See Jenkins, *Exploitation*, pp. xv, 82, 165, 209.
9. Galtung, "Introduction," *EPR*, 3, p. 24.

10. See Higgott, *Political Development Theory*; and Henriot, "Development Alternatives," p. 10.

11. Frank, "The Development of Underdevelopment," p. 112.

12. Mommsen, *Theories of Imperialism*, p. 132. See also Higgott, *Political Development Theory*, ch. 1.

13. STI, p. 437.

14. Galtung, "A Structural Theory of Imperialism: Ten Years Later," p. 183.

15. STI, p. 437.

16. STI, p. 437. By "nation" Galtung clearly means *state,* and I use the two terms interchangeably.

17. A medical analogy is employed to make the point: Smallpox is an example of an epidemic disease, these diseases in turn being understood in the context of "general pathology." STI, p. 438.

18. STI, p. 439.

19. See Chapter 6.

20. STI, p. 713, fn. 2.

21. See STI, p. 441, figure 13.1.

22. STI, p. 713, fn. 3.

23. Brown, "Galtung and the Marxists," p. 221.

24. See "Preface to the French and German editions," in Lenin, "Imperialism," p. 640. Lenin's labor-aristocracy thesis is insistent in its observation that only part of the working class in the imperial states gain from imperialism. See Brewer, *Marxist Theories of Imperialism*, pp. 117–122.

25. STI, p. 442.

26. Galtung, "A Structural Theory of Imperialism—Ten Years Later," p. 185.

27. Galtung does not discuss what Wallerstein calls the "semiperiphery"—those newly industrialized states achieving significant growth rates based on high-technology manufacture rather than the export of raw materials or semifinished goods. Similarly, he does not consider those states that refute his claim that spin-off effects arising from processing generate development, states such as Australia and New Zealand. On this, see Mack, "Theories of Imperialism: The European Perspective," pp. 525–527.

28. See also Galtung, *The European Community*, ch. 3.

29. STI, p. 448.

30. STI, pp. 488–489. In a similar vein, if cheap credit is used to purchase goods and services from Center states, the structure of imperialism remains intact, preexisting consumption patterns will be reinforced, and spin-off benefits will continue to accrue to the Center.

31. STI, p. 450, Figure 13.2.

32. STI, pp. 480–481.

33. STI, p. 451.

34. Van den Bergh, "Theory or Taxonomy," p. 79. See also Brown, "Galtung and the Marxists," p. 226.

35. Waltz accuses Galtung of explaining international phenomena by reference to domestic criteria. *Theory of International Politics*, pp. 31–35. In fact, Galtung describes the behavior of states and sectors of states as being governed by the global structure, a position that shares much with Waltz save for the explanation of the origins of the structure itself. See Brown, "Galtung and the Marxists," p. 222.

36. STI, p. 453.

37. STI, p. 715, fn. 12.

38. See also Galtung, "A Structural Theory of Imperialism—Ten Years Later," pp. 184–185.

39. But note the discussion of the three historical phases of imperialism, STI, pp. 457–459, and *The True Worlds*, ch. 4. Galtung later described imperialism as a "world system," acknowledging the allusion to Wallerstein whose approach is still criticized for being nongeneralizable outside of a historical frame of reference. See "A Structural Theory of Imperialism—Ten Years Later," pp. 194–195, fns. 8 and 9.

40. Waltz has described the convertibility thesis as flawed logically and historically. The invention of tanks and their use in war preceded the opening up of the Middle Eastern oil fields, and in any case, the United States has been largely self-sufficient in oil production. Waltz, *Theory of International Politics*, p. 32.

41. Two cases of nearly perfect correspondence are suggested: the U.S. relationship with Latin American states in the 1950s and 1960s and the relationship between the European Community (EC) and the Asian, African, and Pacific states. Galtung did undertake an extensive case study of the latter. In it he argued that the EC was "a superpower in the making" with the ultimate objective of reestablishing a Eurocentric world order and a united Europe firmly rooted in the West. The study was written in 1973 during public debate in Norway over membership in the EC that led ultimately to rejection of membership in a referendum. In an epilogue, Galtung suggests that the disparate group of "no" voters might constitute the basis for a future political platform based around decentralization, less emphasis on economic growth and more on economic justice, greater national autonomy, and neutralism in international affairs. See Galtung, *The European Community*, especially pp. 159–163.

42. In the STI, Galtung briefly explored the correlations between various indices of development and trade patterns that were seen to confirm a relationship between the level of development and the verticality of trade relations, although he conceded that this was a test only "of a theory along the edges of that theory; it did not prove that the system is working as described." STI, p. 469. See also Gidengil, "Centres and Peripheries: An Empirical Test of Galtung's Theory of Imperialism."

43. STI, p. 470.

44. See STI, table 13.10, p.476.

45. Waltz, *Theory of International Politics*, pp. 31–33. For an ill-tempered rebuttal on Galtung's behalf, see Kaplan, *Towards Professionalism in International Theory*, pp. 13–27.

46. Palonen, "Social Science as Peace Research," p. 114.

47. Van den Bergh, "Theory or Taxonomy," p. 78.

48. Brown, "Galtung and the Marxists," p. 220.

49. Ibid., pp. 223–225.

50. Galtung's diagrammatic representation of "The Structure of Imperialism" (STI, p. 441, figure 13.1) remains a useful teaching aid for illustrating the broad thrust of dependency theory.

51. STI, p. 479.

52. Eide, "Note on Galtung's Concept of 'Violence,'" p. 71; and Brown, "Galtung and the Marxists," p. 225.

5

Constructivism

In Galtung's early work, the model of a science of peace displayed a unity between its elements. As long as the underlying positivist premises were accepted, the relationship between the guiding value of peace, the adopted scientific methodology, and the proposed role of the peace researcher was straightforward enough. Once its foundations were critically scrutinized, the edifice looked decidedly less secure. At the time of writing the STI, Galtung was still reticent to abandon positivism. Empiricism remained an important constraint upon dogmatism, even if the idea of science could not be reduced to the investigation of the factual.[1] Although the stance of objectivity in the form of a symmetrical approach to conflict was now accepted as destructive of the very idea of peace research, which party or actor needed support was to be determined only by its position within the social structure, not by professed ideological sentiments. It was the structure of violence that was to be critically examined and opposed.

A further, less visible theme pervading the discussion of imperialism was futurism. Galtung had concluded the STI by emphasizing the need to examine the present in terms of an immanent potential reality expressed as goals and values. Unlike in some of his earlier forays that largely consisted in extrapolations of empirical trends, Galtung now sought to make the more abstract point that empirical research was too heavily preoccupied with establishing the veracity of knowledge of the present.[2] In his view, good social theory should also be indicative of a potential practice and guide us to the realization of a preferred alternative. Theory should not only be tested against empirical data—that is, the existing or present—but also be judged against posited values that secreted a vision of the future.

At issue was how to reconcile this procedure with the idea of science. Galtung still did not wish to slip into the kind of theorizing that peace research had so explicitly rejected. Science was not simply to be cast aside in favor of a return to reflective, philosophical idealism or traditional

113

peace thinking. Neither could it adopt the antipacifism of its marxist de-
tractors. A sympathy for political struggle against exploitation did not extend to a defense of violence; as Galtung was later to remark, if there was
no taboo on all forms of violence, what was the point of peace research?[3]

The stage was set, then, for a fundamental rethinking of the very idea
of science and its utility for peace research. However, the attempted reconstruction of the concept of science is not to be found in Galtung's writings on peace research. Rather, it took place in some of his lesser known
publications and appears to have attracted a somewhat different audience.
This may account for the lack of reference to it in the few published commentaries and reviews of Galtung's work.[4] The core reference is Galtung's
three-volume study of methodology, the first volume of which was not
published until 1977, although the revised conception of science had been
developed some years before and its central arguments presented in a 1972
article published in *Synthèse*.[5] To a large extent, therefore, the argument
for a reconstructed model of science was published ex post facto, the
main themes already having permeated Galtung's writings on peace and
development.

THE LIMITS OF POSITIVISM

In 1967, Galtung published a monograph in which he explored the
problems of statistical analysis in the social sciences.[6] The book was a
success, becoming widely used in undergraduate courses on social research, especially in the United States.[7] Its contents held few surprises,
being largely a straightforward analysis of the various stages of collecting,
collating, and analyzing statistical data. The fact that it was written by a
leading peace researcher was hardly evident. Nonetheless, the text concluded on a skeptical note in that Galtung characterized the primary limitation on social research as arising not so much from methodological and
theoretical problems as from the social scientist's relationship to society.
Particularly limiting was the concept of "value neutrality." The time had
come for society to "relinquish this value-loaded norm" and recognize the
scientist's right "to be engaged, to participate."[8] In the spirit of classical
positivism, Galtung went on to acknowledge that the other side of the coin
was an obligation on the part of the social scientist to "hand back to society what it will always need most: a true and rich picture of society, past,
present and future—where nothing is taken for granted." Science must
continue to seek verisimilitude, to stand aloof from prejudice, yet it must
also become a purposive activity wedded to the realization of better forms
of social life. It should not be restricted to informing us only how the
world is or was but should also depict what it could become.

The Project Camelot debacle had already alerted Galtung to the potential abuse of so-called value-free social science. Commenting some

years later, Galtung admitted that his response at the time was to advocate "a more symmetric type of project" conducted from the viewpoint of an objective observer: "In other words, I believed that such archimedean fixed points existed and that these were the points from which objective social science should be pursued."[9] Similarly, Galtung's earlier observations on the impact of specific cultural contexts on the scientific enterprise echoed the preference for symmetry and the ultimate need for empirical verification of social scientific hypotheses. In Latin America, for example, he detected among both conservative and radical social scientists a preference for theoretical exploration, or "meta-sociology," at the expense of empirical analysis. Unwilling simply to advocate the wholesale adoption of North American sociological methods, Galtung urged the development of an indigenous sociology that did not consist entirely of "the normative mode of social analysis" conditioned by "church, law and ideology" but also encouraged "fresh inventiveness in empirical sociology."[10]

These comments on Latin American sociology revealed an impatience, even hostility, toward traditional conservatism and scholasticism, coupled with a continuing belief in a redemptive vision of science. According to Galtung, the orthodox scientific outlook was insufficiently concerned with social transformation and the exploration of possible future social orders. In some respects, Galtung was simply offering a milder version of the sentiments expressed by numerous critics of mainstream social science in the late 1960s. However, he differed from other critics in that he did not regard the abandonment of the idea of social science or the adoption of marxism and its cognates (in either scientific or nonscientific variants) as a suitable response to the problem of backward-looking scientific and ideological traditionalism. Indeed, contemporary neomarxism was viewed as particularly prone to scholasticism. If positivism was overly preoccupied with developing methodological tools, then "dialectics" (a common Galtungian euphemism for marxism) was characteristically "verbose, possibly subtle, but incapable of defining clearly (for others) what dialectics is all about." In short, the difference between positivism and dialectics could be expressed as that between "operations without much understanding" and "understanding that has not been made very operational."[11]

The disquiet with orthodoxy of the Right and Left was to become stronger in tone. In a polemical paper, written in 1974 and redolent of Berger's *Pyramids of Sacrifice*, Galtung attacked what he termed a "teutonic intellectual style," examples of which included nazism and "some forms of German neo-marxism."[12] The catalogue of sins he listed was extensive: primarily deductive thinking, insufficient verification of hypotheses, esoteric language, an antagonistic attitude to competing perspectives, a preoccupation with judging and labeling other perspectives, elitism, a hostility to dialogue, ad hominem arguments, and a general humorlessness. Against these tendencies, Galtung argued for methodological eclecticism, the continuing need to engage in empirical research in order to confirm

theoretical assumptions, and a rejection of an assumption of conflict between perspectives. Marxism might provide a useful political and epistemological perspective to juxtapose with liberalism and empiricism, but it
suffered, nevertheless, from two deficiencies: First, as a product of the
West, it had much in common with liberalism and was therefore less novel
than first appeared; second, although strong on critique, it was weak in
creatively developing alternatives as a consequence of a perceived tendency to embrace historical determinism.[13]

Orthodox empiricism could not, however, provide an adequate substitute for marxism's insufficient creativity:

> Empiricism is based on the comparison between theory and data; and
> data can by definition only reflect the past, never the future. Hence, em-
> piricism reflects the past—which is perfectly acceptable as long as one is
> interested only in understanding the past. But peace research is concerned
> with the construction of a better world, to put it bluntly and naively. And
> this world with peace more realized than today, would have to be differ-
> ent from the world so far studied with empirical methods. Hence, have
> we any reason at all to assume that the "laws" discovered by means of
> empiricism will be valid in a world that has transcended the world that
> produced the data for the scientific activity we engage in today?[14]

Galtung was not advocating the wholesale rejection of empiricism. He was
agnostic with regard to the influential debate around positivism then going
on in German sociological circles (the *Positivismusstreit*), preferring to explore the synthesis of dialectics and positivism in a manner that reflected
his attitude toward the political philosophies of liberalism and marxism.
Though he never displayed any interest in the complexities of marxist dialectics, the juxtaposition of present and future within a scientific framework appealed to Galtung.

It was this combination that his new model of "trilateral science," introduced in 1972, was intended to address. The objective was to explore
modifications to orthodox social scientific methodology that would address the problems raised during the debates of the late 1960s.[15] In his
1971 commentary on the Camelot episode, Galtung wrote of now looking
differently at the goal of science. It was no longer seen as "anything abstract or idealistic called 'objectivity'" but as something that could contribute to "a liberation process. . . . It is the task of science to participate
on the side of the dominated party."[16]

The revised understanding of scientific activity hinged entirely on
foregrounding values as a category of equal status to theory and data, the
latter two being seen as the cornerstones of orthodox conceptions of science. Different forms of science could be conjured by variously juxtapos-
ing the three categories of data, theory, and values. Galtung argued that orthodox empirical science was primarily concerned with the production of

propositions and the construction of theories. The production of propositions dichotomized "world space," the Cartesian domain of inquiry representing all combinations of selected variables that is in turn subdivisible into various "world points." The scientist constructs sentences, or theses, about the dichotomization of the world space in which some points are included and some are excluded according to the observation of variables. These data sentences consist in verbal reports or observation sentences that purport to identify empirical reality according to the variables employed. However, the world so observed is not *the* world but the "empirical world," which is only one of many worlds.[17]

Other sets of sentences—theory sentences—also dichotomized the world space according to whether some world points are *foreseen or unforeseen* by the underlying theory. The essence of orthodox empirical science thus consisted in the comparison of corresponding sentences from the two sets, with the objective of establishing consonance or dissonance between that which is observed and that which is foreseen in theory. It is the theory sentence that is being evaluated, and this produces a verdict of the form: true or false. Though sentences of either type—data or theory—can be produced independently, empirical science is meaningless without the comparative exercise, which results in the conversion of theory sentences into propositions.

The construction of theory sentences was a distinctive activity that was also rule-governed. Galtung defined a theory as a set of sentences "weakly connected by a relation of implication" and taking the form of axioms or deductions. The purpose of such a theory is to bring together what were considered disparate aspects of reality. If such sentences are found to be valid (validity being broadly defined as the inverse of a willingness to renounce the sentences), they can be said to define the world. The traditional task of science, therefore, is to define a predictable (static, or dynamic according to unchanging laws) world—not any world but *the* world. Good scientific theory aims for correspondence with the *true* world, this world being conceived of, a priori, as a static image of empirical reality that is arrived at "through patient, laborious efforts to validate and to confirm, to confirm and validate until the hypothetical-deductive system is perfect: all validated theory sentences (and only those) are consonant with validated data sentences."[18]

Intentionally or not, Galtung's account of scientific orthodoxy alluded to Habermas's conception of a "knowledge-constitutive interest." For Habermas, the "empirical-analytical sciences" are teleological insofar as they arise out of a universal interest in the technical control of nature. All scientific inquiry is guided by and defined within an instrumental, cognitive interest that "establishes rules for the construction of theories and their critical testing."[19] Like Galtung, Habermas depicts empirical science as primarily concerned with the production of predictive knowledge. Furthermore, the *meaning* of such predictions is established only by the rules according to which we apply theories to reality. . . . The logical structure of admissible systems of propositions and the type of conditions for corroboration suggest that theories of the empirical sciences disclose reality subject to the constitutive interest in the possible securing and expansion, through information, of feed-back monitored action. This is the cognitive interest in technical control over objectified processes.[20]

In asking what interest guides predictive statements about the world, Galtung gave a response that shared little with the language of Habermas but was comparable nonetheless. He suggested that ruling classes may not necessarily have a vested interest in a static world but may have an interest in a predictable and therefore more easily administered world. The interest in administration forces adoption of an image of the world commensurate with the task. Science comes, then, to reflect its social context. Empiricism arose, in Galtung's view, as a consequence of the development of liberal society, the connected dethronement of God in favor of empirical reality, and the replacement of an ideational with a sensate culture. The replacement of dogmatic rationalism by an instrumental positivism based upon hypothesized, conditional knowledge claims required the development of a process of verification. Observable empirical reality became the secular arbiter of truth—"data became King."[21]

Effectively, Galtung was engaging in self-criticism. Whereas he had formerly presented empirical scientific method as a neutral arbiter of truth, which in the spirit of the early positivists was seen to have an emancipatory potential, it was now cast in the conservative role of a potential agent for the preservation of the social status quo. By excluding normative discourse, empirical science had been transformed from a critique of dogmatic reason into an instance of it. In contrast to the defense of science as the basis of enlightened social engineering, Galtung's reassessment of science highlighted its dogmatic reference to an immutable reality. Furthermore, because empirical reality was characterized by vertical social relations, orthodox empirical science effectively defended exploitation. More specifically, the practitioners of science, being largely confined to the upper echelons of "liberal" societies, were unlikely to have an interest in changing empirical reality that was reproduced within the scientific community itself.[22]

Again it must be stressed that the point of Galtung's critique was the redemption of science. In contrast to the depiction of the orthodox model of science as reducible to "invariance-seeking" activity, he looked to a conception of social science that was concerned with "invariance-breaking" activity. No empirically identified invariance should be taken as sacrosanct because, he now asserted, "there are no laws in social science." Reality was malleable and, therefore, transformable, but the orthodox servility of empirical science to data resulted in the hypostatizing of empirical reality as the only reality. But an age-old problem arises here with regard to what is exactly meant by a malleable reality. A naturalistic application of science to the study of social phenomena cannot capture the mediating effects of human consciousness. Moreover, acknowledgment of the subjective contingency of knowledge claims undermines their authoritative validation for anyone other than those who share the observer's particular account of reality. In that case, how can the reality to be transformed or the invariance to be broken be known decisively rather than arbitrarily? More important, on what scientific basis is an argument for social change to be made? In Galtung's hands, the notion of a malleable reality continued to imply the existence of a knowable realm extrinsic to consciousness. What he appeared to be arguing was that predictive claims about social reality were not of the same status as claims about the natural world. Any claim to have identified an invariance in the social world must be presumed to have ideological content, insofar as it attempted to exclude something that might be valued by some: "To raise a confirmed theory sentence . . . to the level of an invariance is tantamount to saying that something preferred is unobtainable."[23]

An example given by Galtung of an ideologically undesirable variance in social science is taken from the infamous Milgram experiments that attempted to discern the conditions under which participants would administer lethal electric shocks to other unknowing participants. The results suggested that a high percentage of participants were willing to administer lethal shocks within mild authority structures and that the percentage increased with the decrease of social proximity between participant and victim. The set of invariances that these experiments sought to test mirrored vertical social relations in which individuals are assumed to be objects for potential manipulation. As with similar experiments in social psychology, Milgram's procedure was entirely dependent upon the naive subject.

The results of the Milgram experiments were not at issue for Galtung; indeed they may accurately reveal that a lack of consciousness produces submissive behavior. It was, rather, the structure of the experiment that was of concern. In depending upon a low level of participant consciousness, such experiments reproduce in microcosm a social order that operates upon a similar assumption.[24] Thus, the real significance of the experiments may differ from the objective the experimenter intended. The practice of science is predicated upon an ideological assumption of passive subjects around which the wider social order coheres. In reducing humans to unthinking objects, orthodox social science excludes any notion of them as reflexive agents of social change.[25] Social science was, in Galtung's view, replete with such unstated assumptions and the uncritical adoption of specific social values as experimental data. Why should not social science seek out the factors that challenge assumed invariances rather than focus on confirmatory instances?

Galtung acknowledged that his critical remarks about traditional scientific activity may have "the air of the trivial," and he made no claim to originality. He claimed to offer just one version of the critique of positivist social science, a version that, in contrast to Habermas and others, focused on the structure of scientific procedure. Whereas Habermas questions the scientization of social theory through a critical comparison drawn between positivism and other forms of hermeneutic and critical knowledge dismissed by positivism as pseudoscientific, Galtung sought only to redraw scientific procedure. Habermas argues that positivist social science belongs to a scientific culture that science cannot itself explain.[26] Adequate knowledge of the social requires, therefore, other more reflexive forms of knowledge. Only then can empirical science be reabsorbed within a less problematic epistemological framework. By comparison, Galtung retained a positivist residue in his failure to consider other forms of knowledge or recognize that he was effectively smuggling in nonscientific forms of knowledge under the guise of science. Nevertheless, he had a commonality of purpose with the critical social theory of Habermas and others, insofar as both denied positivism's claims to objectivity and located empirical aspects of social inquiry within a wider normative framework.

Galtung's method was to strip science back to what he saw as two indisputable central claims: that sentences dichotomize world spaces, and that science is concerned fundamentally with the comparison of corresponding sentences that have been arrived at in different ways. Traditional science could be attacked through four of its operating principles. The first was the process of disconfirmation that privileged data sentences over theory sentences; the validity of the latter is dependent upon the former. By definition, data sentences refer to the empirical past and result in the primacy of the past being built into scientific activity. For science, as traditionally understood, "it is the world defined by the data sentences, not the world defined by the theory sentences that is the real world."[27]

Drawing an analogy with the concepts of maps and terrains, Galtung argued that in any conflict between the two, terrain preempts map in the search for consonance. But why, he asked, is only the adjustment of map to terrain considered scientific; could not the adjustment of terrain to map be conducted in a scientific manner? Unfortunately, the analogy was quite useless. Intended to illustrate the inadequacy of applying a traditional model of scientific procedure to the study of social phenomena, it conflated this with the larger issue of the relevance of empiricism per se. It is one thing to deem as ideological the uncritical servility of the social sciences to specific data; it is another to question the resilience of the natural or social terrain to change. The natural sciences have always been concerned with and capable of the manipulation of the natural world to suit human interests—the Grand Canyon can be filled. The issue is more for what reason. Some scientists have been all too willing to manipulate terrain to fit their maps, as critics of peaceful-nuclear-explosion engineering technology have pointed out.[28] It is not so much a question of science, as one of ethics and values. So too with social science. The problem with social science is not its inability to explore and realize the adjustment of the social terrain to a preferred map—social engineering of enormous consequence is a marked feature of modernity. The problem is with the maps employed, be they of reality or a preferred alternative.

More effective was Galtung's criticism of a second principle, that of exclusion or experimental closure. He was referring to the scientific endeavor of capturing reality in as narrow a space as is possible. Like a mouse playing with a cat, science marks out a specific behavioral or action space (*Spielraum*), which has a minimal subset of a "rich world space full of possibilities." Whatever problems this raises for the natural sciences (that is, whether results obtained within experimentally closed systems would be obtained in open systems), they are especially acute with regard to the study of social systems. Although Galtung did not say it, the latter by definition have complex human-centered characteristics that can only be excluded at the expense of dangerous simplification of social reality.[29]

A broader conception of the exclusionary tendencies of scientific orthodoxy emerges with regard to the principle of "invariance." Galtung argued that, traditionally, the tenability of any proposition requires that it be invariant of four kinds of additional variable—space, time, subject consciousness, and object consciousness—in order to acquire the status of a law. Invariance in time and space (the "colonization" of time and space) attributes a universality to propositions by discounting geographic and historical variation. Consequently, science tends to privilege singularism over pluralism and universalism over contingency. Putatively universal social laws will, in fact, reflect geographic- and generation-specific images. In contrast to this, Galtung proposed that rather than attempt to reflect time and space invariances, social science should seek to create maximal time and space variation.

The critique of invariance-seeking science was applied to both liberal and marxist models of science, since they shared a "self-perception as each other's unbridgeable contradiction, as well as something filling the universe of social cosmologies."[30] They both held to a naturalist model of science premised upon a relationship of domination (*Herrschaft*) of the social over the natural world. Against this was posited a vision of science as a creative activity in harmony (*Partnerschaft*) with the natural world. Galtung now interpreted the orthodox search for propositions invariant of consciousness as a reflection of a missionary striving for social consensus. Along with Christianity, marxism, and liberalism, science originated within the same civilizational matrix—hence the zealous "claims on space and time and on the images held by all 'normal' human beings."[31] Western civilization secreted a pervasive, quasi-religious, scientistic outlook that transcended superficially distinctive worldviews. Science acted as an ideational cement that bound us in our collective domination of other civilizations and blinded us to non-Western forms of knowledge. Once again, Galtung was providing a foretaste of a significant theme in parallel and subsequent work.[32]

Another consequence of the exclusionary practices of science was the objectification of the human subject, a tendency attributed to both marxism and positivist liberalism, or Galtung's caricature of them at least. Little interest in intramarxist disputes was evidenced in attributing to marxism the view that nothing was an objective law unless it was invariant of human consciousness. The positivist variant was to be found in the assumption that the essence of social reality can only be discovered when subjective consciousness is experimentally reduced to a minimum. The nightmare for many behavioral psychologists, anthropologists, and sociologists, suggested Galtung, would be reflexive subjects who had some knowledge of the disciplines within which they were being studied.[33] There were differences between marxism and liberalism (qua positivism) here: The former emphasized the inner workings or logic of reality (history) over individual objects, whereas the latter's model of social science placed the scientist above experimental subjects deprived of consciousness.

Finally, Galtung questioned the orthodox process of theory construction that privileged the *observed* over the *foreseen*, "the positively existing over the imagined." Data sentences are validated with reference to other data sentences and then integrated within a theoretical structure. The image of reality is narrowly cast in a straitjacket that emphasizes the confirmation of knowledge about reality but excludes the search for a new reality. Science's servile relationship to empirical data resulted in a rejection of theorized alternative realities because of the apparent absence of a means of validation. Within orthodox empirical science, data about the present could not be used to validate a possible or preferred reality. However, Galtung did not consider the complications that might arise if the problem with social science was not just an inability to look forward because of the hegemony of data but was instead the very status of social data.

TRILATERAL SCIENCE

Galtung wanted to construct an alternative model of science that would free scientific procedure from its servility to data. He had identified what Habermas has called a social-technological "guiding interest of cognition" underpinning social scientific orthodoxy. In the process, an alternative conception of science guided by a "social-emancipatory" interest was anticipated. One of the few commentators on Galtung's model of trilateral science depicts it as enabling the user to view reality "through the lenses of the possible and the normative." According to Strasser, conservatism favors concreteness over abstraction, whereas "in progressive thinking the particular phenomena of social reality take on meaning through their relation to a future utopia or a normative code which floats above the factual sub-stratum."[34] This identification of an emancipatory cognitive interest certainly captured the intent of Galtung's advocacy of an alternative model of scientific procedure. Indeed, Strasser's reading of Galtung is acutely accurate in a manner that is ultimately destructive of Galtung's own claims as to the virtues of trilateral science, a point I shall return to later.

Recall for a moment the initial arguments for peace research premised upon a belief in the emancipatory potential of empirical science in the spirit of the founding fathers of positivism. Galtung had not then dissected the process of science; he had taken on board an unreconstructed empiricism guided only by the explicit prior statement of one's values. Thus, radical critics, ultimately including Galtung himself, were able to attack the conservative (if unintended) consequences of the scientific model originally employed. After a bout of self-criticism, Galtung attempted to synthesize more effectively and openly an emancipatory cognitive interest with scientific method. Though sharing much of the spirit of Habermas's critique of positivism, he did not embrace the discourse of critical theory. Instead, he proceeded to explore formally the relationship between social values and scientific inquiry. The benefits of this were twofold: The gist of the radical critique of early peace research could be addressed, and the methodology of peace research could be reconstructed to retain the idea of science at it center. Unreconstructed positivism or vulgar marxist scientism could be rejected without a return to speculative idealism.

The key to the new understanding of science was the introduction of a third category of sentences into scientific procedure. To data and theory sentences were added *value* sentences. The critique of orthodox empiricism hinged on the claim that it secreted a value agenda but was epistemologically incapable of acknowledging the fact. Galtung's response was to build values into the scientific process by depicting value sentences also as dichotomizers of world space into points that are either preferred or rejected. The problem with this procedure was his assertion that such sentences were "more or less valid" in a similar manner to data and theory sentences. However, Galtung sidestepped the issue of how to validate value sentences by claiming this to be the function of something called "axiological science." What such a science entailed was not explained, although consensus, intersubjective acceptability (as for data sentences), and deducibility from "more fundamental values" were canvassed as means for validating norms. More important, Galtung professed to be unconcerned with the problem of precisely identifying what value sentences consisted of (they could, he suggested, refer to either goals or interests or to both), preferring to focus on their dichotomizing function. He conceded, nonetheless, that the addition of value sentences to the scientific process highlighted classical problems associated with the fact-value distinction, to which answers would have to given. Evidently, Galtung's exploration of a new form of science was to be restricted in scope to the manipulation of value sentences rather than determination of their origins.

Galtung saw the introduction of values to normal scientific activity as "epistemologically interesting" in two ways: It challenged the concept of value neutrality in science, and it led to a novel configuration of science as a *trilateral* activity because world space could now be dichotomized in three different ways. This facilitated the definition of observed, foreseen, and *preferred* worlds through the processes of data collection, hypotheses formation, and stipulation of values. The novelty of the proposed model lay in the scientific comparison of data (the observed) and theory (the foreseen) with values (the preferred). Thus, value sentences were accorded a similar status to other sentence types to enable their utilization in a formal analytic manner.

Value sentences were difficult to present with the same level of specificity as data or theory sentences, however, which were premised upon observation protocols or the formal connection of hypotheses. Galtung acknowledged that a methodological implication of the new scientific procedure was the need for precision, even operationalization in the construction of value sentences. To this end, the reader was referred to a research program known as the World Indicators Program that had as its objective the precise identification of suitable values based upon the exploration of basic human needs.[35] This meant, in essence, that the formation of values was still extrinsic to science and could not be explained by it. Thus, the actual focus of most critiques of orthodox social science— the problematical status of specific social values—was left unaddressed, and values were presented as being, in effect, novel sources of data.

The limitations of Galtung's reconstructed science are further illustrated by breaking it into its constituent parts. First, the comparison of data and theory sentences is seen to result in *empiricism*, enabling the generation of sentences of the true-false variety depending on whether the result is consonance or dissonance. Second, the comparison of data and value sentences supposedly produces *criticism*—the assessment of how empirical reality corresponds with values. Finally, the comparison of theory and value sentences is intended to fulfill the task of *constructivism*. In the case of the latter, no reference is made to the observed world. It was, Galtung noted, analogous to the architectural blueprint of an as yet unconstructed house that makes it possible to compare the vision of a structure with a theoretical representation.[36]

All three comparative exercises are examples of bilateral science, but they differ in the conclusions drawn from dissonance between the different sentence types. In empiricism, consonance is achieved through the production of new theory sentences, whereas in criticism consonance is realized through new data sentences. In constructivism, consonance results from the production of either new theory or new value sentences. On closer inspection, however, the description and separating out of these three activities appear quite arbitrary. As I have already argued, empiricism can quite plausibly entail the adjustment of data to theory, terrain to map, and empirical (or social) world to theoretical model. Galtung attributes to empiricism the conservative agenda of privileging the socially given. But the conservatism of empiricism lies in the status attributed to the act of observing extrinsic reality—that is, to the unacknowledged role of values. It is a technical or political question as to whether reality can or should be adjusted to correspond with value-impregnated observations and the theoretical constructs derived therefrom. The assumption that in empiricism "data sentences are stronger than theory sentences" is itself normative.

The account of "criticism" also presupposed that value sentences could be separated out from theory or data sentences, paradoxically a classically vulgar empiricist assumption. In any case, how can values be compared with data to the exclusion of theory? Indeed, the difficulty of distinguishing between theory and values was acknowledged in the brief comment that "highly valid theory sentences function like value sentences, they are normative rather than descriptive."[37] By extension, then, Galtung's empiricism and criticism are only distinguishable because the latter is *intentionally* normative, a point that he conceded. The conflation of criticism and description was amply evident in his account of global structure, wherein the terms *structural violence* and *imperialism* were used as theoretical postulates with which the empirical world was seen to correspond, but their meanings were dependent upon unsubstantiated value assumptions.

Constructivism—the comparison of theory and value sentences—was the category upon which the novelty of the reconstructed model of science supposedly rested. Yet, if theory sentences are inherently value-laden as Galtung admitted they might be, then constructivism becomes an entirely circular process given that no reference is made to an empirical reality. Constructivism merely entails the systematization of values; if realized, the values would produce a social reality that looked like this or that. As Galtung himself described it, constructivism was concerned with "proposal making," and it is difficult to see any novelty in this. It is self-evidently a plausible—and a historically common—activity to construct utopian, theoretical representations of the realization of social values. Equally, the view that values need to be subjected to pragmatic corroboration through their connection with "available and imaginable techniques," lest they die out as ideologies, is found in the American pragmatist tradition.[38] But Galtung's presentation not only claimed that values themselves were scientifically validated through comparison with value-laden theory; it also imputed to constructivism the actual creation of a new reality. Yet, in contrast to the pragmatist model that implies that some connection between values, theory, *and* reality is necessary, Galtung's account did not show how the corroboration of values was connected to the empirical world. Even then, the validity of value sentences existed only insofar as they might correspond with (be realizable within) either the empirical world *or* a hypothesized world. Validity reduces to plausibility.

Galtung acknowledged that the separation of science into these three distinctive activities had an air of artificiality about it. Reality, he averred, "is not so clear-cut because any scientific activity is a mixture of all three, which is one reason why one might just as well be honest and bring them all in explicitly."[39] If in fact science has always consisted of all three activities and the objective is merely to render this fact explicit, then the whole exercise can be understood as a heuristic deconstruction of scientific practice. Indeed, this interpretation of Galtung is adopted by Strasser, who uses Galtung's conception of trilateral science to support the claim that social science always has an irreducible normative component, be it conservative or progressive. Any inquiry into society "converts facts and laws into requisite means and conditions and is unique in being addressed to a system of objectives desired by the formulator or by those in whose service he stands."[40] Thus, contends Strasser, the sociological (for Galtung, the scientific) enterprise is bound to develop into either conservative or radical schools of thought. The explanatory universe and the normative universe are human creations that cannot be deduced from observation. We attempt to explain in order to fulfill human purposes, and it is within this context that our theories of human society are inextricably embedded. The cognitive status of theory is "decisively influenced" by the scientist's guiding interest of cognition, and further, "to actually formulate a social theory that organises what we know about a posed question at any particular time, requires a connecting shaft between the normative perspective—as expressed in terms of axioms, assumptions or value-sentences—and data-sentences."[41] For Strasser, Galtung's conception of science constitutes an effective critique of orthodox social science's self-understanding, providing a succinct formal model of scientific procedure that broadly corresponds with Habermas's critical reading of positivism. From this viewpoint, Galtung's model of scientific method does not therefore refer to a novel scientific activity. It is distinctive only insofar as it confers formal recognition on the incursion of values into the scientific process by openly advocating their presentation in the form of value sentences.

Galtung did ascribe novelty to his model, however, and saw its primary goal as not only a critique of existing scientific practice but also a guide to a preferable scientific procedure. The objective was to move beyond bilateral science to trilateral science, the latter entailing the integration of the three bilateral exercises into "some kind of unity." Its purpose extended beyond the comparative assessment of pregiven data, theory, and values into the "creation of new goals (values), new theory, and new reality (data)."[42] If science consisted essentially in consonance seeking between different sentences, then trilateral science entailed the conducting of science until "the observed, foreseen and preferred worlds coincide."

In spite of the interconnectedness of the components of trilateral scientific procedure, Galtung attempted to describe its conduct sequentially. But in so doing, further problems were exposed. The first step in trilateral science was *criticism*—the comparison of data with values. This was justified on the grounds that the motivation to engage in science was not merely intellectual curiosity but "critical awareness." This implied that some kind of normative activity had taken place prior to science, but Galtung simply asserted that it was preferable that science commenced from the rejection of something about reality rather than a desire to know decisively or confirm that what one hypothesizes is real.

The second stage was *empiricism*—the comparison of data and theory. In Galtungian science this is motivated by a desire to comprehend why reality is as it appears. Thus, empiricism acquires a critical, interpretive function that goes beyond orthodox understanding of the term. It imputes to empiricism a normative function that, if Galtung's own criticisms of empirical science are to be believed, was traditionally never acknowledged and epistemologically excluded. In other words, the two acts of criticism and empiricism appear again to be essentially indistinguishable.

The third and fourth stages entailed the use of values to generate an image of a preferred world and the development of theory suitable to the task of hypothesizing a potential reality that contains the preferred world. The ground is then laid for the fifth activity of constructivism wherein values and theories are compared to assess the viability and attainability of the preferred world. Yet, given Galtung's earlier claim that no reference need be made to empirical reality, the model of a preferred reality can be assessed as either attainable or viable only according to criteria internal to it. In fact, any practicality to the constructivist vision emerges in a sixth, praxeological stage. The previous five stages—critique, analysis, goal formation, theory construction, and proposal making—are classified as "paperwork" and as such are not presumed to go much beyond traditional scientific activity. Galtung's science is, however, in the business of creating new reality; science is politics and "politics is also science, precisely because it is concerned with bringing about consonance."[43] The final stage of trilateral science is "reality creation," when consonance between all three types of sentences is achieved. By this stage, "consonance" has acquired a political content, since it refers to the realization of an alternative and preferred social reality.

Galtung anticipated the retort that all of this amounts to little more than "a paradigm of goal-directed activity." Equally perspicacious but more audacious was his claim that its true novelty lay not in the components of the activity described but in the description of the totality as "normal science." Galtung alluded here to the marxian notion of science as both an epistemic principle and a form of agency.[44] Trilateral science was intended to confront the Weberian division of labor between the politician and the scientist; yet the normative rejection of the distinction was simply a consequence of the rejection of traditional science's claim to value-freedom. Because his reconstruction of scientific procedure still evaded the rational defense of chosen values, it could not go beyond Weber at all. In effect, normative discourse was reduced to a process in which "a decision is made between competing value orders and convictions, which escape compelling argument and remain inaccessible to cogent discussion."[45] What trilateral science offered was no more than a systematic description of a process undertaken *after* values have been decided upon. The analysis of values was purely instrumental: Were they realized within contemporary reality? If not, could a model that might realize them be devised? Of course it can.

A POSTUNIVERSALIST SCIENCE?

There is a further layer to Galtung's discussion of scientific practice that needs to be considered because it helps to explain his apparent unwillingness or reluctance to defend a specific value set. It also leads toward my conclusion that Galtung was actually arguing not for the reconstruction of science but for its dissolution into a form of systematized political discourse, through a rejection of the universalist claims of orthodox scientific practice. Furthermore, the tension between universalism and relativism was to loom ever larger in his subsequent work.

Galtung claimed that the concept of objectivity had not been entirely discarded in his account but partially retained in the procedural rule of consonance between different types of sentences. What was rejected was an understanding of objectivity that presupposes the possibility of the value-free search for universal truth. Though Galtungian science still sought consonance between reality and values and claimed to offer a universally applicable procedure, there was no assumption of a preferred world for all mankind forever. This theme was developed through an imagined dialogue between a "realist" and "idealist" who discursively reiterated the themes of the preceding discussion.[46] Galtung's imaginary idealist repeats the fundamental premise that all sentences, be they derived from data or values, constitute knowledge by virtue of the fact that they dichotomize the world in some way. The status of sentences does not derive from consensual acceptability but from their accordance to a definitional criterion. To the realist riposte that this is tantamount to an argument for pure advocacy, the idealist replies by questioning the logocentric assumption of a single, irreducible, unified reality, with which images of that reality must accord. Against this, the idealist argues for a "pluralistic science" and, in so doing, reduces science to a set of procedural or discursive rules.

The difference between the notion of a singular reality, or its representation in theory, and a pluralist perspective was illustrated by the drawing of two global political analogies. The political consequence of the empiricist assumption of a unified reality was, Galtung claimed, a centralized and conservative world state. In contrast, the political implications of a pluralist perspective would be a decentralized world in which each unit sought through science to implement its particular values, "but there would be no striving for built-in consensus." Furthermore, declared Galtung's idealist alter ego, the idea of an inevitable convergence toward truth is "as false and undesirable as the inevitable convergence toward a world state." A belief in the inevitability of the convergence of knowledge toward any fixed point presupposed that nature was immutable and assumed, therefore, that a single blueprint of the future was ultimately realizable.

The explication of the global political consequences of retaining an orthodox model of science or of adopting a pluralist model required a complex excursion into the sociology of knowledge. But all that Galtung provided at this point was a baldly stated observation that the roots of orthodox scientific universalism lay partly in "monotheistic, missionary Christianity," as reflected in the weltanschauungen of both liberalism and marxism.[47] Such universalism was displaying the symptoms of fatigue along with its political counterpart—an imperialistic Western civilization. The latter, Galtung further asserted, was entering a defensive phase in place of the previous period of apparent perpetual expansion.

Galtung seemed here to be questioning the project of modernity itself. The perception that there was a decline in universalizing forms of knowledge or the view that this was a desirable occurrence was not exclusive to him. It clearly prefigured central themes in contemporary anti-foundationalist thought. But reading Galtung on science it is impossible to know to what extent he was influenced by others who were also arguing for the demise of universalizing discourses or anticipating their exhaustion. It is quite plausible to suppose that Galtung was beating his own path toward an understanding of the possibility of knowledge that would resonate with wider developments in social and political thought. At face value, the dialogue between his two mythical philosophers of science appeared to confirm the postmodern tenor of Galtung's discussion. Thus, to the realist's retort that Galtung's model was not philosophy of science but pure politics, the idealist repeats the claim that science and politics were inseparable. In positing a single empirical and immutable reality, empirical science could not but engage in politics. Against the universalist aspirations of orthodox science was posited an alternative vision of a "nonmissionary," Buddhist model of science, the possibility of which was connected to the declining hegemony of Western imperialism and its theological corollaries.[48] Thus emerged an image of the impending dissolution of a dominant Western conception of knowledge, or legitimizing myth, behind which lay a telos centered around a unified global sociopolitical order. In its place were the shadowy outlines of an alternative scientific practice and consequently another possible reality. Although the new scientific method—the rules governing the comparison of categories of sentences—may have universal applicability (although Galtung was ambiguous on this point), it was not in itself intended overtly or covertly to legitimate a set of universal social values under the guise of truth. Rather, it consisted of an epistemology intended to fit a global social order characterized by value pluralism and the celebration of difference.

At this point there is a danger in overstating the degree to which Galtung had shifted. Like its predecessors—positivism and structuralism—trilateral science exhibited a sensitivity to an emergent intellectual mood, in this case the radical doubting of modernity itself. But to suppose that he was about to embrace antifoundationalism is to forget the continuities between the periods in his intellectual odyssey. The minimal sketch of a different, pluralist global reality spoke to an underlying foundationalism; it was itself a universal value idea. Galtung had not moved as far from a vision of a rational global social order as might be at first supposed. Even the proposed dissolution of the distinction between politics and science continued to be haunted by the voice of Comte: "Savoir pour prevoir; prevoir pour pouvoir." But as was the case with Comtean positivism, Galtungian science failed to give a complete account of itself.

CONCLUSION

As the dialogue between the imaginary realist and idealist endeavored to show, the argument for trilateral science challenged the notion that the search for alternative reality was an inherently idealist exercise: "for could there be anything less realistic than the assumptions on which data-based science have been built . . . [including the assumption] of existing reality as the rock-bottom basis, the final arbiter?"[49] Paradoxically, there was a continuity here with Galtung's original argument for scientific peace research that he had so stridently distinguished from classical philosophical idealism. By way of a reconstruction of the idea of science, Galtung in his peace research was continuing to reject the label of idealism, this time by turning the accusation back on traditional empiricism.

Galtung went on to suggest that what separated the so-called realist from the idealist was the latter's belief in the existence of a potential reality, a potentially knowable other. For Galtung's realist, all that exists outside of empirical reality is "irreality"—the realm of the unknowable. His idealist alluded to a potential reality immanent within the present, a view that suggested a basis for grounding a normative framework within a historical understanding of a human emancipatory interest. As a value-laden mode of inquiry, science could thus be defended within an account of the human species as a "collective history-making subject" seeking knowledge that leads to the reduction of, say, arbitrary constraints upon freedom.

It is hard to tell if Galtung was thinking along such lines. Indeed, to sustain an argument for immanence would have proved difficult within the Galtungian scientific paradigm. Discerning potential reality required no reference to the empirical present. Constructed out of value sentences, it was to be validated by reference to theoretical sentences, the origins of which remained mysterious. Thus, in emulating positivism's analytical separation of fact and value, because of the perceived constraining consequences of the hegemony of fact over value, Galtung could give no indication of how or why the move from the present to the preferred future was to be made—it was quite literally not of this world. Praxis was tacked on as a sixth and final stage, and it was simply asserted that the politics of realizing future social orders could be deemed science because it entailed a search for consonance between a vision of a preferred world and the existing world.

There was a more fundamental problem with Galtung's new science. The idealist's brief comments on the possible decline of Western civilizational hegemony, of which orthodox science was a component, provided a significant pointer to developments elsewhere in Galtung's work where the theme of occidental dominance and its unfortunate consequences was being developed. The existence of a singular account of the existing world was to be resisted—there is no singular truth to fall back upon. But where did this leave the idea of trilateral science? If, as Galtung's idealist suggested, accounts of reality are ideologically or civilizationally framed, then other accounts are a priori possible. Then what is this empirical world so in need of transformation? Equally, on what basis do we select this potential reality over another? In short, what are the values that would enable criticism and constructivism, as Galtung defined them, yet avoid simply creating another totalizing vision? Galtung could have addressed such questions if he had contemplated stepping more firmly onto the terrain of political philosophy and ethics. After all, contemporaneous with his trilateral model of science were emergent discourses also questioning modernity and the unwarranted sovereignty of its truth that showed little interest in trying to work within the stultifying language and method of social science.

As was the case with Galtung's study of imperialism, perhaps it is a mistake to pay too much mind to the ostensible concerns of his reworking of the idea of science. Instead, it might be better understood metaphorically, as a plea for changing the style of utopian political discourse in order to place it on a more systematic footing through the application of a set of discursive rules. It was an argument, then, for the dissolution of the wall between science and politics. Indeed, Galtung closed his discussion with this observation: "People in general observe, foresee and prefer and *have* to do so in order to live. . . . Let the scientist be one among all mankind, with goals built into his daily life and work, making himself accountable to others by telling openly what his preferred world is."[50] Increasingly liberated from the constraints of orthodox protocols of science, Galtungian peace research revealed itself to be what its conservative critics have always suspected. No longer restricted to the exploration of ways and means for eradicating violent conflict, or the exploration of extending systemic tendencies toward global cooperation and integration, it was openly presented as the systematic exploration of an alternative world order—the global good life, made up, it would transpire, of a multiplicity of diverse communal and individual good lives.

There remained, however, that persistent lacuna: the normative framework that guided the search for an alternative reality. Were Galtung truly ensconced within contemporary postmodernist discourse, this might now be dismissed as something beyond resolution without an unacceptable recourse to a teleological metanarrative. But Galtung was endeavoring to ground his normative outlook; there were foundations, and they lay in the concept of human needs.

NOTES

1. Galtung, "Peace Research: Past Experiences and Future Perspectives," p. 256. Written in 1971.
2. For early examples of Galtungian futurism, see his "On the Future of the International System"; "On the Future of the World System"; and with Jungk as coeditor, *Mankind 2000*.
3. Galtung, "Introduction," *EPR*, 5, p. 24.
4. The singular exception is Strasser, *The Normative Structure of Sociology*, who employs Galtung's model of "trilateral science" without any reference to peace research whatsoever. I consider Strasser's usage later in this chapter.
5. Galtung, "Empiricism, Criticism and Constructivism." In subsequent discussion I will be referring to the revised version of this paper, published in 1977 as part of *Methodology and Ideology* (*EM*, 1) and hereafter referred to as ECC.
6. Galtung, *Theory and Methods of Social Research*.
7. See Gleditsch, "The Structure of Galtungism." The popularity of Galtung's text has frequently been mentioned to me by students and teachers of statistics and sociological research methods in Australia, the United Kingdom, and the United States.
8. Galtung, *Theory and Methods of Social Research*, p. 490.
9. Galtung, "Science and Development Assistance," pp. 161–162.

10. Galtung, "Socio-Cultural Factors and the Development of Sociology in Latin America," pp. 158–160.

11. Galtung, "Positivism and Dialectics," p. 214.

12. Galtung, "Deductive Thinking and Political Practice." This paper was never accepted by an academic journal, perhaps because the paper draws analogies between certain forms of left-wing scholarship and nazism, even though it starts off by asking German readers not to take it too seriously. See also Berger, *Pyramids of Sacrifice*, especially "Twenty-Five Theses," pp. 11–15.

13. See Galtung, "Two Ways of Being Western."

14. Galtung, "Peace Research: Past Experiences and Future Perspectives," p. 256.

15. Galtung, "Generalized Methodology for Social Research," p. 230.

16. Galtung, "Science and Development Assistance," p. 162.

17. ECC, pp. 42–43. Galtung does not firmly establish whether he takes a realist or phenomenalist viewpoint. Though he insists upon empirical verification of observation statements, his writing suggests an agnosticism as to whether things exist behind their appearances, as illustrated by his reference to the claims of others concerning *the* empirical world, his preoccupation with the logical connections between types of sentences, and his frequent emphasis on perception of the empirical world rather than the world itself.

18. ECC, pp. 49–50.

19. Habermas, *Knowledge and Human Interests*, p. 308.

20. Ibid., pp. 308–309. Compare with ECC, pp. 41–49.

21. Galtung, "Social Structure and Science Structure," pp. 35–37.

22. Ibid., pp. 24–27, 37. The case is made here in very broad terms with no historical or empirical references. Compare with the more nuanced analysis of the scientization of politics in Habermas, *Toward a Rational Society*, chs. 4–6.

23. Galtung, "Science as Invariance-Seeking and Invariance-Breaking Activity," p. 72.

24. Here Galtung's argument bears comparison with Habermas's concept of "mediatization" (*Mediatisierung*) by which is meant "the suspension of [the population's] substantive decision-making power through its encapsulation in organisations and political parties that predefine its needs with regard to the stability of the political system." *Toward a Rational Society*, preface and ch. 5.

25. Succinctly described by Pusey as the "objectivist illusion of unreflecting science." See his *Jurgen Habermas*, p. 21.

26. McCarthy, *The Critical Theory of Jurgen Habermas*, ch. 1.

27. ECC, p. 51.

28. See, for example, Findlay, *Nuclear Dynamite*.

29. See also Bhaskar, *The Possibility of Naturalism*, ch. 1.

30. Galtung, "Two Ways of Being Western," p. 218.

31. ECC, p. 54.

32. See Chapter 8.

33. See the anecdotal (and possibly apocryphal) reference to two American Indians, overheard by a U.S. anthropologist on an airplane, discussing ways of not disappointing naive young anthropologists, by inventing novel kinship systems for example. ECC, p. 252, note 10.

34. Strasser, *The Normative Structure of Sociology*, p. 6.

35. See Chapter 6.

36. ECC, p. 60.

37. ECC, p. 61.

38. On this point, see Habermas, *Toward a Rational Society*, p. 66.

39. ECC, p. 61.

40. Strasser, *The Normative Structure of Sociology*, p. 11.

41. Ibid., p. 12.

42. ECC, p. 62.

43. ECC, p. 68.

44. Lukacs, *History and Class Consciousness*, pp. 224–225.

45. Habermas, *Toward a Rational Society*, p. 63.

46. ECC, pp. 65–69.

47. Compare this with the idea of "narrative archetypes" in Lyotard, *The Postmodern Condition*.

48. ECC, p. 68. Buddhism becomes much more visible in Galtung's writing during the 1980s. See Chapter 8.

49. ECC, p. 68.

50. ECC, p. 70.

6

From Human Needs
to Global Values

The value idea of a pluralist, equitable global social order was first adumbrated in the revised conception of positive peace, was reiterated within the structural critique of imperialism, and also permeated the argument for an alternative understanding of science. But the sketch of an alternative world order remained unpacked, even though it clearly drew upon a complex set of values. Although Galtung's trilateral model of science could manipulate social values, it could not account for their origins and merely assessed the validity of normative claims in a circular fashion through the comparison of different sets of value-laden statements. The inadequacy of this process was stark enough. After all, the observation, made in "Violence, Peace and Peace Research," that life chances in the extant global structure were unequal was simply an empirical statement; it does not *logically* follow that they should be otherwise. In order to avoid the "naturalistic fallacy," the valuative component of the critique of global structure had to be identified and accounted for.[1] Given Galtung's frequently expressed disdain for deriving social ends from philosophical systems that reflect exclusionary social interests, and his apparent dismissal of purely philosophically deduced values, the source of the values required for the purposes of criticism and constructivism must lie elsewhere.

Galtung rejected the mere dreaming of utopias as too easy a way out. Humans are neither similar nor constant and consistent (factors, he rightly noted, that were often ignored in utopian writing), and he thought there was little value in developing social goals without regard to humanity in all its diversity. But even if his writing exhibited an increasing sensitivity to social difference, a consistent theme also was the acknowledgment that there are universal foundations upon which peace research can be built. Along with numerous other normative writers, Galtung drew upon a conceptual tool that appeared to provide a bridge across the fact-value and is-ought divides: human needs. It was needs-talk that he saw as enabling the connection of the structural critique of imperialism with the blueprinting of an alternative world order. In short, it provided a means for grounding the value amalgam of positive peace.

It is perhaps surprising, then, that the substantive analysis of human needs took up very little of Galtung's voluminous output in spite of its centrality to his project. In his few brief presentations of it, the concept of human needs appears as unproblematic, its putatively nonideological, quasi-empirical qualities and apparent sheer reasonableness suiting his purposes. However, the discussion of needs was always located within a broader concern with "human values" and "world goals" within which the various terms were often used interchangeably.[2] In spite of this imprecision, Galtung's presentation of the values to be realized within a preferred world order was conducted clearly within the spirit, if not always the letter, of needs-talk.

HUMAN NEEDS AND HUMAN VALUES

In a short paper published in 1975, Galtung reviewed ten broad "value dimensions," derived antonymically from a set of negative social conditions, that formed the core of the World Indicators Program (WIP) of the Chair of Conflict and Peace Research at the University of Oslo.[3] The ten values and their antonyms were

1. Personal growth	Alienation
2. Diversity	Uniformity
3. Socioeconomic growth	Poverty
4. Equality	Inequality
5. Social justice	Social injustice
6. Equity	Exploitation
7. Autonomy	Penetration
8. Solidarity	Fragmentation
9. Participation	Marginalization
10. Ecological balance	Ecological imbalance

These value dimensions emerged out of the 1973 world congress of the International Political Science Association that established a transnational group to study and implement a World Indicators Program. The WIP was intended as a contribution to a growing social indicators movement and with which it shared a concern about the overreliance on economic indicators of development. The perpetrators of the latter were, by implication, "national and international bureaucracies" that drew upon a range of models of global development that appeared in the late 1960s and early 1970s, partly as a consequence of widespread concerns over the finiteness of many global resources and partly as a product of substantial improvements in computer-generated data bases and simulated projections.[4] Models such as that of the Club of Rome, the Leontiff model, and to a lesser extent the Bariloche model were seen to be too Malthusian in their perspective. In spite of their commendable function in drawing attention to a number of global ecological crises, Galtung criticized these models for their methodology, ethical assumptions, and tendency to lean toward the middle-class "ideology of ecologism."[5] Under an ostensibly apolitical guise, they depicted the world as conflict-free and devoid of problems of inequality and injustice. He saw the exclusion of war, the arms trade, colonialism, and imperialism as inexcusable deficiencies for models claiming to identify the sources of global crises.

In contrast, the WIP claimed several unique features. First, it was to be world-oriented in applying its indicators to "world society." The definition of *society* employed was, however, rather odd. Acknowledging that strictly speaking a domestic analogy did not hold, Galtung suggested that in "a general sociological sense" the world was a society because it was self-sufficient and, stranger still, because it did not depend upon a "human environment." Presented thus, the idea of world society was seemingly reduced to that of a self-maintaining system.

The term *society* alludes to much more than this. Connoting a set of social relations between actors that goes beyond mere patterned interaction, it is inescapably connected to conscious human endeavor. Galtung's introductory discussion of positive peace, written a decade earlier, at least drew upon the more revealing imagery of a diverse humanity that collectively engaged in rule-governed behavior, premised upon a fundamental species identification. This original argument for the possibility of positive peace invited comparison with the Grotian depiction of an "anarchical society of states" and arguably offered a more substantive basis for claiming the existence of a global society. Like Galtung, the Grotian (English or "rationalist") school of international relations also resists recourse to a domestic analogy, basing its claim as to the existence of an international society on the authority of a number of shared principles that, by and large, are upheld by most states and without which no society beyond the water's edge could be said to exist.[6] Not the least of these is the mutual recognition of the sovereignty of states from which flows the obligation to uphold agreements and property rights. Such features of international relations as positive international law, international organizations, and the very conduct of diplomacy itself are seen to support the claim that at the very least there exists a sufficient level of consensus as to the desirability of international order to warrant speaking of an international society. Unlike Galtung, however, the rationalist perspective takes full account of the state as the primary actor in world politics and remains skeptical of overly cosmopolitan sentiments. Galtung did not elaborate on what evidence there was to support his claim that a world, let alone an international, society existed. He simply chose to treat the global social system as a society, minimally defined.

The flimsiness of this starting point for an exploration of social values was further revealed in the offering of three illustrative concretizations of the idea of a world society. First, the world consisted of approximately 4 billion human beings. If it were a society, asked Galtung, what kind would it be in terms of the levels of justice, inequality, and freedom and with regard to the satisfaction of fundamental needs? Second, the world could be seen as a *system* of collectivities, of which territorial states were possibly the most important. Third, there was also the weakest but also most frequent interpretation—the world consists of a *set* (in the mathematical sense) of collectivities, be they states or organizations, and one could compare and rank them.

If Galtung's first image connoted a cosmopolitan society consisting of a single humanity, then the second image of a system of actors spoke either to an orthodox realist account of international relations or a Grotian image of a society of societies qua states. Which perspective is chosen is of considerable consequence for any normative analysis of global social relations. From the realist point of view, it is debatable whether states have any obligations to take account of the interests of others and, by extension, whether it makes any sense to speak of an international society. For the rationalist, the articulation of international moral obligation must take account of the tension between internal and external obligations and duties. This introduces a certain dynamism in comparison to the realist account. Thus, in earlier rationalist writing, external obligations are limited primarily to the preservation of international order, whereas more recently rationalists have countenanced the idea of the state as a "local agent of world common good."[7] The third of Galtung's images tells us nothing about world society at all.

According to Galtung, the WIP claimed novelty in its effort to develop the first and second images. The interest in the first, the cosmopolitan interpretation, reflected the value orientation of the WIP scholars, insofar as they were clearly engaging in a globally focused needs-based exercise.[8] The focus on the second, the systemic interpretation, supposedly offered insight into the location of peace research. Political science and political sociology have been more concerned with comparing states (as in the third interpretation), he argued, whereas the disciplines of international relations, international sociology, and peace research have focused on the relations between collectivities including nonstate actors. Galtung went little further than this, suggesting that rather than argue the relative merits of adopting one of the perspectives on world society, the WIP intended to canvass all three. Entirely unexplored, however, were the relative merits of the theoretical assumptions that lay behind the three perspectives, their ethical implications, or conflicts and commonalities between them.

The second unique feature claimed for the WIP was a focus on indicators that were not means instrumentally derived from some prior ideological perspective but were ends in themselves: "We are not interested in the number of hospital beds per capita, but in the state of health; not in the production of protein of various kinds, but in the extent to which consumption of protein fulfills fundamental needs; not in industrialisation, but in the general satisfaction of fundamental needs."[9] A benefit of this constraint was the restoration of the value of the term *indicator,* which had become so diluted as to refer to almost any variable. The idea was to force the clarification of basic values as foundations for the construction of "goals."

Galtung was looking to construct goals on as least controversial a basis as was possible.[10] Yet, contrary to the stated objective of developing theory-free indicators that did not merely reflect means, he was effectively arguing for the identification of indicators of something—needs fulfillment—as the bases of goals, which were themselves inescapably normative. If we take the example cited above, indicators of a goal such as "there shall be x number of hospital beds per capita" were unacceptable, whereas indicators of the realization of a condition of "health" were acceptable. The implied distinction between ends and goals was premised upon some special quality of health as a goal—it consisted in a set of human *needs* fulfilled and presupposed that those needs should be satisfied. In other words, the goal or value of health had an irreducible teleological core. To confuse matters, Galtung went on to note that there was no consensus as to what such goals were (the fulfillment of various needs?) but countered this with the observation that there was equal dissent over what were the relevant variables for understanding or changing the world. The argument reduced, then, to a decision to privilege a focus on ends (goals) rather than means (variables), flimsily defended on the grounds that resolving dissent over *variables* was a matter for dispute among social scientists alone and served only to define schools of thought. In contrast, "debate about goals is everywhere (and nowhere!) which is one reason for focussing on it."[11] Galtung's remarks seem largely rhetorical, but if, as I will argue later, the concept of needs necessarily presupposes a given telos, then in fact it is not only the basis for goals or ends but also for *variables* or means for the realization of a wider goal.

It was in such imprecise argument that Galtung reproduced but did not address the problems associated with the concept of human needs. He was making a case for the generation of pure indicators that were not permeated with or determined by prior theoretical assumptions but nevertheless formed the basis for a normative assessment of success in realizing needs-derived goals. These goals provided in turn the basis for constructing a vision of a desirable social order. At no point, however, did Galtung define what he understood by human needs beyond their description and as a consequence could not substantiate their existence beyond a supposition. He drew upon Maslow's well-known "hierarchy of needs" but did not discuss Maslow's depiction of human needs as universal instinctual products of human physiological and psychological makeup.[12] In spite of some evident commonalities, neither did he consider the writings of the young Marx in which human needs are depicted as the essence of what it is to be human, their content changing and diversifying in reflection of "man's incessant productive activity."[13] Yet a similar view of needs as reflective of differing social contexts was evident in Galtung's discussion then, and especially so in his more recent writing. In Marx's account, the fulfillment of the wealth of historically evolving needs is an end in itself, for only then will a situation arise "where man does not reproduce himself in any determined form, but produces his totality."[14] This seems to be what Galtung was also driving at, since he depicted the satisfaction of the whole range of human needs as marking the realization of positive peace, a condition in which individual self-realization becomes truly possible. The concept of human needs acted as a standard against which specific social orders could be judged.[15]

The lacuna in Galtung's discussion can be elucidated by considering a fundamental deficiency identified in needs theory by its critics. Needs-talk appears generally to conflate different forms of utterance. Human needs are presented as empirical statements of necessity but can also refer to statements of logical, analytical, and normative necessity.[16] The realization of the seductive objective of a scientific ethics becomes stranded on the difference between claiming the empirical existence of a need and arguing for its fulfillment.[17] As a consequence, needs theory is inescapably teleological—it requires for its defense a prior standard of human excellence upon which an ethics of needs satisfaction can be grounded.[18] With regard to the most fundamental needs, such as Maslow's "physical" and "security" needs, this is hardly problematic, since few would argue against their existence or the "unqualified claim for [their] satisfaction."[19] In a "normal stating context" the identification of such a need usually implies its fulfillment.[20] However, the content of distinctly social individual or collective needs is far more contestable and their legitimation as candidates for satisfaction more complex. The defenders of different types of social formation would all argue that it is only within their preferred society that human needs are best understood and satisfied. In order for a theory of human needs to have critical effect, it must therefore be able to distinguish between true and false needs, a fact acknowledged by many needs theorists. Beyond identifying the most basic needs—the prerequisites for human existence—needs-talk is necessarily contingent upon a whole host of culturally and ideologically specific categories. Connected with this are

difficulties with distinguishing various needs from the closely related category of wants.

I cannot consider here the variety of responses to these problems offered by needs theorists; suffice to say that in order to argue for the satisfaction of specific human needs, their existence has to be convincingly
established *and* in their defense a deeper stratum of normative argument
must be elaborated.[21] It has been argued, for example, that Marx's understanding of needs and the right to have them satisfied is comprehensible only within a historical account of humanity's striving to be free
from domination. A more contemporary version of this line of argument
is provided by Neilsen, who argues, after Habermas, that the identification of true needs requires a prior consideration of emancipation, for it is
"only under conditions of adequate knowledge and undistorted communication" that humankind's true needs can be known.[22] Neither of these
issues—establishing the existence of needs or arguing for their satisfaction—was adequately dealt with by Galtung. We might suppose that in
utilizing Maslow, he was echoing a theme found in his earlier work by
alluding to a universal standard of societal health. Even if this was the
case, the problem of teleology remains because, as we have seen, trans-
ferring the physiological concept of "health" to the analysis of the social
world carries with it all of the problems associated with organic-analogic
conceptions of society. Given that Galtung rejected, in fact, the derivation of the value of societal health from the presumption of an objective
systemic interest, how then does one determine the substantive contents
of the evaluative standard of health to which the needs of individuals are
relative?[23]

Ostensibly at least, needs-talk dovetails with the trilateral model of
science, since it generates a set of value sentences. Questions about the
origins of such sentences invite the circular response that they reflect,
quite literally, the empirical fundamental needs of humans. Because the
discourse of needs cannot disaggregate needs and values, it supports the
claim—and in Galtung's case the normative rule—that needs and values
are perceptible in an unmediated sense, outside of theory and, presumably,
ideology. The quasi-empirical qualities of "needs" are being called into
play here: A patently normative program is being constructed with the deliberate intent of avoiding debilitating moral and ethical argument. The
dreaded "traditional peace thinking" need not be embraced after all.

Galtung was later to address the implicit universalizing assumptions
of needs-talk by allowing for the possibility of culturally specific needs, a
move that could only weaken the overall argument. In a culturally plural
world it is all the more difficult to determine convincingly who is obliged
to fulfill which needs of whom. Nonetheless, the third supposedly unique
feature of the WIP was its claim to be transideological. Galtung's preference for philosophical eclecticism continued to translate into an argument

for peace research remaining "without a fatherland," divorced from specific ideological and theoretical perspectives. He also noted that the value of "personal growth" opened up an avenue for inquiring into non-Western frames of reference, a theme I will return to later.

The fourth unique feature claimed for the WIP provided a connecting thread with Galtung's earlier work. The goals that underscored the WIP were taken to be isomorphically applicable at all levels of social analysis. In conjunction with the commitment to pluralism, this point was confirmed by the fifth unique feature: The goals should be applicable to several *types* of social collectivity. Clearly, the Galtungian category of needs and values had to establish firmly its transcendental qualities, yet the sixth novel feature confirmed the absence of consistent ethical argument in the discussion and further cast into doubt the actual status of needs or values: The WIP goals were "open-ended" with a consequent "search for legitimation." They may be drawn from existing but unspecified "rich traditions," but in a typical display of candor, Galtung conceded that he simply stipulated the goals.

The desire to avoid relying upon normative argument alone was evident in Galtung's exploration of some sort of public, practical generation of goals. This suggested that his concerns bore comparison with other considerations upon the conditions for and possibility of genuine public consensus.[24] Typically, Galtung made no reference to the work of others in this area. His approach was resolutely populist in its demand that such an exercise must avoid the elitism inherent in the reliance on experts, no matter how transnational their makeup. What was needed was grassroots dialogue, presumably entailing actually asking people what they needed, an apparently difficult task given "our expert-ridden societies." This was no more than a reiteration of the procedure originally proposed to identify systemic functions (or values) in Galtung's earliest papers on structural functionalism, the singular difference being a greater sensitivity to the dominance of elite opinion-makers, such as himself. The proposal also failed to consider whether people can know what their true needs are or know the needs of others, a deficiency that is surprising given Galtung's constant sensitivity to the contaminating effects of ideologies and, in later writings, the constraints of specific cultures upon cognition. The potential conflict between different sets of needs was also not considered. An unexplained normative commitment to egalitarianism, expressed in this instance as a hostility to intellectual domination, determined the direction of his discussion.

Let us return to the ten values offered by Galtung as guidelines to the WIP. The first—personal growth—was identified as the "fundamental value in the sense that all the others are subordinate and seen as necessary conditions for its realisation." Furthermore, personal growth consisted in an amalgam of human needs: "A person is body and soul, *soma* and *psyche*. A person has *needs*, some of them are fundamental, some of them are almost fundamental."25 This wide range of human needs provided a basis for rejecting the narrow economic focus of other models of global social development in favor of a more holistic vision that reflected "the progressive satisfaction of the needs of the body, the mind and the spirit." For Galtung, the concept of development should be connected to a more inclusive understanding of human capacity and desires but remain elusive nonetheless, a receptacle for a variety of ideas but not therefore vague.26 Again, a normative hostility to domination, in this case by too fixed a vision of ideal human social development, was intertwined with quasi-empirical claims as to the existence of human needs.

In Galtung's schema fundamental needs were further subdivided into the categories of physiological, climactic, somatic, community, and culture needs, the latter four also collectively referred to as "ecological needs." All of these needs—but especially those of community and culture—must be realized for properly human life; the alternative is for mere biological life to exist. However, the uniquely human dimension of Galtung's list was not convincingly demonstrated, since he ventured little beyond minimalist descriptions of the more intangible and debatable needs. For example, community was defined as "togetherness, love and sex," and culture was described as an admixture of language and communication. Defined so, it is plausible to suppose that various nonhuman species would equally appear to have such needs (apes and dolphins spring to mind).

The second list—almost fundamental needs—was also intended to capture specifically human needs, such as work—alternatively described as creativity or a means to self-expression—and freedom—the mobility of persons and ideas as "senders, receivers." Galtung's depiction of work echoed Marx's understanding of it as the essential activity of the human species, in that it appears to refer to a lost activity of creative and non-alienated production of desirable living conditions. Obviously, such "almost fundamental" and clearly human-specific needs require more in their defense than the act of simply stating them. That there was more to Galtung's account than meets the eye was in part revealed in the observation that people could in fact survive without their satisfaction, but "in any theory of personal growth they must occupy a prominent position. It may be that politics also belongs here."27 Though central to Galtung's task, this theory of personal growth was left unexplored, as was the implied connection between it and politics: Did politics precede or was it consequent upon the realization of the full range of needs?

The foundational value dimensions were subdivided further according to whether they reflected "distribution-oriented dimensions," such as diversity, socioeconomic growth, equality, and social justice, or "structure-oriented dimensions," such as equity, autonomy, solidarity, and participation. The first set corresponded with "actor-oriented goals" and were intended to reflect the focus of the liberal on the consequences for individuals of the distribution and production of social goods. The structure-oriented values were seen to be compatible with a marxist outlook and were antonyms of exploitation, penetration, fragmentation, and marginalization. This particular subdivision of values continued Galtung's recourse to the methodological principle of utilizing both sides of the Western ideological divide, albeit with a decisive lean to the left. There was, however, a further refinement of the principle looming: Western thought as a whole was to be declared an insufficient source of values. It was in his needs-talk that Galtung began overtly to display an interest, later to become something of a preoccupation, in moving beyond the confines of an occidental frame of reference.

A Note on Gandhi

Given the lifelong influence of Gandhi and his teachings on Galtung, there was a certain inevitability to Galtung's gazing beyond the confines of the West. Yet, tracing Gandhi's imprint on Galtung's work prior to the 1980s is difficult; Gandhi was rarely referred to directly in the earlier writings on peace research, the language of modern sociology inhibiting discursive evidence of an intellectual debt. Still, Galtung's first publication of significance was an analysis of Gandhian ethics, coauthored with Arne Naess.[28] That Gandhi provides the fundamental source of ethical inspiration for Galtung was also evident in a 1959 paper in which the concept of pacifism was explored from a sociological perspective yet equated with Gandhian ethics.[29] A more recent retrospective comment on the founding motivations for peace research confirmed the centrality of Gandhi's ethics from the beginning. Here Galtung speaks of peace research as originating out of a project entailing the mutually enriching interaction of "a moderately rigorous social science" with "the deep insight and moral command" emanating from the writings of Gandhi.[30]

Little discussion of the substance of Gandhian ethics was provided in the 1959 paper, which described Gandhi's pacifism as an ideology, the principle reference group of which was humanity. In common with most commentators, Galtung presented Gandhi as a source of practical inspiration above all, whose life was an example of the technical application of ethical principles to politics in conditions of social conflict.[31] Gandhi's doctrine of ahimsa (literally, nonkilling, nonharming) refers to a form of direct action, a substantive moral force intended to restrain expected violence and comparable to the Pauline concept of love. It is to be distinguished from the mere refraining from violence, or "unviolence," and constituted not only an inspirational ethic but also a guide to constructing a practice of nonviolence—satyagraha. Gandhi's conception of nonviolence was as a practical-moral instrument intended to achieve concrete results.[32]

Galtung clearly was further inspired by Gandhi's equation of peace not only with the absence of physical violence but also with the realization of universal justice. He regarded campaigns for the ending of conscription or disarmament as superficial, aimed at symptoms rather than causes. The primary cause of violence—its essence according to Gandhi—was exploitation, the symptoms of which were submission and servility resulting in a loss of self-worth.[33]

Galtung's subsequent work revealed increasingly numerous but often still veiled hallmarks of Gandhism, in inverse proportion to a declining reliance upon orthodox sociological discourse. Writing in 1971, Galtung identified three significant principles in Gandhian thought: nonviolence (ahimsa), self-reliance (swadeshi), and self-realization, the first two being servants of the latter.[34] Gandhi's work was described as a bridge between the oriental concern with inner well-being and the occidental focus on social structure, although the latter is subordinated to the former. It is from Gandhi that Galtung took the concept of a nonviolent and nonexploitative, or horizontal, social structure, to be contrasted with an occidental tendency to develop vertical social relations that constitute a significant source of alienation and a barrier to self-realization. Furthermore, Gandhi inspired the idea of autonomy as self-reliance coupled with community. The ideal social structure should be such that social detachment as a strategy to avoid structural violence is possible and the opportunities for self-realization are enhanced. It is not difficult to see the translation of the combined values of autonomy and collectivity into the sets of goals promoted in the WIP, although Galtung saw a deficiency in Gandhi's argument for self-reliance arising out of the overriding focus on individual spiritual purity. Gandhi was not a structural pluralist, his vision of a good social order for India consisting of a uniform system of village communities. Against this, Galtung argued for structural diversity as an essential source of external stimulation and a hedge against domination.[35]

Galtung also derived his understanding of alienation from Gandhi as much as from Marx. He drew parallels between the two, insofar as both connect the ownership of machinery with exploitation and alienation. In Gandhi's case it was not just a problem of ownership and work practices but of industrial machinery itself. His well-known aversion to machines and industry was premised upon the perception of their deleterious effects on humans. For Gandhi, "machinism" (Galtung's phrase) impacts upon the human mind by inducing a "craze" (Gandhi's term) that diverts thought away from essentials, reduces control of the palate, encourages sex for other than procreative reasons, and encourages the possession of nonessentials. Galtung displayed little enthusiasm for the philosophy of abstinence but was very sympathethic to Gandhi's antimaterialism. Gandhi did not of course reject all machinery, as his well-known enthusiasm for the Singer sewing machine illustrated, and neither does Galtung. But he did adopt

Gandhi's hostility to rampant industrialism and subsequently built this into the vision of a preferable social order that was taking shape within the exploration of needs-based values. By this time, however, Galtung's interest in the Orient was extending beyond reference to Gandhi.

OCCIDENTAL AND ORIENTAL SOURCES OF VALUES

On face value, Galtung is a man of the Left. Nonetheless, his particular version of progressive politics has always had its idiosyncracies and novelties. As I have already noted in Chapter 5, Galtung's evident empathies with marxism stopped well short of a close embrace. The particular character of his distaste for dimensions of marxism becomes all the more clear if it is connected with his criticisms of liberalism, from which he nonetheless also draws on occasions. Both exhibit a preoccupation with material progress, because they are variants of a single Western social cosmology writ large. Both perspectives evolved in the same historical period and are European products that developed out of the growth of capitalism and a scientific culture. The two approaches reflect a polarity within the capitalist system and cannot, therefore, provide a perspective from without. In short, they are two ways of being Western.

Part of the appeal of needs-talk to Galtung lay, then, in its apparent ability to provide a means for synthesizing values from different ideologies while being beholden to none. The concept of need allowed for the synthesis of egalitarianism and individualism, in reflection of Galtung's abhorrence of domination and preference for autonomy, the latter albeit retaining a collectivist cast. Nonetheless, a synthesis of marxist or liberal themes was still an insufficient basis for discerning the extent of human needs, because of their shared occidentalism. It should be noted at this point that Galtung's excursions into nonoccidental thought were initially occurring separately from the discussion of needs, although their imprint is evident from the outset, notably in the idea of personal growth. The turn to the East connects with another overall shift in his focus, away from structural toward ideational and cultural forms of violence. Although I consider this development in greater detail in Chapter 8, some brief observations are pertinent here.

Around the time he was writing on needs, the mid-1970s, Galtung was also beginning to look to what he calls social cosmologies—the cognitive codes deeply embedded within specific civilizational forms—for the deeper sources of violence and exploitation. All civilizations, he claimed, were characterized by a social cosmology, that is, "vast, ephemeral and deep states or processes close to or identical with the final goal, the ultimate *telos* of mankind."[36] Galtung's concern was neither with examining closely the ontological and epistemological assumptions of different social cosmologies nor with arguing in favor of one particular cosmology, although over time his critique of the West would acquire a greater stridency. His approach was typically taxonomic and descriptive, and he endeavored to extract from various cosmologies different understandings of human needs and visions of desirable social orders. Thus, oriental cosmologies were seen to focus inward on the realization of individual well-being and the achievement of peace of mind. But, if the occidental focus on the outer world was insufficient, then the oriental focus on inner well-being was also inadequate. What was sought was a dialogue between East and West as the basis for developing a richer understanding of the full range of human needs and, by extension, the objective of realizing positive peace. This was illustrated in the value amalgam that Galtung called personal growth, the existence of which required the fulfillment of the complete range of values and needs. On face value, the emphasis on personal growth appears to correspond with a marxist understanding of nonalienated existence, especially if Galtung's definition of work is borne in mind. But Galtung's notion of personal growth also draws upon the liberal concept of individual freedom, read as the antonym of uniformity and expressive of the structural quality of autonomy.[37] In addition, the occidental focus on outer man is to be supplemented with insights drawn from Asian thinking, in particular Gandhi's teachings, and subsequently Buddhism as well, resulting in a more holistic understanding of human development.[38]

Galtung's search for nonoccidental values extended into some cursory descriptive explorations of Chinese and Japanese religions, languages, cultures, and social orders. As to quite what steers these various cosmologies, or indeed what their precise nature is, Galtung initially confessed to uncertainty. However, some clues were provided in the claim that the cosmology of a civilization is analogous to the personality of the individual.[39] This analogy reinforced the antiphilosophical descriptivism that I have identified throughout Galtung's work to this point. Though social cosmologies may regulate the formation of visions of desirable societies, Galtung showed no interest in critically examining the social origins or substantive ethical content of the cosmologies themselves. Visions of desirable world orders were derived from a quasi-empirical realm of civilizational "personality" that, behavioristically, generated images of preferred futures. Social cosmologies acquired the status of a genetic code, safe from philosophical examination but available for inspection. In posing the question of where visions of desirable societies come from, Galtung evaded responding to the more difficult question of where social cosmologies originate.

Galtung did endeavor to identify more precisely those components of social cosmologies that provide the source of visions, citing two in particular: the concepts of nation and class. He imputed to the idea of a "nation" an eschatological quality arising from shared secular and sacred myths (accounts of both life on earth and a possible afterlife). Regardless of their truth value, these provide rich sources of shared visions, or "collective mentalities," of desirable or undesirable societies, perhaps expressed as versions of heaven or hell on or beyond this earth. Irrespective of its eschatological worth, religion has secular significance because it indicates to its believers the sort of life that should be led in order to ensure passage beyond the earthly realm and in so doing offers a vision of a desirable society. This tidy picture was upset, Galtung averred, upon the introduction of the concept of social class, because dominant classes may distort eschatologies in order to serve very earthly ends. Hermeneutic disputes over religious texts often reflected thinly veiled class conflicts, especially if a particular religion advocated acceptance of one's station in life. He thought that such visions were hardly liberating in secular terms. However, the interaction between class and eschatological vision remained insightful because it encouraged heterodox interpretations of religious doctrine, within broad cosmological parameters.

Like human personalities, social cosmologies were deemed to be necessary components of human social existence. Though malleable and subject to distortion, their essence preceded manipulation. This assumption sat uneasily with Galtung's apparent approval of the description of religion as a man-made opiate, a view that appeared to cast doubt upon the utility of religious vision.[40] For Marx, religion was a man-made distortion of man's true being, an expression of an imperfect self-awareness. As such, it could only be a barrier to emancipation and must be removed in order that humanity can truly be free. For Galtung, religion was adopted unproblematically as a source of visions, the utility of which did not require religious belief. Indeed, he went on to make the claim that oriental religious eschatologies provided a much better basis for the formation of visions than their occidental counterparts. He preferred their emphasis on process over structure and their lesser interest in resolving all contradictions in the search for absolute truth. Again, the analysis was restricted to the level of comparative description. Preferred elements could be selected from a range of cosmologies and eschatologies, but the principles of selection remained unexplained outside of a descriptive account of Galtung's own philosophical preferences.

FROM HUMAN VALUES TO DEVELOPMENT

At this point I can begin to bring together the various elements of Galtung's rapidly diversifying oeuvre. Comparing and contrasting oriental and occidental social cosmologies contributed to the expansion of our understanding of the possible range of social values by highlighting certain needs pertaining to the development of "inner-man," insufficiently recognized within Western thought. If we recall the argument for trilateral science, it required a value set against which reality (empirical data) and possible alternatives (expressed as theory sentences) can be assessed. Such a value set could be derived from the analysis of a range of fundamental and "almost fundamental" human needs. This provides, in turn, the basis for constructing paths to human social development—in other words, the fleshing out of the concept of positive peace.

The integration of development studies into Galtung's peace research became inevitable with the introduction of the concept of structural violence and the attendant downgrading of an orthodox focus on such things as arms control and disarmament. The depiction of conflict as a structural problem meant that effective peacekeeping necessitated global, structural change.[41] In contrast to his earlier enthusiasm for interdependence as a basis for extending the realm of peace, an example of an associative peace strategy, Galtung switched to advocating self-reliance as a precursor to interdependence. Structural transformation was now seen sometimes to require disassociation between social units, followed by autonomous development and eventual reassociation on a more equitable basis.

Once again, Galtung appears to have been tapping into an emerging normative and analytical theme evident in wider scholarly and activist discourses. The conflict in Indochina had already stimulated a literature that, recognizing marxism's relative silence on nationalism, was arguing for a defense of nationalism in a global context of uneven development. In prematurely assuming a universalizing process of emancipation, marxism had failed to examine adequately the tenacity of nationalist sentiments and the causes of conflict between nationalisms. Nationalist movements could be seen as agents of emancipation as much as reaction—a response from the global periphery to international inequality. In different ways, Galtung and others were now acknowledging that the extension of moral and political community was an uneven process that could not be taken for granted.[42] The Western cosmopolitan sentiments that pervaded Galtung's early work became increasingly implausible, as he was to admit openly. An emphasis on interdependence failed to consider the multifaceted structure of inequality, just as the orthodox approach to development tended to assume symmetry between social agents and was largely concerned with preventing direct violence and promoting horizontal global development rather than redressing vertical inequalities. Galtung now argued that a superior approach required the analysis of means by which vertical inequality could be overcome, global justice could be realized, and meaningful participation for weaker social actors could be developed. It was only through the integration of analyses of horizontal and vertical development, symmetric and asymmetric conflict, and direct and structural violence that the "theories and indeed the practice of development, conflict and peace can proceed further as tools of human fulfillment."[43]

The image presented in the analysis of imperialism was of a world riven by divisions that crossed the borders between the international and domestic realms. It was within this world political context that the analysis of the problems of development (structural violence) and armed conflict (direct violence) had to be located. It was a context in which the use of arms was not merely a consequence of a capacity to use them, or random events, but arose from basic global conflict formations of which the most fundamental was imperialism. Echoing a polemic that in a different version was also in favor with conservative writers, Galtung spoke of a third world war that had been in existence since 1945. For Galtung, it was a war between rich countries and the masses in which the technological might of the developed world was arrayed against the potential of "people power" in the underdeveloped world. Too great a focus on the East-West axis had masked a more fundamental conflict formation within which the two superpowers were then competing for adoption as the desirable developmental model for undeveloped states.[44] The solution to the problem of armaments and security lay, therefore, in the prior resolution of the problem of uneven global development.[45]

The focus on development at the expense of disarmament was not unique to Galtung. His approach reflected a wider shift of focus in academic thinking about international relations and international political economy during the 1970s from the East-West axis of conflict toward that of North and South. Arguably, this was a consequence of not only a revitalized marxist input into political economy by way of a critique of neocolonialism but also of the combined influences of the vestiges of the very wave of radicalism that had helped spawn a more radical peace research, the period of superpower détente, the rise of the underdeveloped world as a political force in international organizations, and the war in Indochina. Galtung's approach to the question of development bore much in common with the work of other contemporary writers of the period, especially those brought together by the Dag Hammarskjöld Foundation, who were also concerned with the articulation of "another development." They too emphasized the centrality of a broad conception of human needs as the basis for constructing developmental goals, the virtues of self-reliance at all levels, and the ultimate objective of realizing a development strategy that was holistic in approach and sought to bring about the "development of every man and woman and the whole of man and woman." Their target was not only the development of the Third World along these lines but also the directing of the industrialized world away from the dominant developmental model of "the bureaucratic society of programmed consumption."[46] Nevertheless, Galtung and his contemporaries still constituted a small group, distinguishable from other radical critics of the global social order by their emphasis on prescription over complex analytical critiques and on the search for alternative world orders.[47]

Galtung's evolving perspective on human development aimed to go beyond a political economy of development and explore how a particular worldview and developmental goal, the "bourgeois way of life," permeated the globe.[48] This global telos was seen to incorporate both underdevelopment on the global periphery and overdevelopment in the global center. Though not yet universally realized, nor realizable for many, it remained the preeminent vision of the purpose of human striving. It was a developmental goal that emphasized consumption, production, and the realization of material comfort over the fulfillment of nonmaterial human needs. It encouraged the exploitation of humanity and nature and disregarded the finiteness of natural resources, resulting in an increasingly maldeveloped world. Even in the developed world where this lifestyle had most successfully been realized, it had resulted in a developmental curve that has seen societies move from underdevelopment to sufficiency and on to new forms of maldevelopment or overdevelopment. For Galtung, the bourgeois way of life was the very essence of a bankrupted modernity.

In contrast to a stultifying and imposed universality, Galtung reiterated his argument for philosophical eclecticism as the basis for constructing an alternative paradigm of development that aspired to more than the realization of economic justice between and within states. His critique of underdevelopment was wedded to a critique of the overdevelopment of the West, and both were couched in a search for a universal value system that could establish the foundations for global development but, as important, also allow for autonomy in identifying problems and responding to central issues in social life. How, Galtung asked, could one combine "small and big, red and expert" and realize the amalgam of human needs or preferred values? The response to this rhetorical question was to ask how the social formation that generated and nurtures the bourgeois way of life as practice and ideal came about. The answer lay in the analysis of "the real rock-bottom foundation, the deep culture, the cosmology of the Western civilization within which these social formations have taken root."[49]

The idealist direction in which the discussion was heading was evident: By discerning the causative cosmology, its antithesis could be constructed. The causal significance of the dominant cosmology underscored the creative potential of any alternative. Galtung avoided a slide into determinism by insisting that the relationship between cosmology and structure was not simply one of cause and effect; both were coconstitutive of the dominant global vision. Social structures commensurate with the dominant way of life were manifestations of a deep cosmology, at the same time reinforcing it and allowing it to unfold. This appeared to be little more than a descriptive reformulation of the well-known but much disputed marxist topology of base and superstructure. But in Galtung's version there was little attempt to elucidate the nature of the relationship between ideas and practice; the substitution for the term *ideology* of the more elusive *cosmology* rendered such inquiry all the more difficult. It also created a profound problem for the praxeological thrust of Galtung's peace research. Cosmology may offer itself as a richer conceptual tool than ideology, but by using it to displace the origins of domination into the deepest realms of human collective existence, Galtung not only raised the question of how domination could be fully identified but also necessarily exposed the relative shallowness of any alternative.

Alpha and Beta

Recourse to needs-talk was intended to resolve the tensions in Galtung's model of development that emerged in his writing during the 1970s and were expressed in the adopted label of "self-reliance and global interdependence." The Galtungian concept of self-reliance went beyond consideration of issues like trade relations, per capita Gross National Product (GNP), or the introduction of a specific socioeconomic system to focus on the development of "all of man and all men." Authentic development required more than the satisfaction of material needs and had to include the need for freedom, creative work, politics, togetherness, joy, and "a sense of the meaning of life."[50] It was a perspective that reflected what has been called "the dialectic of the specific and the universal," and "the central intellectual antinomy of the modern world," an expression of the threat posed by hegemonic universalism to non-Western civilizations.[51] It is a theme that has been considerably developed more recently as a consequence of a growing emphasis in the international relations literature on the tensions between logics of integration and disintegration and the implications for the politics of identity of accelerating globalization.[52]

In Galtung's view, the problem with arguments such as those for a new international economic order (NIEO)—the paradigmatic critical perspective of the time—was that they were a product of the same intellectual paradigm that generated the old economic order. They both evinced a preoccupation with the economic sphere and a belief that increased growth coupled with a reform of distributive practices would radically transform the global economic order. To the extent that it might, Galtung was supportive. But this was constrained by his belief that it might only result in new forms of economic domination and would contribute little to the ultimate objective of individual emancipation. The call for a NIEO focused primarily on increasing the flow of capital and goods to the underdeveloped states; it was a state-centric reform program that used GNP as its prime measure and assumed that the more produced, processed, and marketed, the better. What was required was a perspective that assessed development in all of its manifestations, particularly the creation of greater national, collective, and individual autonomy.

Galtung's presentation of an alternative development paradigm proceeded in a familiar manner: a critical description of a prevailing pattern of development, from which positive values could be antonymically derived and expressed in terms of the fulfillment of human needs. Two analytical frameworks were employed: a fourfold taxonomy of social structures that captured existing and potential models of social formation; and two broad developmental patterns—"alpha" and "beta." Alpha represented the dominant paradigm of industrialized development. The beta pattern fused ideas derived from Gandhian thinking, oriental philosophy, and the concrete developmental practices of Cuba and Maoist and post-Maoist China that, unlike Soviet socialism, Galtung saw as still providing a genuine alternative to liberal capitalism.

Alpha structures are compatible with Western social cosmology and a dominant bourgeois lifestyle. They are the consequences of an interaction between a particular form of social structure and a specific technological orientation producing the prototypical modern society in its "private capitalist" and "state capitalist" variations. Alpha structures and processes are fundamentally large and highly complex in form. They display all the features of vertical, or imperialist, social relations: inequity, penetration, marginalization, fragmentation, and segmentation. Any social system or social activity, practical or intellectual, that displays these features is included. Alpha structures produce unequal exchange and in-change and induce a centralized administrative, extractive, productive, and distributive network that segments, fragments, and thus marginalizes elements of the overall social order. An alpha model of development places no limitations on size, is dominant over nature, and is highly diversified in the production of goods and services.[53] The primary structural representations of alpha-type social orders are the state and the corporation. Marxism could not grasp the essence of alpha structures, according to Galtung, since it dealt inadequately with noneconomic verticalities and said nothing about the problem of size. Alpha is a hegemonic ethos, which does not necessarily disappear "after the revolution" but transcends specific material or ideological social formations, in reflection of a wider cosmological or civilizational normative order. Above all, alpha development is destructive of a holistic form of human development, providing only for the inequitable satisfaction of basic material needs. In its pure form, then, it constitutes a dystopia —literally a hell on earth.

Beta development is the antithesis of alpha, but since it describes an unrealized future the category is not as well formed. The central features of beta development would be smallness, horizontal social relations, and a low division of labor with a concomitant emphasis on autonomy and self-reliance. Beta development would be more conducive to the fulfillment of the human need for togetherness, participation, and integration.

In its pure form, however, beta development could become another dystopia.

The sole limitation upon the expansion of alpha is the fact of a territorial state system. Lenin's shadow fell again across Galtung's claim that states as alpha structures are checked in their growth by the competitive expansion of other alpha structures. Alpha structures are not restricted to domestic socioeconomic systems but are evident in international organization and interstate relations: Imperialism *is* alpha expansionism. It entails the displacing of the alpha periphery outside of its own national borders, thereby making other nations the objects of multifarious forms of exploitation. Furthermore, the pathology of alpha is deepened by the internalization of alpha values by the oppressed, which leads to attempts to peripheralize others. However, Galtung also saw alpha behavior on an international scale as threatened by its own internal contradictions, for the process of reproduction results in the challenging of First World alpha states by newer Third World states behaving in an alpha fashion. Thus, the call for a NIEO was an expression of the problems of alpha growth in a materially finite world, as developing states acquired a capacity to challenge the hegemony of developed (more accurately, overdeveloped) states over global resources. For Galtung, recession in the global capitalist economy coupled with ecological problems did not simply generate problems in the world economy but produced a crisis of greater proportions. Having successfully globally reproduced itself, the bourgeois way of life was revealing its limitations. The continuing adherence to alpha logic by states and corporations "sets nation-states on collision courses that could not but lead to heavy increases in the levels of direct and structural violence in the world."[54] Alpha may have once provided a vision of a desirable society, but it could not provide the basis for a vision of a desirable world.

Alpha structures are maintained by a particular cosmology that ascribes a naturalness to growth as the progenitor of progress, whereas beta structures do not evince such a reproductive mechanism. The catalyst of alpha to beta transformation lies in the ideational realm—it is the product of the conscious adoption of an alternative cosmology that privileges the nonmaterial over the material, emphasizes internal human development over material development, and undermines the normative foundations upon which alpha ultimately depends. Effectively articulating classically idealist premises, Galtung saw counterhegemonic visions, such as that encapsulated in the idea of beta, as "social forces" of practical consequence. The world was made up of dominant alpha units whose competitive interaction provided the principle source of threats to security and welfare. Yet the millions of villages, typical beta social formations, around the world offered no such threat and suggest, in the spirit of Gandhi, an alternative ethos of much wider application. "Dealphaization" is effectively a form of "structural disarmament."

Galtung was not calling for a neo-Luddite retreat to the village. The replacement of an increasingly pure global alpha system with a pure beta system was not the intended goal. It was all too evident that betalike cosmologies have not been sustained, historically, against the onslaught of the bourgeois way of life. In any case, alpha modes of social organization perform certain functions better than a smaller beta version could hope to do. The need to produce certain things and the preservation of autonomy suggested to Galtung that the retention of certain alpha structures was necessary. In the Third World, for example, a pure beta mode of social organization can result in too much isolation, insufficient structure, and poor security for small social units. High technology provides benefits in the fields of communications and production, which reflects a need for some economies of scale. Isolated beta social units can be become extremely unequal as a consequence of different geographical locations, the uneven global distribution of natural hazards, seasonal extremities, and so on. Alpha levels of social organization and production also accounted for some of the creative dynamism of modernity. In addition, the horizontally structured, supportive and caring, purely communal beta lifestyle insufficiently provided for the evident human need to withdraw and be private.

Because material needs and growth are downgraded within a beta developmental perspective, other nonmaterial needs come to the fore. As we have already seen, Galtung's idea of human fulfillment entailed the fulfilling of nonmaterial, spiritual, collective, and individual needs. It was a mix of alpha and beta—with a strong bias toward the latter—that could constitute a potential counterethos. However, this must "not be missionary, but tolerant and dialogical." Galtung cautioned against those who would simply replace one vision with another: "In all of this the major difficulty will be those who persist with the faith in partial ideologies and visions and false dichotomies, demanding a purity unknown in the real world."[55]

Four Societal Models

The alpha-beta continuum intersected with a fourfold typology of social formations, which also displayed the imprint of Galtung's needs-based social values. Although acknowledging the marxist overtones of his typology, he reiterated his rejection of economic determinism or a linear account of history. As with previous typologies, the emphasis was on ahistorical, abstract description. Furthermore, Galtung claimed that his categories were more general than those of marxism in expressing more than relations of production alone. Consequently, the four societal types were of uncertain ontology, clearly intended to loosely represent historical and extant social formations but also to act as ideal types or generalizations as well as to provide a means for descriptively representing various value combinations.

The typology was generated in Parsonian fashion by the use of two pattern variables: inegalitarian-egalitarian (vertical-horizontal) and collectivist-individualist (uniformity-diversity), although Parsons's "ideological and empiricist bias" was rejected in favor of the derivation of variables from utopian writings "where potential reality has been given maximum play."[56] The combination of the two dichotomizing variables produces four types of society:

Model 1   conservative/feudal (collectivist + inegalitarian, vertical + uniformity)
Model 2   liberal/capitalist (individualist + inegalitarian, vertical + diversity)
Model 3   communal/socialist (collectivist + egalitarian, horizontal + uniformity)
Model 4   pluralist/communist (individualist + egalitarian, horizontal + diversity)

As can be seen, Galtung described each social type in his own sociologically derived terms but confused matters by also using more familiar marxist descriptions based upon historical modes of production.[57] He also did not address the state-society distinction.

Without either substantiating his own classificatory schema or referring to the complex debates over modes of production in underdeveloped societies, Galtung went on to identify examples of the coexistence of differing societal types within various existing societies. He claimed that model 1 feudal societies could be found within the contemporary Third World, although many have elites that display the features of model 2 societies, and Japan was described as a model 1 feudal society. Model 2 societies included the United States and the former Soviet Union and existed in private-capitalist and state-capitalist versions. Model 3 societies were represented by China, Cuba, and Tanzania. The preferred model 4 society was, of course, as yet unrealized.[58] By implication, different social sectors must be able to articulate models contrary to the dominant societal type, a point reinforced by Galtung's own situation as a radical educated in model 2 societies (Norway and the United States) who espouses the formation of model 4.

Even though Galtung asserted that different types of society can exist simultaneously, to further confuse matters he claimed also that his schema was in fact intended to present development historically: Model 1 society represents the past, models 2 and 3 represent the present, and model 4 represents the future, although he continued to disavow any assumption of the inevitability of this specific pattern of societal transformation. The point he was making was normative: The rejection of the necessity of linear development was a denial of the need for a capitalist stage of development. A model 4 society could evolve out of either model 2 or 3 if the correct combination of the principles of equality and diversity was guiding development.

Given its fuzziness, Galtung's typology might be best understood as a symbolic recitation in which desired values (grounded in a specific understanding of human needs) are juxtaposed to produce four rough sketches of societal types, the plausibility of which stems in part from their descriptive correspondence with actually existing social formations. In effect, it constitutes a normative scale of forms, societies 1 to 4 being ranked in order of preference. Each type represents varying levels of satisfaction of specific human needs. Model 1 represents a feudal social order and is decisively rejected. Models 2 and 3 are the two broad groupings into which existing states are deemed to fall (in that respect 2a and 2b might be more accurate notations), although 3 seems preferable, to Galtung at least, because it is egalitarian. The task is, then, to introduce diversity—less uniformity and more individualism—into model 3 social structures thereby producing a model 4 society. Alternatively, if model 2 societies were more horizontally structured, a similar result would eventuate. The intended point was simple enough: Various paths to the preferred world are available, and none of them is to be historically or analytically privileged.

The discussion of needs, the two models of development, and the societal types can now be blended together. Model 2 societies are consummately alpha in form: They are meritocratic, inegalitarian, class-divided, and driven by an ethos of success. Model 4 societies, however, reflect the values that form the core of beta development, the overriding goal being that of self-realization under conditions of equity, diversity, and horizontal social interaction: "One might dream of a society with a kibbutz in one corner, a zen monastery in another, a self-sufficient metropolis, a hippie colony, a people's commune: a collection of horizontal units that in themselves are highly meaningful, built around a certain theme, but respecting other units that are different."[59] It is only within a model 4 society, representing the value amalgam of equity and diversity consistently espoused by Galtung, that the full range of human needs can be satisfied and human potential realized. It is not an unknown vision—it secretes the sentiments of a socialist anarchism and is redolent perhaps of Spanish syndicalism. However, none of the models is irretrievably tied to a specific geographical location, historical epoch, or level of analysis. They are abstractions, deemed to be isomorphically applicable to a number of levels of social development including the global. In other words, the typology also prefigures a model of an alternative to the existing system of states. This theme was to be developed subsequently in *The True Worlds,* the next stopping point in our journey.

CONCLUSION

Three crucial elements were missing from Galtung's vision of an alternative cosmology to challenge the hegemony of the bourgeois way of life: an explanation of the precise relationship between social cosmologies and the empirical social world; a compelling defense of the preferred values that overcomes the limitations of the concept of needs; and a clear indication of how the preferred vision is historically and practically connected to the hegemonic vision—in short, a theory of social change. I shall comment briefly on all three deficiencies.

First, at this stage in Galtung's work the concept of a social cosmology is highly ambiguous and underdeveloped. Galtung appeared to be promoting a theory of cosmological hegemony of sorts, in which social cosmology is historically coconstitutive of the social life-world. The dominant cosmology permeates all aspects of global social life, including scholarly reflection upon it, thereby working to ensure the continuing co-optation of the global and the hegemony of the developed world. In spite of a universalist guise, it is reflective of a select set of ill-defined but deeply embedded dominant interests. On the other hand, in being constructed upon human needs, the proposed alternative cosmology is supposedly discerned *outside* of ideology or theory and selectively draws upon a variety of cosmologies and social practices. This is in spite of the ineliminable normative and teleological content that permeated the catalogue of needs and that also speaks to a select understanding of irreducible human interests. The sole difference lies in the claim of the alternative to capture the *authentic* needs of humanity. What remained unexplained was how such needs could be authoritatively known, beyond those that, if left unfulfilled, were of evident physiological consequence.

Second, though value sentences derived from a set of human needs could either be used to verify a set of empirical sentences about the present world (empiricism and criticism) or be compared with a model of a preferred world (constructivism), the defense of the value sentences was buried within the concept of human needs. In other words, it was internal to the sentences themselves. In the end, the list of needs was no more than a collage of values chosen from a variety of philosophical systems, assumably because they accorded with Galtung's own philosophical outlook. The process involved a double collapsing of the acts of empirical observation and normative critique: in the depiction of the extant imperialist world order and in the presentation of a set of human needs.

Third, no account is given of how the transition from the present world order to the preferred world order will occur or who the principal agents of this transformation might be. Galtung's fourfold typology of societal types takes a bet each way: It leans upon a classical marxist history, but in normatively rejecting both the primacy of the economic and the identification of a specific historical subject, the typology is of taxonomic value only. Analytically, it lacks what Goldmann has called a "historic consciousness"—an understanding not only of the type of society one is in and the social forces operating therein but also of the historical possibilities of altering them.[60]

The only answer to such lacunae lies in the classically idealist assumption that the construction of visions has in itself sufficient causal potency. After all, Galtung was proposing no less than the construction of an alternative social cosmology to supersede the bourgeois way of life in spite of the latter's deep and extensive roots. If that is the case, then the scientific bubble that surrounded the idea of peace research is irredeemably burst. In spite of the scientistic flavor of the concept of constructivism, Galtungian peace research had come full circle and embraced the idealism of traditional peace thinking that it was originally intended to supersede. Although exhibiting a greater breadth of vision and providing a more detailed description of his own normative perspective, Galtung in his constructivist exercises added little of methodological substance to his earlier functionalist account of global values and the belief in the creative potential of the sociological enterprise. He continued to suppose that an actual or potential public consensus existed as to the set of values that underpinned his vision of a desirable society, but at bottom it rested entirely upon our acceptance of a list of essentially contestable human needs.[61] This is not to deny that many of such needs could be compellingly argued for as guiding social values, but Galtung certainly did not show the way.

Galtung's vision was self-consciously offered as just one among many possibilities. However, it did presuppose that a value-plural world, constructed upon a number of universal moral and ethical assumptions arising from the adoption of a specieswide account of needs, was itself a defensible idea. Even if we empathize with its normative premises, there remains the unaddressed question of the practical viability of the vision of an alternative social order, given the use of ahistorical abstract categories in its construction. The preferred world not only consists in a plurality of communities and value systems, but if it is to be consistent with the founding premise of peace research, it must also be without violence. It directly confronts the pessimism of orthodox theories of international relations that depict the threat of violence as the inevitable backdrop to a stable world order composed of discrete human collectivities. More remarkably, it presupposes also the effective dissolution of the modern state, even though the state hardly figured, descriptively or analytically, in Galtung's conceptual lexicon. It advocates the transcendence of national interests by a common global interest, which at the very least consists in universal adherence to the peaceful coexistence of different value systems and social structures, opposition to all forms of domination, and equity as a global operating principle. Yet, the emphasis on the differences between social cosmologies—and by extension on the visions of a preferable world that they generate—only heightens the problem of defending the normative underpinnings of the overall vision, given that we already find ourselves in a value-plural but violent world.

Galtung offered a vision of a preferred world order in which the tension between identity and difference was to be reconciled: not one true world but many worlds true to many people. The possibility of its realization was seen to arise, even if against all odds, in the very acts of imagination and articulation. Whatever one's judgment of it, Galtung's vision, including the manner in which he arrived at it, was echoing and also foreshadowing wider intellectual currents. The distaste for ideological, or cosmological, singularism that began to mark his writing in the early 1970s was prescient, striking a chord with other emerging versions of a radical doubting of the tenability of established discourses of universal emancipation and the modernity that spawned them. Equally, I would happily concede that although the call for the fulfillment of a range of basic human needs—without which the imagining of preferred futures (or any other activity for that matter) simply could not occur—may rest upon shaky foundations, it remains morally compelling nonetheless. Such is the power of needs-talk.

NOTES

1. Moore, *Principia Ethica*, pp. 9–58.
2. Galtung, *The True Worlds*, pp. 19–21.
3. Galtung, "Human Values," pp. 156–159.
4. Galtung, "World Indicators Program."
5. Galtung, "The Limits to Growth and Class Politics," pp. 325–341.
6. See Wight, *International Theory*; Bull, *The Anarchical Society*.
7. See Bull, *Justice in International Relations*, pp. 13–14; and Introduction in this book.
8. All of the scholars are well-known progressives in their fields, and a large number are peace researchers. See the list of participants in Galtung, "World Indicators Program," p. 354.
9. Ibid., p. 355.
10. For example, Maslow argues that human needs provide the basis for a "scientific ethics," Marcuse and Fromm refer to the possibility of deriving universal ethical standards from human needs, and Falk argues that needs add "some objectivity" to moral claims. See Maslow, *Motivation and Personality*, p. 366; Fitzgerald (ed.), *Human Needs and Politics*, pp. viii–xvi., Falk, "Contending Approaches to World Order," in Falk, Kim, and Mendlovitz, *Toward a Just World Order*, p. 155.
11. Galtung, "World Indicators Program," p. 354.
12. Fitzgerald, "Abraham Maslow's Hierarchy of Needs," in Fitzgerald (ed.), *Human Needs and Politics*, pp. 36–51.
13. Duncan, *Marx and Mill*, p. 61.
14. Marx, cited in Duncan, *Marx and Mill*, p. 62. See also Marcuse, *One Dimensional Man*, especially ch. 1.

15. Duncan, *Marx and Mill*, p. 63. See also Bay, "Needs, Wants and Political Legitimacy," pp. 241–242.

16. Fitzgerald, "The Ambiguity and Rhetoric of Need," in Fitzgerald (ed.), *Human Needs and Politics*, pp. 195–212.

17. Taylor, "'Need' Statements," pp. 106–111.

18. Ibid., p. 204. See also Neilsen, "True Needs, Rationality and Emancipation," in Fitzgerald (ed.), *Human Needs and Politics*, pp. 142–156; and Soper, *On Human Needs*, ch. 1.

19. Marcuse, *One Dimensional Man*, p. 19.

20. Neilsen, "On Human Needs and Moral Appraisals," pp. 175–177.

21. Soper, *On Human Needs*, p. 12.

22. Neilsen, "True Needs, Rationality and Emancipation," p. 156. See also Brenkhert, *Marx's Ethics of Freedom;* and Lukes, *Marxism and Morality.*

23. Fitzgerald, "Abraham Maslow's Hierarchy of Needs," p. 41.

24. I am thinking here of Arendt's depiction of politics as the highest form of communicative action by a plurality of equal individuals seeking consensus, Rawls's "veil of ignorance," and Habermas's conception of the "ideal speech situation" and the possibility of undistorted communication. See Arendt, *The Human Condition;* Rawls, *A Theory of Justice;* and Habermas, *The Theory of Communicative Action: Volume One,* ch. 3.

25. Galtung, "Human Values," p. 156. Emphasis in the original.

26. Galtung, "Global Goals, Global Processes," p. 35.

27. Galtung, "Human Values," p. 156.

28. See Galtung and Naess, *Gandhi's Politiske Etikk.* Naess continued to develop a "systematization" of Gandhian ethics and in a later volume acknowledged Galtung's continuing contribution. See Naess, *Gandhi and Group Conflict.*

29. Galtung, "Pacifism from a Sociological Point of View."

30. Galtung, "Introduction," *EPR,* 5, p. 23.

31. "I have called Gandhi's philosophy a pragmatic spiritualism. If this ideology is practically followed there is no reason why man should not be able to bring about lasting peace on this earth." Sharma, *Ethical Philosophies of India,* p. 325. A number of commentators note the ad hoc, inconsistent character of Gandhi's ethics. See Borman, *Gandhi and Non-Violence,* ch. 9; and Woodcock, *Gandhi,* ch. 9.

32. See Gandhi, *Non-Violence,* pp. 107, 121–123. See also the discussion in Borman, *Gandhi and Non-Violence,* pp. 231–232. A more extensive discussion of nonviolence emerges in Galtung's work on cosmologies in which Buddhism is drawn upon extensively. See Chapter 8.

33. Gandhi, *Non-Violence,* pp. 94, 113–118, 283.

34. Galtung, "Gandhi and Conflictology," pp. 126–127.

35. Ibid., p. 129.

36. Galtung, "Social Cosmology and the Concept of Peace," p. 184.

37. Galtung, "World Indicators Program," p. 357.

38. Galtung, "Human Values," p. 159, and "Introduction," *EPR,* 5.

39. Galtung, "Eschatology, Cosmology," pp. 205–206.

40. Ibid., p. 230, note 5.

41. Galtung, "Feudal Systems, Structural Violence," pp. 262–264.

42. For a comprehensive discussion of this theme see Linklater, *Beyond Realism and Marxism.*

43. Galtung, "Feudal Systems, Structural Violence," pp. 163–164, 264.

44. Ibid, pp. 17–18.

45. Galtung, "Disarmament and Environment," pp. 15–18.

46. Nerfin (ed.), *Another Development: Approaches and Strategies;* Galtung provided a small contribution entitled "Alternative Lifestyles in Rich Societies."

47. Note here Higgott's point that dependency theory has failed to adequately replace the prescriptive content of modernization theory. See his *Political Development Theory,* ch. 1.

48. Galtung, Poleszynski, & Wemegah, "Why the Concern with Ways of Life?"

49. Ibid., p. 328.

50. Galtung, *Towards Self-Reliance and Global Interdependence.*

51. Wallerstein, *The Politics of the World Economy*, ch. 15.

52. See, for example, Walker, *One World, Many Worlds;* and Camilleri and Falk, *The End of Sovereignty?*

53. Galtung, "On Alpha and Beta."

54. Ibid., p. 100.

55. Ibid., pp. 102–104.

56. Galtung, "Perspectives on Development," p. 322. See also his "Social Structure and Science Structure," p. 14.

57. The list is taken from Galtung, "Perspectives on Development," p. 323, table 9.1. A more detailed comparison of societal types is provided in table 9.2, p. 325.

58. Ibid., pp. 322–323.

59. Ibid., p. 328.

60. Cited in Neilsen, "True Needs, Rationality and Emancipation," p. 146. For a comparable observation, see also Cox, "Social Forces, States and World Orders," p. 138.

61. Galtung claims that there is near universal consensus over the list of "fundamental needs," and that "many" would also agree to the list of "almost fundamental needs" on paper, if not in practice. See his "Human Values," p. 159.

7

The True Worlds

The present day global set of local sovereign states is not capable of keeping the peace. . . . What has been needed for the last 5000 years and has been feasible technologically, though not yet politically, for the last 100 years, is a global body politic composed of cells on the scale of the Neolithic-Age community—a scale on which the participants could be personally acquainted with each other, while each of them would also be a citizen of the world-state.

—*Arnold Toynbee*[1]

Galtung's *The True Worlds: A Transnationalist Perspective* was published in 1980 as a volume in the series Preferred Worlds for the 1990s, commissioned by the World Order Models Project. Whereas other volumes in the series were commissioned to reflect the regional perspectives of their authors, Galtung eschewed this in favor of a global approach. Much of its content had appeared before, some of it as early as 1971, in various papers, unpublished drafts, and discussion pieces. It can thus be read variously: as an exploration of world politics in its totality; as a contribution to a research project larger than itself; and as the culmination of more than twenty years of peace research.

THE REAL WORLD AND THE POTENTIAL WORLD

The starting point of *The True Worlds* is a snapshot of a multifaceted, global crisis—of violence, misery, repression, and environmental degradation—rooted in the world structure. The crisis is illustrated by reference to a number of empirical trends that, collectively, present a sombre image of the late twentieth century. Data on direct violence—frequency of wars, the casualties of war, exponential trends in arms expenditures—are supplemented with some data on world nutrition, specifically calorie and protein intake. Further analysis of data on infant mortality rates, adult literacy, and world population growth confirms the poverty of the contemporary world order, although in the areas of infant mortality and illiteracy it is conceded that there are signs of incremental improvement. In sum, the extant order is judged as doing a reasonable job in catering to the needs of about one-third of humanity and doing very badly with regard to the rest. Furthermore, these two sectors have very clear geopolitical addresses.

The combination of the finiteness of the natural world and the expansion of the human world has produced both ecological imbalance and social interdependence—the former spawning the twin evils of depletion and pollution and the latter leading, through the evolution of communities and the concept of territorial possession, to the modern states system and expanding economic cycles. These cycles reflect an increasingly complex division of labor that produces uneven accumulation within and between discrete communities, further exacerbating ecological imbalance. The result is structural violence that impoverishes and alienates both rich and poor, albeit in different ways. Direct violence emerges as community is set against community, leading to the regulation of direct violence through the development of international relations.

The upshot of this thumbnail historical sketch is the "hypercomplex" global structure we now find ourselves in: a mix of social relations that extend beyond the realm of states and include relations between non-governments, or "nonterritorial actors." Orthodox state centrism is disavowed; no hierarchy within the various sets of relations or actors is identified, the focus being on a general category of "territorial actors." The summary of contemporary global politics refers to the problems that exist within and between *communities*, of differing kinds and at different levels. A theory of international politics is embedded within the discussion, but there is no attempt to substantiate its various elements or address obvious critical responses. The emphasis is on "this quagmire of a human condition."

The text's character is further revealed in the presentation of two underlying themes. The first is that we all know where real happiness and nonviolence lie:

> in a little boy or girl creeping under the quilt of its parents early in the morning, a bundle of joy and warmth; in the eyes of two in love who know they are going to have each other; in the joy of growing, of creating something, in the joy of being a source of joy and growth for others. All of this is nonviolent, inexpensive, liberating, respectful of nature and future generations.[2]

Not intended to be simply an academic treatise, the text appeals to the critical impact of social structure on everyday life: violence, very broadly understood, connects with the most intimate of individual human experiences. In its varying discursive tone, *The True Worlds* reads as the output of a pamphleteer as much as a scholar.[3]

Furthermore, there is hope. The reader is reminded of how *crisis* is written in Chinese—two characters representing the dialectic of danger and opportunity. In Galtung's eyes, the Chinese have acted in full cognizance of this tension, and hope is expressed that we might too. Recalling a phrase used in his earlier work, he offered up *The True Worlds* as an exercise in peace *search* as much as peace research. Galtung was clearly not interested in dwelling too long on the epidemiology of the global crisis, the primary focus of the book being on diagnosis and cure. The question he posed was simply this: Can the world do better?

Two foci were instrumental in the crafting of a response—the eradication of misery and the realization of equality. A shift in current production toward basic needs coupled with a more egalitarian distribution of productive output would, he thought, produce a more tolerable general condition. Implicit in the assumption that production levels should not be simply raised to address deficiencies was a critique of overdevelopment, and Galtung acknowledged that "tolerable" might not be the phrase chosen by the rich in developed countries whose preferred development strategy was simply growth in demand and supply. In contrast, he favored the suppression of superfluous demand (which may be artificially high due to overstimulation) as well as greater exploration and utilization of resources in order to address artificially low supply. In other words, the fixed (relatively absolute) concept of needs could be used to expose the extreme relativity of notions of supply and demand.

The treatment of needs in *The True Worlds* added little to earlier considerations, with one exception. In contrast to the apolitical tone of the discussion of needs elsewhere, here the concept of needs is overtly politicized. Needs provide the basis for a definition of socialism: "a political and economic system that gives top priority to the satisfaction of fundamental needs; starting with those at the bottom." The ambiguity that I have identified as being characteristic of the concept of needs (which is also central to its appeal) appeared now as an explicit dualism: On the one hand, needs are empirical necessities, the satisfaction of which is a "*conditio sine qua non* of continued [human] existence"; on the other, they provide the basis for an alternative politics. But even if there appeared to be a high level of consensus about the existence of certain fundamental human needs and the rightness of fulfilling them, the limits to such agreement were acknowledged by Galtung. Presciently, he saw the problem as being the dilemma that has confronted most socialist states: They fulfill certain fundamental needs of their citizenry, then tend to "run out of program" and resort to mimicry of capitalist countries.[4] At issue then is the possibility of a consensual image of a global good life that consists in more than the fulfillment of the most basic of human needs.

CONSTRUCTING UTOPIA

The True Worlds responds to this question by way of a descriptive adumbration of a preferred global social structure, in which philosophical differences between communities do not necessarily generate a pathology of direct or structural violence. Moral philosophy is sidestepped in favor of the more constructivist path of envisioning the structural accommodation of difference. The move is stalled, however, by the evident fact that the alternative world order is premised upon a set of universal norms—including diversity, equity, justice, and tolerance—the validity of which is taken to be self-evident. Above all, it is assumed that the global order exists, or should be so constructed, to satisfy the needs of all of humanity.

In some eight pages, the reader is given a summary of a number of epistemological and methodological principles that underpin the role of the text as an exercise in constructivism that seeks to illuminate paths to changing reality and to break empirical invariances. The comprehensiveness of Galtung's earlier writings directly concerned with constructivism may be absent, but practical implications are more forcefully drawn out. The relationship between the empirical and potential worlds is first explained by reference to Kolakowski's observations about the attitudes of Poles toward impending Nazi domination prior to World War II.[5] Kolakowski argues that in spite of the might of Hitler's armies, few Poles doubted that Hitler's triumphs would be short-lived, even though they had no rational basis for such optimism, because the impending horror was so great that few could believe it could continue indefinitely. Galtung interpreted this as recognition of the coexistence of empirical and potential reality: "My basic view is that the potential is always present in the empirical, as its twin brother so to speak and that neither can be understood without the other."[6] In also describing the relationship as "dialectical," he alluded to the idea of immanence—the present containing the seeds of its own supersession. However, a more straightforward relationship is suggested by the observation that the present and future worlds are "at a simplistic level . . . the world of facts and the world of values," a view consistent with his earlier inquiry into the potential and the empirical.[7] Yet, he also acknowledged that neither the present nor the future is fully comprehensible without knowledge of both. It is only in the understanding of the possibility of alternatives that the contingency of the present can be grasped.

Nevertheless, no claim to be able to predict or determine the future is made, and once again Galtung distanced himself from determinist varieties of marxism. Recognizing the historical function of such views, he argued for a position somewhere between determinism and the belief that anything is possible; the past and present could both cloud and enlighten our minds. The fight to be free is at the same time a fight against determinism, a struggle to expand the ideational spectrum within which we can conceive of possible futures. No specific alternatives should be privileged, the possibility of conceiving alternatives at all being at issue. In effect, the possibility of another future reduces to the claim that humans are a priori capable of envisioning alternative social orders. In spite of a sensitivity to constraints that the present imposes upon realizing an imagined future— the impact of "deeper social forces"—Galtung distinguished between the *viability* of a utopia were it to be attained and its *attainability*. "Freedom," he declared, is "insight into sufficiency, not . . . necessity." Liberation lay in the very act of refusing the iron cage of the past and present.

The inadequacies of constructivism remained apparent in this particular introduction to it. After all, Kolakowski's observation only confirms that hope springs eternal and on one occasion was rewarded. Clearly it is possible to conceive of another world that is normatively distinct from the present, yet the critical power of such an exercise is dependent upon establishing its reflexive connection with the claimed empirical world. But in Galtung's account the relationship between the empirical world and the preferred or foreseen world lay in the realm of ideas alone. The "essential tool" for investigating the future was a critical-empirical description of the present, providing only a negative image to be transcended in the envisioning of the future. "Methodologically," Galtung argued, he was "left with no choice. . . . To peer into the future with the methods of empirical science means extrapolation and prediction based on extrapolation today points to catastrophe."[8]

At one point *The True Worlds* does reveal a greater sensitivity to the risks of vulgar idealism than was the case in preceding constructivist explorations. Critical reflection on the present was made possible, Galtung argued, by simultaneously conceiving of alternative futures. Thinking critically about empirical reality casts it in a new light and may induce a desire to change it, although its consequences may also remain unacknowledged or not acted upon. It was neither a necessary nor sufficient condition for social change, but he took the view that scientific thought always impacted in some way upon a social order. The interaction between the empirical world and our reflections upon it was not dependent upon an acknowledgment of the relationship. Societies change whether or not we choose to think about them, because internal contradictions can make them self-transcending entities. Equally, culture (the nature of which Galtung did not define) was not a static realm waiting to be acted upon but was innately capable of self-transcendence, although the process may be slow and fitful. Citing the effects of the 1929 stock-market crash, he noted how liberal economic theory was forced to reassert itself and modify some of its central assumptions in order to rationalize the changing economic structure, a process he saw evidenced by the development of Keynesian economics.[9] Structural forces can determine ideas.

Galtung was not about to deny the value of constructing utopias, but he now emphasized the need to be also mindful of unpredictable, structurally induced change that may inhibit their realization. There is a crucial difference between a political program and a prediction, and *The True Worlds* was presented as a prescriptive exercise premised upon a number of mostly negative *conditional* predictions. While intending to present a set of values combined with theories that might show how they can be realized, Galtung openly conceded that we cannot simply identify a set of values and steer a social structure toward a known goal. Approaches such as vulgar empiricism, idealism, and marxism that appeared to assume that societies were made up of lawlike invariances that allowed for completely planned change were rejected implicitly. A more cautious argument was being made, one that echoed Engels's famous observation that we make our own history but not always in circumstances of our choosing.[10]

If this reading is correct, it undermines the simplistic relationship between the actual (facts) and the potential (values) that underpins the concept of constructivism. A tension exists between the desire to construct a methodology of utopian theory and a recognition of the historicity and contingency of social change. Galtung was now acknowledging that societies are inherently dynamic through the interchange of structure, agency, and values; structurally induced change that cannot be directly attributed to conscious action intersects with conscious intervention premised upon certain social values. Nonetheless, having started on such a cautionary note, Galtung went on to eschew close analysis of the determinants of and constraints upon global change and focus exclusively on describing the present prior to constructing a value-impregnated blueprint of a future. Having acknowledged the need for a historical understanding of the present and its relationship with any future, albeit in a circumspect fashion, Galtung reverted to his habitual practice of comparing a critical image of the present with a disconnected vision of a future.

VALUES AND UTOPIA

With regard to the question of values, *The True Worlds* revealed a novel reticence on its author's part: "Are they [values] extracted from old lists of values, handed down through history, tradition, institutions? Are they some author's own favourite formulations, coming out of his particular life-conditions? Are they based on an investigation of public opinion? Are they arrived at by probing into 'fundamental human needs'?"[11] Galtung now confessed to having "no answer to these disturbing questions," opting simply for the explicit statement of one's value premises in order that they may be subjected to scrutiny. In the long term, the solution to establishing social values lay in the creation of a society "so organised that people in general are more free to formulate their own values."

In the end, Galtung was indeed relying on his own "favourite formulations," in particular a preference for value diversity, although that had its limits. The values emphasized were "not anything but a suggestion" yet were also "to some extent developed systematically, not just chosen as a shopping list."[12] At the very least, the long-term goal of greater freedom for individuals to formulate their own values appeared to acknowledge the minimum requirement of a universal ethic of tolerance, as had already been acknowledged in earlier explorations of the values-needs relationship. Clearly, a good world for Galtung was one in which individuals could develop in a variety of ways, which required in turn a multiplicity of societal forms to ensure autonomy *and* participation. Two large questions emerge out of this: How were the values of consensus and diversity to be reconciled, and at what level of social organization was the analysis to be pitched?

Once again the trilateral model of science was brought into the picture in order to explicate the utility of theory in distinguishing between viable and nonviable utopias. *The True Worlds* offered little concrete indication of the kind of theoretical exercise Galtung had in mind, although some clues were provided. Theories should identify the viability of a potential reality by indicating whether "there would not be built-in contradictions that would make it burst to pieces like a radioactive isotope with a very short half-life." Values, or a value complex such as a utopian blueprint, should be tested for internal consistency and compatibility. In what amounted to the description of moral reasoning in a scientized language, science itself was cast in the role of value realization instead of fact confirmation, and the philosophical assumptions underpinning the exercise remained exempted from external scrutiny.

A second, interventionist and constructivist function of theory was to create opportunities for realizing potential worlds, in contrast to the orthodox view that theorizing was concerned with identifying invariances. If empirical research indicated that a society could not be both rich and egalitarian, then there was no obligation to accept this as invariant. The constructivist approach was to change those parameters that ostensibly determine certain invariances and thereby sunder them. Unfortunately, Galtung provided scant insight into what such invariance breaking activity might entail or how the process of invariance breaking *in theory* connected with the transformation of the empirical world. Again, the resort to a scientistic discourse provided an escape route from the tag of idealism, and the construction of theoretical utopias was cast in a practical, consequential light. To claim that the act of conceiving of social alternatives is at once practical as well as philosophical was, of course, hardly new. In Galtung's case, however, epistemological issues were but a preface to be hurriedly passed over in the move toward exploring the blueprint itself.

The Formation of Goals

Three fundamental changes were central to Galtung's utopia: a shift away from the capitalist mode of production; a shift away from "bigness and verticality," from alpha to beta; and a downgrading of the territorial mode of social organization. His vision could be distinguished from comparable varieties of utopianism by a refusal, in the name of eclecticism, to offer too fixed an alternative vision. But the looseness of his vision had its costs. Other political philosophies (notably marxism) offered an account of the *origins* of undesirable forms of socioeconomic organization that provided a basis for constructing a countervailing praxis. Galtung drew upon a range of critical accounts, including marxism, but his essentially descriptive approach was incapable of identifying a *politics* of social transformation, although he did sketch the outlines of some strategies of transition from the actual to the preferred worlds that I address later.

The "world goals" underpinning his utopian blueprint emerged from the combining of actor-oriented and structure-oriented perspectives, as represented by liberalism and marxism respectively. Whereas earlier considerations of this process had stressed the similarities between the two political philosophies, on this occasion he emphasized their differences. The argument that both perspectives are individually inadequate was also reiterated, although no synthesis was deemed to be available and the two perspectives were cast as complementary conceptual tools, with Galtung clearly leaning toward the structural account. This bias cannot be entirely explained either by the fact that Galtung's analysis of imperialism was structural in form or by his evident sympathies with marxism's focus on exploitation. A full explanation requires the recalling of the influence of Gandhi.

In my discussion of the foundations of the concept of structural violence, I noted that in some of his earliest sociological writings Galtung had emphasized a distinction between "status actions" and "status holders."[13] As a pacifist inspired by the Gandhian conception of universal love, Galtung sought to develop prescriptions that did not advocate violent responses to violence. The concept of structural violence contributed to this purpose by locating the origins of violence in social structure rather than its human agents. This theme was revisited in *The True Worlds* with regard to the origins of the "evil" of violence. Galtung argued that by focusing on human action and intention, an actor-oriented perspective depicts evil as the product of malicious intent. A structure-oriented view, on the other hand, locates evil in the structural context within which humans act. Consequently, the two perspectives lead to differing remedies for violence: The actor-oriented perspective promotes prophylactic or therapeutic remedies that are designed to punish, deter, or treat the wrongdoer (analogies for which can be found in foreign policies premised upon the domino theory and military deterrence); the preferred structural approach invites the singular response of changing the structure. The problem of guilt can be dismissed as metaphysical and the condemnatory institutions of morality and legality condemned as superficial, even detrimental, because they draw attention away from real causes. Galtung's distaste for engaging in moral argument was again evident here, but it arose this time from a prior normative distaste for apportioning blame. No attempt was made to address the implications of ascribing to structures a capacity to do or bear responsibility for evil, even though in considering relations between states as structures, for example, he offered a rich furrow to plough—public discourse frequently attributes moral responsibility to states. Instead, Galtung attributed moral agency to abstracted social structures of uncertain ontological status, in an echo of the populist aphorism "don't blame the victim, blame the system." As I will show in Chapter 8, the possible moral reasoning that lay behind Galtung's stance on evil and guilt emerges more fully only after a subsequent (in terms of date of publication at least) turn to Buddhist philosophy—in particular the disavowal of a personal soul. Even then a characteristic ambiguity would be retained.

Some inkling of an ethics might also be drawn from Galtung's reading of how the two perspectives treat time. From an actor-oriented perspective, time is discontinuous and "dotted with acts." In contrast, a structural perspective focuses on the continuous and apparently permanent.[14] Paradoxically, when it comes to solutions, the two perspectives interchange their time perspective: The actor-oriented perspective responds to evil by advocating the establishment of a moral or legal institution of some permanence, whereas a structural perspective promotes the discontinuous, revolutionary act of breaking down the undesirable social structure. This is seen to reflect contrasting conceptions of the good. From an actor-oriented perspective, what is good for individuals (or the subsystem) is good for the overall system. For the structuralist, the reverse is the case. In the end Galtung refused to choose, a decision that appeared to reflect, on face value at least, a perception of their continuing utility as distinctive sources of analytical or ethical judgment. Notably absent was any interrogation of the claims of structurally oriented accounts to negate the utility of liberal individualism or vice versa. Another explanation, in my view the more plausible, stems from the uncomfortable coexistence in Galtung's unspoken philosophy of an evident hostility to individualism with regard to the critique of the present and the centrality of individual freedom and creativity in his vision of a preferred future.

Actor-Oriented Goals

From an actor-oriented point of view, two facets of individual human existence come into view: being and having. What Galtung wanted was a more developed understanding of the internal and external needs of individuals. "I should like," he said, "to deepen the being side to include more internal characteristics and expand the "having" side to include less material aspects of human life. . . . Sometimes they [individuals] *are* only if they *have* more, sometimes only if they do not have more."[15]

A curious dimension to this theme arises from Galtung's suggestion that the principle of isomorphism could be brought into play here because the distinction between having and being applied also to nations and states, whose internal and external needs were deemed comparable with those of any other social actor. Although he now admitted that the principle of isomorphism applied loosely at best, one of his stated intentions was to construct a unified vocabulary applicable across levels of analysis.[16] In his early work, such a unified vocabulary was developed through the application of functionalist small-group theory to the analysis of relations between states. Although the international system exhibited certain distinctive characteristics (the principle of territoriality being a notable example), these were understood as not reflecting any essential difference but a historical-developmental lag—hence Galtung's characteristic depiction of the international system as a feudal social order. *The True Worlds* did not employ the language of the earlier discussion, but it retained the image of the international system as a premodern social formation amenable to a process of social development comparable to that found within domestic societies. By extension, world goals could be derived from domestic social principles and applied to the global level. Equally, in depicting states as in some sense needy and, furthermore, varying in their preoccupation with being or having, Galtung also was alluding to a moral typology of state forms. It was not a theme that he pursued very far, although, as we shall see, it was to reappear on occasions.

An actor-oriented perspective emphasized the primordial goal of "personal growth" or human fulfillment, the corollary of which was the value of diversity.[17] In spite of the rider that self-realization should not be taken to imply a commitment to Western individualism, Galtung admitted that it was a rather Western notion. It is, of course, a tenet of classical Western liberalism, grounded in the ontological supremacy of the individual. Galtung's individualist sympathies were distinguished, however, by the freeing of the principle of individual autonomy from its origins in an argument for the rights of individuals within a liberal-democratic state and further modified by the emphasis on being over having. But the objective was not to substitute one dimension of personal development with another. The defense of diversity is taken, in part, from Sorokin (whose distinction between ideational and sensate cultures Galtung claimed to resemble his own schema) and his vision of an unintegrated, eclectic culture, with a minimal infrastructure, within which islands of different cultural types could coexist. Given such a setting, individuals should have the freedom to settle within their preferred cultural arena. Nonetheless, the value of *having* requires limitation on ecological grounds because of the finiteness of the material world, the tendency to inequity and injustice in an untrammeled race to acquire material wealth, and the subsequent impairment of other facets of human existence.

Galtung's Nordic origins were reflected in a brief critical commentary on the social-democratic corrective to "untamed, rampant liberalism." Social democracy bridged the realms of having and being by introducing principles of equitable distribution and social justice into the liberal equation. However, the exemplary social-democratic state—Sweden—remained flawed because it fulfilled only the minimal requirements of its citizens, inadequately limited consumption overall, and encouraged social stratification through the unequal provision of resources. The provision of minimal standards of health and education, for example, was insufficient if only a few could exceed the minima and enjoy either genuinely creative work or excellent health. His love of mathematics notwithstanding, Galtung rejected a quantitative definition of equality, preferring a more abstract rendition of it as the "low dispersion of having" in response to acknowledged difficulties in developing paths to the pursuit of equality. The goal was equality as a lasting condition, as opposed to equality at some starting point. Overall consumption could be limited, perhaps, by setting production goals as the multiple of a standardized minimum individual living standard, an impossible goal in a market economy where production is guided by the assumption that demands equal needs. But viewing social rationality as the aggregate of individual rationality revealed "the naivete of pure actor-oriented thinking." Social structure made a mockery of such assumptions, since it distributed the products of labor upward while failing to satisfy the fundamental needs of those at the bottom of the social pile.

A further weakness in an actor-oriented perspective stemmed from its incapacity to capture the necessary structural preconditions of personal growth. Galtung castigated it as utopian, since without significant structural change the values promoted could be enjoyed only by a few. Again, Sweden was criticized for substituting redistribution for structural reform—a "liberal answer to a liberal problem."[18] Classical liberalism acknowledged but could not resolve the tension between having and being, and to this can be added an ecological problem: "Having may stand in the way of having, there may be limits or ceilings on growth."[19] Against the liberal understanding of social justice as an "equality of having" realized through growth, Galtung posited an account of social justice as the independence of what one *has* from what one *is*, again a distinction deemed applicable to individuals, nations, and states.

Structure-Oriented Goals

Galtung's discussion of structurally generated goals in *The True Worlds* essentially reproduces, in condensed form, the main themes of much of his work since the introduction of the concept of structural violence and the structural theory of imperialism. A structure-oriented perspective interrogates the uneven accumulation of resources using the concepts of equal and unequal exchange. This leads to the goal of equal exchange with regard to both the having and being dimensions of all the parties to an interactive relationship. Galtung saw this as ensuring that both accumulation and personal (or national) growth would be equal.[20] However, certain liberal and marxist responses to the problem of exchange had to be rejected because of their occidental "economistic, outer-man oriented thinking." The theme of "in-change" found in Galtung's earlier analysis of exploitation reappears here. Although he conceded that the concept of alienation pointed in the right direction, marxism's critique of exploitation largely focused on expropriation between actors in an exploitative exchange relationship and insufficiently considered the uneven, internal consequences—spin-offs—of unequal exchange whether it be between states or individuals.

A structural perspective highlights the goals (values) of equity and autonomy. For Galtung, autonomy is "power over oneself"—a capacity to inoculate oneself against the power of others. The antidotes to the ideological, remunerative, and punitive forms of power (producing submissiveness, dependency, and fear, respectively) are the attributes of self-respect, self-sufficiency, and fearlessness. In a world order dominated by the powerful, various efforts to develop a philosophy of national self-reliance were already evident, the writings of Gandhi, Mao Zedong, and Korea's Kim Il Sung being cited as examples. In the case of the latter two, Galtung's silence on the absence of his treasured goal of individual autonomy and growth within these collectivist, statist, and profoundly undemocratic models of self-reliant development was deafening. He quite literally took Mao and Kim at their word.

By considering interaction patterns, further structure-oriented values could be identified. Again, familiar themes were being reiterated: Simple asymmetric interaction patterns fragment social actors, and horizontal interaction marginalizes weak actors. What was needed were complex multilateral and horizontal interaction patterns that reflected the values of "solidarity" and "participation," the antonyms of fragmentation and marginalization. By combining these with "autonomy" and "equity," a structurally derived, fourfold lexicon of values can be generated. Furthermore, the four goals were presented as general characteristics of social interaction, applicable at all levels of analysis.[21]

The Taxonomy of Goals

The two dialectically connected perspectives were presented not merely as analytical devices but as reflections of social life itself. Galtung's objective was not restricted to the advocacy of evenly balanced analytical eclecticism, for constructivism's purpose was to transcend concrete social existence through the conceptualization and realization of an alternative global social order. In combination, the values derived from both the actor and structural perspectives enabled the adumbration of a synthetic, normative "theory of society." The list of values was part of "an effort to escape from the current schizophrenia in social analysis whereby different families of terms and concepts are drawn upon for those three aspects [data collection, theory formation, and value realization] of scientific activity."[22]

Unfortunately, the attempt at synthesis proceeded in a convoluted manner, with anything resembling a theory of society hard to discern. The lack of clarity arose from the introduction of a further taxonomy of concepts—power, development, conflict, and peace. Galtung wanted to show how they related to each other as well as to sets of values. Thus, "power" was subdivided into innate, resource, and structural power, which in combination generated what he felt was a plausible image of the contemporary world order. Types of power were convertible into other types, and this contributed to the overall accumulation of power in the hands of specific social actors at the top of a global social structure. Such a world was one in which inequality, injustice, exploitation, penetration, and fragmentation exist, and realization of the preferred values requires us to "work for a reduction of the power differential." This was simply a summary of what Galtung had long been arguing: A better world would be structured more symmetrically, horizontally and equitably. A preferable model of development entailed the realization of all values and therefore a reduction in the power differential. Alternatively, development could also be described as "social growth" in the holistic, Galtungian sense. Again, nothing new was being added here—concepts were defined by reference to other concepts that seemed to mean essentially the same thing. The abolition of unequal power was not, however, an argument for the eradication of power itself but for a shift in its locus. The reduction of power over others results in an increase in power over oneself; the less difference in power there is, the greater autonomy there must be. The objective was to flatten the power landscape, with the exception of innate power, the power of *being*, which because of the decline of dominance could be given freer rein.

Galtung did not elucidate the precise character of innate, or being, power. At one point it is described in terms of certain innate characteristics—such as charisma, intelligence, or strength—that enable an actor (again, not only individual humans) to use bargaining and force to its advantage. But would not a more equitable dispersal of other forms of power simply enable the innately advantaged to use their power to serve their own interests, thereby resurrecting the earlier rugged topography of power? For this not to be the case, innate power must be accompanied by a specific philosophical orientation on the part of actors who possess it. Galtung briefly alluded to such a response:

> There will be diverse personalities as well as diverse societies with varying appeal. Their power will be normative or "moral" as they will not have a resource surplus or structural advantages at their disposal to back it up. . . . This is not so far fetched as it sounds, it is already the case in many places, particularly at the top of the world in countless meetings and committee rooms . . . where ability to project what is inside a person is what counts. It is true to a considerable degree among Nordic countries and to some extent among the European Community countries.[23]

On face value, this comment appears vulnerable to his own argument. In spite of the apparent lack of surplus or structural power, that presence of innate power at the "top of the world" nonetheless suggests that "moral" power is the privilege only of those who are powerful in other respects. Alternatively, the supposedly moral power of the Nordic states might solely be a pragmatic response to a lack of structural power, a common assumption in explanations of the actions of small or middle powers noted for their morally informed worldviews. Good states, it is often said, are small states. In either case, on what basis are we to suppose that moral power would survive in a more horizontal world order?

Galtung's vision of a less rugged global topography of power necessarily presupposed either a constraining institutional framework that is also powerful in some sense or other, or the authentic holding by some states of a philosophy of social action that disavows or at least markedly downgrades the acquisition or employment of negative forms of power. As to institutional formation, Galtung remained open-minded, seeing the shape of any institutional framework as having to respond to varying conditions. With regard to political philosophy he was silent. This was unfortunate because the brief reference to the innate moral power of certain states alluded to more substantive themes that developed further might have added some flesh to the bones of the argument. Two suggest themselves: First, there seems to be a Habermasian assumption about the moral power of reason itself (the unforced force of the better argument) in conditions of meaningful interactor dialogue; second, there seems to be an allusion to an internal cultural account of the behavior of collective actors— to what I would call a theory of the "good state." Regarding the latter, Galtung appeared to be courting a version of what Waltz has pejoratively described as a "second image" argument, in which the behavior of states is explained endogenously rather than exogenously.[24] On this view, certain states can and do acquire authority by virtue not of their material power alone, or even at all, but as a consequence of the externalization of internal moral virtue and consistency and the respect that flows from this.[25] This would provide an interesting corrective to Galtung's structural, primarily exogenous account of actor behavior. However, he got to this point by isomorphically transposing an underexplored individual psychology onto collective actors such as states. A more fruitful route might have been to examine comparatively the political culture and social structures within certain states in order to examine *why* some states appear to act with a greater sensitivity to moral dictates than others—an anthropology of innate power. No such exploration was even tentatively undertaken, hardly surprising given that the state was to have little place in his preferred world.

THE PREFERRED WORLD

The True Worlds makes it clear that, for Galtung at least, peace research cannot be understood as research in the traditional sense, for it no longer is intended to operate under the canons of mainstream social science; its agenda is avowedly programmatic and constructivist. It seeks to realize a world in which the supreme value is self-realization or personal growth, in conditions of structural autonomy.

Galtung's vision of a preferred world order is expressed in terms of the four societal types that we looked at in Chapter 6. The image he had in mind was a *"world that is a model 4 global community of model 4 societies* (which in turn are a collection of model 3 communities). In other words, a world where equity and diversity are the basic rules, a world where exploitation and repression are effectively counteracted—and also a world that would find sufficient two levels of organisation, the domestic and the global."[26] Domestic social orders would be diverse and equitable, acknowledging difference but forbidding any form of exploitation at any level and across any relationship. A prerequisite, therefore, is a postcapitalist economic order, based upon equitable exchange. As a consequence, such a society would not be wealthy compared to contemporary developed societies, but, he boldly asserted, the days of Western concepts of material wealth were probably numbered. Mobility of people and information between communities was essential and should be freely available. Societies would be obliged to guarantee a minimum level of subsistence, with no obligation on the part of inhabitants to sell their labor. Such freedom would be facilitated by the use of automation, the resources for which were available but deployed on such things as military hardware. Leisure and work would blend into each other and both would be enriching processes, with automation also being used as a means for eliminating alienation of labor. Education would have to prepare future inhabitants for all of this, and its tasks would include the promotion of dissimilarity, inconstancy, and inconsistency as social values. It would have to be free and freely available, a feature Galtung sees as potentially realizable (and almost realized) in some existing model 2 (liberal-capitalist) societies. Finally, politics would not be viewed as a profession but returned to the populace for citizens to participate in, but only if they so desired.

This image of domestic societies was presented in the loosest of terms, and it is debatable how much scrutiny it was intended to sustain. Sweeping in its vision and the scale of reform anticipated, many of its themes could be located within identifiable political philosophies, in particular radical forms of liberalism, utopian socialism, and anarchism. Its realization would entail the total restructuring of existing socioeconomic orders, particularly those of the liberal-democratic West. It entailed a blending of two broad value ideas—freedom and equity—but the complexities of the synthesis were explored only with regard to their institutional implications.

The overall vision was also far from precise. Ostensibly developed around two fundamental levels of social organization—the domestic and the global—the vision in fact required three: the global, the societal, and the communal. "Societal" appears to connote some form of poststate organization, whereas "communal" clearly refers to the subsocietal level. Consequently, it is difficult to discern precisely what was meant by the "domestic" realm. Within specific model 4 *societies* would be model 3 (communal-socialist) *communities* some of which might not reflect Galtung's preference for untrammeled diversity and individuation but, in accordance with those same principles, must be allowed to exist. In other words, there is a tension between the commitments to tolerance and to freedom. For example, Galtung's advocacy of sexual liberation might not be shared by all, yet those who would prefer to live by an explicit and restrictive code of sexual conduct must in principle be allowed to do so: "Freedom to practice what one believes would have to be given the status of a human right in model 4 society." Of course, such a freedom might also cut across the taboo on all forms of exploitation. Similarly, Galtung's definition of economic exploitation may be disputed, vigorously defended, subordinated to other ethical precepts, or simply not recognized as such by others. Galtung assumed that no person who truly comprehended his or her situation would wish to be exploited. What was missing was a consideration of the means by which communal or societal values would be publicly generated and, further, how they would coexist across different levels of social organization. After all, certain religious and moral codes enshrine social hierarchies—in Galtungian terms, vertical social interactions—on the grounds that they are part of a God-given or natural order of things. Given that subsocietal communities were defined as type 3, the principle of equity appeared to take precedence over that of diversity at the local level at least. But if the principle of diversity were to be strictly applied, then those who so wished it would have to be allowed to live in inequality. If not, then a preventative structure would have to be created, and that would raise a number of uncomfortable questions with regard to Galtung's consistent taboos on violence and domination.

The escape clause from the tension between equity and diversity was provided in the form of a principle of unhindered movement for individuals between communities. Consequently, Galtung's vision required the decisive abandonment of orthodox conceptions of sovereign statehood and citizenship, although he made no attempt to consider the complex ethical issues emerging out of the conflict between the right to leave and a right to enter, between the cosmopolitan principle of free movement of peoples and the communitarian defense of rights of membership of bounded communities. His preferred world would to all intents and purposes be borderless, apparently without refugees and consisting of numerous small societies. These would be smaller than most contemporary states. Here the concept of beta development comes into play, for it was only in small social units that he thought that the distance between ruler and ruled could be contained in order to preserve "self-expression" for all. Thus, currently large and powerful states should be subdivided, and the resulting multitude of small societies would be enmeshed in a web of nonterritorial organizations. Gandhi was credited with the view that if the fundamental social units were good, then everything else would sort itself out through "oceanic circles of cooperation." But even Galtung had to concede that such faith was hard to share given that aggressive small units could not be ruled out, although they may conduct correspondingly small wars.[27] There would, however, be structural constraints upon the recourse to direct violence within a network of symbiotic relationships—striking out at others could become tantamount to striking oneself. Thus, in spite of the difficulties of conceiving of a global social order entirely devoid of direct violence and aggressive conflict between communities, Galtung proposed the abolition of all restrictions on human movement, such as visas and passports, and the transformation of citizenship into something akin to voluntary membership. The sole acknowledged constraint was that a trial period might be retained. Alternatively, multiple citizenship, or no citizenship at all, might be possible, depending upon individual whim.

Finally, there would need to be some globalization in the form of a "central world authority" designed to carry out the essential planning and administrative functions that would necessarily arise from the territorial and political reorganization envisaged. The institutionalization of the principle of the global commons as a basis for managing global resources such as the seabeds and oceans would be one such function; another would be the development of a policing capacity, although the employment of more familiar "disassociative" approaches to peace designed to keep conflicting parties separate—such as peacekeeping and the enforced border—was not ruled out. Ideally, peacekeeping should henceforth reflect the guiding principles of social organization: It would have to be symmetric, equitable, and unconstrained by traditional concepts of regional and state inviolability.

It would require the training of "some experts in the control of violence" with a transcendent loyalty pitched at the global level, whose "dedication has to be to human beings, to save them and protect them from all kinds of violence."[28] The Hippocratic theme that underscored the founding vision of the peace researcher was being revived here, but Galtung's vision also required an alternative understanding of individual and collective obligation that transcended both existing concepts of citizenship and future loyalties to poststatist forms of societal and communal organization. A peacekeeping force made up of national contingents (the current United Nations model) did not represent a truly global loyalty; rather, there would need to be a prehistory of training and experience during which a global loyalty could be inculcated. This would best be achieved, Galtung suggested, by a permanent force of considerable size, although he paid little mind to the question of the legitimacy of such a monopoly of force.

But Is It Viable?

Viability is to be judged, Galtung averred, partly as a function of stability over time. Viability was possible even if the project ultimately failed: "It may also be argued that if it lasts sufficiently long to give a meaningful experience to its members it has already proved itself to be viable—like many hippie communities."[29] He referred also to the "mechanism of duration," or the *source* of viability: Is it external to the community, or an internal, organic, and self-supporting condition? His preference was for the latter, although during transition periods a limited constraint upon leaving the new social order may be required.

Once again, Galtung missed the opportunity to explore some substantive issues concerning agency and structure—for example, issues arising out of the notion of a "mechanism of duration." Instead he opted for the trivial and anecdotal, thereby creating the distinct impression that when it came to assessing the plausibility of his vision of a preferred world, a world true to his values, his creative energies were running out of steam. If the "hippie community" is taken as exemplary, then global transformation seems not to be seriously contemplated. What would be a global "meaningful experience" that could ultimately fail but have been insightful nonetheless? The only evidence cited in support of claims to viability was the existential capacity of small communities "down to the size of one family or one person" to survive. The assumption of isomorphism was stretched to the extreme in the absence of more substantive argument.

A modicum of realism was restored in the recognition that the principal threats to viability lay in the various forms of violence. Galtung referred briefly to debates about the origins of violence in human social orders (in contrast to his more usual focus on the character of violence itself), in particular the claim that dominance (structural violence) and aggression (direct violence) are the products of indelible biological or psychological human instincts. Such arguments were seen to reflect a Western, actor-oriented, social cosmology and were rejected by him on the grounds that whereas some human instincts—such as the search for food, shelter, and procreation—were independent of historical and social context, the instinct for aggression was not.

Alternatively, it could be argued that innate aggression was triggered by certain external conditions, and the prevention of violence therefore entailed identifying those conditions that would inhibit this. Galtung saw this sensitivity to environmental determinants of violence as a step in the right direction and also testable, although the evidence was inconclusive. Often claimed as determinants of aggression, territoriality, hierarchy, and overcrowding were only correlates of an increase in violence. For Galtung, such explanations constituted rationalizations of a status quo characterized by centralized, hierarchical nation-states and as such, he claimed, were popular with "military and other status-quo oriented groups in status-quo oriented countries." Even so, the connection between environment or structure and aggression had to be retained as part of the argument for the need for an alternative social order. Galtung modified it in two important respects: The definition of violence included structural violence, and it was premised upon a conception of human nature as essentially benevolent. This made us "perfectly capable of living in a non-aggressive, non-domineering manner."[30] Typically, the latter was merely asserted, and Galtung's argument against those who hold to a pessimistic view of human nature can be turned against him: Given that some people are violent under a variety of conditions, can it not equally be assumed that all causes of violence are external to the perpetrator?

Galtung held that our natural human benevolence could indeed be thwarted by certain social structures, in contrast to the view that structures bring out our innate malevolence. The debate between peace researchers and ethologists therefore consisted, he thought, in the identification of what those structures actually are and should be. Thus, Galtung saw the kinds of structures identified by Lorenz and others who depicted aggression as innate to be the opposite of those he preferred. But there is another issue involved here. Lorenz cites Kant's enthusiasm for *Vernunft* (reason and, according to Lorenz, common sense), upon which the categorical imperative is predicated, as an example of emotion creeping into a logical argument. For Lorenz, the belief that it is self-evident that one reasonable human being would not want to kill another—implying therefore that a natural drive would be constrained by the recognition of a logical contradiction—confuses reason with what he sees as moral instinct. He argues that morality derives its energy from primal sources and that reason alone cannot provide goals. Humans respect benefactors more if they feel that acts of friendship reflect a natural inclination rather than a purely rational decision to be friendly.[31] This raises an important question, to which Galtung gave no clear answer. Was he claiming that humans are essentially benevolent because they are rational, or was it the product of a primal, moral drive? The difference between Galtung and the ethologists persuaded by a conception of human nature as consisting in primal drives is that for Galtung, apparently operating upon a notion of a damaged or suppressed innate human goodness, the exercise of discovering other forms of social structure is not preventative but restorative and creative.[32] This view speaks to an emancipatory form of reasoning, upon which rests the viability of his project, but its origin and form were left unexplored.

Strategies of Transition

Armed as he was with only a sketch of the origins of the contemporary global crisis and an inconclusive depiction of human motivation, Galtung offered a discussion of transitional strategies in *The True Worlds* that was particularly weak. He conceded that an extrapolation of existing social trends cast doubt on the attainability of his preferred world but maintained there were grounds for optimism nonetheless. Simple extrapolation was naive; just as forces produce counterforces, so too do trends produce countertrends.[33] Wisely, he acknowledged that it could not be assumed that a countertrend would necessarily lean in the direction of the preferred world: "I believe that society possesses no *Naturgesetzlichkeit* . . . that we are guaranteed neither bliss nor catastrophe, neither Paradise nor Inferno." This led to a second point: We live in a "double world" of empirical and potential reality in which human beings are prone "to develop consciousness of goals as well as existing reality with its instabilities and trends and to engage in concerted action, based on this consciousness." The possibility of a preferred future lay in the combination of "some trends" and "deliberate goal-directed action."[34]

It is the precise nature of the agency-structure mix that matters, however, rather than the banality of simply noting that it exists. Galtung's imprecise notion of a "consciousness of goals" is unsatisfying, reflecting yet again a normative disposition rather than cogent argument. Galtung did not address the self-evidently ideological dimensions of a consciousness deemed to be the progenitor of meaningful political action. This reflected a long-standing refusal to be identified unequivocally with existing ideological labels, although what he understood by an ideology or a perspective has always been something of a mystery, a product perhaps of his preference for a taxonomically tidy two-ness. He frequently appeared to hold the view that reality itself was merely a construct, delimited by the chosen ideology or perspective (actor or structure oriented). All perspectives were criticized for their ideologically driven incompleteness as accounts of the social life-world, even if they offered useful analytical insights. By extension, any "potential reality" must be equally mediated by specific and partial interpretations of the present, unless an escape from the binds of ideology and partiality can be demonstrated. Contrary to the assertions of true believers in a science of the social (including the young Galtung), this would be a remarkable achievement.

For all of their analytical blind spots and silences, political ideologies offer an account of the relationship between past, present, and future within or against which an understanding of the reflexive political subject can be developed. Galtung's purportedly antiideological posture robbed his account of this vital function, in spite of its unequivocally political aspirations. Even though his analysis of the prevailing human condition in *The True Worlds* clearly empathized with specific social groupings, he also declared that any social theory that privileged "a limited category of the inhabitants of society" was to be rejected "regardless of how well it may have corresponded with facts in the past." The truth content of a social theory was thus subordinated to the moral requirement that social theories did not "introduce a new vertical distinction in society between those designated to be the *force motrice* of history and those not."[35] Any theory that did not uphold this antiexclusionary principle could not in his judgment be a peace theory. The imposition of this normative constraint upon theory rendered any systematic investigation and defense of agents or strategies of transformation difficult, to say the least. In the end, the forces for social change were to be determined purely normatively rather than through the analysis of historical possibility.

In *The True Worlds* the preconditions for theorizing the possibility of social change were seen to arise from the existence of unfulfilled human needs, since a combination of perspectives on needs generated an understanding of a social condition marked by multiple contradictions. In specific cases, there may be an overriding contradiction that should be the first target of attack. For Galtung, identification of the dominant contradiction was to be obtained by asking "*how much* it impedes the satisfaction of *how basic* needs for *how many*."[36] On that basis alone he concluded, in a syntactical genuflection to Maoist political discourse, that capitalist imperialism was "contradiction number one." But this offered no substantial indication of a politics of change; within a description of the problem was buried the normative argument for its eradication—courtesy of the ambiguous concept of human needs. Galtung admitted that the prescriptions he offered focused overwhelmingly on what should be done and why, at the expense of considerations upon who should do it, how, when, and where. By and large, his proposals consisted of taxonomies of alternative practices in which analysis of their viability was noticeably absent. The virtues of the various transitional strategies lay simply in the fact that they are supposedly well known (under different names) and some have been tried with success. There is "nothing mysterious or esoteric about them," and they require only that people "understand, organise and act in manners that are perfectly rational and reasonable."[37]

I shall not consider the technical feasibility of the various proposals, given that their presentation was both highly speculative in tone and drawn in very broad strokes. Instead I want to focus on the discussion of the agents of transformation. According to Galtung, they are to be identified by way of two "scanning devices"—motivation and capability. Motivation arises out of a condition of deprivation and despair that only becomes energizing if an alternative can be perceived and therefore individual and collective frustrated expectations will arise. This may result in limited attempts by individual actors to improve their circumstances, but "it may also lead to a more genuine political consciousness and group action. . . . Political man and woman are capable of solidarity, of collective identification beyond private goals."[38] The adjective "political" suggested that a necessary condition for motivation was a specific form of consciousness, but Galtung's understanding of the political was buried within the concept of an alternative vision offered by those such as himself.

In assessing the question of capability, Galtung saw a disjunction between motivation and power. His disinterest in siding with specific social actors resulted in the presentation of opponents of change as being devoid of motivation or insight rather than possessed of a competing and incompatible vision backed by power. A commitment to preserving one's interests by shoring up the status quo is presented in negative terms, in accordance with Galtung's normative disposition, but he offered no critical analysis of the ideological premises of antireformism or its tenacity. He appeared to assume that if alternatives could be articulated and shown to be viable, their appeal was self-evident. In the case of the arms race, for example, he argued that although numerous conferences were held, involving the most significant actors in the military-industrial complex, the results are negligible due not to a lack of power but a lack of motivation. He failed to consider the obvious retort that this supposed lack of motivation can equally be interpreted as a *different* motivation that might well produce results, but not those that Galtung would like.

Galtung located the key to change in the decision by key actors—research scientists working on weapons systems, for example—to upset the equilibrium. Similarly, the oppressed, underprivileged, and exploited should engage in mass action; political space existed and therefore action is possible. The target of such action, however, was not to be other people but the structures of oppression that continue to exist partly because of some complicity on the part of their victims. But why do those whose actions would have such a transformative effect not act, given that they are also depicted as those most motivated to do so? According to Galtung's logic, it is not because they are without power in the orthodox sense but because they are not empowered by any vision of an alternative reality. The ostensible implication, again, is that those who do not seek change are

simply lacking in motivation (i.e., vision), but it is equally plausible to
suppose that their error is that of being wrongly motivated, at least from a
Galtungian point of view. In the attempt both to avoid advocating conflict
and to escape ideological labeling, Galtung offered little more than a presumption of a mysterious capacity of visions to empower.

As I have already noted, Galtung was resistant to the notion that a definitive historical agent could or should be identified. When all was said
and done, this amounted to a rejection of the class politics of the orthodox
Left. Although Galtung did himself subdivide humanity into two broad
groups—the oppressed and nonoppressed, or exploiters and exploited—his
argument also secreted an overriding ethical cosmopolitanism. His depiction of "overdevelopment" painted us all as victims, actual or potential, of
the general phenomenon of "maldevelopment." The principal weapon
against the center-periphery structural formations that were the ultimate
cause of violent maldevelopment was the doctrine of self-reliance. This
carried a large, perhaps an impossible, burden in Galtung's exploration of
an alternative politics. Self-reliance was a general principle of social *action* and the bedrock of an alternative practice; it was the fundamental
principle of peace politics. It was not merely an abstract formula but a historical process that required mass action. Nor was it the same as self-sufficiency or autarchy. Self-reliance was defined as both a "psychopolitical"
and socioeconomic category and appeared in effect to be a substitute for
political philosophy itself. It was concerned with the enunciation of specific principles of social interaction, and it expressed an ideal social
arrangement that reflected a number of normative principles, particularly
equality and personal development (with a further range of normative
themes further subsumed within the latter). Self-reliance was not just a national strategy of action but also an expression of an individual human
condition. Yet, it was not simply a philosophy of individualism because,
for Galtung, self-reliance was a principle of equitable social *interaction*.

How then does one achieve the ultimate tripartite vision of peace, development, and self-reliance? *The True Worlds* concluded by outlining
some broad parameters within which a peace politics could be conceived:

1. History should be seen as a process, not a structure. Current efforts
    to realize preferred futures are part of a historical stream and not
    indicative of an impending and dramatic turning point.
2. There is a need to cultivate a global consciousness that expresses a
    dedication to all of humanity but also recognizes the primacy of
    those most in need.
3. All levels of action are relevant.
4. The drive for peace should avoid creating new vertical divisions of
    labor—different capacities and opportunities should be recognized
    but not translated into terms of power or prestige or both.
5. Both actor-oriented and structure-oriented strategies are relevant.

6. Peace action must be spontaneously generated.

In sum, the model of a professionalized peace research developed in Galtung's earlier work was now depicted as a species of caste formation, resulting in unacceptable social fragmentation. As members of a professional and intellectual elite claiming authoritative knowledge, peace researchers could themselves be carriers of a form of structural violence given that they may set themselves up as monopolizers of knowledge.[39] What was now needed was a set of new "peace-strategic" roles that could "distribute democratically the tasks of peace." These included citizens' initiatives—"a plurality of revolutions at the micro level"; noncooperation with corporations and government agencies; the rendering transparent of the workings of society; and the application of science and technology to the fulfillment of human needs.[40]

CONCLUSION

For all of its activist sentiments and avowedly political tone, *The True Worlds* exhibited residual continuities with the founding conception of peace research in its hostility to any semblance of ideological contamination. Whereas this was previously a corollary of positivism, here it was the product of an overriding normative opposition to any form of ideological domination and a commitment to the value of diversity. As to what constituted the primary explanation of Galtung's version of "anti-political politics," the answer remained unclear.[41]

Galtung resorted ultimately to the restating of a comprehensive set of human needs that could be translated into world goals. True to the requirements of constructivism, this value set was used to criticize the present world order and judge proposals for an alternative world order, one example of which was offered up for scrutiny. But just as the constructivist model of science elided a defense of adopted values, so too did *The True Worlds*. A value set was posited, the present world was critically described (but not explained), and a blueprint of a preferred world was offered. Absent was the philosophical cement that might bind the disparate elements. *The True Worlds* did not provide a compelling argument in defense of its normative foundations, offering little to persuade the skeptical reader. In this respect, it reads as a strangely disengaged text.

Galtung did allude to a foundational philosophical stratum in his claim that diversity—as a creative force and a world goal—was a prerequisite of human fulfillment. Equally, the recognition of a need for a specific form of consciousness in order to effect global transformation suggests that people seek some form of authentic self-understanding. Galtung commendably sought to theorize global transformation outside of any single ideology of change, yet the problems arising from the promotion of social diversity were only shallowly addressed in either their theoretical or structural manifestations. Arguably, realizing the value of diversity on a global scale requires a substantial, even heroic, level of tolerance if it is to result in a global order distinct from the present. Yet, the absence of a historical account of human social and intellectual development or an argument for the possibility of extending political and moral community beyond the water's edge was all too evident in the efforts to develop transitional strategies. A radical transformation of the global social structure was proposed, but a politics of transformation remained elusive. Not only were the social forces that might engender the dissolution of the state system unidentified, but because of normative constraints agents of transformation remained ill defined, and the few political tactics proposed simply articulated a preference for voluntary popular action. Ultimately, Galtung's vision of a desirable world remained detached from the present world, in both theory and practice. As such, it falls prey to Carr's famous criticisms of earlier utopian writings on international politics that, in his view, set up ethical standards supposedly independent from politics and sought to make international politics conform to them.[42] To believe in the possibility of Galtung's vision set out in *The True Worlds* requires either a leap of faith or a resort to the classical idealist assumption that as rational beings, in conditions of crisis humans will come to their senses and act diversely but harmoniously to bring about a new world.

Nonetheless, the various silences and inadequacies of Galtung's sweeping vision do not undermine the undoubted saliency of many of the concerns he expresses. *The True Worlds* espoused an antipolitics of decency that was to resonate with currents of dissident thought that threaded through the momentous revolts against oppression in Eastern Europe during the late 1980s, only to fade with the onset of Westernization. Perhaps now even more so than when he was writing, world order is characterized by integration *and* disintegration—the former occurring primarily in the economic realm, the latter in the political, social, and cultural arenas. Galtung's prescience is reflected in the now burgeoning literature on alternative paths to global and regional security that is reflective of the internal and external challenges to the state as the primary form of social organization and provider of security and welfare in the post–Cold War era.

Galtung was certainly not alone in daring to suppose that we are approaching, or should be seriously considering, the "end of sovereignty"; but few contemporary writers are as willing or bold as Galtung was to make the move from identifying the multiple crises of modernity to sketching a blueprint of alternative world order. One of the principle constraints acting upon them appears to be a heightened sensitivity to the problems of identity and difference as expressed primarily in the realm of culture. Another is an increasing skepticism as to the virtues of the overtly progressivist and programmatic politics that have periodically marked modernity. Galtung tried to avoid modernist teleology but in the end simply buried it out of sight.

The True Worlds was only a stopping point on a still continuing journey. In his more recent work Galtung turns to the cultural realm in his explorations of the sources of violence and the prospects for peace. In so doing, he shifts his peace research even further away from its original positivist certitude and toward what we might now describe as a postmodern ambiguity laced, paradoxically perhaps, with a greater sensitivity to the question of values and ethics. The key to this combination lies in Buddhism.

NOTES

1. Toynbee, *Mankind and Mother Earth*, p. 593.
2. *The True Worlds* (hereafter referred to as *TTW*), p. 6.
3. Galtung describes the treatment of parts of the problem as "technical" but the treatment of the structural whole as "political." *TTW*, p. 3.
4. *TTW*, pp. 19–21, and p. 36, note 22. China and to a lesser extent Cuba are seen as exceptions to this tendency.
5. Kolakowski, "The Opiate of the Demiurge," in his *Marxism and Beyond*.
6. *TTW*, p. 26.
7. See Chapter 5.
8. *TTW*, p. 30.
9. *TTW*, p. 27.
10. Engels, "Letter to J. Bloch in Konigsberg," in Marx and Engels, *Selected Works*, p. 682.
11. *TTW*, p. 28
12. *TTW*, p. 44.
13. See Chapter 4.
14. The difference is illustrated by the preference of the mass media for "news"—changes expressed in terms of discontinuous events—resulting in a tendency to adopt an actor-oriented perspective and promote a liberal point of view. Social structures are much harder to identify and present to an audience in a stimulating and economical manner. See Galtung, "The Structure of Foreign News," pp. 118–151.
15. *TTW*, p. 45. Emphasis in the original. Galtung acknowledges the similarities between his approach and the approaches of Fromm and Allardt but claims his was developed prior to theirs and is superior in its inclusion of a structural perspective. See *TTW*, p. 74, note 14.
16. *TTW*, p. 74, note 17.
17. Bay's claim that individuals have a "basic right" to "develop according to inner propensities and potentialities" is cited by Galtung as an exact expression of his own understanding of personal growth. *TTW*, p. 46.
18 This is an extraordinarily thin reading of Swedish democracy as either philosophy or practice. Galtung appears to adopt the common depiction of the Swedish model as a pragmatic response to the social problems of a market economy. For a contrasting view see Tilton, *The Political Theory of Swedish Social Democracy*.
19. *TTW*, p. 50.

20. Boulding sees Galtung's "passion for equality" as a problem—a truly egalitarian society could not produce a Galtung, for example. Galtung claims to share Boulding's distaste for similarity, seeking only to keep inequality within bounds—a ceiling as well as floor—in line with ideas found in Buddhism, Christianity, and socialism. See Boulding, "Twelve Friendly Quarrels with Johan Galtung," pp. 75–86. For Galtung's response see the introduction to *EPR*, 5.

21. Good research must also avoid exploitation, penetration, fragmentation, and marginalization occurring in the relationship between researcher and researched. See Galtung, "Is Peaceful Research Possible?" pp. 263–279.

22. *TTW*, p. 62.

23. *TTW*, p. 66.

24. Waltz, *Man, the State and War*, ch. 4.

25. This idea underpins recent claims that liberal states are inherently more peaceable. See Fukuyama, *The End of History and the Last Man;* and Doyle, "Liberalism and World Politics." A social-democratic variant that includes conceptions of international justice is critically examined in Pratt (ed.), *Internationalism Under Strain;* and Pratt (ed.), *Middle Power Internationalism*.

26. *TTW*, p. 87.

27. *TTW*, p. 93, and p. 105, note 21.

28. *TTW*, p. 380. Peacekeeping was a fallback position. Such strategies tended to focus on the instruments of violence rather than its ultimate source and were increasingly irrelevant in a world in which distance and geographical separation mean less and less.

29. *TTW*, p. 95. Other model communities include Israeli kibbutzim, Gandhian villages, and Chinese communes.

30. *TTW*, p. 99.

31. Lorenz, *On Aggression*, pp. 212–213. It is difficult to reconcile Lorenz's optimism and humanism with the conservatism that Galtung attributes to him. Although offering an account different from Galtung's as to the origins of aggression, he shares the objective of attempting to understand aggression in order to avoid it. Equally, Galtung's vision of a beta social order seems to share some of Lorenz's assumptions regarding the effects of overcrowding and the sources of conflict between communities. Lorenz argues also for the promotion of values but is more sensitive to the problem of defending them. See *On Aggression*, especially ch. 14.

32. Camilleri points out that the factors peculiar to human psychology and ethnocentricity are too easily dismissed by Galtung. I would add that they need not constitute a problem for Galtung but require a closer look at cultural determinants of and constraints upon violence, a point Camilleri also alludes to. See Camilleri, "Review of *The True Worlds*," pp. 95–96.

33. The notion of opposing forces was probably premised upon a principle of physics rather than social theory. Galtung frequently draws analogies between social and mechanical, biological and chemical systems. For example, see his "Structural Analysis and Chemical Models."

34. *TTW*, p. 100.

35. *TTW*, p. 396.

36. *TTW*, p. 398.

37. *TTW*, p. 103.

38. *TTW*, p. 394.

39. However, Galtung made himself available to both the United Nations and the Canadian government as an expert on development. In his "Twelve Friendly Quarrels with Johan Galtung," Boulding jibes at Galtung for the incompatibility of the principles of equity and his public role as a jet-setting, well-paid academic professor.

40. *TTW*, pp. 413–420.
41. I take the phrase from Havel, *Summer Meditations*, p. 5.
42. Carr, *The Twenty Years Crisis*, pp. 11–12, 21.

8

Peace as Nirvana

Since the late 1970s Galtung has focused increasingly on such phenomena as civilizations, social cosmologies, and cultural violence in an endeavor to discern how violence is embedded in the symbolic and discursive dimensions of social life. A marked feature of this recent work is the greater visibility, in descriptive terms at least, of his own philosophical orientation. This remains something of a mysterious blend of Eastern and Western influences, but over the last decade or so the influence of Buddhism has become very apparent indeed. Although pure Buddhism suffers from certain praxeological deficiencies, Galtung comes to describe it as the belief system that comes closest to "the type of dynamic, highly complex peace theory" that he now wishes to foster. Adopting a positive interpretation of the concept of nirvana as an ultimate condition of collective self-realization, he has suggested that "in a certain sense, peace is nirvana and nirvana is peace."[1]

CIVILIZATIONS AND THEIR COSMOLOGIES

What Galtung understands by civilization and cosmology is bound up with a critique of the West. He has defined civilization as "the culture shared by a large part of humanity, across countries and nations, even across continents, and throughout vast spans of time."[2] This definition is not consistently adhered to, however: At various points "civilization" appears commensurate with national culture; on other occasions it is a synonym for religion that later becomes synonymous with "mega-civilization." Rather than provide detailed analysis of the emergence and evolution of civilizations, Galtung endeavors to grasp their essential idiom. He also adopts the standpoint of the outside observer because one is less likely to become mesmerized by internal ethnic, religious, and linguistic borderlines. A capacity to step outside of a civilizational matrix is also implicit in the objective of identifying the "anatomy and pathology" of specific civilizations, including the Western civilization from which he self-evidently comes. Wisely, Galtung does not claim the status of observer in any strict sense. To do so would, of course, run against his own critique of Western scientific neutralism. Nonetheless, his tendency to objectivize the categories of civilization and culture suggests that, intentionally or otherwise, the mantle of scientism has not been entirely discarded. A plethora of cautionary asides notwithstanding, Galtung's analysis of civilizations and cultures proceeds as if they can be unequivocally discerned independently of discourses endeavoring to interpret them. Galtung moves rapidly from hypothesis to conclusion, or from the critical-descriptive to the constructivist voice. As has been the case with so much of his work, the forays into the comparative analysis of civilizations and their cosmologies are a means for arriving at a creative takeoff point very quickly.

In Galtung's eyes, the West is shifting from expansion to "postmodern" contraction.[3] It is an exhausted, deeply troubled civilization: "vertical, individualist, expansionist, exploitative on the world level, demoralised, full of contradictions." An adequate explanation of the cyclical fortunes of the West requires an investigation of its underlying "social cosmology." By this is meant the "vast, ephemeral and deep" states or processes—what Galtung sometimes calls the "deep ideology," civilizational program, or "social grammar"—of a specific civilization. The cosmology of a civilization may not be apparent at the surface level characterized by facts and artifacts and where the gloss of difference within and between societies may mask underlying invariances. Social cosmology cannot be simply comprehended in Cartesian terms as the realm of the ideal, distinct from the material; it is embedded partly in "the deep structures of the material, human and non-human organisation of the societies in that civilization" and partly in "the deep ideology, the world maps, *Weltanschauungen, cosmovisiones,* of that civilization."[4] Galtung derives from Benedict the analogy of cosmology and personality type: Social cosmology is to a civilization as "the psychological construct of a personality" is to a human being. Within a cosmology lies a civilizationally specific understanding "of the final goal, the ultimate *telos* of humankind." The social cosmology of a civilization can appear as natural, so normal as to be unquestioned and possibly even unknown as such to the inhabitants of a civilization. Indeed, when confronted with an account of their social cosmology, Galtung avers, "they will usually accept some items, have a questioning attitude to others and reject still others."[5]

Three concepts are used to regulate the usage of the term *social cosmology.* First, there is the familiar theme of the isomorphic relationship between social structures, epistemological principles, and global interaction patterns. Second, social cosmologies are holistic; as "deep ideologies" they provide the cement that binds apparently disparate ideologies such as Christianity, liberalism, and marxism. Third, there is a yin-yang aspect to cosmologies: Within a specific civilization can be found dominant and recessive variants of the social cosmology in constant tension with each other; in effect, there is a manifest cosmological core and a latent, peripheral alter ego.

Social cosmology is not, then, a neologism for dominant ideology. Western cosmology is not assumed to be spatially and temporally invariant, but challenges to it—from both within and outside—add up to a potential alternative cosmology that cannot be captured by simple reference to the boundaries of prevailing ideologies. The West constitutes a discernible civilizational form, with a self-image of consistency and order masking a more troubled sea of cosmological undercurrents. The error of orthodox analysis is, then, to fail to look beneath the patina of ideological disputation and intracivilizational variations. To borrow a more contemporary phraseology, it can be said that Galtung is exploring an exclusionary, totalizing metanarrative of the West that threads through all realms of social thought and practice to cement together an apparent cacophony of voices. It is this dominant voice that secretes definitive accounts of intellectual and social practice.

"Ideally," Galtung suggests, "one should be able to invoke a cosmology by one figure alone, an image so powerful that the essence of that civilization is carried in that image alone." But this is followed the caveat that "we are not in possession of such an image so our approach will have to be more analytical." Nonetheless, Galtung frequently attempts to capture the all-invoking key to various cosmologies. For example, in a brief but telling commentary on French civilization Galtung writes:

> A cosmology is expressed in the street patterns of Paris with its centre at the Etoile (Place Charles de Gaulle) and the avenues radiating outwards, the road map of France with its centre in Paris and the routes nationales radiating outwards, the airline network of France with its centre at Roissy (Charles de Gaulle again) and the airlines radiating outwards, above all to the *Communauté Français;* as in certain unquestioned ideas and conceptions French seem to have about the primacy of French civilization.[6]

The description supposedly illustrates the falsity of dichotomizing the ideal and the material and locating social cosmology or its cognates only within the former. This is a reasonable, if hardly novel, point in itself. But what is particularly French about roads radiating out from capital cities, or airline routes reflecting the centrality of a national airline's base airport? Such imagery appears applicable to most, if not all, contemporary civilizations (national cultures more accurately) possessed of capital cities, roads, and national airlines. France may exhibit a higher level of administrative and geographical centralization in comparison to other developed states, but a belief in the primacy of one's civilization is hardly its exclusive preserve. If civilizational arrogance can be detected in states lacking the administrative centralism of France, and this does not seem a too difficult research task, then Galtung's imagery begins to crumble. Equally, is the naming of city squares and airports after dead wartime leaders and long-serving presidents of world renown a peculiarly French activity? Arguably, a similar isomorphism between the material and the ideal—between the (quite literally) concrete structures of quotidian life and the idea of a distinct community—could be detected in numerous non-Western states in which symbolic representations of the social hierarchy of a community figure large. Of course, it may suggest something about the occidentalization (and certainly the industrialization) of non-Western civilizations. But that serves only to muddy the imagery and render it less helpful in telling us much about French civilization.

Galtung's imagery does tell us something about the state, and one might save his argument by suggesting that this is a universal phenomenon of Western origin. In this case Galtung's observations would exhibit commonalities with contemporary postmodern writing on world politics that also focuses on the universal and exclusionary "sovereignty of the discourse of sovereignty" and the manner in which it marginalizes or trivializes alternative forms of community. Such an argument does require a nuanced discussion of the complex interaction of civilizations, logics of globalization, and the hegemony of statism. Galtung does not consider the issues of state formation and nationalism in civilizational terms to any great depth, even though he expresses an intense dislike of the "the ugly ideology of the nation-state, another catastrophic idea." Both the state and nationalism are depicted as secular forms of occidental religious exclusivism: "The state can also be seen as one of the successors to God, inheriting the right to destroy life (execution), if not the right to create it."[7]

Similarly, Galtung describes the "ideology of nationalism" as "rooted in the figure of Chosen People and justified through religion or ideology," to be seen in conjunction with "the ideology of the state, statism." If the ideology of the nation-state is combined with "a theologically based Chosen People complex" the stage is "set for disaster," as illustrated by the "relatively clear cases" of Nazi Germany, Israel, Iran, Japan, South Africa, and the United States. Writing in 1990, Galtung suggested that the Soviet Union under Gorbachev was probably still laboring under the illusion of being a chosen people, chosen by Lenin (a secular but god-like "Him") as the first socialist state. France's arrogance, however, is in a class of its own, as exemplified by Napoleon's taking of his crown from the hands of the pope and placing it on his own head.[8] As such asides illustrate, Galtung's account of civilizations is often anecdotal in form and, in contrast to claims about the investigation of cosmology penetrating to the depths of civilizations, conducted largely in a descriptive and superficial vein.

Although he more usually refers to a generic Western civilization, what appear to be *national* cultures are sometimes described as civilizations or subcivilizations. On the other side of the coin, complex cultural variations are often subsumed under the rubric of a single civilization on the basis of certain structural similarities detected in core beliefs. An example of the latter is the classification of Islam (as religion, civilization, and the ideology of Islamism) as a genus of the species Occident, the latter label used to cover "the area covered by the peoples adhering to, if not believing in, religions of the *kitab* (Old Testament)." To these are added the two "recent secular offsprings" of liberalism and marxism. Thus, a shared hierarchical and universalist outlook, grounded in a particular understanding of the relationship between the individual and God, is seen to warrant the iconoclastic placing of the Christian West, marxism, and the Judaic or Islamic Middle East under the same civilizational rubric.

Galtung establishes the commonalities between occidental discourses largely through a literal reading of brief excerpts of a very select set of (mostly religious) texts and sometimes on no substantive evidence at all. Civilizations are seen to be "in incessant interaction, lending and borrowing, sending and receiving, imposing and submitting as people, things and ideas move in space" and as such are not to be taken as "watertight compartments."[9] Given this, the possibility of isolating out a definitive cosmological key or blueprint from the dynamic interaction of complex civilizational forms to be utilized as an explanatory master category appears to be, at the very least, questionable. Yet, that is what Galtung constantly seeks: the primary, the fundamental, the essential. Even in their interaction, "Occident and Orient seem to act and react differently and these differences are themselves of primary significance in understanding this civilisation." Given the poverty of substantiation, Galtung's taxonomy reflects a subjective and reductionist mapping of cultures that precedes the act of civilizational analysis. This is consistent with the scientistic (and occidental) procedure of hypothesis formation prior to some form of confirmatory or refutational process. In this case, however, the latter is hardly apparent although Galtung frequently suggests it be undertaken.[10] To reiterate an earlier point, the taxonomic exploration of civilizations and their cosmologies appears to be intended not as a definitive contribution to cultural analysis but as a means to a larger end.

THE SOCIAL COSMOLOGY OF THE WEST

In an early exercise in comparative cosmology, Galtung focuses on the hermeneutics of the word *peace*. Two predictions about occidental peace thinking are made: It will distinguish clearly between in-group and outgroup, center and periphery, and it will assume universal application.

Oriental peace concepts are not necessarily more inclusive, but they are deemed to be more benign in their comprehension of the "other." Oriental peace thinking is primarily inwardly focused rather than concerned with either the exclusion or forced inclusion of a lesser periphery: "Their concern is not global architectonics on their own premises or not; their concern is to come to grips with themselves."[11] The outside world is not necessarily unknown, lesser, or awaiting incorporation but is simply profoundly different. As a consequence of its preoccupation with the civilizational self, oriental peace thinking is distinguished by the absence of an aspiration to universalism. In sum, the Occident generates peace plans; the Orient produces peace concepts. But Galtung does not simply advance the case for one side of the occidental-oriental dualism, even if his gaze is clearly eastward. No pure case exists; rather points of gravity differ, and each side of the cosmological divide suffers from overemphasis on either inward focus or planning for universalization.

Galtung's Occident includes Judaism, Islam, the Greek and Roman classical traditions, and the modern period. The Middle Ages is treated as anomalous—an "oriental time pocket in occidental history"—because it produced no peace plans. Christian universalism was constrained by a context of diverse, small political units that were inward-looking and incapable of universalizing their cosmological underpinnings. In contrast, the modern post-Renaissance period produced a plethora of proposals for universal peace, from the fourteenth-century visions of Pierre Dubois and Dante through to various products of the Enlightenment. Even the Western stream of international moral skepticism (what today is usually called the realist tradition) is seen to constitute a variety of peace thinking insofar as the two principal features of occidental cosmology—the inside-outside distinction and universalism—are evident in the assumption that peace occurs within and not between states. Occidental proposals for extending peace across boundaries may appear to transcend realist statism but may, in fact, reconstitute an insider-outsider dualism in the form of a universalism with a Western center. In presuming that the bringing of the Orient into history requires the adoption of norms and practices of occidental origin, both Kantian cosmopolitanism and marxism are deemed to be exemplary of this tendency.

Galtung's explication of occidental concepts of peace is brief. He offers "one possible interpretation" of the meaning of the Hebrew word for peace, *shalom*, derived from two secondary sources, although he adds to them a decisive emphasis on the notion of a "chosen people."[12] Thus, the Judaic idea of peace is seen to be constructed around an image of a tribal rather than universal God. Drawing upon a few excerpts from the Books of Isaiah and Daniel, Galtung depicts the Hebrew God in a vertical relationship with a "divine prince" drawn from the chosen people, beneath whom other nations, races, and tongues are horizontally arranged. Although the emphasis on exclusivity appears to constrain its universalism, Galtung interprets Judaic social cosmology as not precluding the waging of war with others as part of the imposition of God's revealed will.

His analysis of Islam is even more cursory, lacking any reference to primary sources or the evolution of Islamic thought regarding questions of peace and war.[13] For Galtung, the root theology is everything, and he draws from it large implications, not the least being the claim that Islam is "very typical of the general Western pattern" because it hierarchically dichotomizes the world and is of universal aspiration. Islam is seen to cohere around a sacralized conception of space in which the world is divided into the *dar-al-Islam* (house of Islam or peace) and the *dar-al-harb* (house of war). Galtung adopts the familiar but simplistic view that Islam ultimately only offers the unbeliever the choice of capitulation or mortal struggle.[14] Believing in the universal relevance of Islam, the Muslim is seen to be charged with proselytizing the faith with his heart, tongue, hands, or sword in fulfillment of the holy obligation to jihad (striving or struggle). Jihad may not necessarily constitute a form of "just war," but it places relations between the two houses in a state of permanent hostility. Thus, both Judaism and Islam are compatible with aggression but are distinguishable by virtue of Judaism's perpetual exclusivism and Islam's aggressively inclusionary outlook. In either case, Galtung follows Ishida in attributing part of the contemporary antagonism between Israel and the Arab states to "a common tradition of monotheism and a similar militant concept of peace as a realization of justice by the divine will." Absent is any reference to Ishida's subsequent comment that from the Muslim point of view, "the so-called bellicosity of Islam . . . is a biased Christian interpretation."[15]

The classical Greek and Roman cosmologies are significant because they are tributaries to the contemporary Western cosmological amalgam. Classical Greek thought about *peace* is summarized as "an in-group relation" in which a sharp distinction is drawn between Greeks and the "natural enemy." *Homonoia* (harmony) occurs, then, within a clearly demarcated community. In contrast to the Greek understanding of balance of power or even partnership within the center of the Greek world, the Pax Romana emphasized the imperial dominance of a center within the empire. In the modern replay of the Greek model we see the evolution of contemporary statecraft and realpolitik, whereas the Roman model is reproduced in various Enlightenment-inspired peace plans and Eurocentric visions of world order, the objective of which is universal Westernization and the realization of a union of like-minded states. Such visions of global harmony are highly suspect in Galtung's eyes because of the role of direct violence in their realization and the structural violence they are likely to nurture. They comprehended the non-West as a potential outer West, amenable to conversion, incorporation, and exploitation.

Galtung takes it as a given that the dominant conception of peace today is that of the Romans in which peace is defined as the absence of war and is obtained through a series of international pacts that serve to benefit a global core of states. Peace within the state facilitates exploitation; peace between states provides a medium of control and ensures the preservation of a global economic order that benefits the West—the latter to be understood more as a bundle of ideas and practices than a geopolitical location. Such thinking reflects a cosmology that conceives of social space in terms of core and periphery, the sharp demarcation of inside and outside. This is compatible with an epistemological orientation that is atomistic, deductive, and directed toward the precise comprehension and control of reality, utilizing "meticulously theoretical schemes as guides to action." It is an intellectual mind-set that is hostile to contemplation or holism and is obsessed with ordering and classifying as the basis for controlling and steering the natural and social order. Modern intellectual representations of Western social cosmology, such as science and mathematics, discipline us into a "mode of thought highly compatible with black-white thinking and polarisation in personal, social and world spaces."[16] Such observations are neither particularly controversial nor exclusive to Galtung, but in a reductionist stroke he traces occidental epistemology back to the biblical account of creation. For the Occident, "reality is God-made and theory—except for the Holy Bible—is man-made"; to place theory above reality is effectively to commit an act of blasphemy. Thus, the Occident becomes imprisoned in the assumption that reality, the unfolding of God's work, cannot be transcended and once acquired, knowledge of it is permanently valid.

The essential idiom of the Occident is confirmed in its understanding of a trilogy of relationships—person-nature, interpersonal, and person-transpersonal. Occidental cosmology is predominantly anthropocentric and exploitative of nature, preferring *Herrschaft* over *Partnerschaft*; nature is soulless. During its benign medieval, contracting phase, the Occident saw nature in more spiritual terms but still as a repository of evil forces to be expunged. In expansionary mode, it sees nature as a resource ripe for plunder, a realm located below humanity and God in a triangular conception of the order of things.

Galtung interprets occidental cosmology as nurturing highly vertical interpersonal relations, but he also depicts all actually existing civilizations as hierarchical. The implication that future intercivilizational dialogue will of necessity involve existing and *potential* cosmologies should be noted here. The Occident is distinguished, however, by the virulence of its particular form of hierarchy. One of its legacies is the successful exporting of competitive individualism riding on the back of a globalizing capitalism and a dominant model of modernization. Consequently, non-occidental civilizations now exhibit complex hybrids of traditional collectivist and more individualist occidental forms of vertical social relations. Again this is a familiar theme in Galtung's writings, although the discussion of cosmologies makes less of the theme of equity than his earlier work. Given the pervasiveness of vertical social relations, equality appears to be quite literally not of this world, the emphasis now being more modestly pitched at the contrasting of modes of verticality.

The constitutive function of religious interpretations of the human condition is reiterated in the examination of person-transpersonal relations within the occidental civilizational calculus. A generalized occidental monotheism is characterized by an emphasis on the vertical relationship between the individual and an omnipresent God, universalism, and the angst-ridden struggle of the soul-possessing individual to enact God's will. Protestantism represents the extreme of a continuum that moves through Catholicism and Islam on to the more occidental forms of Buddhism that emphasize faith in a God over living the right way as the path to salvation. In the more fully occidental monotheisms, an emphasis on the individual soul underpins private property rights and noncollectivist forms of social life. Religious metaphors emphasizing transcendence and faith are amenable to secularization in the form of fundamentalist ideologies, those "awesome successors" to God, characteristic of occidental modernity. God and Satan, chosen and unchosen are secularized into conceptions of self and other. The contemporary archetype of such thinking is nationalism with the state "as God's successor."[17]

Galtung's description of the pathology of the West reads as a counsel of despair. In fact it foreshadows a prescriptive response in the innocuous-sounding activity of "intercivilizational dialogue." Discerning the idiom of the West contributes to the larger project of transcending a pathological, dominant form of occidental cosmology. Reflecting the enormity of the task, Galtung is circumspect as to what such a project actually entails. Even so, the very possibility of cosmological change arises from the perception of the West as an unstable civilization incapable of reproducing itself in perpetuity. Decisive challenges are emerging such that the West "seems to be the target of a more forceful challenge than ever before in recent centuries" and is now marked by a pervasive disenchantment. Internally, this stimulates recourse to suppressed, more oriental dimensions of the occidental cosmological amalgam as the available repertoire of resources becomes exhausted. But the external environment also presents a decisive challenge as parts of the non-West respond to globalized occidentalism often by turning occidental techniques (aggressive trading policies and the like) against it. The West falls victim of its own success as the "barbarians" learn the techniques of power. Non-Western civilizations entering phases of expansion bear the hallmarks of occidentalization, thereby engendering at the same time both the continuance of much that can be called Western and also the mitigation of (inner) Western dominance. One consequence is a shift on the part of the West from belligerent expansion to a more benign contracting phase characterized by a greater willingness to look within and a posture of withdrawal from confrontation with the outside. The prescriptive task becomes the exploration of nonoccidental civilizations and cosmologies as contributors to the envisioning of a future beyond a modernity, hitherto dominated by a Western cosmology whose "teeth are being extracted or are withering away."[18]

If the West needs a dentist, it is not yet ready for the undertaker. The Occident exhibits a continuing internal vigor and variety that the dominant "inner West" appears yet fully to acknowledge. Galtung depicts two broad civilizational forms within the occidental amalgam. Their distinctiveness can be grasped historically: When the Occident moves into a crisis-driven contracting mode, it engenders the manifestation of a latent, usually peripheral, cosmology comparable to the more inward-looking medieval "oriental pocket" in Western history and with aspects of oriental cosmologies. As a consequence of "structural fatigue" and the exhaustion of cognitive capacity, the "expansive, outward-directed implementation of the usual centre-periphery cosmology with a steep gradient running from the Western top to the non-Western bottom" is replaced with its opposite: "inner-directed, much less concerned with transforming the outside world, engaged in work inside the West . . . and with the inner-life of human beings."[19] It is because of its overextension in the modern period that the inner sanctum of Western civilization "may now be ready to enter a dialogue with less aggressive cosmologies with potentially important consequences for global civilization."[20] Typically, the empirical and the normative are being blurred here. In making the claim over a decade ago, Galtung offered little evidence of the Occident actually exhibiting such openness to the oriental "other," nor did he explore the question of agency in this regard. The idiom of contemporary debate about an emergent new world order suggests that, if anything, the reverse is more probable. Normatively, however, Galtung is clear enough: The Occident should both encourage the emergence of its softer, more oriental alter ego and engage in a more equitable dialogue with the world outside. The praxeological implications for peace research are also apparent: reliance upon any singular civilization and its constitutive social cosmology must be put aside in favor of a dialogic encounter with a variety of civilization-specific discourses on peace as the basis for a "world politics of a richer peace concept."[21] This is to be done in "a spirit of seeking solutions rather than making condemnations," although Galtung proves to be not averse to a large dose of the latter.

So, the instability of the prevailing world order creates a sense of urgency and should reinforce the necessity for change. Yet change does not ensue. Indeed, Galtung sees the anticipation of impending crisis as part of Western social cosmology itself. It reflects a "dramatic," cyclical conception of time with at least seven elements: paradise-fall-darkness-enlightenment-progress-crisis-catharsis. It is, he has recently suggested, a Christian conception of time that post-Enlightenment linearity obscures but does not eliminate.[22] Notions of progress are always connected with a sense of impending crisis or apocalypse, and the source of threats to peace is seen to emanate invariably from outside of a peaceful center. Galtung reads the constant reproduction of an essential dualism—good within, evil without—into such notions as "the triumph of the Lord," the just war, "the glory of the nation," the conquest of nature, the threat of the barbarian, and so on. But the evil outside is also detected within the West in the form of peripheral ideologies and religions, such as Islam, marxism, and Judaism, which are perceived as threats to the dominant cosmology and exhibit different cycles of expansion and contraction.

In terms of deep ideology, then, intraoccidental dialogue can offer only limited benefits. A contracting inner Occident may be more open to dialogue with the periphery of the civilization—the second and third Occidents—but given that this is a dialogue of occidentalisms, the likely consequence is still some form of the Occident in an expansionist mode. The various historical responses to intracivilizational crises—such as marxism, industrialization, a militant Islam, Zionism, and nationalism—ended up generating new crises rather than addressing fundamental problems in the underlying civilizational grammar. In sum, without recourse to nonoccidental values and practices, the Occident will remain as a project, consisting in a process of sorting good from evil and driven by a variously defined telos: the perfect market, pure communism, or redemption in the eyes of a God. For Galtung, the irreducible cosmology of the West can be grasped through the theistic metaphor of the angst-ridden individual struggling to achieve redemption and eternal salvation by the grace of an omnipotent Creator. This would explain the definitive occidental preoccupation with converting the generalized "other" to the right state of mind and social order. Put differently, it is the basis upon which the Occident is deemed to be a civilizational form that engenders violence and, in its expansionary mode, a violent civilization.

Cultural Violence

The prescriptive implications of these sketches of occidentalism emerge more fully with the introduction of the concept of cultural violence. A novel definition of violence usually foreshadows a shift in Galtung's focus, but in this case the concept surfaces a decade after the preliminary surveys of civilizations and their cosmologies. The meaning of cultural violence is grasped through its relationship to the other two categories of violence. It refers to "those aspects of culture, the symbolic sphere of our existence . . . that can be used to justify or legitimise direct or structural violence." In comparison to other forms of violence, cultural violence is an "invariant" or a "permanence"; it flows steadily through time providing "a substratum from which the other two can derive their nutrients."[23]

Again, Galtung appears to be playing somewhat loose with his categories because at this point "culture" sounds like a synonym for "cosmology," that is, the "genetic code that generates cultural elements." In general, he postulates a causal flow from "cultural via structural to direct violence" but also suggests that the cycle of violence can start from any corner of the violence triangle. Although it is usually the case that only certain aspects of a specific culture can be deemed violent, some cultures "could be imagined and even encountered" with a sufficient number of violent aspects to warrant description as a violent culture. Such a culture "preaches, teaches, admonishes, eggs on and dulls us into seeing exploitation and/or repression as normal or natural, or into not seeing them (particularly exploitation) at all."[24] And so to the crux of the matter: Viewed at the level of social cosmology, "occidental culture shows so many violent features that the whole culture starts to look violent." Again, the source of the legitimating power of occidental cultural violence is the "catastrophic idea" of an external, transcendental God—"our father who art in heaven" —and its secular successors. At this point, the very possibility of a *politics* of change—a purpose to peace research—appears to recede dramatically.

The antithesis of cultural violence is cultural peace, a condition engendered by those "aspects of a culture that serve to justify and legitimise direct peace and structural peace." Yet, as Galtung admits, there are some worrisome implications for peace research flowing from this formulation. First, changing the cultural genetic code appears a hopelessly difficult task. Second, peace research is confronted with the unenviable task of identifying an actual or potential "peace culture" that does not simply reproduce occidental arrogance and cultural violence. Yet, passing judgment upon actually existing civilizations, cosmologies, or cultures appears to require a reference set of authoritative values *if* it is also to contribute to the realization of a preferred, peaceful civilizational-cultural form. Of course, there is the ever expanding concept of human needs that remains entrenched in Galtung's lexicon; but as I have already argued, the concept of needs displaces rather than resolves the question of values. The more Galtung expands the range of human needs, especially with the introduction of culturally based "identity needs," the less secure the concept of needs becomes as a foundation for values. As he himself concedes: "Not only do cultures challenge our need-concepts; our need-concepts also challenge cultures in a complex dialogue not yet off the ground. A fruitful contradiction with no simple dissolution in sight."

Galtung's notion of cultural peace does not, unfortunately, help us through this problem because it is philosophically and ethically evasive.

It adumbrates a vision of a nonviolent culture without addressing a number of serious problems. In particular, Galtung offers no exploration of the difficult but very pertinent tensions between communitarian and cosmopolitan claims upon human moral sensibilities. To illustrate: He gives as an example of cultural violence the legitimation of the moral claim that "murder on behalf of the country is right, on behalf of oneself wrong." The use of the term *murder* already presupposes, of course, a viewpoint on the morality of war. Yet Galtung does not attempt to investigate why the distinction between killing *within* a community and *for* a community has come to have wide currency, historically and across cultures. Nor does he explore the possible connections between the realization of postulated "survival," "identity," and "freedom" needs and the recourse to organized violence, for or against the state or other forms of community.

BEYOND THE OCCIDENT

Galtung's more recent work is distinctive not only because of its focus on things cultural but also because that focus has produced an uncharacteristic reticence to move very far down the prescriptive path. Gone are the days of constructing blueprints of preferred world orders or presenting of definitive syntheses of the best features of all ideologies and epistemologies, of which *The True Worlds* was exemplary. Equally, the foundational authority of a taxonomy of needs appears also to be crumbling. It is now presented as a means for constructing images of human beings that are more likely to engender human-centered social theory and practice and for providing an inner circle of concretized values around which theoretical explorations of such things as development, social structures, and culture can revolve.[25] The key word is *dialogue*—between epistemologies, cultures, and civilizations. It is a loaded term; given that the category of cultural violence presupposes a critique of prevailing civilizational forms and cultural discourses, the purpose of such dialogue is equally necessarily political. "Dialogue," writes Galtung, "is not neutral, not above or below politics, it *is* politics."[26] As with all of the categories in Galtungian peace research, the status of dialogue remains ambiguously poised between the analytical, the normative, and the political. The purpose of dialogue is both to further knowledge (it is "a new approach in the social sciences") and to engage in a constructivist act with three goals: consciousness formation; mobilization-organization; and "action-struggle-fight." Here we see the apparent abandonment of objectivity on the part of the researcher although, to confuse matters, at around the same time Galtung was revivifying an earlier image of the peace researcher as paraphysician, guided by some form of Hippocratic oath, neither servant nor aloof expert and beholden to none, be they the peace movement or the establishment. Galtung

still sees value in establishing peace research as an institutionalized profession that could, inter alia, train peace professionals to identify peace
culture.[27] To grasp how Galtung endeavors to bring these objectives together first requires following him through an exploration of the non-West.

Oriental Cosmologies

As to what Galtung means by "oriental cosmology," in the final analysis the answer proves to be concise: Buddhism. Although oriental cosmology is regarded as more heterogenous and eclectic than its occidental
counterpart, the Orient is defined as "essentially the peoples who adhere
to, if not believe in, Buddhism."

Pure Buddhism is rare, however, and of marginal political influence.
Most oriental cosmologies are amalgams of a specific school of Buddhism
with other streams of oriental cosmology as well as significant occidental
components. Nonetheless, the positive values that Galtung extracts from
the Orient are, by and large, Buddhist. Effectively, existing oriental cosmologies constitute a scale of forms, and those with a more evident, or less
tainted, Buddhist content are clearly favored. Whereas in the case of the
Occident he considers the complex interaction between a set of cosmological assumptions and concrete social practices, when it comes to extracting
the idiom of the Orient he is, strictly speaking, working in the realm of the
abstract and utopian. The oriental ideal hardly exists in practice, in contrast to and partly as a consequence of the facticity of a globalized Occident and partly due to the heterogeneity of the actually existing Orient. It
is also a consequence of Buddhism itself, which Galtung argues is relatively underdeveloped as a system of ideas about "social space and world
space"—the primary focus of peace research—in contrast to the insights
it offers to the contemplative individual or devotional community.[28]

Galtung's tracing of the oriental alternative occurs in two overlapping
stages. The first involves abstracting some general features of oriental cosmology to be contrasted with those of the Occident and enable the construction of a taxonomy of civilizations. Little more than this ensues because no unequivocally preferable, actually existing alternative to the
Occident clearly emerges, and the process appears very much to be a
prefatory, scene-setting exercise. The second, still unfolding, stage is the
articulation of Buddhism as both an abstract incarnation of an oriental
challenge to a pathological Occident and a framework for intercivilizational dialogue.

The treatment of oriental civilizations is even more cursory than is the
case with the Occident, Galtung providing little evidence in support of his
descriptive sketches. The initial typology contains only three nonoccidental civilizations: Hindu, Sinic, and Nipponic. Hinduism is placed in the
middle of the Occident-Orient scale by virtue of its perceived transcivi-
lizational eclecticism. It can be understood as either the crossroads or the

cradle of the world, which for Galtung is a very positive feature. None of these cosmologies is embraced as unequivocally preferable to the Occident; equally, none qualify for the condemnation accorded to the worst dimensions of occidentalism. For all of its virtues, Hindu cosmology suffers from its brahminic dimensions that have historically proven highly resistant to change. Being a blend of Daoism, Confucianism, and Buddhism, Sinic cosmology is also seen to embody a concept of peace that appears compatible with both direct and structural violence. The Chinese term *ho p'ing* (and the Japanese equivalent, *heiwa*) offers a conception of peace or harmony that implies both a well-ordered state of mind and a harmonious social order, the connotations of the latter being ambiguous with regard to peace. In both cases the orientation is inward. Sinic and Nipponic civilizations combine internal cohesiveness with a view of the outside as of a distinctly lesser order. Because of its more hierarchical social order and expansionist tendencies, which Galtung attributes to such characteristics as a sense of being a chosen people and nationalistic Shintoism, it is only Nipponic civilization that joins the Occident (in its expansion mode) as a candidate for removal, in principle at least.[29] China might hold the world outside the Middle Kingdom in low regard, but it does not covet it. It should be noted here that the wholesale excision of powerful civilizations is not treated as a realistic prospect by Galtung, nor is it taken as a certainty that they can be changed deliberately rather than as a consequence of cumulative historical circumstances. The point being made is simply that if meaningful change is to occur, then it must do so at the level of cosmology.

Oriental cosmologies are distinctive, albeit to varying degrees, along all of the variables employed in the analysis of the West. With regard to conceptions of sociopolitical space, for example, the Sinic and Nipponic cosmologies share with the Occident a center-periphery image of global space that emphasizes the distinction between the civilizational inside and outside. There remain important differences nonetheless. Unlike the Western view, the Sinic conception of the periphery is that of a "Barbaria" with which little interaction has been sought historically. Thus, in spite of its verticality, Sinic cosmology is largely defensive in contrast to the expansionary aggression of the West. In Nipponic cosmology, the periphery is seen as a resource to be drawn upon, although not necessarily conquered or converted, should Japan's interests require it. Deeper shades of occidentalism can be detected, however, in Japan's relationship with an inner periphery—other Asian states—as historically expressed in notions of a Great East Asian Co-Prosperity Sphere.

Hinduism's centerless holism (figuratively represented by an empty circle) provides the greatest contrast to occidental cosmology.[30] Its virtues include a capacity to absorb and adapt to outside influences and traditions and the absence of a strong perceptual gradient between inside and outside. For Galtung, Hindu universalism supposes "that there is a Hindu in all of us, only that he or she may not be aware of it." Hinduism (and contemporary India for that matter) presents an alternative, oriental model of the encounter with the "other" to that of the West. "Which is stronger," he asks, "the civilization that forces others onto the periphery, or the civilization that encompasses others and absorbs them into its own universe?" Out of the concrete struggle between imperial Britain and a mostly Hindu India emerged two models of intercivilizational interaction: "on the one hand military conquest, economic penetration, cultural imprinting and the imposition of political institutions, and on the other absorption and enhancement."[31]

Galtung is working here with an idealized and abstracted account of Hinduism, which draws upon Jainism and Buddhism (arguably heterodox doctrines) to present a Hindu account of world space. Hinduism is also used interchangeably with contemporary India, another case of the categories of civilization, cosmology, state, and nation being used very loosely. The account of its virtues is derived from an arbitrary mix of mythology and impressionistic observations of contemporary Indian internal social relations. Classical sources of Hindu philosophy of politics can be read as offering a rather different account of world space, as exemplified by the political realism of Kautilya's *Arthasastra* for example. Here little hope is expressed that the "peaceful pattern of well-controlled, harmonious human decency" found within bounded communities "should ever become transferred to the larger field of the nations." Zimmer refers to the "blank pessimism" of classical Indian political philosophy in which international conflict is depicted as a struggle between "fiercely antagonistic super-individuals" and the absence of any higher power ensures that "the primeval law of nature remains in operation, uncontrolled." Against this, he suggests there has long existed "an idyllic compensatory dream" that envisions "a universal world-wide empire of enduring tranquillity under a just and virtuous world-monarch."[32] In the Buddhist version of this pervasive mythical imagery of "the superman turning the wheel" (which can be found also in pre-Aryan, Jaina, and Hindu writings), the Universal Monarch is seen as the secular counterpart of Buddha. Galtung's soft reading of the Hindu worldview privileges Buddha over Kautilya and Mahatma over Indira Gandhi.

Galtung disapproves of the Hindu understanding of caste, but he generously interprets it as an account of social space rather than interpersonal relations. The distinction appears contrived. He also acknowledges that Hindu tolerance of occidental religions has not been matched in the treatment of indigenous peoples or, more recently, Sikhs. Relations between Muslims and Hindus have been uneven, and Buddhism and Gandhism are also depicted as victims of Hindu intolerance. His explanation of all this is that Hindu violence "is directed downwards rather than outwards, as structural violence rather than direct violence"; Hinduism exhibits "horizontal tolerance."[33] Galtung claims, furthermore, that the confinement of Hindu civilization largely within the modern state of India provides further living proof of this. If India is conceived of as a self-contained international system composed of "a number of nations speaking languages as different as those found in Europe," then it is a success in contrast to the history of violent conflict between European states within a single occidental civilization. With regard to intranational violence it is apparently far less successful.[34] It is "tempting," Galtung suggests, to attribute this "success" of India as an international system to the greater tolerance of Hinduism in contrast to European Christianity.[35]

How either the distinction between international and intranational relations within modern India or the superiority of India as an international system in a global context can be sustained is entirely unclear. Galtung makes no reference to the concept of sovereignty that is an irreducible part of any account of conflict in the European state system but not necessarily central to relations between linguistically distinctive "nations" within a state. There is also a history of conflict between Indian states and the Indian state because there is some convergence of political, ethnic, and religious boundaries, the Punjab being an obvious case in point. Overall, given the recent violent confrontations between militant Hindus, Sikhs, and Moslems as well as continuing intercaste conflict, it would be difficult to make the case for any Hindu (or Indian) exceptionalism in Galtung's terms.

Equally, India's external policy could hardly sustain an argument for the ethical superiority of Hinduism's conception of social space. One would have to emphasize India's role in, say, the nonaligned movement in contrast to Indo-Pakistan rivalry (which has led to three wars, a nuclear arms race, and secessionist movements in Kashmir, the Punjab, and Sindh), the dispute with Bangladesh over water rights, the expansion of the Indian blue water navy, or intervention in Nepalese foreign policy.[36] Galtung gives no reason to suppose that India's external relations are governed by anything other than the relativities of power or an astute appreciation of the possibilities available to a large developing state in a context of superpower rivalry. No clearer evidence of this could be provided than the so-called Indira doctrine, proclaimed in 1984, which declared India's role as the region's hegemonial power. If there is a civilizationally distinctive component to the Indian weltanchauung, reflecting a Hindu conception of sociopolitical space, Galtung does not convincingly identify it. Furthermore, if Ishida is right in describing traditional Indian ethics as concerned with escape from the world rather than with developing an affirmative attitude toward it, this is hardly surprising. Ishida emphasizes the distinction between *shanti*—a conception of peace concerned solely with a well-ordered state of mind—and overtly political conceptions of peace such as *samdhi* (the absence of war) and *sama* (a well-governed social order).[37] A more plausible explanation of any novelty to Indian politics is provided in Galtung's own account of Gandhi's contribution to the making of India that convincingly depicts it as being a struggle as much against orthodox Hinduism as for it.[38] Indeed, a comparison of Galtung's generous interpretation of Hinduism as an abstract counterpoint to occidentalism with his more critical reading of it when concretely set against Gandhism suggests that at times Hinduism is simply conflated with Gandhism.[39]

According to Galtung, the Orient is distinguished also by its understanding of time. As compounds of Mahayana Buddhism, Confucianism, Daoism, and Shintoism, the Sinic and Nipponic cosmologies conceive of time as a cyclical or dialectical process involving a spiraling movement toward a final condition, in contrast with the linear progressivism of the Occident. The Orient offers an alternative to the occidental cycle of crisis-ridden but irreversible movement onward toward an end state of either salvation or perdition. The notion of time as revealing a steering process in which humanity is guided toward an unequivocally right destiny is absent. If the Orient has a project at all, claims Galtung, it consists of seeing good and bad as dialectically connected, working upon each other as parts of a complex whole and "of understanding this fact and steering the process towards more distant goals that in themselves must be dialectically conceived."[40] The broad point is clear enough: Oriental cosmologies lack the aggressive desire of the West to incorporate the periphery into a universal model of individual and collective development.

The connection between the abstracted ideal and historical reality is tenuous, given the depiction of actually existing Sinic and Nipponic cosmologies as complex amalgams in which there is an increasing occidental content. Conceding that he is grossly simplifying, Galtung also suggests that the epistemological distinctiveness of the Orient can be brought out by using two dualisms: atomistic-holistic and deductive-dialectical. The first refers to modes of description and the second to modes of explanation. Occidental epistemology is predominantly atomistic-deductive, a characterization that, in the final analysis, is to be attributed to vertical monotheism. In contrast, Sinic and Nipponic epistemologies are holistic and dialectical—a "yin-yang mode of thought." Again, occidentalization has introduced Western epistemology into these civilizations, although Galtung sees little evidence of synthesis. Hindu epistemology is described as closer to the occidental model in that "it is more atomistic than holistic and more deductive than dialectical," although Galtung omits to explain how this is the case.[41] In fact, he provides very little detailed analysis of oriental epistemology, apart from some subsequent explorations of Buddhist epistemology outside of any civilizational reference point and with virtually no systematic reference to Buddhist scriptures or texts.[42] Nonetheless, the oriental mind is depicted as less fearful of inconsistency and ambiguity and less concerned with developing contradiction-free images of reality; in sum, there is less concern with the production of theory. Oriental epistemology draws upon "ancient wisdom" in Hindu, Buddhist, and Daoist concepts and utilizes a discourse that "does not sound like theory-formation to the occidentally trained ear or eye but like verbiage."[43] Examples of the oriental alternative to occidental "deductive rigidity" include the Hindu insistence on the inseparability of elements and the Buddhist usage of circular reasoning. Galtung's reading of oriental epistemology is not entirely uncritical. In its holism, oriental epistemology can be supportive of totalitarian practices. It tends to overstate the interconnectedness of things and presents an image of a cohesive reality to be understood only through a general scheme or master plan, the explanatory key to which is located at a deep or latent level. This can invite submission or, in conjunction with a dialectical viewpoint, revolutionary rejection of that totality. Overall, however, the point of the exercise appears to be not a careful exploration of actual oriental intellectual practices but the postulation of an idealized alternative to mainstream Western epistemology. Given Galtung's long-running and often idiosyncratic dispute with Western positivism, this is very much a case of old wine in new bottles.

The distinctiveness of the Orient is further revealed in its understanding of interpersonal relations and relations between humans and nature, although here Galtung hardly pushes the point. Oriental cosmologies do exhibit elements of exploitation but tend to conceive of our relationship with nature as one of partnership rather than dominance. To greater and lesser degrees, oriental thought sees nature as besouled, "possibly even becoming the abode of human souls in a transmigratory process." In contrast, occidental anthropocentrism underpins aggressive behavior toward other humans (hence the apparently common Chinese observation that the problem with Westerners is that they eat too much meat).[44] Yet, Galtung also sees all civilizations as promoting vertical social relations in some form or other. This is reinforced by the increasing imposition of occidental models of hierarchical social relations upon traditional social structures, just one consequence of the globalized logics of production, management, information control, and capital formation. Oriental cosmologies generally tend to favor the collective over the individual as a primary social unit— of which Galtung would approve—or at least to blend individualism with collectivism to produce complex social formations that combine East and West, traditional and modern.[45] But no existing civilization reaches the ideal. Even Hinduism offers a fertile soil for the reinforcing of caste distinction through the imposition of occidental vertical social relations that are an inevitable consequence of development and modernization. The intersection of primordial and modern forms of vertical social relations is sufficiently powerful to resist efforts by reformers to dismantle them. As Galtung admits, neither Buddha nor the incarnation of Hinduism with a revivified Buddhist egalitarianism in the form of Gandhi succeeded in this endeavor.

Given Galtung's evident distaste for occidental monotheism, it is not surprising that the oriental understanding of what he calls "personal-transpersonal" relations figures large in his survey. The Orient offers up a spectrum of conceptions of the individual's relationship to that which lies beyond the self. At one end lies Hinduism; in possessing a notion of the transmigration of the soul from this world to some other, it has certain affinities with occidentalism. Its multiple variations encompass iconoclastic mysticism (seeking the dissolution of the individual in an impersonal world spirit), as well as a more occidentalist devotional theism that interprets the vast array of representations of God as expressions of the One. Hinduism remains distinguished, nonetheless, by the lesser emphasis on a personal relationship with God. At the other end lie the civilizations (Sinic and Nipponic) that incorporate Mahayana Buddhism. Here "there is no God, there is a plurality of existing faiths, there is no claim to universality, there is no soul . . . and the goal is not eternal life through salvation, but extinction from the cycles, *nibbana*, through enlightenment."[46] The absence of a personal God proves decisive in Galtung's representation of the generalized oriental alternative cosmology.

The primary virtue of oriental civilizations for Galtung is their tolerance of eclecticism: "like being Jew, Christian, Muslim, liberal and marxist at the same time—a combination characterised as insanity in the Occident and as wisdom in the Orient."[47] It is not that any evidence is provided in support of such romanticism; in his paraphrasing of Gandhi, Galtung seemingly forgets certain aspects of actually existing oriental civilizations. True, they may not generally exhibit the aggressiveness of the West, but their eclecticism clearly has its limits, as Galtung goes on to concede. For a foreigner to be accepted fully into Japanese society is virtually impossible. Similarly, the observation that we might all have a bit of the Hindu in us obscures the point that one can only be born a Hindu. Losing one's status as a foreigner in Chinese culture is also notoriously difficult. Even so, on Galtung's reading the Orient offers up a range of conceptions of self and other preferable to the generalized occidental model, even if this tilt is clearly only a matter of degree. Let us concede the point: If the oriental worldview—insofar as it can be identified at all—exhibits some greater tolerance of (or disinterest in) the other, it would plausibly be more conducive to global stability and order and the reduction of direct violence. But the corollary is that it is far from evident that the Orient offers an integrative or embracing vision of humanity as a basis for moving beyond a structurally violent status quo or a decisive alternative to the West.

Of the nonoccidental cosmologies, Hinduism with a strong Buddhist component meets with most approval from Galtung, hardly surprising given his lifelong interest in Gandhi's life and teachings. For the Hindu, "what comes from the outside is received and enveloped, sinking down into the gelatinous, amorphic body of a culture so rich that almost anything is possible, sinking until it meets and blends with its opposite number in Hinduism and is transformed."[48] In particular, Gandhi's blend of Hindu eclecticism and Buddhist rejection of violence not only provides a corrective to the militant tendencies in Hinduism and its structurally violent, sometimes directly violent, conception of caste but also offers a model of oriental values to juxtapose with the pathology of occidentalism. The challenge to the West lies, then, very much in a vision, of which the actually existing Orient gives barely a glimpse.

BUDDHISM, PEACE, AND PEACE RESEARCH

A distinctive Buddhist civilization is a later addition to Galtung's catalogue of civilizations, although its cosmology is not overtly connected to the historical practices of specific states or empires. This would be a difficult task, since the overtly Buddhist state appears to be nonexistent, although the continuing survival of the spirit of Tibet (in spite of the violence of China's efforts to eradicate it) suggests a certain potentiality. Given the diversity of schools of Buddhism and their complex interaction with other streams of oriental cosmology, the very idea of a Buddhist civilization appears contrived.[49] Nonetheless, its introduction points up the third function of the taxonomy of civilizations—as a prefatory exercise to the main game of exploring Buddhism's potential. Effectively, Galtung comes to reduce the contestation of civilizations to a contrasting of Christianity and Buddhism, the two symbolizing the core of the Occident and the Orient, respectively.

Galtung's interest is in the translatability of Buddhism into a practical discourse of peace—a contemporary satyagraha—rather than in exposition of its philosophical substance. In this respect, his work differs little from the bulk of Western writing on Buddhist moral philosophy that has largely been confined to the business of "simple descriptive ethics."[50] Yet, the reading of Buddhism is not entirely passive; Galtung seeks to get beyond intra-Buddhist divisions such as that between Hinayana (or Theravada) and Mahayana Buddhism and the correlative distinguishing emphases on avoiding *dukkha* (the chief characteristic of mortal life—suffering) or realizing *sukha* (bliss or joy).[51] Although he generally avoids judging specific schools of Buddhism Galtung seems less enthusiastic about those that approach the occidental norm of worship and petitionary prayer or emphasize monastic withdrawal and more sympathetic to the more activist Mahayana end of the Buddhist spectrum. Thus Galtung approvingly refers to the Soka-Gakkai (Value-Creating Society) that he has described as having evolved into a "major part of the world peace movement." The Soka-Gakkai's emphasis on such things as social justice, peace action, and the synthesis of capitalism and socialism resonates with themes found throughout Galtung's writings, although he makes no reference to claims that its spread in the 1950s had a violent, authoritarian dimension.[52]

The virtues of Buddhism from the point of view of Galtung's peace research are manifold. Above all, it is the only major system of thought that does not promote some form of direct or structural violence. Galtung describes it as a holistic nonmetaphysical moral philosophy. Whether Buddhism is nonmetaphysical is a moot point, but it has frequently been described as a nontheistic religion with an overtly practical orientation. The Buddha rejected blind faith and likened his teachings to a raft upon which the follower could cross the river from the dangerous shore of the "conditioned world" to the peaceful shore of nirvana.[53] Buddhism acknowledges the existence of personal gods (*deva*), but it denies the existence of an eternal creator or supramundane power. If we bear in mind Galtung's emphasis on all that flows from subservience to a God in occidental religion, Buddhism is clearly off to a good start on this point alone.

Buddhism's nontheistic character is not sufficient to make it unique. At its core lies the doctrine of *anatta*—the denial of the reality of a self or soul—that is peculiar to Buddhism and upon which comprehension of it depends. Without delving into its complexities, Galtung approvingly interprets *anatta* as a counterpoint to the occidental emphasis on the individual as "something unique, specific, detachable and particular." Thus, the second leg of the Christian focus on the relationship between a creator and the individual supplicant is removed. *Anatta* does not, however, "rule out unity in a transpersonal *soul*—in short unity with all humans, wherever they are, transnationally, across any kind of border . . . *and* with nature."[54] Galtung plausibly reads the doctrine as one of universal "identification" that flows in all directions, socially, ontologically, and historically. This underpins the Buddhist understanding of reality, its ethical system, and the very structure of Buddhist thought: "Buddhism does not drive wedges. Buddhism is a religion in the most basic sense of the word, *religio*, a relinking with all that is, out there and in here."[55]

To *anatta* must be added the doctrine of *anicca*, the impermanence of all things including mind and consciousness. Empirically, it connotes an understanding of reality as ever changing, always "becoming," and revealing of new possibilities. Epistemologically, the doctrines of *anatta* and *anicca* conjure an image of a synchronically intertwined reality and consciousness that is resistant to the occidental model of the laborious acquisition of definitive knowledge. Apparent contradictions emerging out of a reality in constant flux do not present an intellectual problem demanding solution but offer a subject for meditative contemplation as part of the process of gaining practical insight. Against the Christian archetype of a tree of knowledge Galtung posits the revolving Buddhist wheel.

The doctrine of impermanence and the nonlinear conception of time—a consequence of the denial of an originating act of creation—do not remove a certain directedness to human action. There remains, especially in the Mahayana school of Buddhism that emphasizes the more missionary objective of the universal achievement of Buddhahood, "a basic optimism that would imbue the cyclical perspective with an element of linearity, somewhat like a spiral moving upward and forward."[56] Replacing occidental teleology in either its theistic or secular variations is the more recondite condition of nirvana that in Galtung's hands emerges as a neologism for peace in the fullest sense: the absence of direct and structural violence (*dukkha*) and the presence of justice and inner peace (*sukha*). Buddhism's interpretation of the "great unity of sentient life" blurs the dualisms of subject-object, reality-consciousness, and creator-created that are characteristic of occidental thought. There is nothing corresponding to "a Prime Mover, some lever or button that can be pressed or pushed starting a chain of processes." Reality and identity are in a perpetual process of becoming: "The world is ebbing and flowing, not a rigid structure of global architectonics—but precisely a process based on diversity in symbiotic interaction."[57] Such an understanding requires the abandoning of a search for the contradiction-free pure social system, a set of unequivocal first principles, or final articles of faith.

The implications for Galtung's peace research are dramatic. There is no certitude of successful mastery of reality, no blueprint that can capture reality in all its dynamic complexity. Instead, peace research and peace action become a constant striving, a series of "many small but coordinated efforts along several dimensions at the same time, starting in all kinds of corners of material and spiritual reality remembering that the system will hit back in a complex web of interrelations."[58] Buddhism's dynamic holism engenders a focus on process over structure. The very organization of Buddhist thought is more conducive to speech and action that "could lead to higher levels of world peace, social development, human enlightenment and nature balance." Against this Galtung acknowledges that the Buddhist outlook can engender calm fatalism and retreat. The Occident and peace research may well need Buddhism, but they can offer it something in return.

It is not just Buddhism's interpretation of reality that is attractive to Galtung but also its ethics. The nonlinearity of Buddhist thought is underpinned by the emphasis on the constant cycle of rebirthing (the process of "wandering on," or *samsara*) as the expression of the universal law of moral retribution—karma. This involves not only individuals but all living things in their interconnectedness. In contrast to the occidental emphasis on the individual soul seeking the path to ultimate redemption in the eyes of a single God, Buddhism offers a complex account of time and moral action as "unbounded" and "infinite, there being no beginning and no end for all practical purposes although there is the transcendence of nirvana to other unknown and unknowable types of existence."[59] The latter suggests to Galtung that time is bounded but in a special sense. Buddhism offers a complex cyclical account of time as exhibiting various processes on the path to nirvana: making and unmaking; the avoidance of suffering (*dukkha*); and realization of blissful happiness (*sukha*). The crucial difference emerges from the doctrine of *anatta*. The movement toward nirvana does not refer to the travails of the highly individualized soul as in various transcendental monotheisms; it is a collective process. No act of creation commenced the cycle of life, yet creation goes on. Human and nonhuman nature are interconnected in a karmic web, or wheel, that links past, present, and future.

Galtung may not tell his readers much about Buddhist morality, but he captures its essence in referring to its "collective ethical budget." Complex though the idea of karma is, it is not entirely alien to the Western mind, especially if we employ Humphreys' description of it as an esoteric, spiritual rendition of the law of causation, of the equality of action and reaction—a universal "law of moral retribution."[60] In the absence of divine authority or its secular equivalent, karma provides the basis for a universal ethics. In its universalism it bears comparison to deontic notions of natural law, and in emphasizing the inescapable consequences of one's actions—consequences that will affect all sentient life caught in the karmic web—it reveals a utilitarian dimension. Yet, by virtue of the doctrine of *anatta* there is little of the occidental emphasis on the attribution of guilt or reward and punishment.

The Buddhist Four Noble Truths provide the foundation for an alternative moral economy. First, all life is dissatisfaction or suffering (*dukkha*). Second, this is not because of the actions or inactions of an omnipotent God but because of the very nature of a mortal realm characterized by human ignorance coupled with craving and desire. In reflection of the interconnectedness of things, desires, and actions, the consequences of ignorance and craving are pervasive: "*No man is an island* and no one escapes the effects of the sum total of evil to which he, among others, contributes."[61] Third, there is a path beyond the evil of suffering to its cessation (*nirodha*) that is open to all humankind. Finally, the fourth Noble Truth declares the way (*magga*) to achieving the release of nirvana: the following of the Noble Eightfold Path.

For Galtung the Christian conception of sin is pervasively vertical: "The sin committed is not against other human beings . . . but against God's law and his son." The Western legal tradition amounts, then, to little more than a secular translation of theistic notions of sin and the reacquisition of grace through submission to punishment. Against this can be posited the horizontal Buddhist account:

> The demerit of an act lies in what it does to other forms of sentient life. That is the relation to be changed. The significant Others do not have to

be alive as identifiable individuals today; the relation of a demerit may also be to life already dead or not yet (re)born. In other words there is no way of individualising the relation. . . . Only through the assumption of full responsibility for the merits and demerits of that collectivity is the illusion of individual separateness and permanence eliminated.[62]

On face value, Galtung's preference is clear and is consistent with his earlier writings on Gandhism and structural violence that focused on the deed rather than the doer. As I have tried to show throughout, the principle deficiency of his preceding work lay in the absence of any philosophical underpinning to the autotelic value of nonviolence that a commitment to the law of karma and the principle of ahimsa might now provide. Yet he equivocates; just as he has previously resisted a total repudiation of personal responsibility for violence, so too does his sympathy with Buddhist ethics have its limits. On the one hand, Galtung embraces the idea of an eternal karmic web in which none of us can escape the consequences of bad karma and retribution has therefore little moral utility. On the other hand, he chides Buddhism for being too symmetric, too gentle in "giving us unlimited time to improve the karma."[63] Galtung wants to synthesize the eternal law of karma *and* occidental notions of limited time frames and accountability. Of course, he is not alone here; various attempts at blending Buddhist and Christian conceptions of responsibility also color the modern history of Buddhism itself.[64] Furthermore, the extent to which Galtung actually assents to the authoritative doctrinal tenets of Buddhism, as opposed to merely viewing them as insightful allegories or metaphors for the human condition, remains typically and conveniently unclear.

When it comes to exploring synthesis, Galtung shifts his attention to secularized representations of religiously inspired civilizational forms. Thus, Christian verticality is reproduced in the Western legal tradition and the substitution of crime for sin. Secularization preserves the form of Christian morality but saps it of its complex spiritual content. Although no directly comparable secularization of Buddhist ethics is identified, a similar process of spiritual evaporation is supposed. Developments in the actually existing Orient suggest that conflict is increasingly viewed in vertical terms and as a consequence "we would expect law, lawyers and litigation to be on the increase in the Buddhist part of the world."[65] Nonetheless, Buddhism offers practical insight into conflict resolution insofar as it shifts our focus away from the individual act or actor toward a relational, or structural, viewpoint. "The closest Western approximation to a Buddhist perspective," Galtung suggests, "would be a multilateral conference with all parties around the table and all issues on the table, articulating and processing all conflicts in the system, past, present and future, without pre-conditions. Highly holistic and dialectic, mature."[66]

The global implications of the Buddhist moral system can also be illustrated by reference to the moral precept of ahimsa—nonviolence to all things. If the idea of the distinctive, elemental self or other is rejected in favor of an emphasis on the interconnectedness of all elements, then violence toward other living things becomes effectively violence against oneself. In this context Galtung refers to Gandhi's interpretation of ahimsa and its premise of an essential unity of humankind. Although the appeal of ahimsa to Galtung qua pacifist is hardly surprising, the simple adoption of this moral precept is resisted. In a violent world ahimsa may be insufficient as a peace policy and in need of supplementation with concepts of defensive defense. Such pragmatism appears also compatible, however, with the Buddhist doctrine of the Middle Way that counsels against the extremes of laxity and rigidity.

Though certainly not entirely implausible, Galtung's reading of Buddhist ethics as supportive of his long-standing distinction between negative and positive peace verges on the idiosyncratic. It is an interpretation that presupposes the privileging of realizing *sukha* (equated with positive peace) over *dukkha* (equated with negative peace). According to Peter Harvey, for example, it is the overcoming of *dukkha*, both in oneself and others, that is Buddhism's central concern, and the primary ethical activity to be developed is that of giving (*dana*) as the basis for further moral development and movement toward nirvana. In pursuit of this, the Buddhist endeavors to cultivate virtue (*shila*) through adherence to the five negative precepts or abstentions contained in the *pancha-shila*. But precisely what adherence entails is variously interpreted between the schools of Buddhism and according to the degree to which Buddhism constitutes part of a larger amalgam of beliefs. It is further constrained by the doctrine of the Middle Way.[67]

There are positive implications in the language of abstention, as expressed in the principles of "lovingkindness" (*metta*) and compassion (*karuna*), and clearly Galtung wishes to emphasize the transformative potential of a Buddhist morality. He is forced to concede, however, that Buddhist scriptures are not terribly helpful here. The claim that Buddhism provides substance to the dualism of positive and negative peace (in other words, that it clearly proscribes structural and cultural violence as well as direct violence) looks especially weak when the move from ethical precepts to social relations is considered. First, as I have already noted, Galtung describes Buddhism as most insightful with regard to intrahuman and human-nature relations but underdeveloped as "a canon of thought and practice for social space and world space." Nevertheless, Galtung attempts to sketch the sociospatial implications of Buddhism: "There is a basic unity-of-man assumption, but also a multicentric construction of space, each centre being restricted to its own area of concern rather than controlling others."[68] This is no more than an idealization in contrast to the concretization of other civilizational accounts through reference to the practices of states. It is, nonetheless, the preferred variety of oriental cosmology. It allows for unity and difference but without the center-periphery gradient of other cosmologies. Developing the point further, Galtung sees Buddhism as promoting the idea of "small is beautiful" because the collective striving for Buddhahood requires a level of interaction that can only be achieved in smaller social units. This connects with his earlier explorations of an alternative beta model of development, which I described in Chapter 6, although it is an open question as to whether Buddhism was an original influence or only discovered later as a supportive source.

Second, Buddhism's tolerance can slide into quiescence toward direct and structural violence. Galtung cites Japanese Buddhism as failing to provide resistance to militarism and the perpetuation of international structural violence in the form of aggressive trade policies. Thai Buddhism has also appeared to accept a concordat with a militaristic state.[69] Of course, such observations raise complex questions as to what Buddhism actually obligates its followers to do in concrete political circumstances, but Galtung is right to note that certain interpretations of Buddhism promote contemplative retreat from the world rather than engagement with it.

This leads to a third more telling point: If decline followed inevitably by revival is seen as an inescapable consequence of the cyclical nature of existence, the turning of the wheel, then fatalism can ensue. Here Galtung's concern shows once again that he has not fully abandoned an occidental understanding of sociopolitical time or the decisive role of purposive individuals dedicated to changing the material circumstances in which they find themselves. Buddhism may provide insight into Galtung's philosophical and moral outlook but not the complete picture. This is perhaps not surprising; even in such sympathetic hands, the substantive contribution of Buddhism to a practical, global politics of peace proves to be thin on the ground.

CONCLUSION

Galtung's writing on civilizations and their cosmologies proceeds through three stages: a critique of the Occident; a survey of actually existing nonoccidental alternatives—the oriental other; and more recently an exploration of a Buddhist counterpoint to occidental Christianity.

The first stage casts his established critique of the West in a novel light through a reductionist emphasis on the theistic underpinnings of occidental civilization. At some analytical cost, Galtung endeavors to capture the "genetic code" of the West as a means to rethinking the problematic that confronts peace research: Occidental social cosmology, in particular the deep ideology of the "inner West" (more recently referred to as Occident I), *is* violence. Given this conclusion, the fact "that there is peace in the Occident, sometimes even emanating from the Occident, is something of a miracle."[70] That miracle is a product of the other "softer," more oriental Occident (Occident II) latent in the first.

The second stage is clearly the shallowest and as such does considerable damage to the normative authenticity of the third. References to such things as "the oriental mind," coupled with anecdotally based generalizations about specific cultures or cosmologies—(especially the Nipponic and Hindu) and simplistic summaries of complex cultural wholes, render the whole exercise suspect. It is tempting to assume that the connections between cosmology and the concrete behavior of states are most apparent with regard to those of which Galtung disapproves. In contrast to the more detailed exploration of the Occident, in which Galtung draws upon much of his earlier work, his treatment of the Orient is far more sketchy and impressionistic. Civilizations or cosmologies are reduced to a few religious epithets, selective reference to events, and potted summaries of historical epochs. In this respect, the essence of Said's fury against those who would suppose that there is a "real or true" Orient or Occident—although cutting across Galtung's particular civilizational partition of the world—is entirely understandable. As Said puts it, "The notion that there are geographical spaces with indigenous radically "different" inhabitants who can be defined on the basis of some religion, culture or racial essence proper to that geographical space is . . . a highly debatable idea."[71]

In Galtung's account of the constitutive assumptions of the dominant Western social cosmology, we might hear the echoes of various postmodern resistances to exclusionary intellectual practices. Yet, Galtung's analysis of cosmology is itself a large exercise in definitive essentialism premised upon a core dualism of Occident and Orient, even when belatedly moderated by the admission that it risks reductionism. The critique of the Occident and the depiction of the oriental other are both marked by the forcing of description and analysis into a limited set of reifying categories justified in terms of the apparent suggestiveness of the exercise.[72] The sometimes insightful, often obscuring, blurring of the line between suggestive abstractions and empirical truth claims is consistent with Galtung's preceding work. In spite of the sketchiness of his presentation of different civilizations, cosmologies, and cultures, there is little reticence to jump from hypothesis to conclusion. Just as modern psychiatry can be accused of forcing a diverse humanity into a limited set of personality types, often for questionable social purposes, so too can Galtung's abstracting of the cosmology of a civilization or culture slide into claims such as imputing cultural arrogance to the French, a preoccupation with being "chosen" to Jews, and a superiority complex to the Japanese. The usage of the categories of culture, civilization, and cosmology tends to suffer from a superficiality, and at times a crassness, that belies the analytical significance of a focus on "deep" civilizational codes. Galtung's choice of in-group or out-group, his preferred "other," may accord more with contemporary progressivist fashion, but in so starkly (re)inscribing the boundaries between inside and outside, or good and bad, he simply perpetuates those features of occidentalism that he apparently despises.[73] In any case, the actually existing Orient proves somewhat disappointing in Galtungian terms; hence my suggestion that analysis of it be treated as a preface to the construction of an idealized oriental other in the form of Buddhist civilization.

Judgment of the third stage is of necessity open-ended, since it is clearly an unfinished project. But it must also be more positive, for it is in the imaginary dialogue of epistemologies and civilizations, rather than in the cruder juxtaposition of the actually existing Occident and Orient, that the creative, suggestive side of Galtungian peace research comes to the fore. Galtung sees Buddhism as having a tremendous if yet untapped potential as a social and political doctrine. It is an ethos, he suggests, "perhaps in search of a concrete structure." Yet the translation proves to be difficult indeed, and the delineation of that structure emerges as an ongoing challenge to both peace research and Buddhism. Thus, "the idea that Buddhahood is something we reach together . . . the self-realisation of all" is seen as a principle that can be applied to "world space." The overall image transposed from Buddhism to peace research is of collective striving through a never-ending myriad of small, coordinated efforts to realize an open-ended condition that can be called peace or nirvana.

Galtung likens nirvana to a condition of "maximum entropy," which has been another long-standing metaphor for positive peace. Of course, he is also playing with the more usual understanding of entropy as the absence of kinetic energy in a system. For Galtung, entropy refers to a condition of messiness or disorder but not in a pejorative sense. The incapacity of a system to crystallize or establish order permits greater complexity and diversity and mitigates the reification of violent structures.[74] Against the occidental Christian image of the conflict cycle as exhibiting genesis-maturation-senescence-death can be counterpoised a Buddhist conception of perpetual conflict energy that does not die but attaches itself to the inevitable conflicts that attend life itself. Conflicts generate more positive (love-nonviolence) and negative (hatred-violence) conflict energy that is "reborn, negatively or positively, into several conflicts . . . as part of the karma of the parties and actors in those conflicts." Seen thus, the notion that conflicts can be progressively and cumulatively solved is illusory. Rather, energy as both consciousness and action is there and always will be, and the question becomes that of transforming conflict from negative to positive rather than endeavoring to resolve it.[75]

Given the increasingly overt adoption of the Buddhist alternative in his more recent work, it is not surprising that Galtung is now reticent to define the purpose and goals of peace research. Such reticence also suits these intellectual times. The very idea of positive peace takes on a more contingent quality, speaking to processes and values rather than structures and final outcomes. In stark contrast to an earlier programmatic certitude, Galtung has now conceded that "I think we shall never come to anything like a final conclusion as to what 'peace' might mean" and, perhaps more tellingly, "nor do I think we should ever hope for that to happen."[76] At this historical conjuncture, the appeal of the diffuse concept of nirvana as a metaphor for positive peace is understandable. It enables the retention of moral and practical purpose, without requiring the identification of some definitive end point that can be authoritatively known. The gentle spiral of Mahayana optimism replaces the certitude of the upward-pointing occidental arrow of progress. Once again, Galtung's peace research adjusts to fit with a shifting intellectual milieu, if never quite to accord with it.

NOTES

1. Galtung, *Buddhism*, p. 27. The "certain sense" refers to the concept of entropy that Galtung sees as central to both peace and nirvana and to which I return subsequently.

2. Galtung, "Western Civilisation," p. 146.

3. Galtung, Heiestad, and Rudeng, "On the Last 2,500 Years in Western History," p. 353. The term "postmodern" is used innocently by them.

4. Galtung, "Western Civilisation," p. 146.

5. Ibid., p. 147.

6. Ibid., p. 147.

7. Galtung, "Cultural Violence," p. 299.

8. Ibid., p. 299. Napoleon was in fact a Johnny-come-lately: In 1697 King Charles XII of Sweden took the crown from the bishop of Upsala and placed it upon his own head. Todhunter (trans.), *Voltaire's History of Charles XII*, p. 16.

9. Galtung, "Western Civilisation," p. 149.

10. In ibid., pp. 150–152, for example.

11. Galtung, "Social Cosmology and the Concept of Peace," p. 191.

12. Galtung's two sources are Bouquet and Murty, *Studies in the Problem of Peace;* and Ishida, "Beyond the Traditional Concepts of Peace."

13. Note Piscatori's observation that between varieties of Islam "the highest common factor is not very high" and "in practical terms, though not theology, there are as many Islams as there are muslims." Piscatori, *Islam in a World of Nation-States*, p. 10.

14. For an account of an intermediate *dar-al-sulh*, see Lewis, *The Political Language of Islam*, ch. 4.

15. Ishida, "Beyond the Traditional Concepts of Peace," p. 137.

16. Galtung, "Cultural Violence," p. 301.

17. Ibid., pp. 296–299.

18. Galtung, Heiestad, and Rudeng, "On the Last 2,500 Years in Western History," p. 352.

19. Ibid., p. 343.

20. Galtung, "Western Civilisation," p. 145.

21. Galtung, "Social Cosmology and the Concept of Peace," p. 196.

22. Galtung, "Conflict Resolution as Conflict Transformation," p. 5.

23. Galtung, "Cultural Violence," pp. 291, 294.

24. Ibid., p. 295.

25. Galtung, "Theory-Formation as Development," pp. 141–157.
26. Galtung, "Dialogues as Development," p. 78.
27. Galtung, "Peace Research, Peace Studies and Peace as a Profession."
28. On this point see Galtung, *Buddhism*, especially the prologue and ch. 1.
29. Galtung, "Cultural Violence," especially p. 299.
30. Galtung, "Western Civilisation," p. 151.
31. Galtung, "Peace and the World," p. 341.
32. Zimmer, *Philosophies of India*, pp. 125–126.
33. Galtung, "Peace and the World," p. 342.
34. Galtung, *The Way Is the Goal*, p. 5.
35. Galtung, "Peace and the World," p. 346, note 19.
36. See Braun, "Asian Power India: A New Equation"; and Rueland, "Europe: A Model for Asia?"
37. Ishida, "Beyond the Traditional Concepts of Peace," p. 138.
38. Galtung, *The Way Is the Goal*, pp. 1–13. Note especially the commentary (p. 13) on Gandhi's murderer—Godse—and the rejection of Gandhism by Nehru.
39. On this point see his religious mapping of the world wherein Gandhism is located at the same point between Occident and Orient as Hinduism in ibid., p. 15, table 2.
40. Galtung, "Western Civilisation," p. 155.
41. Ibid., p. 156.
42. See Galtung, "Methodology, Epistemology, Cosmology," pp. 15–27 (reproduced in Galtung, *Buddhism,* under the curious title "Buddhism and Cultural Adequacy").
43. Galtung, *Methodology and Development*, EM, 3 p. 41.
44. See Galtung, *Buddhism*, ch. 4, especially the chart on p. 107. He advises that his comparison of religious attitudes to nature should be taken "cum grano salis."
45. An example is the Japanese education system, which is ruthlessly competitive but does not threaten the underlying vertical social order. Galtung, "Western Civilisation," p. 160.
46. Ibid., p. 160.
47. Ibid., p. 162.
48. Ibid., p. 167.
49. Harvey, *An Introduction to Buddhism*, chs. 2, 7.
50. Keown, *The Nature of Buddhist Ethics*, p. 4.
51. Galtung, *Buddhism*, pp. 26–27.
52. Galtung approvingly cites the Soka-Gakkai president's extolling of the virtues of Mahayana Buddhism as "further away from the source, . . . freer, more creative, population oriented, directly concerned with laity in everyday life, more practical, down-to-earth." *Buddhism*, p. 147, note 22. Compare this with an earlier version of the same discussion that cites the Mongolian Buddhist Ochirbal thus: "What matters is not hinayana or mahayana but buddhayana!" See Galtung, "Peace and Buddhism," p. 432, note 26. Founded in 1930, the Soka-Gakkai now claims a membership of 1.26 million in 114 countries and promotes the teachings of the thirteenth-century religious figure Nichiren as the true Buddhism. Dator describes the Soka-Gakkai as more Kantian and pragmatist than Buddhist and refers to the past employment of highly intimidatory techniques known as "breaking and subduing" as a means of converting people. Dator, *Soka-Gakkai;* and Harvey; *An Introduction to Buddhism*, pp. 285–286.
53. Harvey, *An Introduction to Buddhism*, p. 11.
54. Galtung, *Buddhism*, p. 14.

55. Ibid., p. 7.

56. Ibid., p. 27. This reading is controversial, although Keown's *The Nature of Buddhist Ethics* provides a more substantive argument in support of a teleological reading of Buddhism.

57. Galtung, *Buddhism*, p. 23.

58. Ibid., p. 24.

59. Galtung, "Conflict Resolution as Conflict Transformation," p. 113. See also Galtung, "Methodology, Epistemology, Cosmology," p. 20.

60. Humphreys, *Karma and Rebirth*, p. 15.

61. Ling, *Buddhism*, p. 18.

62. Galtung, "Conflict Resolution as Conflict Transformation," p. 115.

63. Ibid., p. 116.

64. See Harvey, *An Introduction to Buddhism*, ch. 12.

65. Galtung, "Conflict Resolution as Conflict Transformation," p. 117.

66. Ibid., p. 119.

67. See the discussion in Harvey, *An Introduction to Buddhism*, ch. 9.

68. Galtung, "Peace and the World," p. 336.

69. Galtung, *Buddhism*, pp. 28–29.

70. Galtung, "Cultural Violence," p. 301.

71. Said, *Orientalism*, p. 322.

72. Galtung claims, nonetheless, that in offering at least two readings of the West (a soft periphery and hard or inner core) his method is ultimately not reductionist. "Cultural Violence," p. 304, note 19.

73. For example, after arguing that conceptions of mental disorder are filtered through "all kinds of culturally defined distinctions and discriminations," Galtung goes on to suggest that "a white South African/Israeli behaving to his family like he does to a Black/Palestinian would be considered crazy." The underlying point has undoubted force, but the discourse employed further illustrates the problem in question: By definition, a "white South African" or an "Israeli" becomes racist. See Galtung, *Buddhism*, p. 77.

74. Galtung, "Entropy and the General Theory of Peace." For a critique see Boulding, "Twelve Friendly Quarrels with Johan Galtung."

75. Galtung, "Conflict Resolution as Conflict Transformation."

76. Galtung, "The Next Twenty-Five Years of Peace Research," p. 248.

9

Conclusion

As a visiting professor . . . in the Federal Republic, I was often asked: "Aber wer sind Sie eigentlich?" (Who are you really?) Answers to the effect that "I feel guided by something like 70% Marxism, 70% Liberalism and 60% something asiatic relating to inner man as opposed to the two major Western doctrines" did not alleviate the uneasiness, probably even leading to suspicion about my arithmetic abilities.

—*Johan Galtung, 1973*[1]

Finding a pigeonhole for Galtung is not easy, and his writings consistently suggest that this is how he likes it. This could be interpreted as a sign of healthy eclecticism, but a less generous reading would detect an evasiveness the price of which is a lack of substance—a philosophical glue holding the pieces together. I have argued throughout that the origins of this inadequacy lay in the making of Galtungian peace research within the positivist scientific tradition. In the spirit of the classical exponents of "positive philosophy" (according to Marcuse, itself a contradiction *in adjecto*) he refused to bury his peace research in metaphysics or contemporary ideological debate yet proclaimed the redemptive power of scientific knowledge. The shadow of classical positivism was plain to see in Galtung's application of a technocratic mind-set to the search for a moral and political condition called peace. In so doing he adopted a form of discourse that was incapable of articulating its own normative commitment and could only assert the rightness of seeking global peace on the basis of observable cooperation and integration between discrete human collectivities. In fact, there was little attempt to substantiate even this claim, although it must be said that at the same time sections of the international relations scholarly community were endeavoring to do just that. What Galtung did was to tap into that growing sense of increasing global interdependence and proclaim the empirical extension of community across the boundaries of states as indicative of a potential condition of positive

223

peace, which perforce peace research was charged with bringing about. The impatient dismissal of "traditional peace thinking"—a Galtungian euphemism for all varieties of philosophically oriented reflections on the international system—reflected an overriding interest in the drawing up of a suitable research agenda of practical consequence. The novelty of the very idea of institutionalized peace research appeared to hold sway over the need to develop a more sound theoretical and normative base.

The young Galtung of course was aware of the need to provide foundations for the normative content of his peace research, but his capacity to do this was crippled by his adopted sociological standpoint. As I argued in Chapter 2, although his reading of structural functionalism endeavored to sever the perspective from its original biomechanical systemic assumptions, this was not done convincingly. The functional requisites of a social system were equated with values, to be ultimately derived from the subjective understandings of the members of a social system and not the abstract imperatives of the system itself. But when all was said and done, those values were largely intuited by Galtung himself. For all of his disdain for traditional peace thinking, he shared with a long-standing body of liberal, cosmopolitan thought the view that the trend toward an extension of community beyond the boundaries of nation-states (and the existence of a consensus as to the desirability of such an extension) could probably be supported by empirical research and, in any case, was self-evidently a development to be encouraged and nurtured. The use of "health" as an analogy for the value of peace was intended to underpin the sheer reasonableness of his project. Peace research was portrayed, then, as on a par with the physician's craft: an admixture of social scientific skills applied in accordance with a Hippocratic ethical obligation to improve the health of the emergent world community and not any one of its constituent elements (states, nations, classes, races, and so on). Medical science provided a descriptive imagery that Galtung continued to fall back on nearly thirty years later.[2]

This Saint-Simonian vision of the peace researcher as savant with a higher loyalty to humanity could not last. Intellectual resistance to positivist sociology combined with the countercultural upheavals of the 1960s and particular events within the peace research community to ensure that it would be challenged. But the vision was internally insecure as well. As Herman Schmid had rightly noted, Galtung's peace research had embedded its normative commitment within a systems perspective that imputed to the international system the status of a society—not merely a society of states, moreover—with a capacity to be managed. It had assumed the possibility of reform guided by values that supposedly reflected the universal interests of members of that society. The skepticism of orthodox international relations, which was premised on either the absence or limited presence of an *international* society, was not systematically addressed but simply swept aside. Equally, reflection upon the ideological content of concepts of global interdependence—Schmid's particular concern—figured little.

It is unfair nonetheless to saddle the young Galtung with the limited interest in control and regulation with which Schmid had tarred all mainstream peace researchers. Galtung's methodology was orthodox, but his politics was always transformational in intent. Even his earliest writings revealed the traces of a radical political side to his scholarly persona. Galtung's early work might have employed the barren language of social science, but it was self-evidently morally informed, not to mention playful in its spirit. He was a conscientious objector influenced by Gandhian ethics from an early age. He did leave the sociological community in the United States to establish a peace research institute in Norway at a time when such a move was likely to be seen as foolhardy. Only a few years after proclaiming his peace research, he was inviting critical reflection upon it—the invitation to which Schmid responded. It was his adoption of a particular form of sociological discourse that rendered adequate explication of the guiding moral-political vision of his peace research a necessarily extradiscursive activity. Galtung extensively explored what peace research must do and how it might do it, but in the effort to escape the limitations of legal-philosophical orthodoxy, the reason *why* it should be done was left essentially unanswered. Yet the fleshing out of the ideal end state—positive peace—did require a complex mix of philosophical and normative discussion in defense of its own validity as well as substantive political analysis in support of claims as to its possibility. As Schmid also observed, the positive content of "peace" was in fact so weakly defended that it effectively collapsed into the singular value of "nonviolence."

With the benefit of hindsight, we might engage in reconstruction and substitute the Sanskrit "ahimsa" for "nonviolence," thereby giving Schmid's assessment extra acuity. As I noted in Chapter 3, it could be inferred that Galtung's pacifism was always grounded in Gandhian ethics, and the introduction of the concept of structural violence only strengthened the connection. Gandhian ethics were, after all, compatible with both sides of the violence coin as well as the distinction between negative and positive peace. Unfortunately, Galtung at the time said little about Gandhi beyond the occasional exploration of the translatability of Gandhian ethics into principles of social action. Even the more recent exploration of a Buddhist philosophical counterpoint to the Occident is constrained still by a descriptive frame of reference and the concomitant advocacy of philosophical and epistemological eclecticism, a point I shall return to later.

A second significant flaw in Galtung's foundational model of peace research was the absence of any sustained consideration of collective or individual agency. Hedley Bull's somewhat glib dismissal of so-called idealist aspirations to realize "cosmopolitan" justice comes to mind here. In *The*

Anarchical Society Bull noted that there was "no lack of self-appointed spokesmen of the common good" and that "the views of these private individuals, whatever merit they may have, are not the outcome of any political process of the assertion and reconciliation of interests."[3] Like E. H. Carr before him, Bull argued that a new world order can only arise out of the historical conduct of politics characterized above all, in his view, by the constraining interaction of sovereign states. For many realists, debate about global change terminates at this point, as reflected in Wight's famous aphorism that international relations was a realm of "recurrence and repetition."

Initially, Galtung saw the role of the peace researcher as apolitical, the researcher providing expertise in the service of humanity in contrast to the "crude, idealistic but often naive perspective of the peace movement man."[4] It was the peace researcher armed with a technical understanding of the global social system who would identify the processes of transformation and also promote the vision to be realized, thereby helping the peace activist move from "slogan to the propositional level." For Galtung, the function of the expert was not limited to the suggestion of courses of action once values had been handed down to him; the expert was also to "influence these values . . . [and] if he is worth the title at all, will be able to point to new options never in the mind of the politicians."[5]

But in what did this expertise of the peace researcher consist? In order to realize fully the ambition encapsulated in the drawing of an analogy with medical science, a multidisciplinary and intersubjectively agreed analysis of the physiology of the global social order was required. Galtung did provide some sociological explorations of the feudal global system and the relationship between social rank and the interaction patterns of states, but he rarely extended these beyond the realm of the illustrative. The attempt to wed sociology to the study of international relations relied primarily on a taxonomic approach to concept formation and the use of analogies, the latter often presented as isomorphisms. However, the explanatory value (and hence its value as a basis for political action) of such an approach is contestable without substantiation of the claimed analogies (and isomorphisms) and a precise identification of fundamental interaction patterns.[6] In any case, as Burton observed at the time, what was occurring under the rubric of peace research was also to be found in the work of the "frontiersmen" of international relations in the United Kingdom and the United States.[7] This did not in itself undermine the objectives of Galtung's peace research but did reinforce the point that its novelty lay more in the exploration of its institutionalization and organization.

Most noticeable was the absence of analysis of the state or the power of the discourse of sovereignty as a barrier, or contributor, to peace. The combination of functionalism, systems theory, the principle of isomorphism, and a high level of abstraction facilitated a slide past the issue of the state in a system of states. On occasions Galtung obliquely acknowledged the significance of the state in its various manifestations, but the problem of world order was deemed to be essentially similar to that of organizing domestic social order. "The relations between groups within nations," Galtung averred, "were not too different from relations between nations in the international system."[8] This assumption was reinforced in the application of the concept of rank-determined behavior to the states system and the view that the study of "municipal integration" offered a useful path to the analysis of international processes of integration. The continuum between domestic and international politics was presented as smooth and uninterrupted—or at least potentially so, since the line between empirical and normative statements itself was invariably blurred. In sum, Galtung set peace research on a path that opposed the state centrism and skepticism of the realist interpretation of international relations on primarily normative grounds but that never confronted it head-on. An overemphasis on the distinctiveness of the international realm had been replaced by an uncritical adoption of systems-theoretic holism wrapped around a discursively excluded moral cosmopolitanism.

AFTER THE RUPTURE

What then of the later work produced after the impact of the radical critique—the second phase of Galtungian peace research? Were the two central problems of an inadequately articulated and hardly defended normative perspective or the lack of a theory of global social and political change resolved? On the surface, it certainly appeared as if Galtung had accepted the criticisms of his scientism. Utilizing a mixture of Gandhian ethics and structuralist terminology, he went on to develop a distinctly more critical account of the existing world order that was first signaled in the revision of the concepts of violence and peace. The introduction of the concept of structural violence was destructive of the earlier apolitical emphasis on the symmetry of conflict and decisively recast the peace researcher in the role of defender of the oppressed, no matter who they were. His language revealed a shift in focus away from the problem of direct conflict and its starkest manifestation—thermonuclear war—toward the general problem of social injustice on a global scale. The problems of peace and development became inseparably intertwined.

In spite of the overt discursive shift and the expansion of the lexicon of Galtungian peace research, a residual positivism and scientism remained. This was illustrated in a number of ways. First, the concept of structural violence was presented as a quasi-scientific category that supposedly represented a quantifiable distinction between the actual and potential of human fulfillment. It spoke to the optimal allocation of resources. But beneath the apolitical gloss of the analytical language was a normative layer that remained unexplicated still. Social justice and human fulfillment were the victims of structural violence, and the eradication of direct and structural violence was at the same moment the realization of positive peace. But precisely what this consisted in and how it was to be realized remained unclear. Structural violence was not a concept that came out of a close reading of human history, although a silent reading undoubtedly lay beneath it. Rather it was a blend of an abstract analytical category—a hypothesis of intended heuristic benefit and an unexplicated moral standpoint. Without historical and philosophical underpinnings, it had no substantive meaning outside of the normative perspective of its user. Of course, Galtung's readers were likely to have a reasonable idea of his normative leanings because in descriptive and taxonomic terms, at least, they were abundantly clear in all of his writing after the publication of "Violence, Peace and Peace Research." But if readers could bring a normative theory to the concept of structural violence, they could not derive one from it.

Second, the analysis of imperialism also revealed the remnants of scientism. "A Structural Theory of Imperialism," the most cited of Galtung's writings, endeavored to render explicit the content of structural violence in depicting a global structure whose operating principle was exploitation in various modalities. It invoked the spirit, if not the letter, of critique. More so than the earlier work, it was an intervention, a political act as much as a piece of scholarship. Yet, the global structure under investigation was itself of uncertain status, presented as an abstract analytical concept of wide application and propositional value only but appearing at the same time to lean heavily upon a normatively driven reading of global history. Galtung's theory of imperialism was intended to express a negative condition discernible in various societal formations and all spheres of human social activity from economic exchange to science itself. As such, it had a teleological core that was presupposed in the critical-descriptive sketch of an imperial world order. But, in the overt refusal to tie the analysis to concrete history and the failure to provide substantive evidence of its central claims or adequate defense of its normative assumptions, the account of imperialism was barren as scientific theory and insufficient as normative theory.

Third, the subsequent resort to the concept of human needs as a means of giving substance to the value idea of positive peace confirmed the continuing effort to remain removed from overtly normative discourse. As I noted in Chapter 6, needs offered themselves as empirical phenomena the very identification of which (itself a controversial issue) presumed the obligation to satisfy them. But on what basis can we establish who is obliged to satisfy whose needs and in what order? For Galtung, it was the most needy who had the strongest case, but without a political philosophy to contextualize the understanding of needs, obligations, and priorities, this remained a maxim of limited potency.

Finally, the scientific attitude was most starkly retained in the reconstruction of science itself. Galtung's model of constructivist science openly incorporated value sentences into its procedure, but in continuing to force the distinction between fact, theory, and value it could not improve on traditional social scientific treatment of values as objects of inquiry. It could only suggest the utility of pregiven values in the assessment of the existing world and blueprints of a preferred world. It could not pass judgment on the values themselves or tell us whether they could be realized. Science was reduced to the act of validating one class of sentences with another.

Are we then to conclude that the first two stages of Galtungian peace research are devoid of substantive normative theoretical content, the moral impulse that guides it remaining by and large external to the discourse of peace research? This would be too hasty a reading, for the lacunae in Galtung's earlier work are instructive in themselves. If we peel away the skin of scientism, a normative layer is revealed, the central theme of which is central to contemporary debate in social and political theory. In his equation of science with politics (and scientific practice with political activism) under the guise of constructivism, we can begin to grasp the essence of Galtung's normative outlook, and through a reconstruction of his writings we can understand what science always seems to have meant for Galtung throughout his intellectual odyssey.

Galtung's interpretation of science was born out of an overriding hostility to dominance and intellectual arrogance. In his words, "empiricism was relied upon as a rejection . . . of dogmatism."[9] It offered itself as an intersubjectively communicable form of knowledge that was untainted by the relativism of ideology or geopolitics. The power of science lay, for Galtung, in its apparent capacity to transcend social, intellectual, and ideological boundaries, the same seductive appeal that enticed the classical positivists to proclaim the end of theology and metaphysics. If peace research could conduct itself within the ethos of science, it might escape the contamination of (any) ideology and resist the propensity of nonscientific discourse to legitimate the domination of one part of humanity by another. Science held out the promise of public accountability. Of course, Galtung came to accept the view that the orthodox model of science was incapable of such a laudable goal, if he ever in fact profoundly held to this view. In its enslavement to the world of data, it could only legitimate the existing world and contribute to a practical discourse of social control. But even if he abandoned his earlier advocacy of the utility of peace research as a social science in the orthodox sense of the term, he retained a commitment to the notion of developing peace research as a discourse that could transcend (or at least contain within itself) differences of opinion, belief, and practice. If the history of modern social science is that of a philosophy reduced to a methodology (from positivism to empiricism), then Galtung's thought suggests a desire to move from scientific methodology back to the philosophical sentiments that once guided it. Science becomes a metaphor for an enlightened attitude.

It is in the second phase of his work that the fundamental hostility of Galtung to all forms of domination moves decisively into the foreground. Consider first the continuing refusal to align with an identifiable political philosophy and the related willingness to extract some value from them all. None received his imprimatur; none was unequivocally rejected. We should recall also Galtung's consistent unwillingness to appoint any specific social group as privileged historical agents of social change or to indicate any specific realm of human activity as *the* significant progenitor of global transformation. For Galtung, even if history was cyclical, exhibiting tendencies but revealing no determining pattern of social evolution, it was not without direction either. Though often collectivist in approach, he also constantly reiterated the satisfaction of the diverse needs of all individuals as the ultimate goal of peace research. Indeed, it was this overriding concern with diversity and the eradication of dominance in all of its manifestations that underpinned the revised model of scientific practice. It also provided the normative core of the vision of a preferred world sketched out in *The True Worlds*.

In spite of the absence of moral philosophy, the power of the second phase of Galtung's work resides in the ethical problem that it continually highlights. I referred briefly in Chapter 6 to the "dialectic of the specific and universal" and the suggestion that it was the central intellectual antinomy of our time. Todorov provides another eloquent expression of this antinomy in his proposal that the overriding ideological question confronting Western civilization today is how we might realize "equality without its compelling us to accept identity; but also difference without its degenerating into superiority/inferiority." We aspire, he goes on to say, "to rediscover the meaning of the social without losing the quality of the individual."[10] If there is a consistent theme in Galtung's work until the late 1970s and early 1980s then this is it, and its currency has since gained in strength.

Galtung's understanding of science and his model of the ideal world community were clearly predicated upon the ethical principle that existing moral, intellectual, and communal boundaries were candidates for dissolution in the search for a world free from domination, a sovereignty-free world. Whether it was the enthusiastic initial embracing of science as an ideologically neutral language that could be put in the service of values, the extraction of a model of interconnected global and local social structures from an amalgam of marxism, liberalism, and Gandhism, or the positing of an all-encompassing set of human needs worthy of satisfaction, the normative objective was consistent. Every facet of Galtung's intellectual journey to *The True Worlds* revealed a commitment to an extension of community that would overcome the antinomies (nation-state or world community, citizens or humans) of modernity yet nurture a plurality of identities.

The defense of such visions as contained in *The True Worlds* requires, arguably, an analysis of what Habermas terms the "developmental logics" of "moral and practical reasoning" in order to comprehend the barriers to the global extension of moral and social community.[11] It is this that is missing from Galtung's work up until *The True Worlds*. To paraphrase Cox, utopian thinking needs to be constrained by the comprehension of historical processes if it wishes to guide practice.[12] The investigation of possible world orders requires an understanding of the multiple logics that operate within the international system, simultaneously binding humanity together and keeping it apart.[13] That Galtung has been concerned with the extension of moral community is evident enough; but in the absence of this kind of analysis—as opposed to episodic allusions and brief sketches—Galtung could advance little beyond earlier reformist writings on world order, apart from the restatement of the project in more contemporary terms.

Let me return at this point to Hedley Bull. In contrast to the skepticism that marked *The Anarchical Society*, his subsequent work was to reveal an increasing acknowledgment of the growing cosmopolitan moral obligations incumbent upon states now conceived of as "local agents of a world common good." But this cautious shift was premised on the perception that new members of the European-founded "society of states" were politically employing their membership to shift the global political agenda in the pursuit of greater justice between states; there was a "revolt against the West" through the use of institutions of Western origin. In addition, the emergence of more culturally attuned varieties of rights-talk that acknowledged the tension between rights of states and rights of individuals, coupled with the growing perception of a variety of crises confronting the global community that could not be solved without cooperative action between states and other actors, was now giving political and, therefore, ethical substance to notions of a common good.[14]

For many contemporary critics, Bull's response was inadequate, especially in its statism. Bull took insufficient account of the impact of processes of economic and political globalization (the logics of global capital formation, production, and distribution) or the declining legitimacy and capacity of states authoritatively to represent the national public interest.[15] Nor did he adequately consider the alternative account of the state as "a mechanism for dominating, regulating and reproducing a society under given social relations."[16] In sum, by maintaining the distinction between the domestic and the international realms and by failing to consider state-civil society relations or tensions between state sovereignty and popular sovereignty, Bull continued to reduce the question of agency to that of interstate action. Nonetheless, the main point to be extracted from Bull's approach is simple enough—the need to bring together normative and political inquiry. A second and these days unfashionable point is that for all of their evident deficiencies some states can be a positive force for change in world politics. The state provides a space, albeit a heavily colonized one, for the contestation of ideas and the constitution of novel forms of practice. Blind antistatism risks simply producing a mirror image of uncritical statism.

If the state or statist international institutions do not in fact exhaust the question of agency at the global level, then who might be the plausible alternative agents of social change? Many recent critical explorations of change in world politics emphasize the contribution of still marginalized voices in the discourse of world order and the potential for nonsovereign actors—such as contemporary social movements, national and ethnic minorities, domestic and international nongovernmental coalitions and organizations—to "pose a significant challenge to the political economy of modernity of which the sovereign state is an integral part."[17] Whether such alternative actors and their discourses do offer a plausible counterpoint to orthodoxy is, of course, debatable. Given the globalized networks of power and the hegemony of their textual representations in both the academic and popular literature, the grounds for pessimism are evident enough. Equally, the recognition of cultural specificity of visions of the local or global good life induces a reticence to delineate authoritatively an all-encompassing vision to which to aspire. In exercising such caution, contemporary critiques of international relations orthodoxy, in theory or practice, can no longer be simply dismissed as latter-day varieties of an already caricatured cosmopolitan idealism. Their voices are too ambiguous and varied for that charge to stick. Nonetheless, Linklater's observation a few years ago that "it is not at all clear that any strand of social and political thought provides a compelling account of strategies of transition" continues to ring true.[18] And Galtungian peace research is no exception. A circular problem emerges in these postmodern times: If we should eschew the designing of grand, all-encompassing, and inescapably imperial visions; if we must avoid attributing a culture-smothering universality to our guiding values; if we refuse to privilege a historical agent of emancipation—then what meaning is left to attribute to notions of transition on a global scale? From what to what; by and for whom? We can pose the question more bluntly: What then is the point of peace research?

CULTURE, BUDDHISM, AND PEACE RESEARCH

In the third, most recent phase of Galtung's peace research some of these issues are confronted. The manner of its presentation—its "intellectual style" to use one of Galtung's favored phrases—reveals certain telling, sometimes tedious commonalities with the preceding phases, but it also introduces new significant elements. Indeed, it is arguable that they further contribute to the erosion of any determinant disciplinary boundary between Galtungian peace research and various other contemporary critical analyses of world order, notwithstanding his continuing and by now rather strange evocation of a model of the professional peace researcher.

In reflecting and sometimes anticipating trends abroad in social and political thought more generally, the recent work offers further evidence of Galtung's undoubted ability to "sense new directions of thought and concern in relation to peace research and give them analytical status."[19] As I noted in the introductory chapter, the label *postmodernism* is now applied to a body of literature that, inter alia, emphasizes the cultural dimensions of global social life and problematizes the categories and practices upon which post-Enlightenment reformist discourse has depended. Both of these tendencies can be found throughout the most recent phase of Galtung's writing, and the consequences for peace research are dramatic. Gone are the universalizing visions of an ideal world order. The postulation of a set of guiding values takes on a more contingent, culturally sensitized quality. It was not a case of sudden tectonic shift, for as I have already noted, such movements were prefigured in *The True Worlds*. Emerging out of the third phase is a more open-ended but limited vision of greater intercourse between civilizations and their cosmological or epistemological components. We can borrow from the distinctive language of this work to capture its novel qualities. If the earlier Galtung operated with a Hindu conception of a centerless, all-inclusive political space, then the contemporary Galtung employs from Buddhism the spatial imagery of a spiritually unified humanity in a multicentric sociopolitical order. At face value, the latter does not sound very different from the extant global order composed of states, nations, and peoples. But Galtung's Buddhistic vision is characterized by the absence of hierarchy and hegemony, the logics of power that make the prevailing world order so fractious. Above all, what he takes from Buddhist philosophy is the moral premise that in spite of our differences all of humanity is bound together within a spiritual and moral web from which it cannot escape. There is no need to refer to an omnipotent creator to grasp the necessity of moral action. Though only intermittently visible until the most recent phase of his work, in the final analysis this thread can be traced back through all of Galtung's writings.

It was a stumbling path that Galtung took to his current standpoint. The juxtaposition of actually existing cosmologies suffered from the now familiar problem of categorical ambiguity. Did these civilizations exist as such, or were they abstract idiomatic representations, useful only for purposes of illustration or exploration? The reductionism involved in presenting the dialogue of civilizations as essentially a dialogue between Christianity (albeit in soft and hard versions) and Buddhism ran counter to the supposed cultural sensitivity of a focus on civilizations and their cosmologies. The fallacy of the occidental depiction of the world as composed of a superior core and a lesser periphery in need of enlightenment was being supplanted with a hardly more nuanced division of the world into Occident and Orient. Ostensibly, Galtung's dualism differed in its preference for East over West; yet Galtung's preferred Orient skated uncertainly between the real and the imaginary, sensitivity and sheer prejudice.

In spite of the flaws in its execution, the thrust of the third phase of Galtungian peace research remains, in my view, highly suggestive. The notion that the source of violence lies partly in our cosmologies or cultures is difficult to gainsay. Equally, the implication that peace in the fullest sense requires critical reflection upon the foundational assumptions that pervade political discourse offers a necessary corrective to the assumption that the problem of violence can be resolved at the level of social and political structure alone. Again, this is a theme that resonates with contemporary critiques of modernity. More sobering still is the Buddhist-inspired acknowledgment that the search for peace is a difficult and perpetual process. This is not to say that the third stage is entirely distinctive from the first two. The approach is still avowedly holistic, only now the totality of humankind is expressed more in the spiritually suffused language of Buddhism than in the mechanical atonality of systems-theoretic functionalism or the crudities of a marxian-style structuralism.

The most significant contribution of the third phase of Galtung's peace research, then, is the provision—if not the complete explication—of a moral-philosophic dimension. From an initial rejection of peace philosophy, Galtung he has arrived at a point where he needs to appeal for peace research to open up to the influences of "the humanities, history of ideas, philosophy and theology."[20] There is perhaps an element of tragedy in the fact that Galtung has himself taken so long to openly acknowledge this obvious point. Since serving time in a Norwegian gaol for refusing conscription, he has clearly been influenced profoundly by Gandhian ethics. More recently, Mahayana Buddhism has come to suffuse his writing and his practical-oriented imagination to a degree that suggests that the quantitative account of his personal philosophy, cited at the beginning of this chapter, may be in need of some revision. Oriental philosophy does not provide the complete picture, as I concluded in Chapter 8; the extent of its influence remains somewhat mysterious, since Galtung is not averse to identifying the limitations of the oriental or Buddhist worldview. His continuing advocacy of eclecticism reminds us that occidental philosophical elements continue to be at play.

Such eclecticism is further underscored in the third phase by the combination—strange at first sight—of an overt spiritualism with a return to the more orthodox issues of defense and security, albeit in the guise of defensive defense and transarmament. On closer inspection the combination is not so strange. It is explained in part by the background of Cold War in the early to mid-1980s and the insanity of increasingly grandiose proposals for national defense premised upon continuing belief in technological responses to political conflict, such as the Strategic Defense Initiative (Star Wars). Arguably, this was a context-induced pragmatism in which calls for disarmament are acknowledged to be an inadequate response to public fear of insecurity (although Galtung has rarely enthused about disarmament as a peace strategy), but it also reflects a distinctly Buddhist sense of the pragmatic. The guiding commitment to ahimsa is connected with a sense of the possible and the viable. The Buddhist wheel turns slowly, but it does turn. Nonoffensive defense and cognate ideas such as collective security speak to the practical and the transformational at the same time. They can be construed as having a cosmological dimension—contributions to a sustained challenge to orthodox mind-sets about security and its provision.

To read the first phase of Galtung's writing is to detect the voice of the reformist social democrat–cum–radical liberal. The second phase of his work secreted a considerable debt to Marx, if not to the socialism actually existing. But none of these influences stands alone, not least because of the continuing background presence of Gandhi. A further clue to the occidental dimensions of Galtung's own worldview can be found in a brief discussion on diversity in intellectual styles. Having slated, somewhat flippantly, various Western intellectual styles—the Teutonic, the Gallic, and the Saxonic—Galtung refers to the Nordic intellectual approach. It has none of the elegance characteristic of the Gallic intellectual product, exhibiting instead the combined influence of "saxonic data-gathering and documentation" and "teutonic speculation and theory-formation." But, he says, Nordic social scientists are also distinguished by a desire to be read by society at large and a disinterest in intellectual commentary: "What they read about such things will generally not be mentioned in verbal discourse but kept in the background, in the memory, as something against which to check one's own approach."[21] Part of the explanation for the openness and eclecticism of Nordic scholarship may lie in the fact that the Nordic states are small, "less hampered by imperial traditions and by internal class contradictions" and as a consequence less repressive and more nurturing of intellectual and methodological diversity.

Here Galtung is doing no more than describing himself. But there is also the intimation of a normative theory of the state at play. His comments on the Nordic social scientist allude to the connection between the culturally determined inside and the external orientation of the state. To return to an earlier point, one of the notable omissions in Galtung's work is a sustained interrogation of the state as a social formation, or the place of sovereignty in its discourse of legitimation. In his earlier work, the emphasis on the interdependent global social system pushed the state aside.

In the second phase, the adoption of a structuralist perspective cut across states, rendering them secondary agents—via media—within larger networks of exploitation. The state appears as little more than a site for the reproduction of a global center-periphery structure. In the third phase, the categories of civilization and cosmology perform a similar marginalizing function. It is plausible, then, to impute to Galtung not merely an indifference but an active hostility to the state—that "catastrophic idea"—and the system of states, not least for the obvious reason of their complicity in the perpetuation of horrendous violence. For Galtung, to focus on the state is to avert one's eyes from humans and their needs. But, again, all is not quite as it seems. On occasions, especially when Galtung alludes to his own Nordic origins, he seems to concede that the state is not in fact an unchanging universal form or an entirely negative category. He founded the International Peace Research Institute in Olso, Norway, with grumbling assistance from the state. He has praised certain European states, notably Switzerland and Sweden, for employing innovative interpretations of defense policy that at least in part give the lie to the hegemony of strategic orthodoxy.[22] At certain points he comes close to acknowledging that certain states, like any other social actors, are possessed of an innate moral power. Again, it is the Nordic states that provide the case in point. In a 1989 review essay on Krippendorf's savaging of the state as the evil twin of the military, Galtung expresses sympathy but resists the wholesale dismissal of the armed, bounded state. Both the pacifist route (abolish the military) or the anarchist road (abolish the state) are rejected as ahistorical. For Galtung, the challenge is to "subvert the moral, intellectual and historical legitimacy of the 'higher purposes' of those who hold political power within the framework of states."[23] It is not the state that is the fundamental problem but who "owns" it. More telling is his observation that had Krippendorf made his point of departure Norway rather than Prussia, then a somewhat different conclusion might have ensued.

To suggest that Galtung's philosophy can be described as a blend of Nordic reasonableness and Buddhist ethics is only to hazard a guess, albeit, I would claim, an informed one. To that mix, one could also add a dose of Konrad's and Havel's antipolitical politics. Fundamental questions about the compatibility of these diverse elements remain unanswered. Still, the contemporary intellectual milieu is arguably more tolerant of such esoteric philosophical collages, although in place of Galtung's preferred term—eclecticism—we might now employ that of "pastiche" to describe his oeuvre, citing the self-description with which this chapter commenced in anecdotal support. It is up to the reader to determine whether this is a positive or pejorative attribution. In the final analysis, perhaps Buddhism, the Nordic style, and antipolitics do not make such strange bedfellows. The first two contain within them an emphasis on a middle way, *Madhyama Pratipad* and *Lagom*, respectively. All fit neatly with Galtung's current focus: Two represent softer variants of the occidental norm and the other an idealization of an oriental partner-in-dialogue. In this respect the contemporary phase of Galtungian peace research can also be read as the rendering public of a long-standing private dialogue internal to Galtung himself.

A FUTURE FOR PEACE RESEARCH?

Two concluding points concerning peace research generally can be drawn from the preceding discussion. The first is that, by and large, self-consciously labeled peace research, and not only Galtung's contribution to it, continues to suffer from a philosophical deficit. But the addressing of this deficiency seems hardly to be a task solely for something called peace research unless the label is stripped of meaning. It is when the philosophical and normative content of "peace" in its fullest sense is addressed that disciplinary boundaries necessarily dissolve. If the range of themes found within Galtung's work can be contained within the rubric of peace research, then all contemporary critical writing on the global dimensions of social life warrants inclusion. A distinctive province of peace research becomes difficult, perhaps impossible, to discern.[24] The label *peace research* now indicates little more than an imprecise normative orientation the content of which is continually contested. Alternatively, it can be cast as a rather large exercise in collation. If we consider the conceptual icons of contemporary peace research, most of them introduced by Galtung, we might rightly suspect that much of their substantive content comes from elsewhere. For example, the concept of structural violence would be familiar to anyone working within the marxist tradition of political economy. The concept of positive peace is amenable to a variety of readings and interchanges comfortably with social justice, human fulfillment, or a just world order. In sum, there is little evidence that peace research constitutes in and of itself a distinctive philosophical or theoretical viewpoint. The constant expansion of its purview may be interpreted as a sign of dynamism, the arbitrariness of the label a virtue; but it can also be seen as acquiring the qualities of an intellectual black hole wherein something vital, a praxeological edge or purpose, is lost.

The second point is that to write an obituary for Galtungian peace research would, nonetheless, be premature. Peace research can be conceived of still as a site or as space, be it an institution or a mind-set, in which a critical cognitive intent can be brought to bear upon a range of concrete problems. In this respect an argument can be made for a restoration of focus, a renarrowing of its province but in a context of continuing openness to a range of critical voices. This is not to suggest that peace research simply revert back to the agenda of conflict analysis or the kind of traditional peace thinking that Galtung railed against more than a quarter century ago or, for that matter, the scientism of his foundational model (is the act of re-finement necessarily an act of *re*closure?). But it is to suggest that peace research can serve best as a conduit between developments in the wider fields of social and political theory and the continuing problem of direct violence within and between states.[25] Aspects of that problem are already the subjects of numerous established areas of research that remain of prac-tical value. It seems otiose to deny the continuing need for alternative sources of data on and analysis of the problems of international direct vi-olence.[26] Neither can the rather limited focus on arms control be dis-counted, given the weapons at stake. Equally, the study of the institution of war and its developmental logic remains urgent and incomplete. To these we can add a range of newer areas of a more conceptual and open-ended form, in particular the critical engagement with the discourses of de-fense and strategic studies and the development of alternative security strategies at the national, regional, and global levels. In both cases there can already be detected the impact of iconoclastic postmodern and femi-nist perspectives that serve to open up further the discourse of security to scrutiny and revision.[27]

A renewed pointedness in peace research toward the problem of direct violence does not obviate the need to draw deeper from diverse fields of inquiry including moral philosophy, international relations, social and po-litical theory, sociology, political economy, discourse analysis, historical sociology, and cultural studies.[28] Peace research redefined would remain a tributary to a larger quest, flowing both ways. It might better ensure, however, that insights gleaned from the interchange of ideas have practical consequence. Otherwise, to paraphrase Galtung, what would be the point?

NOTES

1. Galtung, "Deductive Thinking and Political Practice," p. 207, note 23.

2. See Galtung, "Peace Research, Peace Studies and Peace as a Profession" wherein the analogy with medical science is reasserted as well as the value of a Hippocratic oath that commits the peace research graduate to adopting the formula of "peace by peaceful means," a short form of the Gandhian "ethical intuition about the unity of means and ends." See also Galtung, "Twenty-Five Years of Peace Research" and "Scientists and the Peace Movement."

3. Bull, *The Anarchical Society*, p. 85.

4. Galtung's views on the peace movement of the early 1960s can be found in his "International Programs of Behavioural Science," pp. 176–180.

5. Galtung, "Peace Research: Science, or Politics in Disguise?" p. 233.

6. On this point see the review of Galtung's work in Holm, "On a Major Event in the Social Sciences."

7. Burton, "Peace Research and International Relations."

8. Galtung, "Peace Research: Science, or Politics in Disguise?" p. 227.

9. Galtung, "Peace Research: Past Experiences and Future Perspectives," p. 250.

10. Todorov, *The Conquest of America*, p. 249.

11. I take this point from Linklater, "Marxism and International Relations."

12. Cox, "Social Forces, States and World Orders," p. 130. Note also Gidden's observation that an adequate theory of international relations that can continue the project of analyzing the human prospects for increasing autonomy and realizing individual and collective emancipation must not only appeal for a renewal of utopianism but also mix it with "the firmest form of realism." See Giddens, *The Nation State and Violence*, p. 334.

13. On this theme see Linklater, *Beyond Realism and Marxism*.

14. Bull, *Justice in International Relations*.

15. An example of this now common line of argument can be found in chapter 2 of Camilleri and Falk, *The End of Sovereignty?*

16. Halliday cited in Camilleri and Falk, *The End of Sovereignty?* p. 37.

17. Camilleri and Falk, *The End of Sovereignty*, p. 221. See also Thompson, *Justice and World Order*, ch. 9; and Walker, *One World, Many Worlds*.

18. Linklater, *Beyond Realism and Marxism*, p. 172.

19. This incisive comment is taken from Richard Falk's comments on the original manifestation of this work as a Ph.D. thesis.

20. Galtung, "Cultural Violence," p. 302.

21. Galtung, "Methodology, Epistemology, Cosmology," pp. 51–52.

22. On this point see Galtung, *There Are Alternatives*, ch. 4.

23. Galtung, "The State, the Military and War," p. 103.

24. On this point, compare the assessments of peace research offered by Mack and Camilleri in Higgott and Richardson (eds.), *International Relations*, chs. 13 and 14.

25. Note the current research output of the Centre for Peace and Conflict Research, Copenhagen, which focuses on Nordic and European security very broadly defined: nonoffensive defense, military conversion, the idea of "international society," and the social and cultural origins of violence. See its "Research Plan for the Years 1993–1996." See also Øberg (ed.), *Nordic Security in the 1990s*. The prosaic title belies its rich content.

26. Note here the seminal role of the Stockholm International Peace Research Institute (SIPRI). Its foundational commitment was to "a factual and balanced account of a controversial subject—the arms race and attempts to stop it." Twenty years after its establishment, the then director still saw the institution's primary focus as "what is going on in the world military sector." See Blackaby, "Peace Research and the Stockholm Institute of Peace Research (SIPRI)."

27. See, for example, the various contributions in Der Derian and Shapiro (eds.), *International/Intertextual Relations*; and Peterson (ed.), *Gendered States*.

28. An illustration of how peace research can remain both diverse and focused is provided in Camilleri, "The Evolving Agenda of Peace Research," especially pp. 358–368. Camilleri also makes much of the theoretical and philosophical deficiencies of peace research.

Select Bibliography

WORKS BY GALTUNG

Only cited works are listed. They include coauthored or coedited items. Works have generally been cited by short titles. Works frequently cited have been identified by abbreviations, as have the titles of collections of works. The date of essays taken from the collections is that of the original presentation or publication of the specific essay and not that of the overall collection unless they were clearly written for that volume. For a complete bibliography of Galtung's work until 1990 see *Johan Galtung Bibliography 1990*, Oslo, International Peace Research Institute, 1990.

EEC	"Empiricism, Criticism and Constructivism: Three Aspects of Scientific Activity" (1977)
EM, 1–3	*Essays in Methodology*, Volumes 1–3
EPR, 1–6	*Essays in Peace Research*, Volumes 1–6
STI	"A Structural Theory of Imperalism" (1971)
TTW	*The True Worlds: A Transnational Perspective*
VPRR	"Violence, Peace and Peace Research"

"After Camelot," *EM*, 2, 1967, pp. 161–180.
Buddhism: A Quest for Unity and Peace, Honolulu, Dae Won Sa Buddhist Temple, 1988.
"Can We Learn from the Chinese People?" *World Development*, 4(10/11), 1976, pp. 883–888 (with F. Nishimura).
"Conflict Resolution as Conflict Transformation: The First Law of Thermodynamics Revisited," *Estudios Internacionales Revista del IRIPAZ*, 3(6), 1992, pp. 111–119.
Cooperation in Europe, Oslo, Norwegian Universities Press, 1970 (with S. Lodgaard, eds.).
"Cuba: Anti-Imperialism and Socialist Development," *Papers*, 7, 1980, pp. 206–218.
"Cultural Violence," *Journal of Peace Research*, 27(3), 1990, pp. 291–305.
"Deductive Thinking and Political Practice: An Essay on Teutonic Intellectual Style," *EM*, 2, 1972, pp. 194–209.

"Development from Above and the Blue Revolution: The Indo-Norwegian Project in Kerala," *EPR*, 5, 1974, pp. 343–360.
"Dialogues as Development," *EM*, 3, 1988, pp. 68–89.
"Disarmament and Environment: The Dual Purpose Agent," *Papers*, 6, 1972, pp. 14–20.
"The Dynamics of Rank Conflict: An Essay on Single Versus Multiple Social Systems," *EPR*, 3, 1977, pp. 182–196.
"An Editorial," *Journal of Peace Research*, 1(1), 1964, pp. 1–4.
"Empiricism, Criticism and Constructivism: Three Aspects of Scientific Activity" (revised), *EM*, 1, 1977, pp. 41–71.
"Empiricism, Criticism, Constructivism: Three Approaches to Scientific Activity," *Synthese*, 24, 1972, pp. 343–372.
"Entropy and the General Theory of Peace," *EPR*, 1, 1967, pp. 47–75.
"Eschatology, Cosmology and the Formation of Visions," *Papers*, 6, 1979, pp. 205–234.

Essays in Methodology (EM, 1–3)
   Methodology and Ideology (Essays in Methodology Volume 1), Copenhagen, Christian Ejlers, 1977.
   Papers on Methodology (Essays in Methodology Volume 2), Copenhagen, Christian Ejlers, 1979.
   Methodology and Development (Essays in Methodology Volume 3), Copenhagen, Christian Ejlers, 1988.

Essays in Peace Research (EPR, 1–6)
   Peace, Research, Education, Action (Essays in Peace Research Volume 1), Copenhagen, Christian Ejlers, 1975.
   Peace, War and Defence (Essays in Peace Research Volume 2), Copenhagen, Christian Ejlers, 1976.
   Peace and Social Structure (Essays in Peace Research Volume 3), Copenhagen, Christian Ejlers, 1978.
   Peace and World Structure (Essays in Peace Research Volume 4), Copenhagen, Christian Ejlers, 1980.
   Peace Problems: Some Case Studies (Essays in Peace Research Volume 5), Copenhagen, Christian Ejlers, 1980.
   Transarmament and the Cold War: Peace Research and the Peace Movement (Essays in Peace Research Volume 6), Copenhagen, Christian Ejlers, 1988.

The European Community: A Superpower in the Making, Oslo, Universitetsforlaget, 1973.
"Expectations and Interaction Processes," *Inquiry*, 2, 1959, pp. 213–234.
"Feudal Systems, Structural Violence and the Structural Theory of Revolutions," *EPR*, 3, 1970, pp. 197–267.
"Foreign Policy Opinion as a Function of Social Position," *EPR*, 3, 1964, pp. 43–73.
"A Framework for the Analysis of Social Conflict," *Papers*, 2, 1958, pp. 31–80.
"Functionalism in a New Key," *EM*, 1, 1969, pp. 131–159.
"Gandhi and Conflictology," *Papers*, 5, 1971, pp. 107–158.
Gandhi's Politiske Etikk, Oslo, Tanum, 1955 (with A. Naess).
"Generalized Methodology for Social Research," *EM*, 1, 1977, pp. 230–246.

"Global Goals, Global Processes and the Prospects for Human and Social Development: A Prolegomenon to a GPID World Model," *Papers*, 7, 1979, pp. 33–96.

"Human Needs and Human Rights," *Bulletin of Peace Proposals*, 8(3), 1977, pp. 251–258 (with A. Wirak).

"Human Values," *Bulletin of Peace Proposals*, 6, 1974, pp. 156–159 (with M. Cifuentes, A. Guha, A. Loevbraek, S. Sjolie, A. Wirak).

"International Air Communication," *EPR*, 4, 1980, pp. 152–204 (with N.P. Gleditsch).

"International Programs of Behavioural Science: Research in Human Survival," *EPR*, 1, 1967, pp. 167–187.

"Introduction," *EPR*, 3, 1978, pp. 21–27.

"Introduction," *EPR*, 5, 1980, pp. 19–28.

"Is Peaceful Research Possible? On the Methodology of Peace Research," *EPR*, 2, 1974, pp. 263–279.

"Is There a Chinese Strategy of Development?" *Papers*, 6, 1979, pp. 295–311.

"The Limits to Growth and Class Politics," *EPR*, 5, 1972, pp. 325–341.

Mankind 2000, Oslo, Norwegian Universities Press, 1969 (with R. Jungk).

"The Meaning of Peace," *Papers*, 5, 1969, pp. 33–50.

Members of Two Worlds: A Development Study of Three Villages in Western Sicily, Oslo, Norwegian Universities Press, 1971.

"Methodology, Epistemology, Cosmology," *EM*, 3, 1988, pp. 15–67.

"The New Economic Order in World Politics" in A.W. Singham (ed.), *The Non-aligned Movement in World Politics*, Westport, Conn., Lawrence Hill & Co., 1977, pp. 158–174.

"The Next Twenty-Five Years of Peace Research: Tasks and Prospects," *EPR*, 6, 1988, pp. 244–259.

"Notes on Technical Assistance: The Indo-Norwegian Project in Kerala," *EPR*, 4, 1961, pp. 536–599.

"Notes on the Difference Between Physical and Social Science," *Inquiry*, 1(1), 1958, pp. 7–34.

"Occidental Cosmology and the Theories of Peace and Development," unpublished manuscript, 1984, Berlin, Berghoff Stiftung.

"On Alpha and Beta and Their Many Combinations," *Papers*, 6, 1979, pp. 69–112.

"On the Causes of Terrorism and Their Removal," *IFDA Dossier*, 66, 1988, pp. 29–42.

"On the Future of the International System," *EPR*, 4, 1967, pp. 615–644.

"On the Future of the World System: Territorial and Non-Territorial," *EPR*, 4, 1967, pp. 645–672.

"On the Last 2,500 Years in Western History and Some Remarks on the Coming 500," in P. Burke (ed.), *The New Cambridge Modern History, Volume 13*, Cambridge, Cambridge Univ. Press, 1979, pp. 318–362 (with T. Heiestad and E. Rudeng).

"On the Meaning of Non-Violence," *EPR*, 2, 1965, pp. 341–377.

"On the Structure of Creativity," *EM*, 2, 1970, pp. 210–226.

"On the Theory of Theory Construction," *EM*, 1, 1974, pp. 190–213.

"Only One Quarrel with Kenneth Boulding," *Journal of Peace Research*, 24(2), 1987, pp. 199–203.

"An Outline of Structural-Functional Theory Applied to the Analysis of Social Change," *Papers*, 2, 1959, pp. 149–178.

"Overdevelopment and Alternative Ways of Life in High Income Countries," *Papers*, 6, 1978, pp. 113–150.

"Pacifism from a Sociological Point of View," *Journal of Conflict Resolution*, 3(1), 1959, pp. 67–84.

Papers: A Collection of Works Previously Available Only in Manuscript or Very Limited Circulation Mimeographed or Photocopied Editions (*Papers*, 2–7)
  Volume 2, *Papers in English 1958–1960*, Oslo, Oslo International Peace Research Institute (PRIO), 1980.
  Volume 3, *Papers in English 1961–1964*, Oslo, PRIO, 1980.
  Volume 4, *Papers in English 1966–1967*, Oslo, PRIO, 1980.
  Volume 5, *Papers in English 1968–1972*, Oslo, PRIO, 1980.
  Volume 6, *Papers in English 1973–1979*, Oslo, PRIO, 1980.
  Volume 7, *Papers in English 1980*, Oslo, PRIO, 1980.

"Peace and Buddhism: An Evaluation of Strong and Weak Points," *EPR*, 6, 1986, pp. 369–378.
"Peace and the World as Inter-civilisational Interaction," in R. Vayrnen (ed.), *The Quest for Peace*, Beverly Hills, Sage/International Social Science Council, 1987, pp. 330–347.
"Peace, Peace Theory and an International Peace Academy," *Papers*, 5, 1969, pp. 51–102.
"Peace Research as Positive Peace Strategy," *Papers*, 5, 1972, pp. 191–204.
"Peace Research," *EPR*, 1, 1968, pp. 150–166.
"Peace Research, Peace Studies and Peace as a Profession: Three Phases in the Emergence of a New Discipline," in T. Woodhouse (ed.), *Peacemaking in a Troubled World*, New York, Berg, 1991.
"Peace Research: Future Possibilities and Necessities," *EPR*, 1, 1967, pp. 188–223.
"Peace Research: Past Experiences and Future Perspectives," *EPR*, 1, 1971, pp. 244–262.
"Peace Research: Science, or Politics in Disguise?" *EPR*, 1, 1967, pp. 224–243.
"Perspectives on Development: Past, Present and Future," *EPR*, 3, 1976, pp. 315–332.
"Positivism and Dialectics: A Comparison," *EM*, 1, 1976, pp. 214–229.
"Rank and Social Integration: A Multidimensional Approach," *EPR*, 3, 1966, pp. 133–181.
"Science and Development Assistance," *Papers*, 5, 1971, pp. 159–182.
"Science as Invariance-Seeking and Invariance-Breaking Activity," *EM*, 1, 1974, pp. 72–97.
"Science Assistance and Neo-Colonialism: Some Ethical Problems," *EM*, 2, 1976, pp. 180–193.
"Scientists and the Peace Movement," *Bulletin of Peace Proposals*, 17(1), 1986, pp. 79–86.
"Self-Reliance: An Overriding Strategy for Transition," in R. Falk, S.S. Kim, and S.H. Mendlovitz, (eds.), *Toward a Just World Order* (Studies on a Just World Order, Volume 1), Boulder, Colo., Westview Press, 1982, pp. 602–622.
"Small Group Theory and the Theory of International Relations: A Study in Isomorphism," *EPR*, 4, 1968, pp. 27–53.
"Social Cosmology and the Concept of Peace," *Journal of Peace Research*, 18(2), 1981, pp. 183–199.
"Social Position, Party Identification and Foreign Policy Orientation: A Norwegian Case Study," *EPR*, 3, 1967, pp. 74–104.
"The Social Sciences: An Essay on Polarisation and Integration," *EM*, 2, 1968, pp. 15–45.
"Social Structure and Science Structure" (revised 1977), *EM*, 1, 1974, pp. 13–40.
"Socio-Cultural Factors and the Development of Sociology in Latin America," *EM*, 2, 1966, pp. 136–160.

"Sociology 2," *Papers*, 2, 1958, pp. 111–142.

"Sociology 49," *Papers*, 2, 1958, pp. 87–110.

"The State, The Military and War," *Journal of Peace Research*, 26(1), 1989, pp. 101–105.

"Structural Analysis and Chemical Models," *EM*, 1, 1974, pp. 160–188.

"Structural and Direct Violence: A Note On Operationalisation," *EPR*, 1, 1971, pp. 135–139 (with T. Hoivik).

"A Structural Theory of Agression," *EPR*, 3, 1964, pp. 105–132.

"A Structural Theory of Imperialism," *EPR*, 4, 1971, pp. 437–481.

"A Structural Theory of Imperialism—Ten Years Later," *Millennium: Journal of International Studies*, 9(3), 1980, pp. 183–196.

"A Structural Theory of Integration," *EPR*, 4, 1967, pp. 366–392.

"A Structural Theory of Revolution," *EPR*, 4, 1974, pp. 268–314.

"The Structure of Foreign News: The Presentation of the Congo, Cuba and Cyprus Crises in Four Norwegian Newspapers," *EPR*, 4, 1965, pp. 118–151.

"The Structure of Traditionalism: A Case Study from Western Sicily," *Journal of International Affairs*, 19(2), 1965, pp. 333–346.

"A Talk Held at a UNESCO Seminar at Langkollen, Norway, 1961," *Papers*, 3, 1961, pp. 7–18.

"Teaching and Infrastructural Problems of Peace Research: The Role of Universities and Other Institutes of Higher Learning," *EPR*, 1, 1969, pp 280–290.

"Theories of Conflict," *Papers*, 4, 1967, pp. 29–86.

"Theories of Peace: A Synthetic Approach to Peace Thinking," *Papers*, 4, 1967, pp. 87–311.

Theory and Methods of Social Research, Oslo, Universitetsforlaget, 1967.

"Theory-Formation as Development," *EM*, 3, 1988, pp. 133–175.

There Are Alternatives! Four Roads to Peace and Security, Nottingham, Spokesman, 1984.

"Towards a Theory of Freedom and Identity: A New Frontier in Peace Research," *EPR*, 5, 1980, pp. 401–431.

Towards Self-Reliance and Global Interdependence, Ottowa, Canadian Development Agency, 1978.

"Transarmament: From Offensive to Defensive," *Journal of Peace Research*, 21(2), 1984, pp. 128–139.

The True Worlds: A Transnational Perspective, New York, The Free Press/Institute for World Order, 1980.

"Twenty-Five Years of Peace Research: Ten Challenges and Some Responses," *Journal of Peace Research*, 22(2), 1985, pp. 141–158.

"Two Ways of Being Western: Some Similarities Between Liberalism and Marxism," *Papers*, 5, 1972, pp. 215–240.

"A Typology of Peace Thinking," *Papers*, 4, 1967, pp. 13–28 (with F. Van den Burg, S.B. Johansen, A. Egge, I.E. Galtung, H. Hveem, R. Jasica, and N. Shapiro).

Var Nye Verden: Artikler og Foredrag Gjennom Ti Ar (Our New World: Articles and Speeches over Ten Years), Oslo, Institute for Social Research, 1962.

"Violence, Peace and Peace Research," *EPR*, 1, 1969, pp. 109–134.

The Way Is the Goal: Gandhi Today, Ahmedabad, Gujarat Vidyapith Peace Research Centre, 1992.

"Western Civilisation: Anatomy and Pathology," *Alternatives*, 7, 1981, pp. 145–169.

"What If the Devil Were Interested in Peace Research?" *Journal of Peace Research*, 25(1), 1988, pp. 1–4.

"Why the Concern with Ways of Life?" *Papers*, 7, 1980, pp. 307–333 (with D. Poleszynski and M. Wemegah).

"World Indicators Program," *Bulletin of Peace Proposals*, 4(4), 1972, pp. 354–358.

GENERAL REFERENCES

Abrahamson, M. *Functionalism*, Englewood Cliffs, N.J., Prentice-Hall, 1978.

Adorno, T.W. (ed), *The Positivist Dispute in German Sociology*, London, Heinemann, 1976.

Arendt, H. *The Human Condition*, Chicago, Univ. of Chicago Press, 1958.

Aron, R. *Main Currents of Sociological Thought*, Volume 2, Harmondsworth, Penguin, 1967.

Ashley, R.K. "The Geopolitics of Geopolitical Space: Towards a Critical Social Theory of International Politics," *Alternatives*, 12, 1987, pp. 403–434.

Ashley, R.K. "Living on Borderlines: Man, Poststructuralism and War," in J. Der Derian and M.J. Shapiro (eds.), *International/Intertextual Relations: Postmodern Readings of World Politics*, Lexington, Mass., Lexington Books, 1989, pp. 259–322.

Ashley, R.K. "Political Realism and Human Interests," *International Studies Quarterly*, 25(2), 1981, pp. 204–236.

Ayer, A.J. *The Foundations of Empirical Knowledge*, London, Macmillan, 1940.

Ayer, A.J. *Language, Truth and Logic*, London, Victor Gollancz, 1936.

Baran, P. *The Political Economy of Growth*, New York, Monthly Review Press, 1957.

Bay, C. "Needs, Wants and Political Legitimacy," *Canadian Journal of Political Science*, 1(3), 1968, pp. 241–260.

Bellany, I. "Peace Research: Means and Ends," *International Affairs*, 52(1), 1976, pp. 13–26.

Benton, T. *The Philosophical Foundations of the Three Sociologies*, London, Routledge & Kegan Paul, 1977.

Berger, P. *Pyramids of Sacrifice: Political Ethics and Social Change*, New York, Penguin, 1974.

Bernstein, R.J. *The Restructuring of Social and Political Theory*, London, Methuen, 1979.

Bhaskar, R. *The Possibility of Naturalism: A Philosophical Critique of the Contemporary Human Sciences*, Brighton, Harvester, 1979.

Blackaby, F. "Peace Research and the Stockholm Institute of Peace Research (SIPRI)," *Working Paper 68 (Australian National University Peace Research Centre)*, Canberra, Australian National Univ., 1986.

Blau, P. (ed.). *Approaches to the Study of Social Structure*, London, Open Books, 1976.

Boasson, C. *A Prologue to Peace Research*, Jerusalem, Israel Univ. Press, 1971.

Boasson, C. "The Province and Function of Peace Research," in A.R. Blackshields, (ed.), *Legal Change: Essays in Honour of Julius Stone*, Sydney, Butterworths, 1983, pp. 299–315.

Borman, W. *Gandhi and Non-Violence*, Albany, State Univ. of New York Press, 1986.

Bottomore, T. *Sociology: A Guide to Problems and Literature*, 2d. ed., London, G. Allen & Unwin, 1971.

Bottomore, T., and R. Nisbet (eds.), *A History of Sociological Analysis*, New York, Basic Books, 1978.

Boulding, E. "Peace Research: Dialectics and Development," *Journal of Conflict Resolution*, 16(4), 1972, pp. 469–475.

Boulding, E. "Reflections on the Founding of IPRA," *IPRA Newsletter*, 26(3), 1987, pp. 9–14.

Boulding, K. "A Discussion with Harry Redner," *Social Alternatives*, 3(1), 1983, pp. 15–20.

Boulding, K. "Future Directions in Peace Studies," *Journal of Conflict Resolution*, 22(2), 1978, pp. 342–354.

Boulding, K. "Limits or Boundaries of Peace Research," *Proceedings of the I.P.R.A. Third General Conference—Volume 1*, Assen, Van Gorcum & Co., 1970, pp. 5–19.

Boulding, K. "Twelve Friendly Quarrels with Johan Galtung," *Journal of Peace Research*, 14(1), 1977, pp. 75–86.

Bouquet, A.C., and K.S. Murty. *Studies in the Problems of Peace*, Bombay, Asia Publishing House, 1960.

Braun, D. "Asian Power India: A New Equation," *Aussenpolitik*, 41(2), 1990, pp. 167–180.

Brenkhert, G. *Marx's Ethics of Freedom*, London, Routledge & Kegan Paul, 1983.

Brewer, A. *Marxist Theories of Imperialism: A Critical Survey*, London, Routledge & Kegan Paul, 1980.

Brown, C. "Galtung and the Marxists on Imperialism: Answers Versus Questions," *Millennium: Journal of International Studies*, 10(3), 1981, pp. 220–228.

Bull, H. *The Anarchical Society: A Study of Order in World Politics*, London, Macmillan, 1977.

Bull, H. *Justice in International Relations—1983–84 Hagey Lectures*, Waterloo, Ont., Univ. of Waterloo, 1984.

Bullock, A., O. Stallybrass, and S. Trombley. *The Fontana Dictionary of Modern Thought*, 2d ed., London, Fontana, 1988.

Burton, J. "Peace Research and International Relations," *Journal of Conflict Resolution*, 8(3), 1965, pp. 281–286.

Butterfield, H., and M. Wight (eds.). *Diplomatic Investigations*, London, George Allen & Unwin, 1966.

Camilleri, J. "The Evolving Agenda of Peace Research," in R. Higgott and J.L. Richardson (eds.), *International Relations: Global and Australian Perspectives on an Evolving Discipline,* Canberra, Australian National Univ., pp. 343–372.

Camilleri, J. "Review of *The True Worlds*," *Australian Outlook*, 33(1), 1981, pp. 95–96.

Camilleri, J.A., and R. Falk. *The End of Sovereignty? The Politics of a Shrinking and Fragmenting World*, Aldershot, Edward Elgar, 1992.

Carr, E.H. *The Twenty Years Crisis 1919–1939: An Introduction to the Study of International Relations*, London, Macmillan, 1962.

Centre for Peace and Conflict Research, Copenhagen. "Research Plan for the Years 1993–1996," *Working Papers*, 19, 1993, Copenhagen, Centre for Peace and Conflict Research, 1993.

Chalmers, A.F. *What Is This Thing Called Science?* 2d ed., St. Lucia, Qld., Univ. of Queensland Press, 1982.

Comte, A. *System of Positive Polity*, New York, Franklin, 1875.

Coser, L. *The Functions of Social Conflict*, Glencoe, Ill., Free Press, 1956.

Cox, R.W, "Social Forces, States and World Orders: Beyond International Relations Theory," *Millennium: Journal of International Studies*, 10(2), 1981, pp. 126–155.

Dahrendorf, R. "Toward a Theory of Social Conflict," *Journal of Conflict Resolution*, 2(2), 1958, pp. 170–183.

Dahrendorf, R. "Out of Utopia: Towards a Reorientation of Sociological Analysis," *American Journal of Sociology*, 64(2), 1958, pp. 115–127.

Dasgupta, S. *Problems of Peace Research: A Third World View*, New Delhi, Shanti Publishers, 1974.

Dator, J.A. *Soka Gakkai: Builders of the Third Generation*, Seattle, Univ. of Washington Press, 1969.

Davis, K. "The Myth of Functional Analysis as a Special Method of Sociology and Anthropology," *American Sociological Review*, 24, 1959, pp. 757–772.

Dedring, J. *Recent Advances in Peace and Conflict Research: A Critical Survey*, Beverly Hills, Calif., Sage, 1976.

Dencik, L. "Peace Research: Pacification or Revolution?" in G. Pardesi (ed.), *Contemporary Peace Research*, Brighton, Harvester Press, 1982, pp. 176–196.

Der Derian, J., and M.J. Shapiro, (eds.). *International/Intertextual Relations: Postmodern Readings of World Politics*, Lexington, Mass., Lexington Books, 1989.

Diwakar, R.R. "Gandhi: A Social Scientist and Social Technocrat," *Gandhi Marg*, 37, April 1982, pp. 24–28.

Doyle, M. "Liberalism and World Politics," *American Political Science Review*, 80(4), 1986, pp. 1151–1169.

Duncan, G. *Marx and Mill: Two Views of Social Conflict and Harmony*, Cambridge, Cambridge University Press, 1973.

Durkheim, E. *Le Socialisme: Sa definition, ses debuts, la doctrine Saint-Simonienne*, Paris, Felix Alcan, 1928.

Eckhardt, W. "A Brief Review of the Radical Critique of Peace Research," *Journal of Contemporary Revolutions*, 3, 1971, pp. 74–83.

Eckhardt, W. "Pioneers of Peace Research I—Lewis Fry Richardson: Apostle of Math," *International Interactions*, 8 (3), 1981, pp. 247–273.

Eckhardt, W. "Pioneers of Peace Research II—Quincy Wright: Apostle of Law," *International Interactions*, 8(4), 1981, pp. 297–317.

Eide, A. "A Value-Based Approach: Methods and Problems in Peace Research," *International Social Science Journal*, 26(1), 1974, pp. 119–133.

Eide, K. "Note on Galtung's Concept of 'Violence,'" *Journal of Peace Research*, 8(1), 1971, p. 71.

Eldridge, J. *C. Wright Mills*, Chichester, Ellis Horwood, 1983.

Eliav-Feldon, M. *Realistic Utopias: The Ideal Imaginary Societies of the Renaissance 1516–1630*, Oxford, Clarendon Press, 1982.

Emmanuel, A. *Unequal Exchange: A Study of the Imperialism of Trade*, New York, Monthly Review Press, 1972.

Emmett, D. *Function, Purpose and Powers: Some Concepts in the Study of Individuals and Societies*, 2d. ed., London, Macmillan, 1972.

Eurich, N. *Science in Utopia: A Mighty Design*, Cambridge, Mass., Harvard University Press, 1967.

Evans, P. *The Protest Virus,* London, Pitman Publishing, 1974,.

Falk, R. "On the Recent Further Decline in International Law," in A.R. Blackshields (ed.), *Legal Change: Essays in Honour of Julius Stone*, Sydney, Butterworths, 1983.

Falk, R. "The Role of Law in World Society: Present Crisis and Future Prospects," in W.M. Reisman, and B.H. Weston (eds.), *Toward World Order and Human Dignity: Essays in Honour of Myres S. McDougall*, New York, Free Press, 1976, pp. 132–169.

Falk, R., S.S. Kim, and S.H. Mendlovitz (eds.). *Toward a Just World Order* (Studies on a Just World Order, Volume 1), Boulder, Colo., Westview Press, 1982.

Findlay, T. *Nuclear Dynamite: The Peaceful Nuclear Explosions Fiasco*, Rushcutters Bay, New South Wales, Brassey's, 1990.

Fink, C. "Editorial Notes," *Journal of Conflict Resolution*, 16(4), 1972, pp. 463–467.

Fischer, L. *Gandhi: His Life and Message for the World*, New York, Mentor, 1954.

Fitzgerald, R. (ed.). *Human Needs and Politics*, Rushcutter's Bay, New South Wales, Pergamon Press, 1977.

Frank, A.G. "The Development of Underdevelopment," *Monthly Review*, 18(4), 1966, pp. 17–31.

Friedrichs, R.W. *A Sociology of Sociology*, New York, Free Press, 1970.

Fromm, E. *The Anatomy of Human Destructiveness*, Harmondsworth, Penguin, 1977.

Fukuyama, F. *The End of History and the Last Man*, London, Hamish Hamilton, 1992.

Galbraith, J.K. *Economics, Peace, Laughter*, London, Andre Deutsch, 1971.

Gandhi, M.K. *Non-Violence in Peace and War—Volume 1*, Ahmedabad, Navajivan Publishing House, 1942.

Gantzel, K.J. "Dependency Structures as the Dominant Pattern in World Society," *Journal of Peace Research*, 10(3), 1973, pp. 203–215.

Giddens, A. *Capitalism and Modern Social Theory*, Cambridge, Cambridge University Press, 1971.

Giddens, A. *Durkheim*, Glasgow, Collins, 1978.

Giddens, A. *The Nation State and Violence: Volume Two of a Contemporary Critique of Historical Materialism*, Cambridge, Polity Press, 1985.

Giddens, A. *New Rules of Sociological Method: A Positive Critique of Interpretative Sociologies*, London, Hutchinson, 1976.

Giddens, A. *Politics and Sociology in the Thought of Max Weber*, London, Macmillan, 1972.

Giddens, A. *Positivism and Sociology*, London, Heinemann, 1974.

Giddens, A. *Studies in Social and Political Theory*, London, Hutchinson, 1977.

Gidengil, E.L. "Centres and Peripheries: An Empirical Test of Galtung's Theory of Imperialism," *Journal of Peace Research*, 15(1), 1978, pp. 51–66.

Glasenapp, H. von. *Buddhism: A Non-Theistic Religion*, New York, Braziller, 1966.

Gleditsch, N.P. "The Structure of Galtungism," in N.P. Gleditsch et al., *Johan Galtung: A Bibliography of His Scholarly and Popular Writings 1951–1980*, Oslo, PRIO, 1980, pp. 65–84.

Green, T.H. *A Prolegomena to Ethics*, 5th ed., Oxford, Clarendon, 1904.

Habermas, J. *Knowledge and Human Interests* (trans. J.J. Shapiro), Boston, Beacon Press, 1971.

Habermas, J. *The Theory of Communicative Action: Volume One—Reason and the Rationalisation of Society* (trans. T. McCarthy), Boston, Beacon Press, 1984.

Habermas, J. *Toward a Rational Society: Student Protest, Science and Politics* (trans. J.J. Shapiro), London, Heinemann, 1971.

Hamilton, P. *Talcott Parsons*, Chichester, Ellis Horwood Ltd., 1983.

Harle, V. (ed.), *Essays in Peace Studies*, Aldershot, Gower Publishing Co., 1987.

Harre, R. *The Philosophies of Science: An Introductory Survey*, 2d ed., Oxford, Oxford Univ. Press, 1985.

Hart, H.L.A. *The Concept of Law*, Oxford, Clarendon Press, 1961.

Harvey, D. *The Condition of Postmodernity: An Enquiry into the Origins of Cultural Change*, Oxford, Basil Blackwell, 1989.

Harvey, P. *An Introduction to Buddhism*, Cambridge, Cambridge Univ. Press, 1990.

Havel, V. *Summer Meditations*, New York, Alfred A. Knopf, 1992.

Hearn, F. *Reason and Freedom in Sociological Thought*, Boston, Allen & Unwin, 1985.

Held, D. *Introduction to Critical Theory: Horkheimer to Habermas*, London, Hutchinson, 1980.

Henriot, P.J. "Development Alternatives: Problems, Strategies, Values," in C.K. Wilber (ed.), *The Political Economy of Development and Underdevelopment*, 2d ed., New York, Random House, 1979, pp. 5–22.

Higgott, R. *Political Development Theory*, Beckenham, Croom Helm, 1983.

Higgott, R., and J.L. Richardson. *International Relations: Global and Australian Perspectives on an Evolving Discipline*, Canberra, Australian National Univ., 1991.

Hinsley, F.H. *Power and the Pursuit of Peace: Theory and Practice in the History of International Relations*, Cambridge, Cambridge Univ. Press, 1963.

Hodgson, G. *America in Our Time: From World War Two to Nixon What Happened and Why*, New York, Vintage Books, 1978.

Holm, H.H. *Johan Galtung: "Superstar" eller "Vaekkelsespraedikant"?* (Johan Galtung: "Superstar" or "Preacher"?), Århus, University of Aarhus, 1975.

Holm, H.H. "On a Major Event in the Social Sciences," *Cooperation and Conflict*, 1, 1978, pp. 61–74.

Holm, H.H., and E. Rudeng. (eds.), *Social Science—for What? Festschrift for Johan Galtung*, Oslo, Universitetsforlaget, 1980.

Holmes, R.L. *On War and Morality*, Princeton, Princeton Univ. Press, 1989.

Homans, G. "Bringing Men Back In," *American Sociological Review*, 29(5), 1964, pp. 809–819.

Homans, G. *Social Behaviour: Its Elementary Forms*, New York, Harcourt Brace, 1961.

Horkheimer, M. "Traditional and Critical Theory," in M. Horkheimer, *Critical Theory: Selected Essays* (trans. M.J. O'Connell et al.) New York, Herder & Herder, 1972.

Horowitz, I.L. (ed.). *The New Sociology*, New York, Oxford University Press, 1964.

Horowitz, I.L. (ed.). *The Rise and Fall of Project Camelot*, Cambridge, Mass., MIT, 1967.

Horowitz, I.L. (ed.). *The Use and Abuse of Social Science: Behavioral Research and Policy Making*, 2d ed., New Brunswick, N.J., Transaction Books, 1975.

Humphreys, C. *Karma and Rebirth*, London, John Murray, 1943.

Husserl, E. *The Crisis of European Sciences and Transcendental Phenomenology* (trans. D. Carr), Evanston, Ill., Northwestern Univ. Press, 1970.

Huxley, J. *Memories II*, London, G. Allen & Unwin, 1973.

Ingram, D. *Habermas and the Dialectic of Reason*, New Haven, Yale Univ. Press, 1987.

Isard, W. "Introduction," *Peace Research Society (International), Papers X, Cambridge Conference, June 1968—Vietnam: Some Basic Issues and Alternatives*, U.S.A., PRS(I), 1968.

Ishida, T. "Beyond the Traditional Concepts of Peace in Different Cultures," *Journal of Peace Research*, 6, 1969, pp. 133–145.

Jahn, E. "Peace Research and Politics in the Federal Republic of Germany," *IPRA Newsletter*, 14(4), 1981, pp. 2–9.

James, W. *Pragamatism*, New York, Meridian Books, 1955.

Jenkins, R. *Exploitation*, London, Macgibbon & Kee, 1970.

Johnson, B. *Functionalism in Modern Sociology: Understanding Talcott Parsons*, Morristown, N.J., General Learning Press, 1975.

Kaplan, M. *Towards Professionalism in International Theory: Macrosystems Analysis*, New York, Free Press, 1979.

Keal, P. "Can Foreign Policy be Ethical?" in P. Keal (ed.), *Ethics and Foreign Policy*, Canberra, Allen & Unwin/Australian National Univ., 1992, pp. 1–20.

Keal, P. (ed.). *Ethics and Foreign Policy*, Canberra, Allen & Unwin/Australian National Univ., 1992.

Kelman, H. *A Time to Speak: On Human Values and Social Research*, San Francisco, Jossey-Bass, 1968.
Kent, G. "The Application of Peace Studies," *Journal of Conflict Resolution*, 15(1), 1971, pp. 47–53.
Keown, D. *The Nature of Buddhist Ethics*, London, Macmillan, 1992.
Kolakowski, L. *Marxism and Beyond*, London, Paladin, 1971.
Korhonen, P. "The Dialectics of Power in the Thought of Young Johan Galtung," in V. Harle (ed.), *Essays in Peace Studies*, Aldershot, Gower Publishing Co., 1987.
Korhonen, P. *The Geometry of Power: Johan Galtung's Conception of Power*, Tampere, Tampere Peace Research Institute, 1990 (Research Reports No. 38)
Krippendorf, E. "The Dominance of American Approaches in International Relations," *Millennium: Journal of International Studies*, 16(2), 1987, pp. 207–214.
Krippendorf, E. "Peace Research and the Industrial Revolution," *Journal of Peace Research*, 10(3), 1973, pp. 185–201.
Krippendorf, E. "The State as a Focus of Peace Research," *Peace Research Society, Papers, XVI, The Rome Conference, 1970*, pp. 47–60.
Kuhn, T.S. *The Structure of Scientific Revolutions,* 2d. ed., Chicago, Univ. of Chicago Press, 1970.
Lawler, P. "The Good Citizen Australia?" *Asian Studies Review*, 16(2), 1992, pp. 241–250.
Lawler, P. "New Directions in Peace Research," in H.V. Emy and A. Linklater (eds.), *New Horizons in Politics: Australian Perspectives*, Sydney, Allen & Unwin, 1990, pp. 101–131.
Lawler, P. "Peace Research and International Relations: From Divergence to Convergence," *Millennium: Journal of International Studies*, 15(3), 1986, pp. 367–392.
Lehman, H. "R.K. Merton's Concept of Function and Functionalism," *Inquiry*, 9, 1966, pp. 274–283.
Lenin, V.I. "Imperialism, the Highest Stage of Capitalism," in *V.I. Lenin: Selected Works in Three Volumes*, Moscow, Progress Press, Volume 1, pp. 634–731.
Lentz, T.F. *Towards a Science of Peace: Turning Point in Human Destiny*, London, Halycon Press, 1955.
Lessnoff, M. *The Structure of Social Science*, London, G. Allen & Unwin, 1974.
Lewis, *The Political Language of Islam*, Chicago, Univ. of Chicago Press, 1988.
Lichtheim, G. *Imperialism*, New York, Praeger, 1971.
Ling, T. *Buddhism*, London, Ward Lock Educational, 1970.
Linklater, A. *Beyond Realism and Marxism*, London, Macmillan, 1989.
Linklater, A. *Men and Citizens in the Theory of International Relations*, London, Macmillan, 1982.
Linklater, A. "Marxism and International Relations: Antithesis, Reconciliation or Transcendence," in R. Higgott and J.L. Richardson (eds.), *International Relations: Global and Australian Perspectives on an Evolving Discipline,* Canberra, Australian National Univ., 1991, pp. 70–91.
Linklater, A. "Realism, Marxism and Critical International Theory," *Review of International Studies*, 12, 1986, pp. 301–312.
Linklater, A. "What Is a Good International Citizen?" in P. Keal (ed.), *Ethics and Foreign Policy,* St. Leonards, New South Wales, Allen & Unwin, 1992.
Lipset, S.M., and N.J. Smelsor (eds.). *Sociology: The Progress of a Decade*, Englewood Cliffs, N.J., Prentice-Hall, 1961.
Lorenz, K. *On Aggression* (trans. M. Latzke), London, Methuen, 1967.
Lukacs, G. *History and Class Consciousness: Studies in Marxist Dialectics* (trans. R. Livingstone), London, Merlin Press, 1971.

Lukes, S. *Emile Durkheim: His Life and Work*, New York, Harper and Row, 1972.
Lukes, S. *Marxism and Morality*, Englewood Cliffs, N.J., Prentice-Hall, 1982.
Lundberg, G. *Can Science Save Us?* 2d. ed., New York, David McKay & Co., 1961.
Lyotard, J.F. *The Postmodern Condition: A Report on Knowledge* (trans. G. Bennington and B. Massumi), Manchester, Manchester Univ. Press, 1984.
Mack, A. "Australia and Peace Research," in R. Higgott and J.L. Richardson (eds.), *International Relations: Global and Australian Perspectives on an Evolving Discipline,* Canberra, Australian National Univ., 1991, pp. 373–393.
Mack, A. *Peace Research in the 1980s*, Canberra, Australian National Univ., 1985.
Mack, A. "Theories of Imperialism: The European Perspective," *Journal of Conflict Resolution*, 18(3), 1974, pp. 514–535.
Mackie, J.L. *Ethics: Inventing Right and Wrong*, Harmondsworth, Penguin Books, 1977.
Malhotra, S.L. "Gandhi and the Scientific Outlook," *Gandhi Marg*, 37, April 1982, pp. 40–49.
Marcuse, H. *One Dimensional Man,* London, Sphere Books, 1972.
Martindale, D. *Functionalism in the Social Sciences*, Philadelphia, American Academy of Political and Social Sciences, 1965.
Marx, K. *Early Writings* (trans. R. Livingstone and G. Benton, intro. by L. Colleti), Harmondsworth, Penguin, 1975.
Marx, K., and F. Engels. *Selected Works in One Volume*, London, Lawrence & Wishart, 1968.
Maslow, A. *Motivation and Personality*, New York, Harper & Row, 1954.
Maus, H. *A Short History of Sociology*, London, Routledge & Kegan Paul, 1962.
McCarthy, T. *The Critical Theory of Jurgen Habermas*, Cambridge, Polity Press, 1984.
Meadows, D.H., D.L. Meadows, J. Randers, and W.W. Behrens. *The Limits to Growth: A Report for the Club of Rome's Project on the Predicament of Mankind*, London, Pan Books, 1972.
Mehta, V. *Mahatma Gandhi and His Apostles*, Harmondsworth, Penguin, 1976.
Merquior, J.G. *Foucault*, London, Fontana, 1985.
Merton, R. "The Position of Sociological Theory," *American Sociological Review*, 13(2), 1948, pp. 164–168.
Merton, R.K. *Social Theory and Social Structure*, Glencoe, Ill., Free Press, 1957.
Mills, C.W. *The Sociological Imagination,* Harmondsworth, Penguin, 1970.
Mommsen, W.J. *Theories of Imperialism*, London, Weidenfield & Nicholson, 1981.
Moore, B. *Political Power and Social Theory: Six Studies*, Cambridge, Mass., Harvard Univ. Press, 1958.
Moore, G.E. *Principia Ethica*, Cambridge, Cambridge Univ. Press, 1903.
Morgenthau, H. *Politics Among Nations: The Struggle for Power and Peace*, 5th ed., New York, Alfred A. Knopf, 1978.
Myrdal, G. *Objectivity in Social Research*, New York, Pantheon Books, 1969.
Naess, A. *Gandhi and Group Conflict: An Exploration of Satyagraha*, Oslo, Universitetsforlaget, 1974.
Naess, A. "A Systematisation of Gandhian Ethics of Conflict Resolution," *Journal of Conflict Resolution*, 2(2), 1958, pp. 140–155.
Nagel, E. *The Structure of Science*, New York, Harcourt, Brace & World, 1966.
Neilsen, K. "On Human Needs and Moral Appraisals," *Inquiry*, 6, 1963, pp. 170–183.
Nerfin, M. *Another Development: Approaches and Strategies*, Uppsala, Dag Hammarskjöld Foundation, 1977.
Newcombe, A., and H. Newcombe. *Peace Research Around the World*, Oakville, Ont., Canadian Peace Research Institute, 1969.

Øberg, J. (ed.). *Nordic Security in the 1990s: Options in the Changing Europe*, London, Pinter Publishers/TFF, 1992.

Olsen, O.J., and I. Jarvad. "The Vietnam Conference Papers: A Case Study of the Failure of Peace Research," *Peace Research Society (International) Papers XIV, The Ann Arbor Conference 1969*, U.S.A., PRS(I), 1969, pp. 155–170.

Overend, T. *Social Idealism and the Problem of Objectivity*, St. Lucia, Qld., Univ. of Queensland Press, 1983.

Palonen, K. "Social Science as Peace Research: An Interpretation of Johan Galtung's Intellectual Odyssey," *Current Research on Peace and Violence*, 2, 1978, pp. 104–125.

Papineau, D. *For Science in the Social Sciences*, London, Macmillan, 1978.

Pardesi, G. (ed.). *Contemporary Peace Research*, Brighton, Harvester Press, 1982.

Parkin, F. *Max Weber*, Chichester, Ellis Horwood, 1982.

Parkinson, F. *The Philosophy of International Relations: A Study in the History of Thought*, Beverly Hills, Calif., Sage, 1977.

Parsons, T. *Essays in Sociological Theory*, 2d ed., New York, Free Press, 1954.

Parsons, T. "Some Problems Confronting Sociology as a Profession," *American Sociological Review*, 24, 1959, pp. 547–559.

Peterson, V. Spike (ed.) *Gendered States: Feminist (Re)visions of International Relations Theory*, Boulder, Colo., Lynne Rienner, 1992.

Pisar, S. *Coexistence and Commerce: Guidelines for Transactions Between East and West*, New York, McGraw-Hill, 1970.

Piscatori, J. *Islam in a World of Nation-States*, Cambridge, Cambridge Univ. Press, 1986.

Popper, K.R. *Conjectures and Refutations: The Growth of Scientific Knowledge*, 4th ed., London, Routledge & Kegan Paul, 1972.

Popper, K.R. *The Logic of Scientific Discovery*, London, Hutchinson, 1980.

Portis, E.B. "Max Weber and the Unity of Normative and Empirical Theory," *Political Studies*, 31, 1983, pp. 25–42.

Pratt, C. (ed.). *Internationalism Under Strain: The North-South Policies of Canada, The Netherlands, Norway and Sweden*, Toronto, Univ. of Toronto Press, 1989.

Pratt, C. (ed.). *Middle Power Internationalism*, Montreal, McGill-Queens Univ. Press, 1990.

Pruitt, D., and R.C. Snyder (eds.). *Theory and Research on the Causes of War*, Englewood Cliffs, N.J., Prentice-Hall, 1969.

Pusey, M. *Jurgen Habermas*, Chichester, Ellis Horwood, 1987.

Rapoport, A. "Can Peace Research Be Applied?" *Journal of Conflict Resolution*, 14(2), 1970, pp. 277–86.

Rapoport, A. "Various Conceptions of Peace Research," *Peace Research Society (International) Papers XIX The Ann Arbor Conference 1969*, U.S.A., PRS(I), 1971, pp. 91–106.

Rawls, J. *A Theory of Justice*, Cambridge, Mass., Harvard Univ. Press, 1981.

Reisman, W.M., and B.H. Weston (eds.). *Toward World Order and Human Dignity: Essays in Honour of Myres S. McDougall*, New York, Free Press, 1976.

Rex, J. *Key Problems of Sociological Theory*, London, Routledge & Kegan Paul, 1961.

Richardson, L.F. *Arms and Insecurity*, Pittsburgh, Boxwood Press, 1960.

Richardson, L.F. *Statistics of Deadly Quarrels*, Pittsburgh, Boxwood Press, 1960.

Robinson, R.H. *The Buddhist Religion*, Belmont, Calif. Dickenson Publishing, 1970.

Rock, P. *The Making of Symbolic Interactionism*, London, Macmillan, 1979.

Rosenau, P. *Postmodernism and the Social Sciences: Insights, Inroads and Intrusions*, Princeton, Princeton Univ. Press, 1992.

Roy, R., R.B.J. Walker, and R. Ashley. "Dialogue: Towards a Critical Social Theory of International Politics," *Alternatives*, 13, 1988, pp. 77–102.

Rueland, J. "Europe: A Model for Asia?" *Aussenpolitik*, 43(4), 1992, pp. 392–401.

Russett, B.M. (ed.). *Peace, War and Numbers*, Beverly Hills, Calif., Sage, 1972.

Ryan, A. (ed.). *The Philosophy of Social Explanation*, Oxford, Oxford Univ. Press, 1973.

Said, E. *Orientalism*, Harmondsworth, Penguin, 1985.

Salmon, W.C. *The Foundations of Scientific Inference*, Pittsburgh, Univ. of Pittsburgh Press, 1967.

Savage, S.P. *The Theories of Talcott Parsons: The Social Relations of Action*, London, Macmillan, 1981.

Schmid, H. "Peace Research and Politics," *Journal of Peace Research*, 3, 1968, pp. 217–232.

Schmid, H. "Peace Research as a Technology for Pacification," *Proceedings of the International Peace Research Third General Conference—Volume 1*, Assen, Van Gorcum & Co., 1970.

Schumacher, E.F. *Small Is Beautiful: A Study of Economics As If People Mattered*, London, Blond & Briggs, 1973.

Senghaas, D. "Conflict Formations in Contemporary International Society," *Journal of Peace Research*, 10(3), 1973, pp. 163–184.

Sharma, I.C. *Ethical Philosophies of India*, London, Allen & Unwin, 1965.

Shils, E. "Imaginary Sociology," *Encounter*, 14(78), 1960, pp. 78–81.

Simey, T.S. *Social Science and Social Purpose*, New York, Schocken Books, 1969.

Simon, W.M. *European Positivism in the Nineteenth Century: An Essay in Intellectual History*, Ithaca, N.Y., Cornell Univ. Press, 1963.

Simovitz, R.L., and B.L. Price. "Progress in the Study of International Conflict: A Methodological Critique," *Journal of Peace Research*, 23(1), 1986, pp. 29–40.

Smith, A.D. *The Concept of Social Change: A Critique of the Functionalist Theory of Social Change*, London, Routledge and Kegan Paul, 1973.

Soper, K. *On Human Needs: Open and Closed Theories in a Marxist Perspective*, Sussex, Harvester Press, 1981.

Stein, M., and A. Vidich (eds.). *Sociology on Trial*, Englewood Cliffs, N.J., Prentice-Hall, 1963.

Stohl, M., and M. Chamberlain. "Alternative Futures for Peace Research," *Journal of Conflict Resolution*, 16(4), pp. 523–530.

Strasser, H. *The Normative Structure of Sociology: Conservative and Emancipatory Themes in Social Thought*, London, Routledge & Kegan Paul, 1976.

Suganami, H. *The Domestic Analogy and World Order Proposals*, Cambridge, Cambridge Univ. Press, 1989.

Szacki, J. *History of Sociological Thought*, Westport Conn., Greenwood Press, 1979.

Sztompka, P. *Robert K. Merton: An Intellectual Profile*, Basingstoke, Macmillan, 1986.

Taylor, C. "Neutrality in Political Science," in P. Lasslett and W.G. Runciman (eds.). *Philosophy, Politics and Society*, Oxford, Blackwell, 1967.

Taylor, K. (trans. and ed.), *Henri Saint-Simon: Selected Writings on Science, Industry and Social Organisation*, London, Frank Cass, 1975.

Taylor, K. *The Political Ideas of the Utopian Socialists*, London, Frank Cass, 1982.

Taylor, P. "'Need' Statements," *Analysis*, 19(5), 1959, pp. 106–111.

Thompson, J. *Justice and World Order: A Philosophical Inquiry*, London, Routledge, 1992.

Thompson, K. *Auguste Comte: The Foundation of Sociology*, London, Nelson, 1976.

Tilton, T. *The Political Theory of Swedish Social Democracy: Through the Welfare State to Socialism*, Oxford, Clarendon Press, 1991.

Todhunter, W. (trans.). *Voltaire's History of Charles XII King of Sweden*, London, J.M. Dent, 1908.

Todorov, T. *The Conquest of America: The Question of the Other* (trans. R. Howard), New York, Harper & Row, 1984.

Toynbee, A. *Mankind and Mother Earth: A Narrative History of the World*, Oxford, Oxford Univ. Press, 1978.

Tudor, A. *Beyond Empiricism: Philosophy of Science in Sociology*, London, Routledge & Kegan Paul, 1982.

Van den Bergh, G. "Theory or Taxonomy: Some Critical Notes on Galtung's Theory of Imperialism," *Journal of Peace Research*, 9(1), 1972, pp. 77–92.

Veblen, T. *The Theory of the Leisure Class: An Economic Study of Institutions*, London, Unwin, 1970.

Vidich, A.J., and S.M. Lyman. *American Sociology: Worldly Rejections of Religion and Their Directions*, New Haven, Yale Univ. Press, 1985.

Walker, R.B.J. *One World, Many Worlds: Struggles for a Just World Peace*, Boulder, Colo., Lynne Rienner, 1988.

Walker, R.B.J. "The Prince and 'The Pauper': Tradition, Modernity and Practice in International Relations," in J. Der Derian and M.J. Shapiro (eds.), *International/Intertextual Relations: Postmodern Readings of World Politics*, Lexington, Mass., Lexington Books, 1989, pp. 24–48.

Wallerstein, I. *The Politics of the World Economy: The States, the Movements and the Civilisations*, Cambridge, Cambridge Univ. Press, 1984.

Waltz, K.N. *Man, the State and War: A Theoretical Analysis*, New York, Columbia Univ. Press, 1959.

Waltz, K.N. *Theory of International Politics*, Reading, Mass., Addison-Wesley, 1979.

Wasburn, P.C. *Political Sociology: Approaches, Concepts, Hypotheses*, Englewood Cliffs, N.J., Prentice-Hall, 1982.

Westergaard, J.H. "Sociology: The Myth of Classlessness," in R. Blackburn (ed.), *Ideology in Social Science: Readings in Critical Social Theory*, Glasgow, Collins, 1972, pp. 32–44.

White, S.K. "Poststructuralism and Political Reflection," *Political Theory*, 16(2), 1988, pp. 186–208.

Wight, M. *International Theory: The Three Traditions*, London, Leicester Univ. Press, 1991.

Willer, D., and J. Willer. *Systematic Empiricism: Critique of a Pseudo-Science*, Englewood Cliffs, N.J., Prentice-Hall, 1973.

Williams, R. *Keywords: A Vocabulary of Culture and Society*, London, Flamingo, 1983.

Woodcock, G. *Gandhi*, London, Fontana/Collins, 1972.

Wright, Q. *A Study of War*, Chicago, Univ. of Chicago Press, 1965.

Zimmer, H. *Philosophies of India* (ed. J. Campbell), New York, World Publishing, 1961.

Index

Action space (*Spielraum*), 121
Actor-oriented perspective, 143, 171–173, 185
Aggression, 93, 197; disequilibrium and, 62; innate, 181
Ahimsa, 44n47, 144, 145, 225; commitment to, 82, 235; Gandhi on, 216; moral precept of, 215. *See also* Nonviolence
Allardt, Erik, 188n15
Almost fundamental needs, 143, 149, 162n61. *See also* Fundamental needs
Alpha development pattern, 152–155
American Social Science Association, social reform and, 20
Amin, Samir, 110n2
Anarchical Society, The (Bull), 225–226, 231
Anarchy, 2, 5, 178
Anatta, doctrine of, 212, 214
Angell, Robert, 12
Anicca, doctrine of, 212
Antihumanism, 7
Antipolitics, influence of, 236
Arendt, Hannah, on politics, 161n24
Arthasastra (Kautilya), 206
Ashley, Richard K., 8, 14n18
Atman (self, soul), realization of, 82
Atomistic-deductive dualism, 208
Atomistic-holistic dualism, 208
Autonomy, 147, 174; collective, 152; national, 152; structural, 177

Balance of power, 49, 81
Bariloche model, 137
Behavioral revolt, 15
Behaviorism, 22, 110n8
Benedict, Ruth, 192
Benton, Ted, 20; on morality, 19
Bernstein, Richard J., on positivism, 16
Beta development pattern, 152–155
Bildungsprozess, 16, 43n5
Boulding, Kenneth, 12, 70, 72; on Galtung, 189nn20, 39

Brown, Chris: on Galtung, 110; on STI, 107–108
Buddha, 206, 209, 212
Buddhism, 134n48, 147, 171, 188, 189n20, 199, 204, 205, 206, 208, 221n52; Christianity and, 217, 233–234; conflict resolution and, 215; doctrines of, 211, 212; Galtung and, 216, 217, 219; influence of, 191, 236; moral system of, 215–216; peace and, 211–217; peace research and, 211–217, 219, 232–237; sociospatial implications of, 216–217; structural violence and, 212, 217; teleological reading of, 222n56; tolerance of, 206, 217
Bull, Hedley, 225–226; on moral obligations, 231; on new world order, 226; on normative/political inquiry, 232
Burton, John, 60, 226

Camilleri, Joseph: on Galtung, 189n32; on peace research, 239n28
Capitalism, 146; alternative to, 153; globalizing/homogenizing, 9
Carr, E. H., 187, 226
Castes, conception of, 206, 209, 211
Center for Research on Conflict Resolution (University of Michigan), 12
Center states, 95; democracy in, 104; dominance by, 100, 105; exchange relations and, 100; imperialism and, 97, 98; interactions between, 101; transforming, 106
Central world authority, 179
Centre for Peace and Conflict Research, Copenhagen, 239n25
Change: critical explorations of, 232; key to, 184; politics of, 202. *See also* Social change
Chicago school, empiricism of, 21, 22
Chosen People complex, 194, 196
Christianity, 189n20, 215; Buddhism and, 217, 233–234

257

About the Book and Author

In this first comprehensive and critical account of the development of Johan Galtung's thought, Peter Lawler places Galtung's work in the context of past and contemporary debates in international relations, political theory, and the social sciences more generally.

The starting point of the book is an examination of the young Galtung's writings on sociology and the foundational model of peace research that emerged from them. Going on to survey subsequent periods, Lawler sees each of the distinct phases of Galtung's work as the reflection of a shifting wider intellectual milieu, ranging from the positivism of North American sociology in the 1950s through the postmodern sensibilities central to contemporary social theory. Throughout, he scrutinizes the conceptual icons (e.g., "positive peace" and "structural violence") that Galtung has contributed to the discourses of peace research and international relations, as well as the broader philosophical and methodological underpinnings of his work.

Providing the most extensive survey of Galtung's work to be published in English, Lawler also shows how Galtung's prolific and often iconoclastic writings, in their weaknesses as much as in their strengths, can shed light on a range of difficult questions about values and their place in the theorizing of global politics.

Peter Lawler is lecturer in international relations in the Department of Government at the University of Manchester, Manchester, England.